PIETER GEYL

The Netherlands in the Seventeenth Century

PART TWO
1648–1715

LONDON · ERNEST BENN LIMITED

NEW YORK · BARNES & NOBLE INC.

1964

First published by Ernest Benn Limited 1964
Bouverie House · Fleet Street · London · EC4
and
Barnes & Noble Inc · 105 Fifth Avenue · New York 3

© Pieter Geyl 1964

Printed in Great Britain

THE NETHERLANDS
IN THE SEVENTEENTH CENTURY

PART TWO

1648–1715

Contents

Maps

Preface

AFTER *The Revolt of the Netherlands, 1555–1609*, and *The Netherlands in the Seventeenth Century, Part One, 1609–48*, re-issued in 1958 and 1961 respectively, following their first appearance in the thirties, I can now lay before the public the English translation of a further section of my *Geschiedenis van de Nederlandse Stam*, covering the period from 1648 to 1715, a period when relations between the Netherlands and England, whether hostile or friendly, were of particular importance.

I must again express my heartfelt thanks to Mr. L. Russell Muirhead. With unwearying devotion he went over the English text resulting from the labours of my daughter Catherine and myself, making suggestions from which I am sure the work has benefited.

P. G.

Utrecht, April 1963

VI

The Republic between France and England

A. THE ESTABLISHMENT OF THE REPUBLICAN RÉGIME: 1648-54

I. SHORT-LIVED AMBITIONS OF WILLIAM II, 1648-50

THE young Stadholder William II had not been able to prevent the conclusion of the Peace of Münster, but soon—as I observed in the preceding volume[1]—he was busily working against it, and his father's policy, which had seemingly suffered a total eclipse in 1646, rose again in his own. The partition with France of the South and the restoration to power of the Stuarts remained the twofold goal. The States of Holland still stood in the way of this adventurous policy so largely inspired by dynastic motives. To counter their opposition William II, like his father, looked towards France. When it was still only a question of preventing the peace, the new Stadholder, a very young man, much given to frivolous pastimes, had by his negligence aroused the annoyance of the French Ambassadors. But in the course of 1648 his interest in political matters awoke and from then on he continued his father's questionable tradition with an impetuosity that offered a sharp contrast to the latter's circumspection.

For a policy of aiding the Stuarts William II could count on sympathies which Frederick Henry had had to do without. The rise of the Independents in England, that is to say of the religious individualists who set their faces against the Presbyterian church system, was observed with indignation by the Reformed in the Netherlands, who were indeed, both on theology and church order, of one mind with the Presbyterians. So when the King fell into the hands of the Independents and had in the end to mount the scaffold (30 January 1649), there

[1] See *The Netherlands in the Seventeenth Century*, Part One, p. 156.

was a general outcry in the Northern Netherlands, no less than all over the continent, and the objections felt so recently against Charles I's episcopalianism and despotism were forgotten. The young Prince of Wales, acknowledged as King by the Scots, was, with a horde of exiles, staying in The Hague, the guest of his sister and brother-in-law. He now received whole-hearted support from William II in ventures to make his way back to England, in 1649 by way of Ireland, in 1650 by way of Scotland, both equally doomed to fail. The connection between the Houses of Orange and Stuart could not but strain relations between the English Commonwealth and the Dutch Republic. The Stadholder was out for war and his influence on the deputies from the landward provinces in the States-General was sufficient to bring about what amounted to a severance of diplomatic relations. That peace was maintained was solely owing to the States of Holland who in the general turmoil against the regicides quietly held to their opinion that war with England could serve no national interest and would cause trade to suffer. When the ambassador of the Commonwealth was not admitted to the States-General, the States of Holland received him in their own assembly and in May 1650 they even sent Gerard Schaep of Amsterdam to London as 'commissioner' on behalf of their own province in order to allay the resentment caused by the hostile attitude of the Orange party.

The Orangists raised a great clamour against this diplomatic mission on the part of a province, which according to them was tantamount to breaking up the Union. And although it was only the conclusion of 'confederations and alliances' by the separate provinces that was explicitly forbidden by the Act of Union of 1579, there is no doubt that this action of Holland did imply a very real danger. Yet these high-sounding appeals to the Union were no more than a party manoeuvre. Less than ever did constitutional theorising touch the heart of the dispute now that the States-General had become a corrupt body in which the deputies of several provinces carried out the orders of the Prince of Orange, actuated by the interests of his wife's family and by his personal ambitions, rather than be guided by their principals (the States of Gelderland, Overijsel, etc.).

That he himself had entered into private relations with a foreign state, and this earlier and much more deeply than

Holland had done with England, contemporaries could only suspect. Already in February 1649 he had sent Mazarin assurances to the effect that in the six provinces outside Holland his influence was sufficiently great to get them to resume the war against Spain. In the event of Holland continuing to stand out against the majority in the States-General, the Prince requested that France might recognise the six provinces as the Republic and give financial support: in that case he would be able to subject Holland with the aid of the army and lead all seven provinces into war. That was not quite what was to happen, particularly because the Fronde troubles made it impossible for France to interfere actively in Dutch affairs. Nevertheless later in the year Mazarin at William's urgent request refrained from calling back the French troops stationed in the Republic. It was on those French troops that the Prince would have to rely in the case of a clash with Holland. In the summer of 1650 he considered himself strong enough to risk a trial of strength even without any other, more direct, help from France, which still remained in a state of disturbance.

The disbandment of troops was the point round which the quarrel in the Republic had come to centre. Not only did Holland and the Captain-General supported by his faithful followers in the States-General hold different views regarding the extent to which, now that peace had been restored, the reduction of the army had to be carried, but this matter, too, developed into a constitutional issue when Holland, without waiting for the approval of the general assembly, took it upon herself as 'paymaster' to disband part of the troops 'assigned to' her for their pay.[1]

This procedure was patently unconstitutional, yet that it was resorted to becomes understandable when we remember what was the reality of the situation. It was that the Prince, by means of his hold over the smaller provinces, was trying to force Holland to spend her money towards a policy which she cordially detested.

William II now thought the moment had come for decisive action. On 5 June 1650, he obtained from his compliant States-General full powers for taking the measures required for the maintenance of the Union. There had been protests, this time,

[1] See explanatory note in Part One, p. 60.

from others besides the Hollanders, but the States-General's Greffier, Musch, had lent effective help. To begin with William contented himself with 'visiting'[1] the eighteen voting towns of Holland. At the head of a delegation from the States-General, and with a large following of high-ranking officers, he journeyed from town to town admonishing the magistracy in each that they should for their part try to induce the States of the province to range themselves with the six others. In several towns the authorities would not receive the delegation of the 'allies', and the Stadholder, too, had to stomach an evasive or cool answer, or even a flat refusal. In Amsterdam, although the civic guard had been called out to do the Stadholder honour, the municipal council refused to receive him, but let him negotiate with the Burgomasters, the very people about whom he had wished to complain. William took this in very bad part and refused to sit down to the dinner that had been served up for him in the Prinsenhof:

Six to seven tables that had already been laid were cleared again, His Highness saying that he could not feast with people who refused to hear him speak.

The 'visit' had only served to increase bitterness on both sides. At Dordrecht, Delft, Haarlem, Hoorn, Amsterdam and elsewhere it had been suggested that it was all directed against 'the sovereignty and rights' of the province of Holland. The Stadholder, in fact, working with the majority in the States-General against Holland and trying to get into contact with the towns over the heads of the Provincial States in the States-General's name—this was a spectacle that revived the shocking memories of 1618. The Prince and his supporters, for their part, felt personally affronted, and suspected the Hollanders more positively than ever of evil intentions against the Union. The rumour was spread abroad that Schaep in London had entered into a secret alliance with England on behalf of the province of Holland. Still basing himself on the vague resolution of 5 June, William decided to settle matters once and for all.

[1] 'Visiting a town' was the term used for sending a solemn delegation to remonstrate with the town's 'government' and persuade it to comply with a majority decision in a matter where unanimity was required. Normally it was the provincial States that resorted to this procedure. For the States-General to 'visit', not the States of a recalcitrant province, but, over the head of a provincial States assembly, one or more of its component 'members' (as was done in this case), was in itself irregular.

It would be wrong to think that the dispute about the disband-ment of troops was his real incentive. At bottom it was the question of whether the Prince of Orange should be free to conduct the foreign policy of the country in accordance with his personal pleasure. A pro-States pamphleteer was soon to sum it up in party language, but nevertheless not incorrectly, as follows:

(*Basing himself on the resolution of 5 June*) he had resolved to remove in all the towns of Holland, and also in some other provinces, several magistrates who had scorned to look up to him like slaves, and to fill their places with others of a slavish disposition. And if he had succeeded therein we should have been dragged into two wars at once, to wit against the Parliament of England to help the King of Scotland, and against the King of Spain in order to please the frivolous Frenchies, to whom he had wholly lost his heart.

A medal, which was struck at about that same time at Amsterdam, simply declared that the town had displeased the Prince *quia bella vetabat* (because it opposed war).

On 30 July six deputies to the States of Holland were arrested at The Hague by the colonel of the Prince's bodyguard and taken to the castle of Loevestein the next day.

The deed recalled the attempt made eight years previously by William's father-in-law, Charles I, to have the leaders of the opposition in the House of Commons arrested—a far from auspicious example, because it had served as the signal for the civil war and for Charles's downfall.

And although William's coup was carried through success-fully, it was only the preliminary to a much greater and, as it proved, riskier undertaking. A strong army, commanded by the Stadholder of Friesland, William's cousin William Frederick, unexpectedly made its appearance before the gates of Amster-dam. Cats, still Grand Pensionary, received the startling news from the Prince himself so that he might be able to communicate it to his masters, the States of Holland, and he later sketched the attitude he adopted towards the 'youthful hero' in verse revealing both for the statesman and the poet:

At this I stood amazed as by an unheard-of miracle:
My brains were all upset as by a heavy thunderclap.

The plan to take the town by surprise failed, however. Burgomaster Bicker led a stout resistance. The loyalty of the civic guard did not waver for an instant. The Prince, who had

by now come over from The Hague in person, began preparations for a regular siege, a perilous undertaking in the opinion
of his entourage, especially if the town were to resort to
inundation. But the magistracy shrank from extremities which
might have led to a civil war. Negotiations were started, and on
3 August a treaty was signed in which the Prince undeniably
had the best of it. The town promised compliance on the
point of the disbandment; the brothers Bicker were to resign
their offices. The gentlemen at Loevestein for their part were
released only after they had withdrawn from their several town
governments. The mood of the States' Party was one of
dismay.

'He who controls the army is master', so a German captain of
horse had said to one of the six prisoners. Many were of the same
opinion and prostrated themselves before William. But in fact
William was far from having attained his goal. Amsterdam and
Holland were still holding firm, resolved to oppose his plans for
war. This became apparent in September when William wished
the States-General to intervene in order to check a Spanish
invasion in Northern France. Holland refused to give its consent
to resorting to menaces which the Prince had already represented to the French as being an introduction to a declaration of
war against Spain. And for the time being he had to acquiesce
in this refusal. In the long run he might have been able to carry
his point, especially if Mazarin, after having restored order in
France, had been able to back him up. But in November 1650
he suddenly contracted small-pox and died, only twenty-four
years of age. A son was born from his marriage with the Stuart
Princess a few weeks afterwards.

His death was of incalculable moment to the course of Dutch
history. William II represented a trend which perhaps would
not in any case have been able drastically to reform North
Netherlandish society and civilisation, but which certainly ran
counter to all its most ingrained traditions. He was the exponent
of the monarchical principle which was then prevailing all over
the continent: centralising and militaristic, no longer leaning on
the nobility as an independent power, but using it all the more
as an instrument and for its own more resplendent lustre. Also,
in William's hands all this took on a cosmopolitan, predominant-
ly French tinge—and indeed monarchism, centralisation, and

court nobility had never sprung willingly from Netherlandish soil. It had been the greatness of William the Silent that he had known how to work with the forces native to the Netherlandish community, that is to say with the burgher regents thrown up by the provinces and towns, and obstinately clinging to their several particularisms. Imbued with the true spirit of the revolt against Spain, he had helped to found a republic in which that spirit had acquired its own form and substance. An odd form no doubt, full of anomalies and inner discrepancies, so that the six Loevestein gentlemen could never be identified with a national conception of freedom as had been the case in England with the 'Five Members' who had only just escaped Charles I in 1642.

In monarchical Europe at all events the North Netherlands state was generally looked upon with scoffing unbelief. The consolidation of its future, so it was thought there, could only result from a strengthening of the power of Orange, in the way William II himself had wished it strengthened. In the 'Stadholderless Period' of over two decades that was now opening, the Dutch regent class was again, after the great days of Oldenbarnevelt, given an opportunity to show what it could do.

With respect to the Dutch Republic's foreign policy, at least, the death of William II had one immediate and drastic effect. There was no longer any question of a renewal of the war against Spain in alliance with France, nor of a partition of the Southern Netherlands on lines that would have delivered up Flanders[1] to France. The peace of Münster was consolidated. Relations with England, on the other hand, were not so thoroughly improved as might have been expected. Indeed, two years had hardly elapsed before the war which the States had begrudged William II broke out all the same, and this at a time when their influence on the country's foreign policy had become so much greater.

2. THE GRAND ASSEMBLY: JANUARY TO AUGUST, 1651

THE impotence of the Orange Party after the death of William II and during the childhood of his posthumous son was in part due to the quarrels that divided the Illustrious House. The

[1] That is, the county of Flanders, situated between the duchy of Brabant and the sea (see map, Part One, p. 152). In modern usage Flanders can also mean the entire Dutch-speaking area of Belgium: Flanders, Brabant, Limburg.

Frisian Stadholder, William Frederick, was the only member of that house who might have maintained its political position during the little Prince's minority—although the Hollanders were particularly hostile to him on account of his share in the undertaking against Amsterdam. But he was distrusted also by both the mother and the grandmother. The two widows themselves fought for the guardianship of the new scion of their house with great animosity. The royal pride of the Englishwoman had made her an object of hatred to her mother-in-law and the rest of the family. The old Princess looked to the Elector of Brandenburg (her son-in-law) for support. Unedifying squabbling took place at the christening ceremony. The two Princesses brought their differences before the Court of Holland and the Supreme Court (of Holland and Zealand), each trying to gain against the other the support of the States of Holland, the opponents of the House of Orange it is true, but the rulers in actual fact. A settlement was reached at last by which the grandmother and the uncle (Amalia of Solms and the Great Elector) were recognised as co-guardians; the mother nevertheless practically remained mistress of the field. It could only make patriots more distrustful to see the future of the House of Orange thus fallen into the hands of a young woman of no personal ability whatsoever, but with a considerable share both of the obstinacy as well as of the levity of the Stuarts, a woman moreover who recognised as head of her House—even to the extent of asking for his 'orders'—an English King who, after his attempts first on Ireland then on Scotland, was soon to be a fugitive on the continent again. She felt indeed English, she preferred to speak English and otherwise French. As the years wore on she even came to hate her son's country and people, at the same time sorely trying the patience of her followers and friends by her indifference and chilly pride.

In the face of this confusion the States of Holland acted with discernment and resolution. The gentlemen who had been dismissed at William's request were at once reinstated in the various dignities they had held in their respective towns. But the States did not stop at their own provincial affairs. The discontinuance of the power of Orange brought about a constitutional crisis for the whole of the federation. The Hollanders became the self-constituted leaders. Without engaging in recriminations over the immediate past, they on the contrary declared in the States-General that it was

the sincere intention of Their Noble Great Mightinesses[1] to revive and maintain the unity, love, friendship, and complete correspondence and trust existing among the Provinces, keeping it up and cultivating it faithfully and indissolubly for ever.

To forestall insinuations that were to be expected, they presently declared that they wished to uphold religion according to the Synod of Dort (no Arminianism), honourably to preserve the Union of Utrecht (no secessionist policy), and to continue the militia in accordance with former resolutions (no disbandment). Meanwhile they requested the other provinces to come to The Hague with large deputations or even with plenary States assemblies in order to be able to deliberate and decide on the three points—religion, union, and army—without having to consult the principals. In this way they managed to by-pass the States-General, which were still largely filled with creatures of the Prince, and get directly into touch with their 'allies'.

This was to become the famous Grand Assembly. In January 1651 it was opened with due pomp in the Ridderzaal on the Binnenhof (decorated with all the banners captured from Spain) by the Grand Pensionary of the inviting province, Cats. In a way it was a constituent assembly, in which Netherlanders met to discuss the mutual relations of their provinces under more peaceful circumstances than seventy years earlier at Utrecht: Netherlanders this time, however, from the regions north of the rivers only. Yet in that conservative age, in which established rights were held in such high regard, and whose favourite argument in political palaver was historical precedent and the wisdom of one's ancestors, a really free assembly which would have been able to reform and construct was hardly thinkable. This becomes plain at once from the form the deliberations assumed. No more than in the States-General, whose place the Grand Assembly was in effect taking for some months, were there any genuine debates in which opposing opinions combat each other, an orator hopes to convince his hearers, and every member may in the last instance yield to the force of argument. Instead of this, the Grand Assembly was a congress where seven

[1] This was the title the States of Holland had assumed. The States of the other provinces contented themselves with *Noble Mightinesses*, without the *Great*. The States-General were *Their High Mightinesses*.

groups met and where the speakers did not act for themselves but each only as representing his group. In fact they usually only read aloud long memoranda, handing them in afterwards in writing, full of quotations from the Bible and the classics and from old States resolutions. When the pile of documents had become utterly unwieldy, a committee was appointed to look for the highest common denominator, and then, after endless conferences, statements, and counter-statements, the Assembly agreed on the 'conciliatory advice' proposed, or left the matter where it was.

What Holland really wanted was in fact something negative. She wished to safeguard herself against the sort of attacks to which she had been exposed at the hands of Orange. For that reason she not only meant never again to appoint a Stadholder herself, but brought all her influence to bear to restrain the other provinces from so doing. For that reason, too, she no longer wanted a Captain-General for the Union.

> Their Noble Great Mightinesses (*as Cats expressed it*) would rather think of a form of military government after the example of the oldest republic the world has ever known, namely that of the Hebrews, that is to say God's own people, who from the time they were led out of Egypt until the time of the Kings, being about 450 years, never appointed a regular Captain-General, notwithstanding that they were continually engaged in warfare, but chose a head or general for each separate campaign.

Finally, Holland wanted to make her safety doubly sure by weakening the Generality's power over the army, which actually had proved a tool in the hands of an ambitious Captain-General, and by strengthening her own hold over it. So the Hollanders now produced a detailed plan and, as a result of the deliberations in the Grand Assembly, the consent of any province in which troops were stationed was henceforward required for marching orders (patents), the appointment of officers was largely laid in the hands of the States of the province to whose 'apportionment' a given regiment fell, and the soldiers were made to swear allegiance not only to the Generality but also to such provincial States (the paymasters). The States of the province in which troops were stationed (not necessarily that of the paymasters of course), as well as the magistrates of the garrison towns, were likewise mentioned in the oath, which thus became a tremendously detailed and complicated document. This multiple oath of allegiance was apt to cause conscientious soldiers a great deal of heart-searching. The result of the arrangement was that unity in the management of the army was lost; and also that the noble officers' families of Utrecht, Gelderland, and Overijsel now started looking up to Holland (the province with the largest 'apportionment'—fifty-six to every hundred!) in the way they had used to look up to the Prince of Orange.

It was no small triumph for the Hollanders that unanimity was reached at the Grand Assembly on all these matters. The 'disorders' which had manifested themselves in 'the government' the year before were buried. For one last moment there was a flare-up of old passions. A document drawn up by the Greffier of the States-General, Musch, who had died shortly before (probably by his own hand), was made public, in which he painted Holland's conduct in the blackest hues. Holland now succeeded in getting the Grand Assembly itself to annul the resolution of 5 June 1650, which William II had advanced in justification of his action; it was declared to be considered

as not adopted, wherefore null and void and of no value, which goes also for anything that has in any way been done on the strength of and in accordance with it.

All this meant that Holland no longer had any need to carry on a particularist opposition. The province on the contrary became the leader of a confederate system; one, indeed, in which particularism reigned supreme. This was no more than a natural reaction to the abuse of the Union slogan under the previous régime, but that the army became the victim of this development is an undeniable fact.

North-Brabant noblemen and town magistrates had again tried to get their district recognised as an eighth—or rather the first!—province, but their demand was disregarded. North Brabant, or the Generality lands in general, had only been mentioned at the Assembly by the strictly Contra-Remonstrant provinces (Zealand, Friesland, Groningen) in order to support the request of the ministers of religion that the 'political reformation' there, that is to say the dismissal of papist officials in towns and villages, should be taken more rigorously in hand.

In 1648, when by the peace treaty the States-General had at last become the undisputed masters of the whole of North Brabant, including the rural districts, that policy had been decided upon immediately. In practice, however, its execution was impeded by the peculiarities of the *ancien régime*, the absence of an obedient bureaucracy and of an adequate police force, the stubborn feeling of respect for ancient rights and personal property, not to mention the practical impossibility of applying the Protestant programme to the Brabant region since the Counter-Reformation had consolidated Catholicism there. Yet the Grand Assembly now, at the ministers' request, readily affirmed the principle.

Five ministers had appeared in the Ridderzaal as delegates of the Synods of the provinces,

all standing bare-headed. Ministers of temporal princes are given a seat and allowed to cover their heads (*so rails Aitzema*). Shall Christ's ministers (II Cor. v. 20) stand bare-headed?

The religion of Dort was upheld. Regarding the repression of papist idolatry, superstition, and hierarchy it was possible to point not only to the resolution of two years previously with respect to the Generality Lands, but also to the vigorous action taken at Zijdewind, North Holland, at the same time. There 3,000 Catholics had gathered together (now that peace had come) to be confirmed by Rovenius' co-adjutor, De la Torre. Not only had that meeting been broken up, but to set an example the States had afterwards imposed heavy fines and had had the place of worship razed to the ground. Were not the ministers' imputations of too great lenience unjustified? Yet it is a fact that orthodox and libertinist regents with all the greater unanimity went on to combine and make the Reformed Church feel that the States were masters of the land. The 'true republicans' in Holland and elsewhere fully realised the importance of being on good terms with the Reformed Church, but apart from their obligations to the non-Reformed sections of the nation they knew very well that not all the ministers considered Cats' praise of the Hebrew Republic a conclusive argument in favour of a Stadholderless régime. Even among the five delegates themselves there was one, named Maximilian Teellinck, son of Willem Teellinck, 'the godless Zealander', as Vondel had scoffed, who had, with the help of other biblical texts, glorified William II's *coup d'état*.

However that may be, the States were masters of the situation; Holland's system triumphed in the Generality. And in the now Stadholderless provinces the oligarchy could still more tighten its cohesion. Everywhere the towns, that is to say the town corporations, took into their own hands the appointment of magistrates, in which until then the Stadholder had had a say,[1] thus becoming independent of all outside influence. This was what the regents themselves called Freedom. However clearly the features of a narrow class egoism may be visible through this mask, we need not therefore look upon the leaders of the Grand Assembly as hypocrites. The idea of Freedom inspired generations of regents with a genuine political faith. And in one respect this was strikingly apparent. The Assembly passed rigorous resolutions against bribery and every kind of corruption. This had a truly purifying effect. In that respect the period which now opens contrasted favourably with the preceding one.

One heavy shock the régime had to withstand almost at once.

3. THE FIRST ANGLO-DUTCH WAR

THIS shock came from outside. The sudden death of William II, the protector of the Stuarts, had seemed like a judgment of God to the English Republicans. In March 1651 Oliver St. John and Strickland appeared in The Hague. Accompanied for the greater glory of their masters, as was the custom of the times, by some hundreds of gentlemen, they came to propose a new policy of close co-operation between the two Protestant republics. What they really desired was a merging of the two into one State, but at the very least they hoped for an alliance against the Catholic world. To attain this they would have been willing to restrain their own commercial-interest party at home, which looked upon the Dutch as the chief obstacle to England's economic development. They soon discovered, however, that they had been mistaken about the spirit now prevailing in the Netherlands. The idea of a Protestant crusade, which apparently was what the English enthusiasts had in mind, did not in the least appeal to the Holland regents, while the populace of The Hague gave utterance to plainly hostile feelings. Incited by the Duke of

---

[1] The corporations, or municipal councils, whose members (between twenty and forty) sat for life, every year drew up a 'double number' for the appointment of Burgomasters (at most four in every town) and 'schepenen' (échevins, aldermen; seven), out of which list the Stadholder made the appointments. This enabled him at least to bar particularly objectionable opponents.

York and Prince Edward of the Palatinate and the 'domestics' of the Princess Royal, they demonstrated their abhorrence of the regicides by shouting abuse and even by violence. What made things worse was that the Orangists were still proving strong, not only in the streets, but in the States of the landward provinces as well, where they could obstruct and impede the negotiations in which they considered only the interests of Holland and Zealand to be involved anyway. The ambassadors returned home in a mood of irritation, and now that it became clear that nothing could be done with the Dutch, politically speaking, the party in favour of unbridled economic competition came to the fore in England.

Whilst the Hollanders, with their strong capitalistic development and their lead in shipping, desired only *freedom* in Europe with respect to England, the rising trading class in England felt a need of *protection*. Protection, and protection specifically against the Dutch, they now obtained through the famous Navigation Act, which aimed at excluding foreign, and practically that meant Dutch, shipping from intercourse between England and her American colonies as well as between England and other European countries. At the same time the claims of the monarchy to supremacy at sea were revived, and pursued a great deal more forcefully. English men-of-war, invoking the old maritime law which the Hollanders were always trying to relegate to the background (they had done so again in the abortive negotiations at The Hague), started molesting merchant vessels. England in fact was inviting war. War with England was the very last thing the Holland regent class desired, and it was they who were now directing the policy of the Republic. But public feeling in Holland was rising to fever heat. Urgent missions to London were still tried. First went old Jacob Cats, who had by that time relinquished the post of Grand Pensionary; he was followed by his successor, Adriaan Pauw, who had already shown himself a 'true Hollander' in the same post in Frederick Henry's time. But an incident at sea, occasioned by Tromp's refusal to lower the flag for Blake and resulting in an exchange of cannon shot, made it difficult to continue diplomatic relations. Many supporters of the States were inclined to censure Tromp's unyielding attitude and put it down to his well-known Orangist sentiments. By the beginning of July it was war.

At England's challenge others who suffered from or envied Holland's trading monopoly pricked up their ears. Extremely alarming possibilities appeared on the diplomatic horizon; Sweden and Spain—the latter as lord of the Southern Netherlands—seemed to be drawing together as well as looking for a rapprochement with England.

Nothing is more understandable than that in the Southern Netherlands means were being devised to revive overseas trade, in spite of the prohibitive restrictions laid down at Münster. The towns of Flanders especially, which were not under such immediate North-Netherlandish supervision as was Antwerp, started bestirring themselves. At the beginning of 1652 Bruges had sought to get into contact with the Hansa towns. Their resident at The Hague, the North Netherlander Lieuwe van Aitzema, well known to us through his voluminous chronicle of the times, was received by the town. How the inhabitants in the midst of so much decayed glory loved to look back towards the past! A convention dating from 1360 was unearthed from the archives and now renewed. In these plans Ostend was probably thought of as the port of entry from the sea. In ordinary circumstances the tariffs laid down at the Peace of Münster formed an effective hindrance, but now that the North Netherlanders were trying to cut off traffic between England and the Baltic, while the English were trying to cut out the North Netherlandish ports, there seemed to be an opportunity for Flanders to become the staple of Baltic trade, at least for England.

In the Baltic it was not only the politically powerless Hansa towns, but more particularly Sweden which hoped to put that combination to advantage. Since the events of 1644–45[1] Holland, which at the time had looked upon Sweden as first and foremost the adversary of the despot of the Sound duties, had gone over to the side of Denmark, now definitely the weaker party. Now suddenly, the loss of the Baltic through a resuscitation of Flanders seemed to have become an awful possibility.

In the field of trade (*Aitzema reflects*) the downfall of one means the rise of another. The destruction of Brabant and Flanders spelt the prosperity of Holland and Zealand.

The Republic, however, reacted against this menace with complete success; Denmark's aid was bought to 'nail up' the

[1] See Part One, pp. 139–41.

Baltic against the English; and a policy of trade restrictions carried through against all the neutrals—the Hansa towns, Sweden, and Spain—directly contrary to the principle of the freedom of the seas which Holland had just been advocating in the negotiations with England. During this crisis diplomacy was all that was required in the Baltic, although the young Amsterdammer, Koenraad van Beuningen, who had been sent to Stockholm as ambassador, had had to keep on warning all the time that Sweden might at any moment take the side of England.

From other more distant areas the English also were excluded, and there simply by force of arms. In the Indies the Dutch East India Company eagerly made use of its superior position, in no way dismayed by the fact that the ten years' truce with Portugal had run out shortly before. Even in the Mediterranean, where the English possessed the older and the larger interests, the Dutch were in complete control after a naval battle off Leghorn. But in the heart of the position, in the home seas, things went less propitiously. There, in the summer of 1653, a truly disastrous situation developed.

In any naval war with the Republic England started off with an invaluable natural advantage. A glance at the map is enough to make one realise how much easier it must be for the English navy to cut off Dutch commercial activity than the other way round. In those days the overseas trade of the Dutch was much larger than that of the English, and on that account alone the Republic was the more vulnerable. The task of protecting and escorting the merchant fleet bore very heavily on its navy. The southward route by way of the Channel was almost impracticable—and the alternative, the circuitous route round the north of Scotland, remained fraught with danger—unless the Dutch navy were in complete possession of the command of the sea. For that reason their fleets had to seek out the enemy again and again to try and drive him from the seas. While on the other hand, as soon as the Dutch fleets were compelled to fall back on their bases—the Wielingen in the South and Texel in the North—and abandon the seas to the English, the country practically found itself in a state of blockade.

Now the British Commonwealth was a redoubtable opponent. Ambitious and enterprising with the violence of a young régime, it was a military state *par excellence*. Cromwell had subdued

Ireland and quite recently Scotland also; Charles II was again in exile. From the start Parliament had held the seas as against the Royalists. The strongly centralised régime, ever more free of democratic supervision, had a formidable navy at its disposal. Indeed, the actual belligerent navy of England was stronger than that of the Republic, which, just as in 1639, had to increase its nucleus of national and 'direction vessels'[1] with merchantmen hurriedly equipped for fighting purposes. Even the States' proper men-of-war were smaller, and especially were less well furnished with heavy artillery (iron instead of copper cannon) than those of the Commonwealth. Tromp sailed out with bigger fleets than he had had at the Downs, but every time he came to grips with the enemy this inferiority of equipment proved an immense disadvantage, to the great chagrin of the States, who had cherished the hope that it would be in Tromp's power to shut up the English in 'the river of London'.

Those naval wars were a savage business. Hardship and privation accompanied by continuous ill-payment were the lot of the crews, while the horrors of battle were terrible beyond words. These uncouth fellows, undisciplined and crazy for spirits, were difficult to manage. Many of the captains, no less brutal than their subordinates, would snatch at the bottle in the hour of danger, or simply turn tail. Shirking duty in the face of the enemy was of common occurrence on both sides, and after every battle punishments had to be meted out right and left.

Yet what strong and noble characters emerged from these horrible trials, seemingly more than human nature could endure, characters which could inspire the men to incredible acts of heroism. None is more attractive than the intrepid and yet gentle 'grand-dad' Tromp. His devoted service under the new régime, with which he did not sympathise, and which after the Blake incident had treated him with scant consideration, was all the more precious at a time when party spirit often got the better of love of country.

His powers were taxed to the utmost in the course of that year. Months were spent in fruitless cruising, frequently harried by bad weather. The English were in the early phase of the war

---

[1] In 1631 the States-General had for the first time authorised some of the leading trading towns to found Directions for the equipment and management of men-of-war. These Directions were to some extent financed out of an imposition on trade and had to work in close conjunction with the Admiralties.

still keeping their navy divided for chasing merchantmen, and so Tromp could in December 1652 inflict a really severe blow on Blake and his squadron (off Dungeness). This gave him for a time complete supremacy at sea and convoys of hundreds of ships could sail to France unmolested. But while convoying a return fleet, Tromp was attacked by the repaired, and by that time united, English fleet; after three days of heavy fighting (28 February, 1 and 2 March 1653), in which much of his fleet, and especially many of the convoying vessels were lost, Tromp was able to save his sadly battered 'main squadron' in the Wielingen just before the defeat was on the point of becoming disastrous through lack of powder and shot. The English fleet was not able to keep the sea either, so that in April Tromp was once more to be seen setting out with a hastily repaired and reinforced fleet. First he conducted it northward in order to escort the 'circumnavigators' who were expected home; returning, he went south to look for the enemy, who had failed to find him anywhere. And again the undivided English fleet, which came upon him on 15 June off Nieuport, proved too much for him. He suffered even more severely than the previous time, because the English, rapidly learning by experience—the world had never yet witnessed a naval war on such a scale—did not give his ships a chance of boarding, but, staying at a safe distance, made them feel the full power of the superior English guns. This time the English remained in possession of the seas, and to the intense dismay of the Dutch people their shipping was deprived of ways of either sailing out or in.

The country's danger occasioned an outburst against the new régime which seemed to be bringing it to the verge of collapse. A 'frenzy' of Orangist feeling swept the country. Civic guard companies arrayed themselves with orange. Everywhere attempts were made to force the drummers who were recruiting men in the name of the States-General to mention the Prince of Orange's name as well. Inevitably the commotion often led to rowdyism and sedition. Matters took a serious turn when in August, at Enkhuizen, where the fishermen were once again, just as in 1572[1], reduced to idleness, the city gates were closed against the States' troops summoned by the anxious Burgomasters: guns were levelled at the soldiers outside, the town

[1] See *The Revolt of the Netherlands*, p. 124.

government was deposed and the Orange flag flown from all the towers. Similar disturbances were occurring in Zealand. Everywhere the people were demanding 'a chief'.

In later years it will seem unbelievable that a warlike nation in its embarrassment sought refuge with a small boy not yet out of his swaddling-clothes (*so wrote an indignant States of Holland man in a pamphlet*).

But people imagined that the Stadholder of Friesland might act as lieutenant for a Captain-General under age. They did not know how profound the disunity between the leading personalities of the family still was, so that both the mother and the grandmother of the young Prince were working against the candidature of William Frederick, which was regarded with sympathy by several of the provinces. But what, indeed, could William Frederick have done? English annoyance at the continued influence of the pro-Stuart House of Orange had been a contributory cause of the war. The States of Holland were conducting it as vigorously as they could, but with the definite intention of ending it as quickly as possible, for after all the country had nothing to gain by it. On 5 June, shortly before the defeat off Nieuport, Holland had managed to induce the States-General to send ambassadors to England to negotiate peace. In England there happened at that moment to be a reaction in favour of peace. Cromwell, to whom the Protestantism common to both Republics meant more than the rivalry of their merchants, was consolidating his power. But if William III were now to be appointed to the posts of his forebears, then feeling in England would become more than ever implacably eager for war. That is what the English royalists were hoping for, and that is why they were continually offering to assist the States. But the latter were wiser than to respond, and Charles II was not even allowed to enter the Republic's territory. The leaders of the Orange party, too, were looking out for this development, men like William Frederick and Sommelsdijk, who had joyfully welcomed the war on account of the confusion into which they hoped it would throw the hated 'Loevesteiners'.

In the circumstances prevailing in that summer of 1653 the recklessness of this policy was so obvious that William Frederick himself had made his provinces join in the vote for the mission to England. But that did not mean that party passions were abated. The systematic poisoning of popular opinion with the suspicion that the regents did not mean well by the country was now having its effect. It had once been alleged that Pauw, the Grand Pensionary, had instructed Tromp to spare the English. Later on the same slander overtook Wassenaer van Obdam, a pro-States member of the Holland Nobility, who sailed with the fleet as deputy of Their High Mightinesses. And even more reckless things were said:

Good evening, neighbour Cornelis, good evening. (*With these words Jan opens the conversation in a pamphlet in which Cornelis, the pro-States writer and mouthpiece, in the end convinces his credulous friend of his error:*) What say you now? Do you still not believe that our country has been sold, and that they are already arranging for the delivery? (*In their talk Jan at first persists:*) Only a short while ago I called at a bookseller's shop and heard it said in so many words that the gentlemen of Amsterdam and the Loevesteiners had come to an understanding with the English Parliament. They were to allow our merchants to be despoiled at sea, and with that aim in view they were to make our men-of-war sail in small squadrons and give our merchantmen niggardly convoy, so that they might the more easily be captured and conquered. And then, having lost our naval strength and our commerce, and the merchants being destitute, we could the more easily be brought under English subjection and the House of Orange and Nassau be cast off for ever. (*Cornelis, after having given vent to his feelings in some heartfelt imprecations, says:*) That such idle talk is greatly in vogue among the ignorant commonalty is not unknown to me.

Unable to produce an alternative régime or even an alternative policy, the Orange party in the crisis of the first Anglo-Dutch War could create nothing but confusion. Fortunately the States régime showed itself equal to its responsibility and with admirable energy stood up to the difficulties assailing it from within as well as from without. At this very time it found a statesman of uncommon ability and strength of character to conduct affairs in the post once filled by Oldenbarnevelt and to give a lead which was no longer to be expected from the ailing Pauw. This was Johan de Witt, still a young man—he was born in 1625—and a Loevesteiner by birth, for his father, Burgomaster of Dort, had been one of William II's six prisoners. Johan was Pensionary of his home town and in that capacity not only attended the meetings of the States of Holland but, since Dort was the first in rank of the eighteen towns, did duty for the Grand Pensionary in the latter's absence.

As I see it, the situation of our common beloved fatherland (*his customary term to indicate the Union of the seven provinces*) is at present in a very distressing not to say desperate condition, it being as it were blockaded and besieged. Since people always want to explain evil by some cause, all our

disasters are very generally attributed to the bad management of the regents
. . . and, as is generally the case, there are people now who are trying to fish
in troubled waters, giving the commonalty the impression that a chief is what
is needed, or else matters will never prosper, an opinion which is so deeply
rooted in the general mind that of the common rabble hardly one in a
thousand is free of it.

Thus did De Witt, in a private letter, describe the situation
just before his appointment. But amidst this commotion he saw
his line of conduct straight before him and followed it unwaver-
ingly.

First of all the fleet must be enabled to sail out again to break
the English blockade. At all the harbours and wharves the workers were hammering with a will. Not that the shortcomings of the
States' form of government did not make themselves abundantly
felt. The Admiralties remained responsible for the execution of
the plans, although they were stripped of their revenue owing
to the blocking of trade, so that the States had to come to their
aid. Boards and commissions were continually at loggerheads,
conferences without number, differences between Holland and
Zealand, Amsterdam in favour of one strategy, Rotterdam of
another, with Zealand protesting that nobody gave a thought to
her trade interests—in fact one is surprised that anything at
all could emerge out of such confusion. Tromp complained
that on the voyage which was to prove his last he was sent out
with a much too weak, an unnecessarily feeble, fleet.

It grieves me to see (he wrote to 'Their High Mightinesses' on 12 July 1653)
that the fine new ships everywhere remain ashore, having only partly been
finished; they might so well have reached completion if only everyone to a
man had done his share, in which case we should have been able to stand up
to the enemy properly. Yet, as for me, I shall not be lacking in my duty of
living and dying for my dear country as beseems an honest man. Please rest
assured of this.

It should not, however, be concluded from this complaint
that the leading men in the States had not worked to the best of
their ability. Actually the obstacles presented by particularism
and the spirit of faction had been overcome with surprising
success. The Hollanders and the Amsterdammers and the new
Grand Pensionary had developed a driving force which was in
no way inferior to what had been accomplished in 1629 for the
siege of 's Hertogenbosch, and the defence against the invaders
from Germany, and for the battle off the Downs in 1639.[1] And in

[1] See Part One, pp. 89 and 126.

c

fact the fleet was able to do what was expected of it. Brilliant seamanship helped. The junction Tromp was able to effect with Witte de With's squadron created the most favourable circumstances for the new battle, at the outset of which he was killed (off Terheide, on 10 August). De With, who took over the command, fought with heroic pertinacity, but left in the lurch, as he was, by a number of captains, he was finally obliged to fall back on Den Helder. The English, however, had suffered so greatly that they too had to put back to port. Holland and Zealand breathed again.

More vigorous resistance against the English therefore, but at the same time—that was both De Witt's and Holland's policy—attempt to bring the peace negotiations to a successful conclusion: these two matters were interconnected, because after their defeat off Nieuport Cromwell had thought that the Dutch would submit to any conditions. Nothing was further from the minds of De Witt and his friends, however, and the fleet's comparative success in August was thus most welcome to them. But at the same time they felt it necessary to show the English that in the Republic it was not the Orangists but the States of Holland who were in control. The States of Zealand, not so much from inclination as because they were less independent of their citizens than were those of Holland, came forward with a proposal in the States-General to appoint a Captain-General. De Witt attached the greatest importance to the fact that even the Orangist magistrates of Haarlem and Leiden allowed themselves to be persuaded, so that he could obtain a unanimous recommendation from Holland against the proposal. As regards Enkhuizen, it was not the Dutch way to deal severely with civil disturbances, but the States evinced neither fear nor weakness and the insurrectionary movement in that town soon collapsed.

Now the four envoys in London could enter into serious talks with the Protector. The negotiations followed almost the same pattern as had those of 1651. Again Cromwell started off with the idea of a union, proposing an offensive alliance next. Not even the prospect of an economic arrangement which might have meant getting rid of the Navigation Act could tempt even the Hollanders among the envoys to consider either of these proposals seriously. When Cromwell had realised that his ideal programme was unattainable, he nevertheless desired the reestablishment of peace between the two Protestant nations; but economic concessions were now out of the question. And besides, since the Republic could sympathise so little with his international policy, he insisted all the more strongly on guarantees against a restoration of the House of Orange, whose adherents had proved still to possess only too much influence. The constitution of the loosely knit confederation must always enable the landward provinces to prevent guarantees that would satisfy him on this point from passing the States-General, but rather than let the peace negotiations break down, the two Hollanders among the four ambassadors—of whom Van Beverning acted in close communication with De Witt—now entered into a secret settlement with the Protector, whereby only *their* province promised never to take any member of the House of Orange as Stadholder nor to allow any of its members to be appointed Captain-General by the Generality.

This was the famous Act of Seclusion, which De Witt in May 1654 managed to extract from an expressly convened meeting of the States of Holland (who were sworn to absolute secrecy). The vote was not unanimous this time, but the dissent of the few Orangist towns was passed over. So the document was handed to Cromwell by the two Holland members of the mission in London, and only then did he ratify the peace that had already been concluded with the States-General. But even before that happened the secret had leaked out. The Princesses of Orange— for once working in unison!—requested the States-General to protect their son and grandson against Holland, and a veritable storm of indignation broke out in the Union. Holland was accused of having broken the federal covenant by having thus negotiated on its own with a foreign power, of having humiliated the State by allowing foreign intervention in its domestic affairs, and of having, by the exclusion of the young Prince, violated the national duty of gratitude towards the glorious House of Orange. De Witt was highly vexed at the state of nerves to which some of his political associates were reduced. Even Dort, he wrote to his father, in undisguised anger,

which has never on any such occasion been known to fail, has sent people hither (*as deputies, namely, to the States of Holland*) who have allowed themselves to be so intimidated by the empty sound of a child's name and by the dead letter of two widows' humble request that they have shamefully deserted their posts.

Such timidity was indeed unnecessary. When it came to the point even the Orangists, especially those in Holland and Zealand, no longer dared jeopardise the peace. They never got beyond protests, and to these De Witt returned an uncompromising reply in a *Deduction* published in the name of his masters, the States of Holland. The transaction with the Protector did not come under the description of 'confederations or alliances', forbidden by the Union of Utrecht, so he argued; and he recalled certain actions at least equally near the border-line of constitutional propriety of which some of the protesting provinces had been guilty in the past. As for the debt of gratitude due to the House of Orange, that had been fully acquitted by generous payments to the successive Stadholders, and he appended a list of these running into a staggering sum of money. In fact Holland was in an unassailable position, and what paralysed the opposition, when it came to acting rather than raising a clamour, was the fear, to which even the landward provinces and 'the rabble' in Holland could not be insensible, that to upset the private arrangement between the Protector and the powerful province would mean to upset the peace. So the upshot was that the Republican régime had withstood the shock of war and faced the future with redoubled self-assurance.

It goes without saying that no Dutchman of to-day can look upon the Act of Seclusion with feelings other than of regret. Technically it was not perhaps a breach of the Union, nor had the Prince of Orange hereditary rights to the official posts his forefathers had held. Yet, to abate, by a secret settlement with England, the country's freedom to arrange its government according to its own ideas was certainly not an act redounding to the credit of De Witt's conduct of his office. It would be most unfair, however, to charge him with all the odium. The circumstances that drove him to the transaction—after he had honestly tried to avoid Cromwell's demand—were not of his own nor of the States of Holland's creating. The Act of Seclusion was the fruit of the unhappy alliance between Orange and Stuart by which Frederick Henry and William II had allowed their foreign policy to be dominated. It was that which had prompted England to choose sides in the party conflicts in the Republic, and it was that which had turned the relationship with England in the Republic into a party matter. How this and the accompanying poisonous mutual distrust could at moments weaken the Dutch State was to appear anew, and tragically, in the subsequent course of De Witt's administration.

Meanwhile the Peace of Westminster was more than a stabilisation of the States' régime; it was at the same time the deliverance of the country from a deadly danger. It contained stipulations which were not palatable to the Republic. Thus, besides the fact that the Navigation Act was upheld, the States had to promise that those 'guilty' of the Amboyna massacre of thirty years before[1] (if there were any still alive . . .) would be punished. The Protector thereby not only triumphed over the States but also over the monarchy, which had had tamely to let the matter be consigned to official oblivion. But England not only wanted to avenge Amboyna, she also wanted to put an end to the position the Dutch held there. The English Company still had in the Archipelago to be content with a remote position in Bantam and was wholly shut out from the Moluccas. England's political ascendancy in Europe now had to serve to take her back there: near the Banda group, on the most sensitive spot of the Dutch East India Company's monopoly, the sovereign rights over the small island of Pulu Run were transferred. Moreover it was laid down that the Dutch should strike the flag for British men-of-war on the seas which the more powerful party considered its own, whereby yet another of the monarchy's old ambitions was realised.

But in the summer of 1653 the English had wanted to go much further than that. Demands which would have made the seas a British possession by more than the mere symbolism of the flag, the Hollanders had resisted. A regular tribute for fishing along the Scottish coast, an extensive right of visitation, an indemnification involving the admission that the war itself was only a rightful re-establishment of England's position—by a settlement on those lines the Republic would have been reduced to unmistakeable inferiority, and the attempt had been frustrated by its powers of resistance. The ability of its naval commanders and the determination of its statesmen had preserved its future possibilities intact. The first trial of strength between England and the North Netherlands State had decided nothing.

[1] See Part One, p. 179.

B. THE SOUTHERN NETHERLANDS
BECOME A EUROPEAN PROBLEM

THE split in the Netherlands had not created a stable state of affairs. The Republic, entrenched behind the rivers and justifying its existence by its Protestantism, had become a clearly outlined and respected figure among the powers, whereas the Southern Netherlands (let alone the universally forgotten Generality lands) remained a fragment without a clear national character, with frontiers difficult to defend, and subject to a distant, once redoubtable, but by now decrepit master—in fact a tempting morsel to all conquerors. This created a European problem, and so little could the Peace of Münster be considered a solution that for none of the powers did it constitute so urgent a problem as for the severed and now independent North. The Republic's very existence seemed involved. Not that the danger seemed to be continuously imminent; the Republic was threatened from other quarters and distracted by other interests. Yet what is striking in this period is how in the long run everything came once more to be dominated by the South Netherlands question, which it had been thought in 1648 could be shelved.

1. THE REPUBLIC ISOLATED; THE BALTIC QUESTION

The Southern Netherlands Threatened

THE Peace of Münster had secured peace to the Southern Netherlands on the north side only. France for the time being had acquired what it wanted in the exhausted and disintegrated German Empire, and the peace she concluded there meant among other things that the Austrian Habsburg had to leave his Spanish cousin to his fate. We already know, however, that while the peace concluded with the Republic allowed the Spanish armed forces in the Netherlands to be concentrated against France, at the same time France's powers of aggression were crippled by the civil disturbances of the Fronde. The highest nobility in France, men who could still play lord and master over entire provinces, still appeared to subordinate the modern concept of the sovereign State to the old feudal idea of their personal rights and liberties. Turenne, son of the turbulent Huguenot Duke of Bouillon (and cousin of Orange), who in the German war had brought as great glory to French arms as had Condé in the war against the Spanish, in 1649 and the years following fought at the side of the Governor of the Netherlands, the Archduke Bishop Leopold William, against the French armies. On his return to French service he soon became young Louis XIV's most important commander, because Condé himself, the hero of Rocroi and Lens (1643 and 1648), a prince of the blood royal, now fought on the Spanish side! If the malcontents in France had been able to co-operate, the French monarchy could hardly have escaped a shattering disaster.

Even as things were, the Spaniards in 1649 reconquered Ypres, which they had lost the year before. In 1650 the invasion of Northern France which had acted as a spur to William II in his attempts at getting the States-General to join the side of France,[1] came to nothing. But in 1651 the Spanish general Fuensaldaña retook Furnes, Bergues, and Bourbourg; and in 1652 Dunkirk. Thereby the last small fragment of the Dutch language area was once again recovered from French occupation. But although that was the moment when Condé came to reinforce the Spanish forces in the Netherlands with his adherents, France had recovered from its worst depression. In 1653 Mazarin firmly assumed control again. At the same time Condé proved so unmanageable a person that he did not at first bring anything but confusion to the camp of his allies. Nevertheless in 1654 a bold stroke was undertaken, namely the siege of Arras, but Turenne heavily defeated Condé and Fuensaldaña and relieved the town. In 1656, it is true, Turenne suffered a similar reverse at the siege of Valenciennes; a new Governor, Don John of Austria, a bastard son of Philip IV, with a new general, Caracena, in that way happily inaugurated their rule. But now a third party joined in the fight and the tide turned against Spain.

This was Cromwell. After having settled the war against the States-General, there the Protector stood at the head of his strongly ordered and fully armed State, thirsting for action. A Protestant alliance under his leadership was ever his dream, but the independence of the North Netherlands statesmen, who

[1] See above, p. 18.

were guided rather by economic considerations, impeded its realisation. With the new Swedish King, the enterprising Charles X, Cromwell was better able to come to an understanding; the Swiss Protestant Cantons also looked up to him. But even though the two great Catholic powers, France and Spain, were continuing to destroy each other, he was still a long way from having the lead in Europe. His joining one side in the inter-Catholic conflict meant a compromise with his warlike religious ideal. When in 1655 he sent an expedition to conquer San Domingo, he had only intended an energetic denial of Spain's right to shut England out of the New World: it was not that he wished to side with France, indeed he treated her at sea equally roughly. But the expedition was unsuccessful—even though Jamaica was conquered—and Philip IV, notwithstanding the sad plight he was in, took the insult in very bad part and declared war. This presently brought France and England into closer contact, but not until the spring of 1657 did Cromwell take a new and important step by concluding an offensive alliance which with the help of France was to give England a firm footing in Spain's Netherlands. It was agreed that England should co-operate in conquering the Flemish coastal towns with a fleet of 6,000 men and herself retain Dunkirk and Mardyck. At the same time, through Mazarin's diplomacy, a possible impulse on the part of the new Emperor to come to Spain's aid was prevented by a league of German Rhine States under France's leadership.

Circumstances were thus too much for the new Spanish rulers in the Netherlands. Mardyck fell in that same year 1657 and was handed over to the English. In 1658 the campaign (after Cassel had first been taken) started with the siege of Dunkirk by Turenne. An attempt by Don John and Condé to relieve the town led to the defeat of the Dunes, in effect the death-blow for the Spanish army, once reputed invincible but which for the last fifteen years had repeatedly been beaten (the first time by Condé himself!). It was a worse and more sudden collapse than had been the case in 1646. Dunkirk capitulated on 23 June. The young King Louis XIV made his victorious entry, but after that the town was given up to the English. In the following weeks the French took the whole of the west corner of Flanders—this time for themselves!—Bergues, Turnes, Dixmude, Gravelines;

next Turenne turned his attack eastward, crossed the Lys and took Gavre and Audenarde on the Scheldt (Ypres, Menin, and Comines in his rear he did not secure until later), pushing forward to Grammont and Ninove on the Dender, at the extreme eastern boundary of Flanders, on the road to Brussels. There consternation reigned, but winter had set in, the rain made the roads impassable, and Turenne contented himself with the advantage he had gained.

Naturally these events were watched by the North Netherlanders with uneasiness. During Frederick Henry's last years France's northward push had already roused fears, and now, instead of being an ally, she was still nursing her grievance about what she considered the defection of Münster; in the previous year the vigorous action taken by the States fleet against the lawless French privateers in the Mediterranean had almost caused a rupture. That England was taking part in the conquest of Flanders was far from improving matters in the eyes of the leaders of the Republic. Their relationship with the rising trade rival remained difficult, and it was not without anxiety that the Dutch saw him establish a foothold in the Southern Netherlands, which they had managed to render commercially impotent at Münster in the treaty with Spain. What made the situation even more perilous was that the Republic had just proceeded to take military action against Portugal in Europe; the ten years' armistice had come to an end as early as 1652, and as we shall see there had been lively fighting in America, but especially in Asia, from that moment onward: and Portugal, the enemy of Spain, was the protégé of both France and England.

Even so not everything has been mentioned that made the relations of the Republic with the new allies so very delicate. In the Baltic, too, conditions were going through a crisis. The man after Cromwell's heart, Charles X, through the tradition of Gustavus Adolphus and of Münster associated with France also, had started a war against Catholic Poland in 1655 in order to conquer the largely Protestant and German-speaking coastal area, i.e. Prussia, the eastern part of which was held as a fief by the Elector of Brandenburg. The Republic could not look on in idleness. Without going so far as to ally herself with Poland, of old a member of the Habsburg party in Europe, it was her obvious course to seek an understanding with the other Baltic

powers—Brandenburg and Denmark—in order to press Sweden
to moderation. Brandenburg, whose elector was an uncle of the
young Prince of Orange, Denmark, whose King was a kinsman
of the Stuarts—this policy could not but arouse distrust in
England. De Witt and most of the 'members' (that is, of the
voting towns) of Holland considered that extreme caution was
required, but the Amsterdammers, supported by the other
maritime towns, thought the moment had come to teach
Sweden a lesson. Van Beuningen, who was at this time on a
diplomatic mission in Denmark, pushed this policy through,
practically against the officially accepted one, and in 1657
Frederick III, trusting to Van Beuningen's urgings, had plunged
into the war which was soon to lead him to disaster. Charles X
came rushing up from Poland with his army and by crossing the
ice made his way into the Danish islands. All this happened with
such rapidity that Frederick had to give up the game for lost,
before others could think of intervention. In February 1658 the
Peace of Roskilde was concluded and the Danish King was
compelled to cede Scania and Halland, the districts on the
southernmost point of the Scandinavian peninsula, the possession of which had given him the control of both banks of the
Sound. That shift in territorial power was not unpleasing to the
Hollanders, to whom free entrance to the Baltic was ever the
first consideration, but for a moment Frederick III seemed
to be thinking of closely allying himself with his enemy of
yesterday so that they might jointly close the Sound. This was
an extremely undesirable situation from the point of view of
Netherlands diplomacy. Van Beuningen did all he could to upset
the peace just concluded. In vain did De Witt, always apprehen-
sive of the consequences of a breach with Sweden or with
Sweden's friends, urge him to observe caution.

Short-lived Plan for 'Cantonment'

IN THESE circumstances the French, shortly after the conquest
of Dunkirk and while they were still triumphantly pushing on
into Flanders, made a surprising proposal. Mazarin let it be
known in The Hague that it was his intention to drive the
Spaniards out of their Netherlands altogether. He did not,
however, wish to annex the country, but to turn it into a Free
Republic. If the States-General were willing to help him in this

project, France would evacuate the part of the Netherlands she already occupied, 'even including Arras', and rejoin it to the rest.

De Witt eagerly fastened upon the idea, and nothing is more natural. Here was a chance of rescuing the Republic from its dangerous isolation by a reconciliation with its old ally France, while the South-Netherlands question would be solved in a way which seemed to serve the Republic's security excellently. De Witt was all zeal to insure the life of the contemplated South-Netherlands State by a defensive alliance and by guaranteeing to it the promises France was to make.

But the Amsterdammers thought differently. Their minds were wholly taken up with plans for action against Sweden, and, besides, they did not trust France and feared that by joining in they might be displeasing Spain and England. The Grand Pensionary saw better than they did that the South-Netherlands question could not be evaded and that if the chance of reaching an agreement with France were allowed to slip by, it might later prove necessary to co-operate closely with Spain against France. And this at first sight meant a startling break with tradition. Public opinion did not yet clearly recognise the Peace of Münster as the end of an era: would it be possible to make such a policy acceptable? Would not the ministers of religion denounce it?—to say nothing of Spain's apparently incurable exhaustion.

However that may have been, the French gave up the idea of a 'cantonment' as suddenly as they had suggested it. Does this prove that they never had any other intention than of amusing the Northern Netherlands with the prospect whilst continuing to help themselves to the Southern Netherlands? Perhaps an adequate explanation of their crying off is supplied by the hopeful turn now being taken by the peace negotiations with Spain, which had already been going on, somewhat fitfully, for some years: I shall return to that presently. But it is also possible to connect their change of front with Cromwell's death (13 September—3 September O.S.—1658), which rid Mazarin of the worry a powerful England as a factor in the situation had meant to him.

Dutch Intervention in the Baltic

CROMWELL's death gave greater liberty of action to the Republic also. Under the continual and vigorous insistence of Amsterdam

—although it was in fact De Witt, with the diplomatic map of the whole of Europe before his mind, who shaped the policy— the Republic took advantage of the occasion to intervene energetically in the Baltic.

There Charles X, apparently expecting a Dutch-Danish attack, had himself broken the Peace of Roskilde and in the summer of 1658, after another lightning expedition, had appeared on Zealand to take Copenhagen. But now Copenhagen put up a gallant resistance and Charles X was delayed by a long siege. In October the States' fleet under Obdam sailed northward with auxiliary troops. In November they beat the Swedish fleet in the Sound—when Witte de With was killed—and sailed on to Copenhagen. The Swedes continued the siege from the landward side, however, occasioning a lengthy crisis, in which large European interests were involved and European peace endangered. De Witt managed to set on foot an action on a European scale for the purpose of controlling that crisis. He succeeded in getting England and France to join with the Republic in the so-called Hague Concert. The three Western powers took it upon themselves to dictate a settlement whereby Charles X was to keep Halland and Scania, while ensuring that the Sound was to remain open.

De Witt's policy demanded great reserve and patience from the commanders of the fleet—in 1659 De Ruyter also appeared in the Baltic, and to him Obdam later left the supreme command. De Witt's task was all the harder because of the continual insistence on the part of the Amsterdammers that more vigorous measures should be taken against Sweden. When, however, the increasing confusion in England caused the English fleet to be recalled, the chances of dissension among the signatories to the Concert were lessened. In spite of the treaty, the English fleet had in the Baltic been looked upon as the ally of Sweden while the Dutch fleet was regarded as the ally of the Danes. The Dutch now had to carry out the provisions of the Hague treaty alone, and, since Sweden refused to submit, this involved action in conjunction with the Danes. De Ruyter distinguished himself uncommonly, especially in the conquest of Funen in the Autumn of 1659. The sudden death of Charles X in February 1660 in the end facilitated the restoration of peace by a settlement which answered to the Hague programme entirely.

Before this the Grand Pensionary's successful financial operations had impressed opinion abroad and had stimulated his compatriots' self-confidence. He had been able to convert outstanding loans and had managed to get the interest on the enormous war debts, which weighed on the province of Holland particularly, lowered from five to four per cent.

Holland will profit two million florins annually (*so one young regent wrote to another in 1655*), and if that be true and Holland being increasingly disembarrassed should in course of time become free in her movements so that she could enjoy her great income clear of encumbrance, I would have you reflect whether she will not be able, with God's help and protection, to attain such a position in the world as to make herself feared.

He added: 'provided there be the supervision and guidance of a good chief', and there is no doubt that many continued to distrust the Stadholderless régime on principle. But the States' vigorous and yet prudent intervention in the Baltic had raised their prestige both in the world outside, and with their own people. Their Minister De Witt and their Admiral De Ruyter had become figures of the first magnitude on the European stage. At home De Witt had strengthened his personal position by his marriage to a daughter of the great Amsterdam family of the Bickers. Her uncle, De Graeff van Zuidpolsbroek, henceforth saw to it that the town should keep 'good correspondence' with the Grand Pensionary.

2. THE SOUTHERN NETHERLANDS AND THE PEACE OF THE PYRENEES

MEANWHILE, as we saw, France and Spain had come closer together. Philip IV at last had to recognise the increasing exhaustion of his Empire and to draw the consequence from the long series of calamities on the war theatres of the West Indies, Portugal, and the Netherlands. Before the end of 1658 he consented to a marriage between his daughter Maria Theresa and the young French king as the price for a tolerable treaty. It had long been known how greatly the French desired this marriage. They were moved by the purely dynastic reflection that through the Infanta Louis XIV, or at any rate his successors, might in course of time be entitled to lay claim to the Spanish monarchy. It is true that in 1657 a sickly little son had been born of Philip IV's third marriage, which hitherto had only brought forth daughters who had hardly survived infancy. Moreover, before the wedding Maria Theresa was made to renounce in the most stringent form her right to the succession. But the French jurists were ready with a variety of arguments to prove the invalidity of any such renunciation. At all events it was with an eye to these dynastic possibilities in the future that Mazarin not only gave up the chance of an immediate conquest of the Spanish Netherlands, but even evacuated part of the territory already conquered. The Peace of the Pyrenees was not concluded until November 1659: the delay had been chiefly caused by Spain's demand that Condé should be reinstated in his position in France. As far as the Netherlands were concerned, Spain ceded to France the province of Artois almost in its entirety as well as bits of Hainault and Luxemburg and a small piece of Flanders (Gravelines and Bourbourg). England was not included in the peace (an arrangement which Cromwell would not easily have put up with), but she kept a tight hold on Dunkirk and Mardyck (as well as on Jamaica). The French, to sum up, abandoned almost the whole of Turenne's conquests in Flanders, and by the new boundary-line many more Walloons than Flemings were withdrawn from the governance of Brussels.

The Netherlands towns which thus escaped from the French—little did they know for how short a time!—beheld them leave with joy. That held good for French-speaking places like Lille no less than for Dutch-speaking like Bourbourg, where, when the French had been forced to evacuate the little town in 1652 after the Spanish had recaptured Dunkirk, the inhabitants had mockingly given them a send-off with a fiddler playing the march of Bergues. What the people, Flemings and Walloons alike, hated in French rule was the stricter and more centralised absolutism; besides, they were attached to the Habsburg dynasty out of sheer habit and because to them it was the champion of the Catholic religion, as they were taught by the priests and especially the monks.

A strongly developed sense of nationality, which might have felt the separation from fellow-countrymen and language partners as a disaster, was not to be expected after the long alien rule which had drawn to itself all political responsibility and extinguished independent intellectual life. If one surveys the eleven years that had elapsed since Münster, it is remarkable to find how difficult it is to catch sight of the people of the Southern Netherlands. They are of even less account than in the preceding period. From its very beginning in 1635 the war with France had interfered with their prosperity more profoundly than had the war with the Republic, which had by then already been going on for fourteen years: Münster, therefore, which brought peace with the Republic and left the war with France going on, had not done much to give relief. Especially in Flanders the coming and going of the French armies had had a disruptive effect on economic life. Trade and business languished, there was considerable distress. This passive role is about the only one in which one sees the people appear. Less than ever had they had any opportunity of acting, or even expressing themselves, politically.

Immediately after his arrival at Brussels Leopold William had placed the central government, the management of finance and of the army, still more exclusively in the hands of foreigners. Even President Roose had not been sufficiently submissive and had therefore been dismissed. Under Don John, with the war going even more disastrously, the government had imposed its immediate needs with increasing urgency as the overriding law. The war makes up the whole history of the Southern Netherlands, and it was not their war. They suffered from it, but it was fought over their heads by Spaniards, Frenchmen, and Englishmen, and it was again foreigners who put an end to it without one South Netherlander having been asked for his opinion. Nevertheless the Peace of the Pyrenees and the claims it created were to exercise a profound influence on the national future of the people of Flanders and Brabant—because all that fell to France during Louis XIV's time was destined to lose its Dutch character. But the people of Flanders and Brabant, who had so violently resisted Spanish rule less than a century ago, and whose own kin in the North were at that moment, under their own burgher-regents and deliberating in their own language, making their influence felt so vigorously in the councils of the world, lacked not only the power but the will to assert themselves. Nobody asked about their wishes, but indeed they were hardly aware of having any. Peace, that was all they craved.

The Netherlands (*the Lierre notary De Bie wrote in his 'Book of Painting, in 1662*) have attained their greatest happiness and joy through peace. For what more fortunate or better or more useful can happen to man in this world than to possess peace ...

In the great events which determined the destinies of this people, they had neither soldiers nor statesmen of their own, nor did they any longer have any poets or writers, only theologians and lawyers.

All this does not mean that the rule of the foreigners was interfering more profoundly than before in the affairs of the population. On the contrary, while it was conducting the war with the intensity of despair and made everything yield to its requirements, the Government bestowed less attention on them. Little was left of the reforming zeal which had characterised the administration of the Archdukes in the religious and social sphere. At most the Governors still occasionally meddled with the struggle which the secular clergy and the theologians of Louvain, mostly inclined towards Jansenism, carried on with the Jesuits—with great bitterness on both sides—and then it was always to enforce the papal denunciations of Jansenism. The Archduke, Bishop Leopold William, in particular strongly favoured the Jesuits, to the great grief of the old Archbishop Boonen, who in vain invoked the King's support. These disputes hardly roused the attention of the people, or at least they took no active part in them. We shall consider their importance later on when dealing with the cultural life of the period.

Taking it all in all, the decay of the foreign monarchy to which the Southern Netherlands were subject and which exposed them to the danger of conquest by France at least had the advantage of protecting their local self-government against further encroachments of extra-national absolutism. To the people these local liberties meant all the more because they had lost any real self-determination, and we have already seen that their attachment to these liberties helped to make them prefer Habsburg to Bourbon. It was always in Brabant above all where the spirit of opposition was able to make itself felt, because there the nobility, the clergy, and the towns had retained the free disposal of their finances more completely than elsewhere. With great political questions, however, the resistance put up by the Brabant classes was never concerned; at most it attached itself to local interests, or was just simply an aversion to paying taxes. This much is certain, that their rights in this matter compelled the government to practice a good deal of circumspection and patience.

Not that the Spanish rulers had to take everything lying down. The story of the action they took against the civil disturbances at Antwerp in 1659 deserves to be briefly related here. It helps one to realise the town's impotence in a serious clash with royal authority; worse even, one feels what a schooling in humiliation the long period of foreign dominion must have meant to the once proud Brabanters and Flemings.

There was considerable similarity between these disturbances and those that had taken place in Brussels forty years earlier.[1] Here too the leaders were the deans of the guilds, who had already in 1656 been able to get their way in a controversy over taxes. Now they stood up for the town privileges, which, according to them, had been violated by the postal monopoly granted to the Count of Thurn and Taxis. The Council of Brabant, however, confirmed the right of the royal Postmaster, and when the deans continued to make the town messengers maintain the service with Holland (for that was what the dispute was chiefly about) and started using violence in preventing the bailiffs of the Council of Brabant from carrying out the Council's pronouncement, the Council, on 25 August 1659, sentenced eight of them with their henchmen to exile. No more than formerly at Brussels did the magistracy dare follow the lead given by the 'third member' of the government (which was what the guilds were, as also at Antwerp). They did hedge for a time, but when summoned by the Council of Brabant they delayed no longer in promulgating the verdict and prepared to carry it out. A tremendous outburst of popular anger was the answer. Burgomaster Van Halmale was assaulted in the Town Hall. His house and the houses of the deans who had not taken part in the action were ransacked. Soon the leaders lost control of the movement, and 'the scum', 'the scoundrels', and 'the beggars' came to the fore. For days on end the town was in a tumult; well-to-do citizens sought safety elsewhere. The margrave, Burgomasters, and sheriffs took a strong line, however, first with the help of the armed guilds in so far as these were willing, and then with the regular mounted guards, composed 'mostly of the principal citizens of the town, but also of wage-earners'. In addition 1,500 foot-soldiers—'waardgelders' they would have been called in the North[2]—were enlisted. 'The

[1] See Part One, p. 23.   [2] See Part One, p. 59.

D

lower people' were still in a dangerous ferment, however, not least as a result of the complete standstill in trade occasioned by the disturbances.

> Workmen go up to their merchants, for whom they have worked year in and year out, saying: 'It's now time for the merchant to be silent and for the workman to speak up. You people have coerced and tormented us often enough, but now it is our turn. Come on, give us money to live, or we shall know what to do.'

But the town government proved to be strong enough to have houses searched every day and have those who were guilty of the looting seized. It was in control of the situation.

Nevertheless the central government now intervened. Don John's successor, the Marquess of Caracena, had no intention of leaving the magistracy of a town like Antwerp, situated so near the frontier of the United Netherlands, in possession of troops of its own which might make it feel dangerously independent. The obstinacy of the deans, who it is true were profuse in professions of allegiance, but for all that delayed in subjecting themselves unconditionally to the decisions of the Council of Brabant, afforded a ready pretext. Thus on 18 October the Governor—indeed with the full consent of the Council of Brabant—suddenly appeared before the town at the head of an army 10,000 strong, and accompanied by Condé, the Dukes of York and Gloucester, and the inevitable Duke of Aerschot. The Peace of the Pyrenees had not yet been signed, but a truce had been arranged, so that he disposed of greater freedom of action than had his predecessor in 1656. Resistance—such as Amsterdam had offered to William II's army nine years before —was out of the question. Not only did the town authorities lack the necessary determination, but in fact the citadel with its Spanish garrison rendered the town defenceless. The magistracy disbanded its mercenary troops without awaiting orders to do so. The deans who had been sentenced fled along the river; one of them, after having taken shelter with the Minorites for a whole week, disguised in a monk's habit. The others soon begged for pardon in a humble document (worded in French of course). The clergy went to the citadel, where the Governor and his retinue resided, to intercede for them, and the dean of the chapter, who knew Spanish, delivered an address in that language. The Governor answered not without condescension, and so that all the bystanders might understand him the better, he gave this answer in the French language, to everyone's astonishment; since he had not done so often.

Meanwhile, outside the town walls, the soldiers were committing the most atrocious excesses,

stealing, robbing, murdering, and destroying almost everything, and presuming (*so Aitzema relates*) to shout at the people of Antwerp that if they were allowed to enter the town they would make things even hotter for them.

No wonder that a nervous feeling prevailed there, which turned into panic when the false rumour got about that the Spaniards had captured the Ro and Cronenborch gates. The recollection of the Spanish Fury of 1576 must still have lived on at Antwerp. The worst crimes were done this time by the English and Irish royalist troops, but the alarmed populace cried: 'the Spaniards!'

All the Marquess of Caracena wanted, however, was to break the spirit of independence, and to that end, once fear had been instilled, it was mercy that was called for after due submission. The submission left nothing to be desired. The magistrates, wardens and deans took an oath before the Council of Brabant on the conditions the Marquess had laid down for a general pardon. These conditions comprised in the first place the acceptance of the disputed verdict, next a curtailment of the deans' rights, trial of the looters by the Council of Brabant (instead of by the town, the excuse being that their misdemeanour was *lèse-majesté*), and removal of the chains which the citizens had thrown across the streets in self-defence.

The commonalty felt nothing so badly as this.

The Council of Brabant, installed in the Town Hall (a cleverly devised insult), sentenced seven of the looters to death. The next day, 30 October, they were hanged (with the exception of a few who were pardoned) in the market-place in front of the Town Hall, the armed guilds securing order. But assurance was made doubly sure:

The soldiers are drawn up behind the castle so as to be in readiness in the case of tumult arising among the rabble, when they see their fellows being led to their death.

The Council, the Marquess, and the troops now left, although the garrison of the citadel was reinforced. A placard was issued threatening punishments in the case of insults directed against the Marquess, the clergy, the magistracy, and the 'present government'; floggings were actually meted out to singers of defamatory songs. Antwerp's pride was wounded the most by

the derision and ridicule of the surrounding towns and villages. From various quarters all sorts of squibs, abusive rhymes and songs are finding their way into town.

Thus complains a well-to-do Burgher of Antwerp, from whose account the foregoing quotations have been taken, and one such squib he has preserved for us. It takes the form of a 'litany', in which the people of Antwerp are supposed to invoke the mercy of a long series of gentlemen and notabilities:

> Marquess of Caracena have pity on us.
> Gentlemen Chancellors, have mercy.
> Gentlemen of the Council of Brabant, have pity on us.
> We have sinned, we confess it.
> Prince of Condé, Duke of York . . .
> (*Pastor of this, Abbot of that*)
> All you gentlemen clergy within and without,
> We go down on our knees before you,
> We wear out the cloth of our breeches.
> We offer you our liberties,
> We renounce our privileges,
> We give you our lives and our children . . .

In Madrid serious alarm had been felt lest Antwerp might be driven to complete rebellion and (who knows?) might throw herself into the arms of her Northern neighbours. As we can now see, the conditions for such a contingency were hardly present, but it is certain that it was the fear of this that contributed to the moderation which the Marquess of Caracena preserved in his triumph and which his successors also exercised. The Peace of the Pyrenees left Spanish rule in the Netherlands in an anything but stable position. Not only for the population and their local authorities were the times inauspicious, Castilian pride and Counter-Reformation confidence themselves were severely tried. Even more incongruous than the complaisance shown towards the subjected provinces was it for Spain to have to woo the friendship of her erstwhile rebels, the free North. But with European relationships as they were, the Republic was the only state of whom anything could be hoped if it came to having to keep France out of the Southern Netherlands.

Not that the Republic would necessarily act in alliance with Spain. We saw how much the Grand Pensionary was opposed to being pushed into the Habsburg camp and how the idea of solving the question in concert with France had appealed to him. Even after that plan had come to nothing, and in the situation created by the Peace of the Pyrenees, his aim still was to arrive at a satisfactory settlement with France without consulting Spain—in opposition to Spain if necessary. What drove him to seek an understanding with France was especially the Republic's relationship with England. As we have seen, this had caused less worry for a time on account of the confusion following on the death of the Protector. The Restoration, however, brought its own dangers along with it.

3. HOLLAND, ORANGE AND CHARLES II

IN MAY 1660 Charles II travelled from the Spanish Netherlands through the Republic to go and set himself at the head of his penitent subjects. The States-General, who in accordance with the Peace of 1654 had up till then meticulously kept him out of their territory, now received him with every mark of honour, and he on his part needed them too greatly for the time being to do otherwise than pretend cordiality. The Act of Seclusion naturally lapsed together with the régime at whose demand it had been passed, but the King permitted himself no more than a discreet recommendation of his nephew to the benevolence of the States. In the Republic, on the other hand, there was an outburst of popular joy at the change in England, which was naïvely looked upon as the beginning of a friendship in which Orange was as a matter of course associated. The Princess Royal for a moment believed that her son's 'designation' for the Captain-Generalship of the Union might now be forced from the States-General. In her opinion the authoritative word of the King, her King, should be conclusive for them too.

The States of Holland on the contrary were the more keen to withdraw the ten-year-old Prince from the foreign influences surrounding him. They were willing to hold out the prospect— they never thought of a binding pledge—of high office some day, on condition that his education were entrusted to them. After first having mobilised for the 'designation' the Orangist party among the regents in the landward provinces—and indeed the return to power of the Stuart dynasty seemed to have given the party new life—Mary suddenly gave in and contented herself with 'education' according to the Holland plan. At bottom all those complications of Dutch domestic politics were a matter of complete indifference to her, and so when her brother, still seated somewhat uncertainly on his new throne, did not wish to support her against the States of Holland, she hurriedly entered into an arrangement which placed her son entirely in the power of the Loevestein party, and herself rushed overseas to enjoy the resuscitated greatness of her House. On their part, Their Noble Great Mightinesses solemnly declared William to be

a worthy pawn and an instrument of great hope to this State.

What Mary found in England, however, was her death of the smallpox, and therefore in the spring of 1661 new provisions had to be made for the guardianship of young William III. The States of Holland, energetically led by De Witt, were willing to continue the education, which had barely begun, only if they were recognised as the chief guardians. But these few months had brought about great changes. Charles II not only felt more certain of his kingship, but he had learnt that his people expected of him a powerful continuance of England's 'economic' policy with regard to the Hollanders. The Act of Navigation was renewed. Moreover the King had meanwhile married a Portuguese Princess, who brought him Bombay and Tangier as her dowry; the English therefore penetrated further into India through alliance with the colonial power with which the Republic was in those parts still waging war. Complaints and objections against the conduct of Dutch naval captains in the colonial world were put forward with great vehemence. Negotiations were started in which ominous rumblings might be detected. In those circumstances Charles II saw in the Orange party a useful weapon against England's rival, and, not out of family feeling therefore, but in the interests of English policy, he was unwilling to give up the 'worthy pawn'. It is true that he still tried to come to an agreement with the Hollanders, especially on account of the financial support they might lend the House of Orange, impoverished as it was by its long protracted aid to the

Stuarts. But De Witt had written at once after Mary's death:

If the matter cannot be settled in that way or in some similar manner (*recognition of the States of Holland as 'supreme guardians'*), then it seems best to me for Their Noble Great Mightinesses to wash their hands of it and to let the high pretenders (*there were also Frederick Henry's widow, the boy's grandmother, and his other uncle, the Great Elector of Brandenburg, married to a daughter of Frederick Henry's*) worry it out as it comes and settle the affair as they think fit.

And that was how matters turned out. In September 1661 the States of Holland divested themselves of all responsibility towards the young prince, whom they now naturally no longer wished to be considered as 'an instrument of great hope'.

From this account it will be clear that the policy of neglect and exclusion with respect to the scion of Orange, which was now, after so short an interruption, resumed by De Witt and his political associates, cannot be put down solely to their oligarchic Republicanism. No doubt they believed wholeheartedly in the system of Liberty which had prevailed since 1650, but among the best of them class-feeling was combined with a profound consciousness that it was in their hands that the responsibility had been laid for

a Republic so glorious, built up by the blood of our brave forebears, and not only preserved through the mercy of God in a long war of over eighty years, but even grown from small and weak beginnings into a great and mighty State. Only with a feeling of the utmost shame can we reflect that we should let this Republic be lost by faint-heartedness, negligence, and blindness on our part and be robbed of all its splendour. I should rather die than witness such a thing.

Thus wrote Van Beuningen from Sweden in a letter to De Witt during the dark days of the first Anglo-Dutch War, and in this 'outpouring of his melancholy into the lap of so good and worthy a friend' we can catch the spirit which inspired that generation, who had all of them been young men at the beginning of the Stadholderless period. That zeal for the honour and independence of the country was apt now to be pointed against the House of Orange as a result of its ill-fated alliance with the Stuarts.

William II's subordination of the national interest to that of his English relatives and the thoroughly un-Dutch appearance of the Orange court under the Princess Royal—this was now all put in the shade by the spectacle of an English ambassador who had come to mobilise the Orange party on behalf of his master's policy. And what an ambassador! Sir George Downing, who had previously served 'the usurper' in the same capacity, but who—changing sides at exactly the right moment—had been knighted by the King and was again sent to The Hague in June 1661, represented under both the Puritan and the Royalist régime the commercialistic imperialist trend in English political thinking to which the Dutch Republic was the chief adversary. A man of unbounded energy and an expert in matters of maritime law and trade, he was not a mere tool but a fervid supporter of that policy. He hated the Hollanders. Words of condemnation, envy, and contempt flowed naturally from his pen whenever he wrote about them. Unceasingly he incited his principals against them.

Immediately on his return to The Hague this man began building up intimate relations with the Orange party. Several gentlemen from the smaller provinces—for instance from Friesland, Overijsel, and Gelderland—accepted his money. A leading Orangist politician like Sommelsdijk consulted confidentially with him. In reality Downing became the leader. No doubt he was sincerely anxious to promote the Prince's interests, but only because, as he himself remarked, without Orange the King will never have reason to be satisfied with Dutch policy. And as a matter of fact, in the negotiations about the trading disputes, which dragged on far into 1662, De Witt's policy was paralysed in the States-General again and again by the opposition of the landward provinces (always dominated by the Orangists).

Those negotiations did result in 1662 in a treaty, which could not really reconcile the economic contrasts, but only postponed the clash for a time by removing grievances that had been piling up. The cession of Pulu Run had been stipulated as early as 1654 in the peace treaty. When soon afterwards the English raised new complaints and claims, the Dutch East India Company, all-powerful as it was in those waters, had failed to carry it out. That had naturally become a grievance the more, and once again the cession was promised. On one disputed point where the English case was certainly less justified than it was on several others—it concerned two English ships, wrecked twenty years previously and already compensated for—the

Orangist opposition made it impossible for De Witt to demand a definite settlement.

'What concern is this of ours' (*said the landward provinces according to Downing's report*). 'We do not wish to quarrel with the King about two ships.'

Is it surprising that De Witt began to consider the elevation of Orange as equivalent to subjection to England? The Orangists' reckless procedure in the meeting chamber of the States-General made a bad impression in wide circles outside. It was at this time, with the appearance of De la Court's *Interest van Holland*, followed by *De Stadhouderlijke regering* (*The Government of the Stadholders*) of his younger friend and admirer Uytenhage de Mist, that we can see the beginning of a systematic assault on the Orangist tradition and of the building up of a doctrinaire Republicanism, often allied with Holland provincialist feeling. It is true that De Witt had already, in his *Deduction*, eight years before, indicated the leading motifs. But now for the first time a theory was formed which, for all the violent opposition it called forth at once, was yet to continue to count in political thought. Thus the influence of the Orange party, so recently revived, was seriously impaired. Nevertheless it still possessed plenty of reserves of power and its connection with the Stuarts was apt to weaken the North-Netherlandish State in its struggle with English rivalry.

4. THE REPUBLIC IN ALLIANCE WITH FRANCE

As HAS been said, the English menace made the Grand Pensionary anxious to come to an agreement with France, and all the more so since the danger was by no means imaginary that France would otherwise join England against the Republic. The French civil war was a thing of the past. Through the Peace of the Pyrenees France had triumphed over the Spanish Habsburgs as she had already triumphed over the German Habsburgs through the Peace of Münster. Under her young and ambitious king she cut a formidable figure in the Europe of that day. In French policy, moreover, there was an economic trend (represented in the King's Council by Colbert), which, just as inevitably as in the case of England, must clash with Holland's superiority in trade and shipping. In Holland there was a clear perception of the dangers to which the country's prosperity exposed it now that the surrounding powers seemed to have a freer hand.

Since it is notorious (*a merchant of Dort wrote in 1663*) that envy and jealousy steadily grow as blessings increase, like a shadow with its body, we could not very well imagine otherwise but that our good fortune, being envied on all sides as it is, should suffer on that account; as in fact appears already from the attitude of England and of France.

For Louis XIV, however, the traditional policy of territorial expansion came first, and in pursuing it he kept his eyes fixed on the Southern Netherlands. He knew well enough that neither of the two Maritime Powers, England and the Dutch Republic, would care to see him penetrate into that quarter. Their mutual rivalry suited him perfectly. After some hesitation it seemed to him that the wisest course to take was to support the Republic against England, and not the other way round. The Dutch statesmen, however, were not so eager as not to make sure that their own interests were cared for in the close alliance of friendship with France that was concluded in April 1662. In a commercial treaty bounds were set to Colbert's protectionist policy. There was also a mutual guarantee regarding the territory and rights of the contrasting parties; here Louis only conditionally included the Dutch occupation of Cleves, which was still being continued; on the other hand he allowed himself to be prevailed upon to extend his obligation to the protection of Dutch fishing on the Scottish coast, against which at that very moment a clamour was again being raised in England. We have already observed the first effect: the English showed themselves a little more accommodating and a treaty had been concluded, albeit far from settling everything.

It is certain that Louis meant to make sure, by this alliance, of the Republic's connivance when the moment had come to strike his blow in the Spanish Netherlands. In how strong a position it placed him was at once apparent when he added his first piece of territory to Mazarin's acquisitions. This was Dunkirk, Cromwell's conquest, with which Charles II, starved as he was financially by Parliament, was at a loss to know what to do. So in 1662 he had let Louis purchase it. And now, in order to get the alliance with Louis ratified, the States, much against their inclination, had to include Dunkirk among France's guaranteed possessions.

Yet there is no doubt either but that De Witt hoped the treaty would afford him a chance to press the King, in an amiable exchange of views, to come to a compromise, to a solution which would avert the disaster of a complete absorption of the inter-mediate land by France.

In March 1663 he obtained certainty about Louis' ambitions. He himself had taken an initiative by informing D'Estrades, who was again the French ambassador in The Hague, that he had received a secret visit from two Flemish gentlemen who had come to tell him on behalf of six towns of their province that they were sick of Spanish domination, requesting the support of the States for founding a Catholic Netherlandish Republic. The old idea of a 'cantonment', so often discussed since 1632, only seems to have been an opening gambit in the diplomatic game. No more at least is heard of the two Flemish gentlemen, but De Witt now learnt from D'Estrades that the latter's sovereign, in case the male line in Spain might come to fail, did indeed con-sider his queen's claim as still valid. In view of the sickliness of Philip IV and of his small son Charles born in 1661 (the little Prince of 1658 had already died, just as had all the baby daughters born of that marriage), De Witt now impressed upon his confidants in Holland the necessity of strengthening the Republic against that eventuality by expanding its territory as well. And as the only possible way of accomplishing that end he pointed to amicable negotiations with France. An engineer and a merchant had been sent out to travel through the Southern provinces in order to be able to furnish advice of a strategic and politico-commercial nature. On the strength of military and economic considerations De Witt came to the conclusion that the Republic might content itself with a frontier running from Ostend to Maastricht, and if possible still further up the river Maas as far as Liège.[1]

It may indeed be deemed fortunate that Amsterdam once more opposed this deceptively attractive plan. The larger part of the Dutch language area still remaining to Spain would thereby have been ceded to France (more even than in the 1635 plan, although certainly with a strategically less impossible frontier). Not that this was among the considerations submitted by the town. The feeling of solidarity with the Flemings and Brabanters

[1] See map on p. 153, Part One.

had receded still further; moreover nobody probably realised how much more irresistibly gallicisation would proceed under French than under Spanish domination. No, just as did De Witt himself, the Amsterdammers argued purely from the point of view of the economic and political interests of the North Netherlandish state—not forgetting, of course, the interests of the city of Amsterdam. The traditional aversion to having France as a neighbour, the fear that once Antwerp had been admitted into the States-General's territory it would no longer be possible to keep it cut off from the sea, the dislike of an adventurous policy which might entail turning Spain into an enemy and the effects of which it would be difficult to estimate—here are some of the arguments represented to De Witt. In his talks with D'Estrades, in which he had already moved some way in that direction, he now had to draw back to some extent and tried instead to persuade the French to listen to the cantonment plan: at the death of Philip IV and of his small son the Southern Netherlands were to become independent, but only after France and the Republic had both nibbled off some bits for themselves. France was to take the Dutch-speaking districts of Nieuport and Furnes in addition to the French-speaking area of Cambrai, St. Omer, and Aire, whilst the Republic claimed for herself the north-western corner of Flanders (Ostend, Passchendaele, Bruges, Blankenberghe) and, on the other side of the Netherlands, Upper Gelderland (which after all had already been as good as promised at Münster) and places in the neighbourhood of Maastricht. The economic bondage of the Southern Netherlands was not of course to cease: whether it was to be division or cantonment, the North wanted to be assured with respect to its 'trade, custom, and industry'; the occasion was even to be used to prohibit any further construction of canals in the South.

No doubt De Witt, too, would have preferred the solution of the cantonment to that of division, even though he had begun by proposing the latter himself; but he had known from the start that although this was 'the safest' solution, there was but 'small hope' of getting Louis XIV to accept it. Indeed what could possibly be the attraction to the King in helping the Southern Netherlands to become independent when according to his Queen's right of inheritance they would fall to her and his son in their entirety? The co-operation of the Republic might be

worth a strip in the North to him, yet it was hardly to be expected that he would buy it at the price of nearly the whole area.
And the less so because Louis' lawyers, as De Witt gradually
began to perceive, had discovered a theory by which the Queen
would not have to wait for the death of her half-brother, but
could claim immediate possession on the death of her father,
not of the whole of the Spanish monarchy, but precisely of the
Netherlands. There, so these clever gentlemen pointed out,
obtained the 'law of devolution', according to which daughters
from the first marriage inherited before sons out of a second
marriage. In fact that law did not hold good in all the South-
Netherlands provinces and besides related only to private
individuals; but Louis considered it sufficient for his purpose
and intended to have recourse to it at the right time. It was
therefore out of the question that he should allow himself to be
kept within certain bounds in the Netherlands of all places, and
De Witt's policy was more certainly doomed to failure than ever.
The slightest warning that the States might after all prefer to
come to an understanding with Spain drew from the King
ominous utterances of irritation.

As a matter of fact De Witt never intended seriously to take
up with Spain. Spanish diplomacy, greatly alarmed, exerted
itself to detach the Republic from France. The first ambassador
to reside in The Hague on behalf of the King of Spain—the first
since Spain had recognised the independence of the Seven
Provinces in 1648—Antoine Brun (from Franche Comté), had,
in the days of William II, mooted the idea of an alliance of the
Seventeen Provinces as against the Stadholder's plans for war in
conjunction with France. At the time little attention had been
paid to that proposal because it would have meant taking part
(on the other side) in the war that was still going on between
France and Spain. But now that there was peace between the
two crowns, outwardly at least, Brun's successor, Don Esteban
de Gamarra, plied the plan for all it was worth. What precisely
the Spaniards meant, what was to become of Spain's sovereignty
in the Southern provinces if these were to take part in such a
league, does not appear. They referred to the Pacification of
Ghent, but was this more than an empty phrase? So much is
certain that in 1664, when there was very little chance any
longer of inducing France to acquiesce in a settlement, De Witt

urgently warned the States against the Spanish alternative,
and this on the ground that it was not really an alternative.

Surveying Europe, he was of opinion that only an alliance consisting of the
Epmeror, the King of Spain, the King of England, and the Republic would
be in a position to keep the redoubtable Kingdom of France in check. Such
an iallance, however, was unattainable. The Emperor was impeded by the
German Princes allied to France; the German Empire was not a live body
but a puppet whose limbs were worked by brass wires; and the King of
England could not and would not take part. To rely on Spain alone would be
madness, because Spain, enfeebled and exhausted, and bound to lapse into
the utmost confusion at the very moment when through the death of Philip IV
its help would be needed, was no more than a broken reed. As regards the
Netherlands, both North and South, it was true that the Burgundian state
had at one time proved a dangerous enemy for France; but how were
circumstances changed! The Dukes had enjoyed the support of England;
their territory had stretched much further south, and now recently France
had captured new strategic forward positions. The population of the
Southern provinces, moreover, who at that time were attached to their rulers,
now hated the Spaniards and would preferably seek peace, prosperity,
and protection of their religion under the powerful Louis, whose language
they spoke almost everywhere and to whose ancestors they had once belonged.

This is a free summary of the note (preserved in a French
translation only) with which De Witt tried to convince his
masters the States of Holland of the emptiness of the Spanish
proposals. One cannot read without amazement the assertions
about the Southern Netherlands. That they longed for French
domination was almost as untrue as that the majority spoke
French and had once been under the French crown. But it
cannot be denied that the other points made were only too
sternly true. It is certain that the Southern provinces, even if
they were not at all anxious to be absorbed by France, could
hardly be expected to co-operate vigorously in their own
defence. For that both their national sentiment and their
political energy were too feeble, while moreover they were
animated by too keen a distrust of their Protestant Northern
neighbours, who even in their greatest embarrassment never for
a moment thought of giving up the economic stranglehold to
which they subjected the Southern provinces. The split disastrously weakened the capacity of the once united Netherlands
to resist France's advance. And the discords in Europe, Spain's
helplessness, the confusion in the German Empire, and
England's hostility—all this did indeed create the worst possible
circumstances for the Dutch Republic.

It was unfortunate that De Witt's note fell into the hands of D'Estrades. It could not but strengthen the King's confidence that the States were indissolubly bound to him. Firmly determined to keep his hands free, Louis did not think it worth his while to go on with the negotiations, even though he ended them with no lack of amicable words and gracious assurances. De Witt put on an appearance of satisfaction. Indeed he and the States no longer had any choice. The Southern Netherlands continued to constitute a problem, so long as Philip IV was still alive, and for the future. But a rupture with England threatened immediately, and, with an eye to that, friendship with France was indispensable.

c. COLONIAL EXPANSION AND THE SECOND ANGLO-DUTCH WAR

THE first Anglo-Dutch War had largely been caused by the dynastic entanglements between Orange and Stuart, but the second Anglo-Dutch War was economic in character and origin. In itself the political position of his young nephew did not interest Charles II very greatly; it was only when he was at loggerheads with the Republic for other reasons that he bethought himself of Orange as being a useful weapon in the struggle. The root of the disagreements and the aim of the war alike lay in the field of trade, particularly of colonial trade. Before considering the war I shall therefore introduce a chapter about the activities of the Dutch East and West India Companies—about some indeed that were not directly connected with the war.

1. THE DUTCH EAST INDIA COMPANY

Settlement at the Cape of Good Hope

ON THE long voyage to the Indies a place for provisioning was indispensable. Scurvy, which used to cause such ravages among the crews, could only be prevented by unsalted meat and fresh vegetables. The Portuguese, who in the beginning of the sixteenth century had found the tribes in the country behind the Cape of Good Hope difficult to deal with, usually anchored at St. Helena. The Dutch and English often put in there too, the Dutch sometimes going to Mauritius as well, but their fleets repeatedly called at Table Bay also, where they bought cattle from the Hottentots if any showed themselves, and where beneath large inscribed stones they used to leave letters for their fellow-countrymen coming from the opposite direction. Un-favourable changes at St. Helena and fear that the English might forestall them prompted the Directors to found a 'rendez-vous' at 'Cabo de Boa Esperança'. On Christmas Eve 1651 two ships and a yacht sailed from Texel under the thirty-four-year-old Commander Jan van Riebeeck with artisans and soldiers on board; on 7 April 1652 they arrived at Table Bay; an unusually speedy voyage. Van Riebeeck's orders instructed him to build a fort capable of holding eighty people, to lay out vegetable gardens, and to buy cattle from the natives.

The first months of this great undertaking—though no one foresaw how great indeed it was—were difficult. The only near-by inhabitants were some fifty poverty-stricken Hottentots, whom the Dutch called the Beach-runners (Strandlopers). The cattle-owning tribes on their slow wanderings kept behind the mountains. The rains and the terrible north-easterly storms of the Cape winter washed away the new vegetable gardens. Van Riebeeck needed an iron hand to enforce discipline and to keep the enfeebled and discouraged men at work, until at last the Hottentots with their herds appeared. There were again difficult moments when a year later all the cattle bought were stolen one Sunday while the colony was listening to the 'comforter of the sick' (there was not yet a minister of religion). The offenders were of all people the same Beach-runners whom the strangers were accustomed to employ as intermediaries in their traffic with the nomadic tribes. From then on the newcomers hated the blacks. The Directors' orders, however, were to deal leniently with the natives, and for a long time Van Riebeeck acted accordingly. The Hottentots had their own grievances, however. Although their wanderings over a wide area took them only rarely to the Cape peninsula, they looked with anger at the fort and the ever-increasing buildings, vegetable gardens, and plots of land, encroaching on what they considered to be one of *their* pasture-grounds.

Before long the settlement could fulfil its immediate purpose.

It was possible to provide the passing fleets with abundant vegetables, if not perhaps at once so regularly with meat. But the settlement cost the Company money, especially because the corn grown on the spot did not yield enough for the subsistence of the small population. Ways and means had to be thought of for reducing expenses. Van Riebeeck, who had got to know the Chinese during his service with the Company, thought of them as being the most industrious and the soberest agricultural workers. Fortunately there were none available. The Directors were thus driven to offer to their own servants an opportunity of settling there as 'freemen'. Between 1657 and 1662 as many as 200 tried this freedom, as agricultural workers, cartwrights, carpenters, or fishermen. Their freedom, however, was of a limited order, just as in New Netherland. The Company wished to keep trading relations with the natives, as well as with the fleets to and from the Indies, as much as possible in its own hands. The problem of unskilled labour it attempted to solve by importing slaves from Angola and from a number of places round the Indian Ocean. The Portuguese language was thereby imported at the same time, or at least the Portuguese-Malay mixture in which the uprooted slaves could best understand each other. Rycklof van Goens, who inspected the new colony on his way to the Indies, urgently warned Van Riebeeck against this:

> With the coming of the slaves, Your Honour shall be very careful not to introduce the Portuguese language, but to prevent it with all the means at your disposal, setting a good example, you and the officers, since so much depends on this; and Your Excellency shall use no other language with the slaves than our mother tongue only, nor allow them to speak in any other way; which in course of time will give security.

But no more than in the Indies[1] was this evil suppressed so readily as that. At first indeed the free farmers did not find it an easy matter to govern their slaves. In 1659, moreover, fresh troubles with the Hottentots led to open conflict. In connection with this the peninsula was at last shut off from the mainland by a thorn-hedge and some blockhouses, stretching over a distance of twelve miles or more. Soon now a regular peace was concluded with the various tribes, to which these ceded the land already occupied and promised to provide cattle. In this way the development of the colony was assured for a considerable time

[1] See Part One, pp. 186/7.

E

to come. Van Riebeeck did some excellent pioneering work by introducing all sorts of crops—among others the vine—and animals. His relations with the freemen were much better than what we saw was the case in New Netherland.[1] Not only did he zealously look after their interests, but from the beginning they had representatives on his Council. Their number was still too small and their dependence on the Company's support too great for them not to feel satisfied with simply being consulted. Not that there were not plenty of difficulties and privations to be struggled with. Again and again freemen gave up and returned to the Company's service. There were also always a number who returned home after their time was up, and there had to be a continual strict supervision lest freemen or soldiers should stow away on board the Indies vessels. In vain were expeditions sent inland in search of the rich towns and silver mines in the fabulous land of Monomatapa, of which vague mention had been made in old descriptions like Van Linschoten's *Itinerario*. Those courageous explorers had nothing to show as the result of their bold undertakings but accounts of deserts and bogs, wild mountains and immense plains peopled with wild animals and wandering Hottentot tribes.

When in 1662 Van Riebeeck was 'released' and went to seek promotion in the Indies, he left a colony behind him in which the Directors had but little faith. The first Commander had in their circle gained the name of being an optimistic visionary. Contraction appealed more to them than expansion. Van Riebeeck's successor, Zacharias Wagenaar, judged that, with some possible exceptions,

most of our freemen and farmers are sodden, lazy, clumsy louts, who, since they do not pay proper attention to the servants lent to them, nor to their work in the fields, nor to their animals, for that reason seem wedded to their low level and cannot rid themselves of their debts.

He too (who had spent almost forty years in the Indies) sighed for Chinese farmers, but the Supreme Government at Batavia was still unable to furnish any. It should be remembered that the settlers were still leading a sort of camping way of existence, without the comfort and discipline of family life. Wagenaar exerted himself to trying to get 'some poor domestic servants or farmer's daughters' as wives for his citizens, and not without

[1] See Part One, pp. 204, 206/7.

success. Greater stability and order was the result. A school-master was now teaching the children of the slaves and citizens. A minister of religion was appointed. After some time the Amsterdam Chamber of the Company began to encourage the settlement of farmers' families from the home country, but even so the Cape attracted but few immigrants.

One event, however, took place during Wagenaar's administration which suddenly caused the Directors to pay greater heed to their new possession. This was the war with England which started in 1664 with the capture of the settlements of the West India Company in West Africa and North America. By the authority of the Directors 300 soldiers were retained from passing ships to help in replacing the first fort and its earthen walls by one of stone. At the inauguration on 2 January 1666 the following poem was recited:

> Thus far we managed against the Hottentots with earthen walls.
> Now we take pride in walls of stone against all others.
> So we strike terror into the hearts of the European
> As well as of the Asian, the American and the wild African.

Whether through fear of the new fort or not, the English, who had captured St. Helena a few years previously, left the Cape undisturbed.

Van Goens and the Conquest of Ceylon, Negapatam, and Malabar

THE fortunes of the small band of settlers at the Cape of Good Hope will always arouse our interest on account of what they were preparing for the future. But in the history of the East India Company between the first and second Anglo-Dutch Wars as seen by contemporaries, they constituted but a very small incident. To them the big event of those years seemed to be the continuation of what had been started under Van Diemen: the demolition of the Portuguese Empire in the Indies.

When the truce[1] expired in 1652 the two powers at first did nothing more serious in Europe than bombard each other with notes, but the East India Company, not in the least alarmed—in the consciousness of its overwhelming naval power—by the circumstance that there was a war on with England at the same time, instructed its servants to injure the Portuguese wherever they could. The West India Company meanwhile lost its last

[1] See Part One, p. 187.

foothold in Brazil. The only result of the obstinacy with which the States-General nevertheless continued to support its claims was that the other Company gained time to complete its conquests at the expense of Portugal in the Indies.

For a few years there were only skirmishes at sea, on the coast of Ceylon (where the Company, as we know, had gained a firm footing in Galle and Negombo), and even on the coasts of the Great Mogul, whose neutrality was not respected by either party. The Portuguese naval forces, however, received a severe blow in 1654, when Rijcklof van Goens, returning from a tour of inspection in the 'Western Quarters' at the head of a small fleet, met, off Goa, five heavy galleons one after another and destroyed or captured them all. But not until 1655 did the Supreme Government at Batavia—where only a short while ago Joan Maetsuycker had started the twenty-fifth year of his governor-generalship—feel strong enough, after the arrival of reinforcements from *patria*, to make a decisive attempt. 1,200 men were landed in Ceylon under the command of the Director-General, Gerard Hulft, who instantly laid siege to Colombo. When they stormed the town, however, the Dutch were beaten off and suffered heavy losses. Reinforcements had to be moved up and the siege became a long-drawn-out affair, the fleet cutting off all relief coming from Goa. Hulft had been killed before the town surrendered to his successor in May 1656. The garrison had dwindled to one-fifth of its former strength, and the population had been decimated by hunger and disease. Officials and officers, and the clergy with their church-ornaments and relics, were transported to Tuticorin or Cochin. The remaining Portuguese were offered the choice of recognising Dutch rule or leaving. The provisions of the capitulation could not prevent plundering, and after that a strong occupation force had to be left behind in Colombo because 'the inhabitants in their hearts remained devoted to and affectionately disposed towards the Portuguese'.

The Company was now in possession of the coveted cinnamon region. Rajah Singha, however, who had welcomed the enterprise because he still counted on taking possession of the conquered town in accordance with the treaty of 1638, but who had done no more than look on with his army, was greatly put out when the Dutch simply took the place of the previous intruders. Even though the 'Emperor' imagined himself to be the 'Lord God', he yet did not dare attack Van der Meyden and withdrew sulkily into his mountainous interior. From there he not only did his best to incite the population of the cinnamon regions against the conqueror, but it was to be feared that his ruffled feelings might lead him to seek a *rapprochement* with the Portuguese, and so it became advisable to drive these out of their last strongholds in the north of the island and on the south-easterly point of India opposite.

Rijcklof van Goens, who was to become the executor of this policy, had been all through its most zealous supporter; quite recently, during a stay in *patria*, he had recommended it to the Directors. In 1657 he was sent out from Batavia as commander-in-chief. After having conveyed Commander Roothaes to Goa to shut in the Portuguese galleons and troops there, Van Goens went to carry out his own mission on both sides of the Gulf of Manar.

Tuticorin was hastily evacuated by the Portuguese, the small island of Manar after some days of fighting. Van Goens wrote glowingly of the importance of those two places for pearl fishing; friendly relations were cultivated with the neighbouring native princes and grandees. What remained of Portuguese in or near Ceylon had now drawn together on the peninsula of Jafna, and even after the town of that name had been conquered, street by street, they put up a desperate resistance in the castle, which was bigger than that of Batavia. Another three months passed before the surrender took place, on harsh terms, on 23 June. The castle was found to contain 3,500 people, of whom 800 were Portuguese; of these sixty were priests and 200 white women. The remainder of the 3,500 were half-castes ('tupasses'), natives and slaves. Only the officers were granted a passage to Goa, the rest remained prisoners until they could be transported to Europe. They were not even allowed to take with them any silver and gold that they might possess.

Thus (*Van Goens wrote triumphantly*) has the Noble Company (by the special mercy of God) become lord of the Kingdom of Jaffanapatnam and ruler of the beautiful island of Ceylon, from which all the popish crew with the whole of their idolatry have now been driven away.

Domine Baldaeus, the minister who later was to write a famous description of Ceylon and Malabar and of their conquest,

preached in the main church on the following text from Exodus:
'And Moses built an altar, and called the name of it Jehovah-
nissi'—that is, the Lord is my banner.

The army was then sent to Negapatam under a sub-comman-
der. This place used to be the connecting link between the
Portuguese force in Ceylon and the mainland of India. In itself
a town of some importance, it formed the key-point of the
Portuguese position on the Coromandel coast. It surrendered
without offering resistance in July 1658. The Portuguese and the
clergy with all their possessions and church appurtenances were
allowed to take themselves off.

It was impressive, but it had cost a great deal of money. For
some years arms were laid aside while Van Goens, as Governor
of Ceylon, tried to organise the new conquests, the Directors
meanwhile trying to procure financial support from the States-
General. The States-General, however, were now more inclined
to drop their claims regarding Brazil and to conclude peace with
Portugal. And so the Company braced itself to use the remaining
space of time for a mighty effort to wrest the Malabar coast too
away from its enemy. Towards the end of 1660 reports began to
get round of the negotiations about Charles II's marriage and
that Portugal seemed inclined to hand over all its Indian
possessions to England. This rapprochement between Portugal
and England might well prove a 'dire blow', and this the
Company wished to forestall.

It was again Van Goens who led the expedition which left
Batavia in October 1661 and conquered Quilon and Kranganur,
again only after stout resistance. But Cochin it was that mattered.
The native Queen and her nobility, the Nayars, used to rely on
the Portuguese against the ever threatening aggression of the
Prince of the interior, the Samoryn. The Dutch had to start by
taking the Queen of Cochin prisoner and then laid siege to the
Portuguese town. The Portuguese defended themselves so
bravely that the siege had to be raised, a difficult operation,
which Van Goens accomplished with great skill. Another
attempt had to be made. Again a fleet was sent out from Batavia,
in September 1662, and now at last, in January 1663, after a
fierce bombardment, the town capitulated. In Europe a peace
treaty had been signed as early as August 1661, but the ratifica-
tion dragged on until 14 December 1662. The Portuguese

nevertheless had some grounds for demanding the restitution of Cochin as having been conquered in peace-time. Lengthy negotiations were carried on, but the Company kept what it had.

That this replacement of the Portuguese by the Dutch was most unwelcome to the English is just as natural as that the Dutch had heard with alarm of the plan for transferring the Portuguese possessions to England. As a matter of fact what the English had in mind was, by means of their protégé Portugal, to penetrate further into Indian trade without striking a blow. If, on the contrary, the Portuguese possessions were to fall into the hands of the Dutch, the English would have less chance of making their way into the Indian trade than ever.

The situation is illuminated by an incident in the military operations that gave rise to much bad feeling. To the south of Cochin lay the Kingdom of Porakad, or Porka, where the English had recently established a trading station for the pepper trade. During the siege of Cochin, Porka, which had sided with the Portuguese, had at once been blockaded by the Dutch, and an English ship which came from headquarters in Surat to fetch pepper was politely but firmly refused admittance. This ship, the Hopewell, was high up on the list of grievances which Downing presented at The Hague in '63 and '64. After the defeat of the Portuguese, the Prince of Porka, like many another, was compelled to sign a treaty in which the right to the export of pepper was reserved to the Noble Company. Nothing was left to the English but to close down their trading-station. So little was the Company, at the height of its power, inclined to make room for the English that at the same time, in quite a different quarter, namely in the Banda group of islands, the English official sent from Bantam to take belated possession of Pulu Run in accordance with the treaty of 1662 was on some pretext detained.

The loss of Cochin, which happened to coincide with the loss of San Thomé on the other side of India to the King of Golconda, was no less a tragedy to the Portuguese than had been the loss of Colombo, Jafna, and Negapatam—or of the Moluccas, Malacca, and Galle. 4,000 men, women, and children of Portuguese blood were shipped to Goa.

According to and by virtue of the agreement (*thus Van Goens reported to Batavia*) a tremendous number of people, something like 8 to 10 thousand tupasses (half-castes) and natives, remain in the town, most of them being craftsmen and of such trades that they will be very useful to us in our possession of this town, since it is impossible to found a colony of our own people here straight away. And since these people have been brought up in the popish religion, they have been allowed to keep five Franciscan monks—until Your Excellencies should signify your disapproval—and they will be permitted to practice their religion behind closed doors, without giving offence by holding public processions . . . since after all it will not be possible at once and by forcible means to introduce the Reformation there. But whilst the said monks will be tolerated for a time, without being allowed to entice any one of our people to their religion, it will be possible for our ministers to give the popish natives better instruction so that gradually papacy will disappear there.

In yet another corner of its enormous territory the Company at about this same time disposed of the Portuguese. The warlike princes of Macassar, who arrogated to themselves the overlordship over the smaller potentates in the south-west corner of Celebes, not only protected the trade of their own subjects with the Moluccas so jealously guarded by the Company, but they also granted hospitality to trading settlements of the Portuguese, English and Danes, also trying to evade the Dutch monopoly. The Portuguese occupied a very exceptional position at Macassar. Their number, half-castes included, was estimated at 2,000. There were rich merchants among them, who lived in great state. The economic life of the court and capital largely depended on them, and they consorted on a footing of equality with the native grandees. These latter spoke Portuguese, and negotiations between the Company and Macassar were usually conducted in that language.

Friction was of frequent occurrence. The unnatural policy maintained by the Company in the Moluccas inevitably led to clashes with any neighbouring independent power. The relentless grip of its monopoly was indeed reaching ever more widely. De Vlaming van Oudshoorn, the unbending Governor of the Moluccas, ruled through a man of straw, the Sultan of Ternate, who let his rights over the Amboyna group of islands be bought off and obediently permitted the destruction of the clove-trees on his own group of islands. The attempts of Macassar to exploit the despair of the inhabitants of the Moluccas were followed with suspicion by Batavia, and after a number of previous skirmishes the Supreme Government at last, in 1660, sent out an expedition. The Sultan was forced to assent to a treaty in accordance with which he had to expel the Portuguese and allow a Dutch trading post by the side of those of the English and the Danes. This was still only the beginning of the end of Macassar independence.

However, in a place far from this region the Company suffered a severe loss in these same years. The island of Formosa, which was of great importance for the Chinese trade, and where moreover it had to do with a submissive and malleable population, was conquered by the redoubtable pirate Coxinga (to use the Dutch version of the somewhat complicated Chinese name). With Domine Hambrouck's martyrdom, and the undeserved disgrace of Coyet, the Governor, it all forms a tragic story which made a deep impression on contemporaries. Yet it did not seem more than a spot on the sun of the Company's prosperity, and the embittered English at any rate saw only Van Goens's triumph.

2. THE WEST INDIA COMPANY

THE picture presented by the West India Company during these years offers a sharp contrast to the success story of the East India Company. Not only had it by its settlement in Brazil struck the Portuguese in a spot where they were able to offer a surprisingly strenuous resistance, but, also in this Company's area of activity, England was already to prove a more formidable rival than in the East. We shall first cast a look at the completion of the loss of Brazil, and next watch the downfall of New Netherland, which we already know was sandwiched between Virginia and New England.[1] Furthermore, along the coasts of Guinea and Guiana and in the Antilles (all on their respective sides of the Atlantic forming one shipping area), the English trading and colonising spirit had been strongly developing ever since the days of Drake and Raleigh. The French too, as a matter of fact, and even the Danes and the Swedes (who in the East Indies were much less able than the English to assert themselves against the Dutch claim to monopoly), had settled in various places on the African and American coasts of the Atlantic Ocean in positions of undeniable strength.

The Evacuation of Brazil

WITTE DE WITH'S expedition[2] had set sail for Brazil in a highly expectant mood, so much so that the Directors refused to have

[1] See Part One, p. 199 ff.   [2] See Part One, p. 196.

anything to do with Portuguese proposals for buying them off. But on the spot the Dutch leaders soon found that catastrophe was not to be averted. The army that started out from the Recife to seek out the rebels was crushingly defeated. There was nothing for it but to go on clinging to the small corner near the coast under the protection of the fleet and to suffer discomforts and privations as patiently as possible.

The organisation of the food supply encountered such difficulties that in 1649 the Admiral, at his wits' end, took the unauthorised decision to return home with a number of ships. He was put on trial, and it was fortunate for him that Holland and the Generality did not see eye to eye about the case. His final acquittal was no doubt perfectly justified. Yet it is easy to imagine the bitterness felt by the Council on the Recife at De With's leaving in the lurch the colony entrusted to his protection, 'thinking only of his own belly'. In the mother country there was some thought of sending out a third expedition, but the outbreak of war with England, which necessitated concentration of forces nearer home, was the death-blow to the settlement on the Recife. In January 1654 a capitulation had to be signed. The Portuguese Commander, General Barretto, was received in the town and conducted to the Town Hall. Then, amidst the most frightful confusion, there followed the evacuation of the town by the Dutch officials and merchants and by the Jewish population, who were carried off in overcrowded vessels to Holland or to other Dutch possessions in the West Indies. It was a scene such as had already been staged at Malacca and Galle, and as was still to follow at Colombo, Jafna and Cochin, with the Portuguese in the role of the victims. Schoonenborch, his fellow-councillor Haecx, and the Commander Schkoppe were prosecuted on their arrival in Holland, a far from generous reward for the constancy they had shown through all those years under the most impossible circumstances.

The Brazil adventure was at an end. As we know, the quarrel with Portugal dragged on for some years more, to the great advantage of the East India Company. In order to obtain peace and to be left in the undisturbed possession of Brazil, Portugal in the end had to allow a certain amount of trading facility and to pay several millions by way of damages. But the West India Company, whose clinging to Brazil had hampered it for twenty-four years from expanding in any other direction, was incurably exhausted now that it had lost this deceptive treasure.

The Loss of New Netherland

IT HAS been related in the preceding volume[1] how greatly the Nine Men in New Netherland felt encouraged in their conflict with Governor Stuyvesant by the protection which the States-General had afforded Melyn. In the summer of 1649 three delegates embarked for the home country in order to submit a petition from the citizens to the High and Mighty Assembly.

It was much more than a question of complaints against the Governor. The spokesmen of the New Netherland citizens presumed to take quite a violent line against the Directors of the Amsterdam Chamber, against the High Directorate of the Nineteen, and in fact against the entire system practised by the Company. They had their own ideas, and set them out plainly, about the policy that should be followed with respect to 'the province of New Netherland'. The leading spirit of the triumvirate was Adriaan van der Donck, and not only the contents but also the style of the petition, as well as of the *Vertoog van Nieuw-Nederland* which the deputation published in print to arouse public opinion, make us feel that here was a remarkable man. The West India Company never found a Coen or a Van Goens among its officials in New Netherland, but the settlers themselves produced in Van der Donck a man with a statesman's vision.

What a case for the prosecution those documents make! The governor playing the tyrant, the self-seeking of the Directors, the neglect of systematic colonisation, the deterrent effect caused by trade restrictions and lack of civic freedom—it is all exposed —and the languishing state of a colony where all the conditions necessary to growth and prosperity seemed present was uncompromisingly attributed to mismanagement. The situation called, nay shouted, for an influx of Dutch colonists to keep the Indians in check and to resist the English; that alone could save New Netherland. Save—for indeed the petition warned urgently that the very existence of the colony was at stake.

The most terrible ruin will follow and this province will become the defenceless prey of its neighbours. The Dutch free burghers already living

---

[1] See Part One, p. 207.

there will be forced to seek refuge elsewhere or to subject themselves to a foreign nation. The very name of New Netherland will be lost and no Dutchman will any longer have any say in affairs here.

These calamities, however, could be averted, so the New Netherlanders asserted, by means of the following threefold policy. In the first place the States should take over the colony from the Company and place ships at the disposal of emigrants, who would sooner venture overseas under their authority than under that of the Company. In the second place they should institute for the colony,

a civic government, somewhat after the manner of the praiseworthy government of our fatherland,

while trade should be encouraged by exempting it from impositions and otherwise. In the third place the States should arrange for a frontier settlement with the surrounding English colonies and station a few companies of soldiers in New Netherland.

Unfortunately, the States-General did not show to the best advantage in their handling of this matter. The documents were given to a committee to be studied, which in turn asked the Chamber of Amsterdam for its comments, and, after a great deal of writing to and fro and numerous meetings, the committee elaborated a proposal in which the soundness of Van der Donck's criticism is implicitly admitted. No wonder that the Gentlemen Directors felt offended. Yet the committee itself shrank from so drastic a measure as the transfer of the colony to the direct administration of the States would have been. The Amsterdam Chamber continued to be heard at every stage. Obstinacy and incapacity made themselves felt all along. For example, when directions were given to the effect that 15,000 guilders should be spent annually on the transport of emigrants, the Chamber replied that their creditors would never allow it. Stuyvesant was recalled, and the recall was immediately revoked. When Van der Donck wished to return after two and a half years of petitioning and negotiating, he was refused admittance to the Company's ship. It was certainly an important innovation that in 1653 New Amsterdam was given its own town government with Burgomasters and aldermen, but the Governor continued to treat the Burghers with suspicion and severity.

Before any decision had been taken in The Hague about the

wishes of the citizens, Stuyvesant had done his best to come to a frontier settlement in direct negotiation with the New England colonies. In 1650 he went to Hartford in person, on the Verse Rivier (Fresh River), called the Connecticut by the English, who there held land that had once been occupied by the Dutch and where there had been a fort called Goede Hoop (Good Hope). There was no possibility of either driving away the English there or of subjecting them, and Stuyvesant certainly acted wisely (although Van der Donck counted it against him as one offence the more) when he agreed to a treaty in which that neglected bit of land was ceded, but in which New England at least recognised the existence of New Netherland, even though only within narrow boundaries. What was worse was that the States-General could not induce the English government to ratify the treaty. To the English the settlement on the Hudson remained an infringement of James I's patent and the land English land, to be appropriated at the first suitable opportunity. This came very near to happening in the war of 1652-54, but the expedition which was on the point of setting out from Boston was stopped in the nick of time by the peace then just concluded, although, as has been said, the States' claim to New Netherland was not recognised in the peace treaty.

So, taking it all in all, the situation continued to be a somewhat uncertain one. The mission of Van der Donck and his colleagues had undeniably had some effect. The attention of government circles and of the general public had been directed towards New Netherland. The introduction of at least some measure of self-government, together with the rumour that the country's high assembly was concerning itself with the colony's affairs, did encourage emigrants. In 1651 Van der Donck had helped to arrange an organised crossing. Since then the influx had continued, in moderate fashion. The Company now supported the movement as far as its financial resources permitted. Yet in 1659 a certain Jacob Steendam in a 'Klagt van Nieuw-Amsterdam tot haar moeder' (Complaint of New Amsterdam to her mother) still made the little town sigh out:

> Could I but obtain farmers,
> I should not yield to the powerful.
> But I suffer from a dearth of workers. . . .

By no more than a show of force Stuyvesant, in 1656, had

brought the Swedish settlement on the Zuidrivier (the Delaware) under the authority of the Company, which had never given up its claim to that area. The city of Amsterdam now undertook its systematic colonisation. Religious policy was important in this connection. Stuyvesant was just as much inclined to take sharp measures against religious deviations as to suppress civic liberties, but on the first-named point at least he did not have the backing of the Directors. They reminded him of the praiseworthy and advantageous tradition of the mother town in that respect, and amidst the surrounding English colonies, each of which was in its own way strictly orthodox, New Netherland became a sanctuary for sects of all sorts. Amsterdam sent Mennonites to the Zuidrivier; Steendam helped by writing an enthusiastic eulogy on 'that blessed province, where milk and honey flow'; German Lutherans and French Huguenots betook themselves to New Amsterdam. Quite a number of Englishmen continued to arrive, attracted also by the opportunities for trade. The town, in fact, was becoming a new smuggling centre where the English Navigation Act, intended to keep the colonies in too strict a dependence on the mother country, could be evaded. It has been estimated that between 1647, when Stuyvesant entered upon the Governorship, and 1664, when the English storm at last broke, the population of New Netherland increased from 2,000 to 10,000 souls. How large was the admixture of foreign elements it would be difficult to say. It is certain that New Netherland was much less purely Dutch than either Virginia or New England were English. By 1664 the population of those English colonies was already estimated at 100,000.

The relations with the English neighbours, particularly with those of New England, with Hartford (Connecticut), and the eastern part of Lange Eiland (Long Island), were continually being disturbed by incidents. In 1663 armed men from Hartford under a certain Captain Scott occupied the small village of Oostdorp—to them it was Westchester—and attacks were made on places on Long Island. The Directors at home were beginning to be alarmed. They now felt colonisation was the best means of strengthening the position, but how long had that policy been neglected! And even now the Governor and Council of New Netherland kept lamenting that the authorities at home failed to rise to the demands of the situation! More men, more money, and more munitions would be necessary if the frontier was to be maintained against the English. The Directors meanwhile addressed serious complaints to the States, requesting them at long last to get the English to recognise the frontier settlement of 1650.

The English government had very different plans. It had come to the conclusion that the existence of New Netherland made it impossible to carry out the Navigation Act in North America. The leaders of the westward movement in Connecticut and Long Island were in touch with the government at home, and it was provided with royal letters, so that Scott was able in the beginning of 1664 to persuade the English villages under Stuyvesant's authority on Long Island to rebel. It was already rumoured that the King was thinking of making a grant of the whole of Long Island to his brother, the Duke of York. In spite of the treaty of Hartford, Stuyvesant had to acquiesce in the defection of Westchester and places on Long Island. At the same time he wrote to the mother country, once more urgently requesting aid. But the English government struck first.

The gift to York, not only of Long Island but also of the whole territory between Verse Rivier (the Connecticut) and Zuidrivier (the Delaware), was effected in secret; and quite as secretly an expedition was sent out to take possession of his property for him. A royal writ commanded the Governors of Massachusetts and Connecticut to offer assistance in subjecting the Dutch, who had recently (some fifty years ago!), 'unlawfully and to the great damage and inconvenience of his Majesty's good subjects, taken possession of rivers and lands within our territory'. In late August 1664 the English fleet from Boston suddenly appeared before New Amsterdam with upwards of a thousand men on board. Against these Stuyvesant could oppose only 150 soldiers and 250 burghers—if they would obey him. The fort was in bad condition, and there was a shortage of gunpowder.

Old Stuyvesant with his wooden leg wanted to fight. The burghers however, thought the invading force too vastly superior to be resisted. The English circulated promises that property and rights and freedom of trade would be respected. For days their vessels lay in the harbour without any shots being exchanged, while Stuyvesant was angrily disputing with his

own people, his council as well as the burgomasters and the
citizens' spokesmen. Finally a petition to prevent needless
bloodshed was handed over to him, and among the ninety-three
signatures was included his son's. Women and children crowded
about him with supplications. So he gave in. On 4 September
the surrender was signed, by which the rights and liberties of
the Dutch inhabitants were to the fullest extent guaranteed.

One cannot reproach the colonists with having too readily
allowed the tie with the mother country to be broken. On the
contrary, it is understandable enough that they were feeling
abandoned by the mother country. Had they not through Van
der Donck, fifteen years ago, warned against the very thing
that was now happening? Had they not since then, just as had
the Governor, repeatedly urged the Directors at home and
the States to send reinforcements? Resistance *was* impossible,
and would only have led to their having been taken by storm, a
horror sufficiently terrible in the seventeenth century to explain
the citizens' trembling at the prospect. If one wishes to realise
how acceptable the conditions of the overpoweringly strong
enemy must have appeared to the terrified New-Amsterdam-
mers, one need but recall the fate of the 4,000 Portuguese who
had been driven from the conquered town of Cochin by Van
Goens the year before; or that of the Dutch who had had to
leave the Recife after their surrender to the Portuguese twelve
years earlier. The contrast makes us feel at the same time how
different was the relationship between the Dutch and the
English, in spite of all their trading rivalry, from that between
the Dutch and the Portuguese. Religion counted for a great deal
in this.

Thus it also becomes explicable why the Dutch population of
what was now called New York resigned itself so easily to its
fate, and how, more and more mingled with English elements
from the surrounding colonies and from England, it was
gradually anglicised. Would the preservation of the Dutch
character of the settlement on the Hudson have been impossible
in any case? If one compares the narrow strip inhabited by the
Dutch on the map of North America with what has now become
a wholly English-speaking area, one would almost think so. But
the capitulation of 4 September 1664 was the final fruit of a
neglect that had been going on for years, and it is that which

makes it a sad spectacle to a Dutch beholder. When speculating on what might have been, however, it should not be forgotten that the English colonies of the east coast started gradually expanding into the hinterland only much later, and that to do so they had to engage in severe struggles, first with the French, from Canada to Louisiana, and then with the Spaniards, in Florida, Texas, and New Mexico, a struggle in which they might not have been so completely victorious if they themselves had remained split in two by the supremely well situated New Netherland area. The early downfall of that Dutch colony on the Hudson is therefore a fact of far-reaching importance.

We shall see later that the Dutch flag was not lowered for good on 4 September 1664. But the return of the Dutch in 1673 was of short duration.

The West Coast of Africa, Guiana, and the Antilles

In 1630 the West India Company still held important posses-sions on the tropical coasts of the Atlantic Ocean, although the exhaustion of its financial resources prevented it from deriving the full benefit from them. Usually the Company borrowed money for each separate voyage and lost a good part of the returns in interest and insurance premiums. A good deal of the trade, moreover, it left in the hands of private individuals, contenting itself with claiming, as holder of the monopoly, a duty in proportion to the tonnage of the vessels concerned.

Just as the East India Company in *its* territory, so too had the West India Company attained its position on the west coast of Africa largely to the detriment of the Portuguese. In 1648 St. Thomas and St. Paul de Loanda had been reconquered for Portugal from Bahia, but St. George d'Elmina was preserved and had become the centre of a Dutch sphere of influence along the Gold Coast. More to the north both the Portuguese forts, on the islands of Goree off Cape Verde and Arguin off Cape Blanco, were in Dutch hands. The former was administered by the Chamber of Amsterdam, the latter by the Zealand Chamber. In 1634 the patron of Berbice, Van Pere, had had Arguin occupied by a private fleet under the command of his son. Privateering and warlike activities seemed naturally wedded to the spirit of enterprise animating those Zealand merchants.

F

There were a number of 'factories' scattered along the coast as far down as the Congo, some fortified and some not as the case might be, and most of them under the rule of some native prince, occasionally together with factories of other nations, notably of the English of course. Gold, ivory, rubber and ostrich feathers were obtained from Africa, and tools, arms, and textiles were brought there. One article became increasingly important, namely slaves, who were in various places bought by the thousand every year from their black conquerors, particularly on the Gold Coast and the so-called 'Bocht' (Bend).

The Company's position was strongest on the Gold Coast. There was a Director-General at Elmina—at this time his name was Valkenburgh—and although the direct authority of the stations did not extend very far inland, it was possible nevertheless to aim at a very real subjection of the whole coast by means of alliances with negro kings. It is true that the English also were still active here. Their chief stronghold was at Cormantin, somewhat east of Elmina. Moreover Swedish and Danish companies were pushing in, for example at Cape Coast Castle, between Cormantin and Elmina, where they harassed each other and were at times used by the English against the Dutch West India Company. Those sailing under the Swedish or Danish flag were as often as not Dutchmen, whose spirit of enterprise could not content itself with the monopoly of the patented Dutch Company. All these white traders incited the surrounding negro tribes against their rivals and tried to exclude the latter from trading in those waters. There was plenty of occasion for friction.

On the other side of the Ocean the whites did not get in each others' way quite so much. The Dutch settlements on the Wild Coast increased but slowly. Brazil's needs had impeded their development: almost the whole of the slave supply they needed had been directed to that country. Nevertheless groups of plantations were to be found all along that unhealthy coast, on the Pomeroon, the Essequibo, and the Berbice, each group under the protection of a fort right in the middle of the wilderness. In Cajana (Cayenne), where a similar attempt had been tried more than once, the Dutch colonists had been driven out by the French in 1664. Berbice still remained under the patronage of the Van Peres. Essequibo had been taken over by the Zealand

Chamber when the Company, alarmed by its adverse experience in Brazil, was thinking of abandoning it. In 1657 the worries involved grew to be too much for the Zealand Chamber also, but the Zealanders were too keenly interested in South American and West African affairs to leave the colonists to their fate: the towns of Middelburg, Veere, and Flushing adopted Essequibo. At the same time, in Surinam there was a similar English colony.

The Dutch Company was even less sole master of the islands than of the Wild Coast. The big islands had been thoroughly colonised by the Spaniards, although the French had ensconced themselves on San Domingo, while the English had conquered Jamaica. The Dutch had likewise, in 1633, robbed Spain of the Curaçao group. Of the smaller islands which the Spaniards had neglected, the West India Company had occupied some and given them in patronage: St. Eustatius and Saba to Van Pere and Van Rhee, and St. Martin and Tobago to Lampsins, a Zealander like the other two; Lampsins' islands had as a matter of fact to be shared with the French. St. Thomas and St. Cross (Santa Cruz) were soon abandoned to the Danes, but here again the Danes were Dutch in disguise. French and English islands were scattered between the ones mentioned. The importance of their possession was not measured by their surface area, for even though the sugar plantations became valuable later on, they served first and foremost as key-points for contraband trading with the Spanish colonies.

From the point of view of trade there was the closest connection between these twin areas in America and West Africa. Very often vessels sailed via Arguin or Guinea to the Wild Coast and from there past the Antilles homewards. But besides this the slave trade forged a close link. The black cargo would often be brought first to St. Eustatius and distributed thence. The import of negroes was to govern the development of those regions for generations. The Dutch took a very active part in this. The abominations inherent in the whole business were regarded with composure, because heathens were not looked upon as fellow-men. Later on we shall observe the moral corruption with which slavery infected the slowly growing white communities in the Dutch West Indies.

The French, as we have already seen, drove the Dutch from Cayenne, and later from St. Martin and Tobago as well. The

English first directed their attention to West Africa. Just as in North America, the Restoration of 1660 meant a more vigorous policy here. A Royal Company was founded, which was granted a trade monopoly for West Africa. Court circles, and here again more particularly the Duke of York, were deeply interested. A fleet, including some ships of the Royal Navy, was sent out in 1661. The leader, Holmes, occupied some posts on the river Gambia, opposite the island of Goree, and warned the Dutch that from there downward as far as the Cape of Good Hope only the English were entitled to trade. One can imagine that the West India Company protested. Charles II did not openly support Holmes, but neither did he punish him. The treaty of 1662[1] wiped out these disputes, but soon new ones arose. The English—understandably enough—resented particularly the pretensions of the West India Company in excluding them from regions which it ostensibly kept blockaded in the endless little wars with and among the negro kings, in which the European law of nations did indeed cut a strange figure. It will be remembered that the same problem occurred in India—at the sieges of Cochin and Porka. Downing's violent notes only led to interminable discussion, and meanwhile the Dutch under Valkenburgh strengthened their hold all along the Gold Coast.

In 1664 the English proceeded to enforce their claims by warlike procedures, just as they had done in North America. A list of grievances presented by Parliament to the King made it clear that in his struggle against the Dutch he would be able to count on the support of his people. In May the States responded to the demonstration by equipping thirty 'stout men-of-war', yet negotiations went busily on. In July, however, it was learnt in The Hague that Holmes had again sailed for Africa, with a much stronger fleet this time, and had started open hostilities against the Dutch. Ships had been captured, Goree had been taken as well as Fort Tacorany in the neighbourhood of Elmina. Whilst Charles II continued to disclaim responsibility for Holmes's depredations, the leaders of the Republic hastened to assist the helpless Company with more than diplomatic action. An order was issued in the name of the States-General to De Ruyter, at that moment cruising the Mediterranean, to go and restore the Company's position in Africa; Orangist members

---

[1] See above, p. 5s.

of the assembly, who might have informed Downing, had been
kept in the dark by De Witt by means of a ruse. The English,
taken unawares, now suddenly became the weaker party. Not
only did they have to evacuate Goree and Tacorany again, but
after some hard fighting De Ruyter and Valkenburgh captured
Cormantin. In accordance with his orders De Ruyter now
crossed over to the Antilles. The acts of violence on both sides
had by degrees led to open war. Off Barbados De Ruyter had to
give battle to English men-of-war. Unfortunately his fleet,
although increased by several prizes, was no longer strong enough
to call, as prescribed in his instructions, at New Netherland
(quite recently passed into English hands); he sailed on to New-
foundland (Terre Neuve), then still French, and from there viâ
Bergen in Norway back home, where such a state of emergency
had developed that his arrival had been eagerly looked out for.

3. THE WAR AND THE PEACE

Obdam, C. Tromp, De Ruyter; the Bishop of Münster

THE occupation of New Netherland and the attack on Guinea
were undeniably acts of aggression on the part of England. But
the fact should not be overlooked that the policy of exclusion
applied by the Dutch East India Company in the Malay
Archipelago and on the coast of Malabar, and which was also
applied by the West India Company in Guinea, could not fail
to be felt as a provocation by a people aspiring to take part in
world trade. What the States were getting ready to defend was
not only established possessions, but also the claim to expansion.
The 'regulation of overseas trade' proposed by the other side in
the negotiations seemed to them an intolerable attempt at
throttling the forces and energies still abounding in Holland,
for the very reason that it would have made expansion difficult,
an expansion which in the regions mentioned could not yet
dispense with the exclusion of European rivals. There was
indeed in the outburst of popular fury in England against the
presumption of the Dutch an element of spontaneous reaction,
and Downing was not far wrong when he said, scoffingly, that
what the States wanted was:

mare liberum in British waters, but mare clausum on the coast of Africa and in
the East Indies.

It was the same contradiction that had come to light in the dispute with James I about the Moluccas[1]. With quite as much sincerity the English were looked upon in Holland as sea tyrants.

The States stood firm to guard sea law.
They (*the British*) fought for themselves, we for the whole of Europe.

Thus rhymed Jan Vos. And De Witt wrote with some acerbity about 'the insupportable temper of that nation' and of their 'greed'. Downing's manners and the unpredictable changes of the King's moods did not make the exaggerated demands of the English interested parties any more acceptable. Downing made the mistake of underestimating his adversary and thereby contributed not a little to the clash. He kept on assuring his government that measures of vigour would always make the States climb down. And certainly they were as little anxious for war as they had been twelve years earlier. But they could not submit to challenges indefinitely. It was partly his intimacy with the Orange party which caused Downing to speak so boldly: the Orangists did indeed constitute a weak spot in the Republic when it came to a show-down with England. But the States party felt themselves in command of the situation. The French alliance afforded a backing. The hard work done by the Admiralties under the constant urging by Holland's Grand Pensionary had moreover borne fruit: the navy was no longer inferior to its English rival.

All the more galling therefore was the disappointment when the first encounter, off Lowestoft in June 1665, ended in a heavy defeat. The fault lay with the poor co-operation between the sub-commanders and their lack of confidence in the high-born admiral Wassenaer van Obdam. He was killed in the battle when his ship exploded, after which several captains had taken to flight. Popular fury, unfairly enough, was directed against the Zealand admiral Johan Evertsen, who was even thrown into the water by the people of The Brill. The main body of the fleet was safely stowed away in Texel by Cornelis Tromp (Maarten's son), who displayed masterly skill on that occasion. He was now temporarily invested by the States with the supreme command.

The dark days of 1653 seemed to have returned. The people's alarm was loudly voiced in the two conflicting assertions, that

[1] See Part One pp. 56, 177.

the war was due to the States party's having angered Charles II by the exclusion of his nephew, and that the war could only be successful under the leadership of that nephew.

I will go and return to my first husband; for then was it better with me than now;

on this text (Hosea ii, 7) the Reverend Mr. Lantman, minister at The Hague, preached on an officially decreed day of prayer, and he was seriously reprimanded by the States of Holland for his impudence. To the preacher's voice a foreign monarchist supplied the echo:

You may be sure (*wrote a Frenchman*) that the States' fleet will next time be beaten still more easily. Waging war is no job for merchants.

It was a good thing for the development of Dutch national self-confidence that deeds gave the lie to these utterances. With splendid courage and strength of mind De Witt faced the situation. We have here the unwilling testimony of his greatest enemy, Downing, who remained in The Hague as long as France continued making attempts at mediation and from there, plotting with the Orange Party all the while, kept his government posted about the situation in the Republic. Not for a moment did the Grand Pensionary and his supporters falter amidst all the confusion and consternation. Soon De Witt went to Texel in person to help restore discipline there—three captains who had fled from the battle were shot and others rewarded —and to strengthen the fleet and get it ready to sail. How profound was the general dismay can be gathered from the outburst of popular enthusiasm in August at the news that De Ruyter, who had been thought lost, had fallen into the northern port of Delfzijl from his Ocean voyage, with ships, prizes and all. Never had an admiral been more vociferously welcomed back, and the States-General at once appointed De Ruyter commander of the fleet at Texel. Cornelis Tromp, quick-tempered, rash, and an Orangist into the bargain, was not a man after the hearts of the leading regents. Nevertheless it was De Witt who persuaded the bitterly disappointed admiral to stay on under De Ruyter's command. De Witt was the only man in the country who possessed real moral authority over sailors and naval commanders and the courage required to make use of it. However ill he could be spared at home, the States yet appointed him as deputy in the fleet. It was a disappointment to him that for the rest of that year, while he sailed the seas on board De Ruyter's flagship, the enemy was not again encountered.

Meanwhile the support of the great ally Louis XIV had been most valuable. This in spite of the fact that the king was not to be prevailed upon to declare war on England straightway, and he had at first hoped to be able to obtain, as the price for his aid, support for his plans in the Southern Netherlands. But this De Witt had vigorously opposed, simply demanding the execution of the treaty of 1662 now that the Republic had been indubitably attacked. France, once the patron of the Oranges, had turned away from them since they seemed to have become the clients of the restored Stuarts, and so, if for no other reason than to oppose England's influence in the Republic, Louis was anxious to save the States' régime from a collapse. In itself the declaration of war on England came at a most inopportune moment for Louis. In September 1665 the Southern Netherlands problem had reached a critical stage: Philip IV of Spain died, the wretched little Carlos II became king, and really 'the rights of the Queen' should now have been brought into play by the French. But now that he had to choose the side of the States in the Anglo-Dutch War, Louis thought it necessary to bide his time so as not to drive England and Spain into each other's arms.

The aid he gave the States' régime against another assailant cost him less worry. I am alluding to the warlike Bishop of Münster, with whom there were disagreements about the frontier (his principality was contiguous with the provinces of Overijsel and Gelderland) and against whom Holland was now belatedly sorry not to have supported the town of Münster more energetically, shortly before. That town indeed, in its constant quarrels with its overlord, used to look for Dutch assistance as had Emden some time earlier. To the bishop, on his part, possibilities of finding supporters in the States' territory also seemed to present themselves in the dissensions troubling the Eastern provinces. A Groningen Burgomaster, Schulemborch by name, who in the town of his birth had mixed himself up with guild movements not unlike those in Antwerp some years previously, had sought refuge at the bishop's court. Immediately before the invasion, designs on Doesburg and

Arnhem were discovered, for which two citizens paid the death penalty, while the Registrar of Doorwerth also fled to Münster; the bishop denied the plot, asserting that innocent Catholics had become the victims of cruel persecution. The Vicar-General of the North Netherland Catholics, Bishop Neercassel, who now, very unlike Vosmeer and Rovenius at an earlier date, could sojourn in the country and who could even have discreet relations with the States—to that extent at any rate the situation had grown less tense—urged his co-religionists to remain loyal to the States' government. Yet we can see here again how the continuance of the edicts against the Catholics rendered their attitude in a case of emergency an uncertain factor; although of course to the Calvinist zealots the war with Münster was on the contrary an occasion to press for a strict application of those edicts.

That a French auxiliary army was required to get rid of this enemy made a humiliating spectacle. The fortified towns in the east proved to be in bad condition, and during the years of peace, and without the attention and authority of a Prince of Orange as Captain-General, the army had gone slack. John Maurice the Brazilian, now advanced in years, showed himself far from enterprising. The French as a matter of fact did not exert themselves very greatly, and if the bishop consented to a peace in 1666, it was due to the States' diplomacy having succeeded in setting up his other neighbour, Brandenburg, against him.

Even though Louis had now also declared war on England, he did not take it seriously, and the powerful fleet with which De Ruyter sailed in 1666 (for the first time on the flagship *The Seven Provinces*) had again to face the English without any help from the French.

The two fleets met at once, off Lowestoft, and in a bloody battle lasting four days the English were heavily defeated. De Ruyter put into port at the Wielingen with six English prizes and 3,000 prisoners, among whom was Vice-Admiral Ayscue De Ruyter's fleet indeed had also been too badly battered to keep the sea. After another supreme effort on the part of the Admiralties, he could set out to sea again a few weeks later, but the English fleet had also been put in fighting trim once more. In August the two fleets encountered each other anew in the same region, and this time, after a two days' battle, it was the

English who came out on top. De Ruyter imputed the defeat to
Cornelis Tromp, who, as things were going well with his part of
the line, had in the heat of his pursuit failed to assist the main
body. After a violent quarrel Tromp was relieved of his
command and threw himself into intrigues against the States'
régime.

Buat's Conspiracy

As SOON as its quarrel with the States-General had come into the
open, the English Government bethought itself of the existence
of the king's nephew. In the declaration of war it had, with
obvious intent, already suggested that the quarrel was more
particularly one with the States of Holland. And now presently
Downing got to work in league with his friends in the Orange
party to discredit the States with the public at large. The insolence of his activities in full war time is remarkable. In the end,
in fact, he went too far. One of his servants, Oudart, a Dutchman, who had been secretary to the late Princess Royal, was
imprisoned in the autumn of 1665 and Downing himself had to
leave the country. But soon a fresh attempt was made to force
the Republic by means of the Orange party to conclude peace.
The Secretary of State, Lord Arlington, recently married to
Nassau-Beverweert's daughter, and his agent Sylvius, from the
principality of Orange in southern France, who had also been
a servant of the Princess Royal, conducted the affair from the
English side; their henchman in the Netherlands was the
Seigneur de Buat. The latter was a States' officer of French
descent, brought up at the court of Frederick Henry, married
to a daughter of the late Greffier of the States-General Musch
(who had been so closely linked to the Stadholder), and still
accounted a servant of the young Prince of Orange. Buat
approached the Grand Pensionary with proposals of peace. The
States had already let it be known in England that they were
willing to conclude peace, on the basis either of mutual restitution of conquests or of *uti possidetis*. The proposals now made
were vague in the extreme. An indemnification was demanded,
also once more a regulation regarding trade with the overseas
world, and a united front against France; it was implied that the
indemnification might be reduced if the Prince of Orange was

elevated. Sylvius (now in England) had indeed represented to the English government that to claim an indemnification was sure to cool the enthusiasm for complying with England on the point of the Prince of Orange, and yet, so he had written:

the influence which the King will be able to exercise in future through this Prince and his party is worth a great deal more to the King than if he were now to receive several millions.

De Witt understood quite clearly that it was the aim of the manoeuvre:

firstly, to impart to the commonalty here, and perhaps also to some ignorant regents, the impression that peace with England could be had if we so wished; and that it is the fault of this Government itself that peace is not concluded; meaning in that way to promote dissension and factions throughout the country and to make the people unwilling to pay the heavy contributions which at this juncture are demanded of them by the times and the circumstances; and secondly, to separate this State from France, or at least to make jealousy and distrust grow between the two.

He was careful therefore not to turn the proposal down bluntly. While De Witt meticulously kept France informed, he authorised Buat to continue the correspondence. By the side of the correspondence meant for De Witt's eye, Buat, however, secretly communicated with Arlington and Sylvius about his attempts to propagate in a wider circle the English proposals, unacceptable as these were to his Dutch principal, and to form among the States members a party 'for the peace and my little master'.

His chief helpers were two regents from Rotterdam, Burgomaster Kievit, brother-in-law to Cornelis Tromp, and Van der Horst. Their connections branched out into the nobility and voting towns of Holland. The quarrel between De Ruyter and Tromp, about which public opinion was violently taking sides, deepened the discord. The Prince and peace with England, or the States and alliance with France; that became the contrast. But while De Witt and his adherents were on their guard with regard to France, Buat and his confederates on the contrary allowed themselves to be used as blind tools by England. They did not even know England's actual conditions for peace, but what was in Buat's mind can be gathered from what he wrote to Sylvius:

I dare assure you that the King will be the greatest monarch in Europe, because he will be able to do as he likes here.

De Witt meanwhile had already come to realise that it would not be possible to keep the Prince of Orange, now approaching the completion of his sixteenth year, out of all office for ever, but this took him back at once to his train of thought of 1661, namely that the young man must be withdrawn from his Anglophile environment. The Princess Grandmother (Amalia) received his suggestions for a revival of the education scheme with favour—the financial consideration no doubt weighed heavily with her—and in April 1666 William III had been adopted by Holland as 'Child of State'. His governor, Nassau-Zuylesteyn (whose wife was an Englishwoman), and other courtiers were replaced by trustworthy Hollanders and a committee was instituted to superintend his education. De Witt, who was on the committee, took this task seriously. According to the decree of the States of Holland the Prince had above all to be well and properly instructed and taught in the true Christian Reformed Religion, as well as in the salutary rights, privileges, and maxims of the State.

The development of the Buat affair makes one feel that this change in the position of the young Prince was a most fortunate occurrence for him and his house. When the plot came to light, in August 1666, through Buat's carelessness (by mistake he had given De Witt a letter from Arlington meant for himself only), William and his grandmother could truthfully say that they were ignorant of the whole affair and disown the conspiracy. The discharged governor Van Zuylesteyn belonged to those in the know. Only a short while ago the Prince, when on a visit to Rotterdam, had been made to dine at Kievit's house. Now everything came crashing down. Buat was arrested, Kievit and Van der Horst fled (Kievit to England). Buat was brought before the Court of Holland and beheaded in October. Forming a party for peace in consultation with the enemy and against the country's ally—it was a clear case of treason. That many Orangists saw in Buat a martyr and in De Witt a murderer only goes to show how faction had weakened the Dutch people's power of resistance against English intrigues.

After the Two Days' Battle the English had for a moment been in control of the sea and had turned it to account by destroying a Dutch merchant fleet in the Vlie and plundering Terschelling. In September, however, the Dutch fleet sailed out again and in October, since De Ruyter had fallen ill, De Witt, as deputy of the States-General, to all intents and purposes assumed the command. In the summer, when the two big battles had been fought, official duties had kept him ashore. Now he eagerly sought out the enemy, but a battle was averted by the autumn storms.

Chatham and the Peace

THE combatants were fairly matched. The war asked for a tremendous effort of each of them. More than half of the expenditure of the province of Holland (which had to defray the costs of the war almost alone) was swallowed up by interest payments. England was ravaged by the plague and the fire of London. In May 1667 peace negotiations were opened at Breda among the three belligerents under the mediation of Sweden. The failure of the Buat intrigue had caused the English to moderate their claims—first they had even hinted at towns in Zealand to be ceded in pawn—but in the end they agreed to a peace on the basis of *uti possidetis*. The situation was complicated, however, by the fact that Louis now seriously began making preparations for taking possession of the Southern Netherlands on behalf of his wife, and by the incorrigible fickleness and ambiguity of Charles's policy.

In his Council one party was in favour of co-operating with the Republic to keep France out of the Southern Netherlands; the other party wanted to give France free play in the Southern Netherlands so as to obtain her help in plundering and breaking the Republic. What was worse was that both lines of policy were tried in secret negotiations with each of the allies separately and simultaneously. The Austrian statesman Lisola, always trying to convince Europe of the paramount danger of France, was eager to mediate in the former direction. That De Witt did not just simply accept Lisola's good offices becomes understandable when we know that the Grand Pensionary and the French kept each other informed of Charles II's secret negotiations with the other. Unaware of this, the English assumed an arrogant tone at Breda. They again cited the notorious two ships, and demanded the reinstatement of Kievit in his offices. And they played this dangerous game without having taken due care for their safety in the new summer season, which they assumed was to bring peace. Entrapped as he was in lack of cash and internal dissensions Charles II had not had the fleet made ready for action, while the States, whom he had thought would be reduced to a state of confusion and impotence by his intrigues, had been again working with all their might at theirs.

In the middle of June the States' fleet, with English republicans familiar with the English waterways on board, as well as troops, sailed across from Schooneveld (Walcheren) to the mouth of the Thames. De Ruyter had Cornelis De Witt at his side, or rather above him, as deputy of the States-General. The deputy's written instructions were to sail up the Thames and then up the Medway in order to damage and destroy the English ships lying at Chatham and the wharves and warehouses there. This was the Grand Pensionary's plan, who, knowing the sailors' aversion to an undertaking of that nature, had let his brother be ordered (the instruction was supposed to emanate from the High and Mighty Assembly itself, but it was the Grand Pensionary who had drafted it):

to work and proceed with all possible resolution and rather to take some risks than to return without having effected anything notable.

The Deputy did indeed need that backing. In the full Council of War, which it was the custom to consult on all decisions and which was informed of the plan on the 18th when the fleet lay at anchor in the *Koningsdiep* (King's Deep), criticism and doubts were expressed on all sides. Not only was it considered dangerous, but 'ridiculous and impossible'. De Ruyter himself hesitated, and without the insistence of Cornelis De Witt nothing would have come of it. And indeed it was an extremely hazardous undertaking. There was a danger of being shut up in the Thames by English fleets coming from the Channel or from the North; and the narrow, winding Medway was a difficult fairway even for the English. But in the execution of the scheme skilful management was as conspicuous as daring. The fort of Sheerness was taken by landing troops on the 21st and was set on fire. Small craft under Van Ghent and De Witt then went up the Medway, harassed by the enemy from the banks and with fire-ships. The chain that had been thrown across the river was rammed asunder, after which the expedition could start destroying the half-dismantled English navy and burning the warehouses bordering the river. Two of the biggest English men-of-war, one of them the *Royal Charles*, were captured. Along the banks the English made desperate attempts at defence under the leadership of York and Albemarle. Behind them, in London, panic reigned. But under the command of De Ruyter himself, who had joined De Witt on the 23rd, the Dutch on the 24th sailed down the Medway again to rejoin the main body of the fleet, which now set sail to drop down to the mouth of the Thames.

The impression made by that successful attack was enormous. The prestige of the States' régime rose immeasurably. Charles's government felt, and was, disgraced. Pepys, the diarist, a highly-placed Admiralty servant himself, notes down, weeks after the event and after much bitter comment:

> Thus, in all things, in wisdom, courage, force, knowledge of our own streams, and success, the Dutch have the best of us, and do end the war with victory on their side.

Never did the Dutch State make a more powerful appearance in the world than in the expedition to Chatham. And not the least striking feature was the accuracy with which the Grand Pensionary, who had called Cornelis 'the best plenipotentiary', had calculated the political effect of the blow to England's pride. For one moment Charles thought of recalling his ambassadors from Breda, but presently on the contrary they received instructions that peace was indispensable, and on 26 July the treaty was signed.

A treaty whereby—according to the *uti possidetis*—New Netherland was ceded by the original founders seems to us a somewhat surprising anti-climax, even though on the strength of the same principle Surinam was acquired, having just been taken by a Zealand fleet under Crijnssen. But North America had never touched the public imagination in the Netherlands as it had in England. A few years previously a book had appeared, which had met with a certain amount of success, and in which the delights, the riches, and the pleasant climate of Guiana were praised above anything New Netherland had to offer. From the purely financial point of view the Dutch had not indeed made so bad an exchange, and but few contemporaries saw with any clearness what a huge difference there was in possibilities for popular settlement and national expansion between Guiana and

New Netherland. In West Africa and the East Indies, the countries about which more than anything else the war had started,
the two Dutch Companies maintained their positions and their
claims. Pulu Run was definitely abandoned by the English, and
without so much as a by-your-leave the East India Company
moreover seized their last stronghold in the neighbourhood of
the Moluccas: but of Macassar, which even after 1660 was still
a thorn in the side of the Company's most jealously guarded
monopoly, I shall speak later.

D. TRIUMPH AND FAILURE OF THE
BALANCE-OF-POWER POLICY

I. THE TRIPLE ALLIANCE AND THE PEACE OF AIX

WHILE the Republic was engrossed in its war with England,
Louis XIV had finished the careful diplomatic preparation of his
plans regarding the Southern Netherlands. Treaties had been
concluded with Portugal to keep Spain busy in the rear, and
with German rulers in the Rhine area to block the Emperor's
path. In May 1667 the King then notified the Spanish court of
what, in his opinion, should be the Queen's rightful share in the
Netherlands according to the law of devolution—it embraced
especially Hainault and Brabant—and forthwith sent his army
under Turenne to take possession of those provinces.

Never had the Southern Netherlands been so defenceless.
The years that had elapsed since the Peace of the Pyrenees had
not been used to any purpose. The government in Madrid,
under a weak regency, was paralysed by administrative confusion and lack of money, and the government in Brussels was
no better off. Since 1664 the Marquess of Castel-Rodrigo had
been Governor, a man who wholeheartedly wished to resist the
French advance, but whose burning zeal only showed up his
impotence the more pitifully. He received but small comfort
from Madrid in response to his appeals for help, and in the
Netherlands itself he was not only alarmed by the wretched
condition of the means of defence and of the beggarly army,
but also by the general dejection of the people. Despairing of

the government's ability to defend them, many South Netherlanders, so long unaccustomed to independent action, were
inclined to range themselves under the impressive power of
France rather than suffer the terrors of invasion and war all
over again. Castel-Rodrigo noticed with displeasure the gallicisation of social and cultural life in the land he was to govern.
But the pressure he brought to bear on courtiers and officials to
dress and have their hair done in Spanish rather than in French
style did no more to arouse the national spirit than the strictly
formalistic legal argument which Stockmans, a member of the
Privy Council, opposed to the claims of Louis's queen.

When the invasion came, Castel-Rodrigo was forced to fall
back on Brussels without striking a blow, and Turenne in the
course of some three or four months conquered Armentières,
Charleroi, Douai, Courtrai, Oudenarde, Lille and Alost without
one of those towns putting up a serious defence. But European
diplomacy stirred into feverish activity. Louis did not make it
too difficult for his opponents. He soon announced that he
would content himself with an equivalent of his wife's rights,
and mentioned areas which were less terrifying to the States
than was the adjacent province of Brabant. It was De Witt's
tactics to tie the King to this proposal, and in the way most
pleasing to him, namely by pressing Spain to a speedy acceptance and if need be to assist in forcing her. This was still the
policy of 1663, which aimed at combining the preservation of
the French alliance with keeping the French northern frontier
as far removed as possible. This latter aim, however, had now
become something of a delusion because all that might be
attained this time was persuading France to allow the devolution
right to be bought off: nothing was decided about her further
claims should the little Carlos II (as was ever expected) die
without issue. No wonder that a strong inclination became
manifest in the Republic to side with Spain, and De Witt himself felt inclined to do so when Castel-Rodrigo made an offer
of cautionary towns in return for possible support. Negotiations
were carried on in which Ostend and Bruges and towns in
Upper Gelderland were mentioned, but the Governor had to
take back his suggestion when Madrid failed to sanction it.

The English meanwhile were not idle either, and just as they
had done two years previously they tried simultaneously

G

opposite lines of policy, namely: support to France on condition that she should allow herself to be used against the Republic (France might be found willing to leave Ostend to England);
and support to Spain (again with Ostend as a reward if possible!)
in co-operation with the Republic. Both in England and in the
Northern Netherlands, however, public opinion was so violently
anti-French that Anglo-Dutch trade rivalry seemed to recede
into the background, and the King of England, feeling how
much the outcome of the naval war had damaged his prestige,
decided to follow opinion rather than defy it. Not that he really
gave up his preference for an alliance with France against the
Republic! Perhaps even his apparent change of front was
actually intended to create the first condition that would bring
this about, namely a breach between the allies of 1662. Sir
William Temple, however, the young diplomat who was now
sent to The Hague to conclude a treaty for joint intervention,
was personally a convinced supporter of the policy of setting up
a united front against France.

In De Witt's view, the Triple Alliance which was thus
brought about in January 1668—the participation of Sweden,
won over by bribes under a King who was a minor, was of little
practical significance—had its objectionable aspect. But for
months now, the States' ambassadors had done their utmost to
wean Charles II's divided government from its dangerous tendency to join hands with France. It was impossible to rebuff
Temple when he positively assured the Dutch that that tendency
had been overcome. Yet De Witt did not want to rebuff the ally
of 1662 either. And on the face of things it did not seem impossible to avoid this. The mediation outlined in the Triple
Alliance was to adhere to the basis indicated by Louis himself:
Spain was to resign herself to ceding an equivalent for the
Queen's rights. In a secret clause, however, it was laid down that
if Louis were to be tempted by his military success to go further,
force should be brought to bear on him too and an attempt be
made to push him back to the frontiers of 1659.

When that clause became known at the French court—and
that was soon—there was a violent outburst of indignation
against the ingratitude and conceit of the States-General. For
the time being Louis resisted his generals who assured him
that the Netherlands were ripe for garnering; even after the easy

conquest, in midwinter, of Franche Comté—one of the regions which had been mentioned as an equivalent—Louis remained willing to be content with the areas indicated in July. His moderation becomes less surprising when we realise that in that same month of January he had concluded a secret treaty with the Emperor—the master of de Lisola, the propagandist against France!—whereby in the case of the death of Carlos II of Spain the Spanish heritage was to be divided between the two of them, both of them sons-in-law of Philip IV, and whereby Louis would get a great deal more than the conquests parts of which he now declared himself ready to evacuate, in particular the whole of the Southern Netherlands. But the King's displeasure about the Triple Alliance was in no wise diminished, and it was wholly directed against the Republic: while he had carefully adhered to their treaty, the Republic now proved to be contemplating a war against him rather than acquiescing in his obtaining the Netherlands on which he had set his heart.

Nor did De Witt get any thanks from Spain—and is it any wonder? He resisted all Castel-Rodrigo's efforts to push the Republic into direct conflict with France, and in the end Spain had to agree to a peace, at Aix-la-Chapelle, which England and the Republic had previously prepared in consultation with France at St. Germain. Spain was given the choice of ceding Franche Comté or the regions Louis had conquered in the Netherlands the previous year. With bitterness in his heart Castel-Rodrigo chose what would be most obnoxious to the Naval Powers, namely the latter. As a result not only Lille, Tournai, and Ath, but also Courtrai, Oudenarde, and Thielt fell into French hands, and that new frontier, which considered as such was an absurdity, pleased Louis only too well: it could serve as a springboard for further conquests. Nobody asked for the opinion of Flanders thus cruelly lacerated, but with his unexpected choice Castel-Rodrigo had intended to declare the Naval Powers as it were in default for the next occasion, which could not be long in coming.

In the Republic the Triple Alliance was nevertheless celebrated as a great diplomatic victory. De Witt arranged a banquet which the Prince of Orange diligently honoured with his presence: was it not a treaty which set the seal upon the reconciliation with his uncle? The States, fresh from their triumph over England, now seemed to act as the umpires of Europe. They felt themselves prodigiously important.

> After having reconciled Kings, preserved the freedom of the seas, brought about a glorious peace by force of arms, and established order in Europe, the States of the United Netherlands had this medal struck; 1668.

Thus did the States commemorate the Peace of Breda and that of Aix in accordance with the custom of the times by means of a medal. The phrase they employed cannot have been read with any great pleasure in either England, Spain, or France.

2. THE DOVER PLOT

THE figure the States' government cut in the world was impressive enough in all conscience. And yet it rested on a weak foundation. The Triple Alliance seemed to be the triumph of the policy of the balance of power. It was by no means De Witt's intention to turn from France to England. He continued to resist all Castel-Rodrigo's blandishments to conclude a treaty with Spain: the arguments he had used in 1663 were reinforced by the demonstration of impotence and inactivity which Spain and the Emperor had just given. But that France had been estranged soon became apparent. Just as in England, the party of economic competition, whose advocate was Colbert, had gained free play there, now that political grounds no longer dictated considerations of the States' interests. In 1668 Colbert introduced his stringently protectionist tariff. This caused the Dutch to look towards their new ally, who was now soon found to have already disengaged himself from the bonds he had himself so eagerly suggested shortly before.

Nothing could be stronger than the assurances Temple had given the Grand Pensionary to allay the uneasiness with which the latter envisaged the Triple Alliance.

> M. De Witt said (*so Temple wrote from The Hague in a confidential report on the critical negotiations*): 'That, if they should break all their measures with France and throw themselves wholly upon his Majesty (*of England*) by such a conjunction, any change of counsels in England would be their certain ruin'. (*To which Temple had replied:*) 'That I should not have made this journey, if I had not been confident that the unsteadiness of our counsels had been ended and we now bottomed past any change or remove'.

And with a charming faith in the reality of what he wished, he had exclaimed after the conclusion of the treaty:

At Breda reconciled enemies, now brothers! . . .

But economic rivalry soon made itself felt again. The Peace of Breda had not settled anything about the real conflicts in the colonial world, and Temple's promise at the conclusion of the Alliance to the effect that a trade convention to the liking of the States would be passed, proved impossible to carry out in the teeth of the protests of the City of London. Negotiations were therefore resumed, sometimes of a heated character, especially as regards the East Indies, where the British East India Company did not cease to oppose the policy of exclusion applied by the rival Dutch Company. It will be remembered that this Company's ambitions were not satisfied with the acquisition of Ceylon and the Malabar Coast and that it had already set out to lay hands on more, in the Malay Archipelago this time, namely on Macassar, the last remaining refuge of free trade in the neighbourhood of the Moluccas. But apart from these questions of interest, which at certain moments could outweigh the feeling of community in Protestantism which had been roused so vigorously by Louis' advance in the Southern Netherlands, there was the King, who might give way before that feeling, but who could never really share it. For Charles the Triple Alliance had been no more than a sacrifice to the spirit of the nation, which he had offended by his mismanagement of affairs. It did not mean that he had banished from his heart the alternative policy, so often tried after 1661, of joining France against the Republic. Nor would he be withheld by any feeling of having to stand by his word given in January 1668. The very displeasure felt by Louis against the Republic on account of the Triple Alliance offered Charles a wonderful opportunity, for until then Louis had always firmly abided by the alliance of 1662. And, as has already been hinted, it is not improbable that it was exactly this that the cunning monarch had aimed at when he made his proposals to the Republic. It was he, in fact, who had betrayed the secret clause of the Triple Alliance to Louis, well knowing that the latter's resentment would be directed especially against the Republic. While Temple, therefore, as the regular ambassador in The Hague, represented England's policy of friendship, a *rapprochement* was taking place, under cover of the greatest secrecy, between the two courts of England and France—a *rapprochement* having in view the destruction of the Republic.

In May 1670 a treaty was signed at Dover through the mediation of Charles' sister, wife of Louis' brother the Duke of Orleans, which had to be kept secret from even some of Charles' chief ministers. In fact, in it French support was promised for Charles' intention, even so no more than vaguely indicated, of leading England back to Catholicism. More positively the two Kings agreed to start a war against the ungrateful and arrogant Republic for the purpose of dissolving and dividing it. Charles II stipulated for Walcheren, Sluis, and Kadzand: the ambitions which had made Elizabeth in 1585 demand cautionary towns situated on the estuaries were still alive. Moreover it was his special wish that the interests of the Prince of Orange should be seen to. The idea was that the latter should, under the protection of the two Kings, be raised to the sovereignty over what remained of the North Netherlands State, after France had also taken her share.

Before striking, Louis XIV wished to isolate the Republic. To that end Sweden, the remaining partner in the Triple Alliance, was bought off and pacts were concluded with German rulers, notably with the Bishop of Münster and the Archbishop of Cologne. Louis was thinking of sending his army to the Republic through the lands of the latter, who was at the same time Bishop of Liège. He wished to avoid directly violating the Spanish Netherlands, in order to keep Spain out of the war as long as might be. Moreover the only means of striking a blow at the heart of the Republic was by way of the east—the examples of 1572 and 1629 were there to prove it.[1]

This plan is only seemingly in contradiction with Louis' policy during the early years of his reign. The Southern Netherlands were still his real goal, but whereas at that time he had tried to get the Republic to reconcile itself to his ambitions by means of a show of friendship, he now, after these efforts had failed and she was proving herself a most determined opponent, wanted to eliminate her as an effective factor in the international power game. Already Colbert's protectionist tariff of 1668 was

[1] See *The Revolt of the Netherlands*, pp. 120 and 131; and *The Netherlands in the Seventeenth Century*, Part One, p. 89.

hitting Dutch interests severely and led to counter-measures which aggravated relations not a little.

Colbert, quite as much as his master, considered the Republic France's chief opponent, although in another field. He had his eye on the naval power and financial strength of Holland, which, once the country had been brought into subjection, would be able to serve France's late, but now powerfully aroused, trading and colonial ambition. Therein lay danger for England, as Temple, who towards the end of 1670 was recalled from his post in The Hague, pointed out to his government; but Temple was no longer listened to.

The alliance could also be considered as an attempt on the part of the forces of Catholicism to strike a blow at the Netherlands Republic as being the chief *point d'appui* of Protestantism. As early as 1668 the Bishop of Münster had pointed out to the Pope, with elaborate detail, the importance of this aspect. But what he desired, namely that France and Spain should settle their mutual conflict for the sake of this great goal, had not come to pass. Louis still coveted the Spanish Netherlands, and so the Republic was to find Catholic allies in its hour of need. Nevertheless the attack which was now being prepared again placed the religious antithesis on the map of practical European politics.

Very gradually De Witt began to understand that there was something afoot. During these years the indolence of Dutch diplomacy contrasted sharply with the unceasing activity of French diplomacy. Yet in the end the Dutch could not but notice the cool and often unfriendly tone adopted by the English. The English government protested against medals and paintings celebrating the expedition to Chatham; it provoked incidents involving the saluting of the flag; and more serious still, it opposed the admission of the Emperor to the Triple Alliance. For the Emperor's understanding with Louis was already at an end, and nothing was more natural than for the Republic to turn to him. At last, in the summer of 1671, England sent Downing to take Temple's place, and the selection of that hated quarrel-monger spoke only too clearly. By that time a veritable tariff war had sprung up with France. Moreover, at the end of 1671 the new ambassador to the French court, Pieter de Groot, son of Hugo Grotius, had been able to pass on fairly accurate information about the Dover plot.

The intention is said to be (*so he wrote to De Witt*) not simply to declare war on our State, but to sap its strength to its very foundations and to overthrow the whole constitution of its government. This line of action has been deemed necessary here not only to give no ground for jealousy to the King of England, but on the contrary to excite his affection and to ruin, in the interest common to both, the commerce of a State which draws all trade to itself and wishes to lay down the law to all kings. To combat this successfully they here deem it best to turn the Republic into a Monarchy, putting the sovereignty in the hands of the Prince of Orange, who thus, being under an obligation to his promoters, is expected to conform to their interests.

The Prince of Orange was now twenty years old and had become a personage of importance in the Republic. The promise implied in his adoption as Child of State was defined more specifically in 1667. Almost immediately after the peace treaty had been signed at Breda, the States of Holland had passed the Perpetual Edict which declared the Stadholdership abolished, in so far as the province was concerned, and the office of Stadholder in any province incompatible with that of Captain-General of the Union. A great deal of opposition had to be overcome before all the other provinces could be got to accept the latter proposition. In 1670 the Act of Harmony effected this, after which the young man was admitted to the Council of State. The significant part of the compromise was that William III was now designated for the Captain-Generalship as soon as he should have completed his twenty-third year.

When in the autumn of 1671 war with the two powerful neighbours of the Republic was unmistakably threatening for the coming summer, many of the regents, even in the province of Holland, were beginning to feel inclined to have that appointment take place immediately. Proposals to this end were made by Gelderland in the Generality and by Enkhuizen in the Assembly of Holland. De Witt wrote to Pieter de Groot, scornfully:

The supporters of the Prince of Orange and also many good patriots (*meaning the States-party men*), whom God has not armed with any remarkable steadfastness of purpose or courage, are doing their utmost and are openly haranguing that it is impossible for this State to withstand the might of France alone . . . [and] that there is no choice but either to fall a prey to France and utterly to go under, or to throw ourselves into the arms of England, who (these men say) they are certain will take upon herself vigorously to defend this State, if only we will do a number of things of our own accord which they asseverate will greatly please the King of Great Britain; namely the promotion of the lord Prince of Orange to the Captaincy-General over the armed forces of this country. They maintain, moreover, that by this measure greater harmony will be effected in the State, that it will be obliging six provinces, will put heart into the soldiery, and will make the commonalty more willing to pay for these heavy charges; with many other such specious and plausible arguments. I frankly admit that I believe the remedy to be worse than the evil itself.

After the report De Witt had received from Pieter de Groot in Paris, the meaning of these last words will be understood. Shortly afterwards the Prince paid a visit to his uncle in England. During his absence, the three votes (out of seven) in the States of Zealand, over which he had control since his recognition as First Nobleman in that province, obstructed in the most unreasonable manner the Generality project for strong armaments on land and sea, which De Witt promoted for all he was worth. It is true that the Prince on his return at once put an end to this opposition, but how must not all this have stimulated De Witt's suspicions aroused so long ago! Many months later, as a matter of fact, when the war was on the point of being declared, Gelderland and Overijsel in their turn wasted precious time by withholding consent to new recruiting measures, suddenly professing themselves to be convinced of Charles II's friendly intentions. Yet Charles was at this very moment complaining about the insults implied by the glorification of the victory at Chatham in Holland and was clearly forcing a breach. De Witt could not but look upon the Prince as a tool in the hands of England. To exalt him meant:

to fall under the protection of England and to become wholly dependent on her.

It is certainly true that good Hollanders, who could not be reproached with lack of 'courage', had long wished for more vigorous action by taking the side of Spain against France and hoping through the Prince, without in the least wanting 'protection or dependence', to win England's support. Such for instance were the Amsterdammers, among them Van Beuningen, De Witt's friend indeed, but apt to take his own way, as had appeared in Northern affairs only too plainly. Led by a powerful Burgomaster, Gillis Valckenier, Amsterdam at this time escaped from De Witt's guidance altogether. This had appeared most clearly at the young Prince's appointment in the Council of State. The appointment had not been effected without fierce dissension in Holland about the question (in itself not very important) as to whether he should be given a vote in the Council or not. The question had in the end been decided in the affirmative, partly through the influence of Valckenier and Van Beuningen, and for De Witt, who had in vain urged the contrary course, it had been a defeat hard to stomach. The appointment as Captain-General could no longer be held up either, but here De Witt at least managed to have it arranged that the command should be for one campaign only. It was unfortunate that time was wasted by these bickerings, once again, and that the army, neglected as it had been in any case, did not in this way obtain from the Prince's appointment the full moral value it might have meant. And how tragic does the great Grand Pensionary's inability to co-operate wholeheartedly with Orange appear when we shall see that his suspicion was groundless. The 'education' had done more for William III than De Witt, who had had the greatest share in it, realised.

Not that it had turned William into a willing servant of the Loevestein party. He grew up as a pretender, as the leader of a particular tendency in the State. His importance was not solely due to the fact that he might become the rallying point for all who still hoped to be able to detach England from France. He also seemed able to provide a remedy against all the weaknesses inherent in the existing régime, weaknesses which showed themselves only too clearly in these years.

3. WEAKNESSES OF THE STATES' GOVERNMENT

Relation to Reformed Orthodoxy

As HAS already been said, the Republicans (or States-party men) were very well aware that it was to their advantage to keep in with the ministers of religion, and at first they had succeeded pretty well. The orthodox tenet about the Reformed character of the State continued officially in force, however much qualified in practice. When De Witt in his *Deductie* of 1654 argues that an eminent head is not necessary to keep the Seven Provinces together, since there is enough binding material of a different nature, he curiously enough omits to mention the feeling of unity on the basis of community of language; he mentions material interests, political arrangements, and 'above all' religion:

And are not above all their hearts and souls united and bound together by the spiritual and divine bond of one and the same religion?

It was indeed a difficulty that the ministers were not content with such generalities, but that they untiringly insisted on measures which at least the States of Holland could not bring themselves to pass. Their Noble Great Mightinesses were ready enough with fair words in response to the ever-recurring requests of the North and South Holland Synods for

a speedy and adequate remedy against the enormous and excessive effronteries of the Papists;

but when in 1655 the Synod proposed

that public and free residence of all Romish Mass priests and other such clerics should without exception be terminated, forbidden and if need be forcibly prevented,

they met with a very definite negative. For years committees consisting of States' Deputies conducted an investigation into the evil of Catholic officials in country districts; it appeared that in the villages large numbers of Burgomasters, sheriffs, and aldermen still belonged to the old religion; but nothing like vigorous action resulted. In the matter of Cartesianism the States let themselves be driven more readily: a quarrel among scholars is what it must have seemed to them, which it would be possible to suppress by a word of authority. Thus, acting on remonstrations on the part of the South Holland Synod in 1656, they adopted a resolution to the effect that

after mature deliberation and consultation upon the subject, they considered it necessary to take care by proper means that the true Theology and Holy Scripture should not be offended through liberty of philosophising or by any abuse of it;

with which end in view they went on to order the professors of philosophy and theology to stay each within his own bounds and set limits;

Moreover, to hold as fixed and indubitable, as being the most certain, that which has been by the Lord God revealed to man through Holy Scripture; ... (and) for the sake of order and peace to leave off propagating the philosophemata drawn from Dr. Cartesius' philosophy, which to-day give offence to a number of people.

It was not without some jibbing that the Leyden professors in the two dangerous subjects took the required oath before the Chairman of the Board of Curators (himself, as was customary, a member of the Committee of Noblemen in the States of Holland). Among the resisters Professors Coccejus and Heidanus were undoubtedly to be found. The latter was an ardent admirer of Descartes. The former, who had come to Leyden from Franeker, had now become the leader of a theological system in which the scholastic method was replaced by a philological exegesis of Scripture, proceeding from the meaning and inter-connection of the words. Although what he searched for in the Old Testament was above all symbolism reflecting the New Testament, yet here was a break with pre-conceived notions in the most hazardous field of all. In any case it was the orthodox—Professor Hoornbeek, a pupil of Voetius', and Bondius, who a little later was chosen by the Princess Dowager to teach William III—who were soon to appeal to the States' resolution when they opposed the conferring of the doctor's degree on a pupil of Heidanus', whose theses were clearly Cartesian. Coccejus, who was 'Rector' of the University that year, allowed himself to be intimidated by the critics, and the candidate had to offer other theses, but apart from the fact that these were not free from objection either, it seemed scandalous to the orthodox that a man of Cartesian leanings should receive the Leyden title of Doctor of Divinity at all. Words ran high in the Senate meeting, where Bondius, with the resolution of the States in his hand, *magnis et immodestis clamoribus* cried out that he would travel to The Hague the next day, and *contumeliose cum insana vociferatione* threw at his colleague Colius the words: 'you miserable time-server!'[1] The States gave no other answer to the lengthy memoirs with which the two parties bombarded them than that the resolution of 1656 was to be observed; which did not mean anything. Indeed, when the consistory joined in the conflict and decided that in future it would insert in the certificates of theological graduates a note about their views regarding Cartesianism according to the resolution of 1656, the Senate (without the concurrence of Hoornbeek and Bondius presumably) drew the attention of the States to so

---

[1] The minutes of the Senate meetings were kept in Latin, but these last words were noted down in Dutch.

intolerable an encroachment upon their authority, and the States ordered the consistory to refrain from such an innovation until they, the States, should have found time to go into the problems involved. And there the matter rested. That is to say with the Cartesians really, in spite of the resolution, in possession of the field.

These incidents happened in 1660. Feeling rose very high. And it is not solely on account of what happened at Leyden that this year can be regarded as a turning-point in the relations between the Republican States' Party and the Reformed Church.

Voetius had in 1660 already passed his seventieth year, but his unbending personality still formed the real centre of the Republic's ecclesiastical life. In all the long-drawn-out controversies and sudden storms he or his influence are in evidence. The man's activity was amazing. In the course of the years his series of heavy Latin tomes with theological expositions and disputations kept growing, and at the same time tracts and disputations in Dutch flowed from his pen. He was not only *primarius theologiae professor* in his university, but also honorary minister of the Word in the city of Utrecht and in fact the heart and soul of the consistory. Several of his younger colleagues had once been his pupils. It was he who usually composed the memoirs to the magistracy and the States, or the public treatises required in the numerous disputes carried on sometimes by the Utrecht church, sometimes by the theological faculty of the Utrecht university.

Utrecht had become a stronghold of that new trend strongly marked by English influence—of which Amesius and Willem Teellinck had been pioneers—which without abandoning the dogmatism of Dort, admitted the insufficiency of 'holiness through doctrine' and stressed the importance of a saintly *life*. In 1653 a man thirty years younger was called to Utrecht, who, always working in perfect harmony with Voetius, represented the pietistic spirit in a way of his own and, one might say, more purely. This was Jodocus Lodenstein. Sprung from a Delft regent family (which was unusual for a minister, almost all of them being of lowly birth), this remarkable man combined in himself the characters of the mystic and of the prophet. As a writer of songs, in which he glorified 'blessèd solitude' and (like Hugo and à Bolswert) the love between Jesus and the soul, he belongs to Dutch poetry. At the same time his gloomy awareness of the profound chasm separating not only profane society but his own church itself from his exalted ideal left him no peace: tearing himself away from his meditations and his transports he worked for improvement, admonishing and rebuking, both in writing and by word of mouth. His detestation of sin made him severe, but he was equally so to himself, always serious, living an ascetic, celibate life.

Had he been one of us (*a Catholic is said to have declared after his death*), we would consider him a saint.

And at his funeral an admirer exclaimed:

Not only did his voice thunder, but his holy conduct of life was like a lightning shaft.

Such a figure could not but arouse at the same time much ridicule and aversion. That grim invective against small human weaknesses was denounced as 'loveless'. And the unbending application of ecclesiastical discipline as practised at Utrecht (and imitated by consistories in other towns of the province) met with resistance. Lodenstein might argue that ecclesiastical penalties (admonition, exclusion from Holy Communion) were not meant to entail any social or political consequences; that, for instance, if they were applied to a man in public authority, it would be no less incumbent on the faithful than before to show him respect and obedience in his office; yet in practice such distinctions were not possible. And not only that, but was the ministers' judgment in every case reliable? Lodenstein himself was once attacked in public on account of what was, indeed, a most objectionable case of 'intimidation by threatening with God's judgment'.

In 1658 there had been a sudden upsurge of animosity against the whole Voetian system, when Heidanus and Coccejus got involved in a debate with their old colleague at Utrecht, backed by Hoornbeek, about the Utrecht punctiliousness (really British, as was suggested by Heidanus and the anonymous pamphleteers who joined in the fray) with respect to Sabbath observance.

Let a Cromwell, a Pharisee, sabbatise (*thus one reads in the 'Den Schotsen Duyvel'—'The Scottish Devil'*); no good Christian can bind himself strictly to keep the Sabbath. (*'Strictly', it should be remembered, meant:*) no cooking no laying of the table, no making of beds, no honest gaiety, no going out for a walk . . .

Only the deeper background of theological and philosophic difference explains the violence of the conflict between Leyden and Utrecht, to which the States of Holland, always on their guard against ecclesiastical disputes, put an end by admonishing their professors to hold their peace, but which as we already know was immediately followed by mutual dissension at Leyden. Not only did the Leyden Voetians suffer defeat in that conflict, but at about the same time Voetius himself lost the support of his own Utrecht authorities.

Less than any other party could the Voetians do without the support of the authorities. Just as in Holland, so in Utrecht, they continually petitioned the provincial States to enforce the system: Sunday observance, prohibition of one thing and another, suppression of heterodox opinions. Just as in Holland, relations between the consistory and the town authorities had for a considerable period been fairly good, although inevitably there yawned a gulf between the practice of the worldlings and the ideal of the ecclesiastics. But one problem now obtruded itself which led to a complete breach.

In Utrecht there existed a flagrant class abuse—in a less glaring form not unknown in other provinces—with regard to the estates of the old church. In Holland such estates had been nationalised for public purposes, but in Utrecht their revenues, or a large part of them, served to endow certain members of the ruling oligarchy—nobility from the countryside, and citizen regents from the town corporations. A chosen few of the men so benefited, the *Geëligeerden* (Elected), then paraded under the old ecclesiastical titles of canon or provost in the provincial States, where they formed one 'member' beside that of the Nobility and that of the Towns. Men who rendered services to the State—that had originally been the justification. It is true that contributions were levied from these Protestant prebendaries out of which the salaries of the ministers were paid, but for anyone having so high a notion of the Church's mission as had Voetius and his friends, who moreover considered worldly fear of the authorities beneath them, these abuses were in the long run unendurable. The case was indeed worse than that of the 's Hertogenbosch Brotherhood referred to in the previous volume.[1] Asked for advice by the Town Council, eight out of the twelve ministers of religion, led by Voetius, expressed their undisguised disapproval in a memorandum which, after having occasioned a great deal of whispering, was ultimately printed. Several ministers began stirring up the flock's feelings against the practice from the pulpit. In 1659 a member of the Town Council proved so troubled in his conscience that he refused a prebend when his turn came. No other member wished to accept after that, so that the prebend had to be sold; nevertheless the Council was not to be moved to pass a resolution such as the majority of the consistory desired them to do: that the property should be used for the purpose for which it had originally been intended, the promotion of religion.

All this gave rise to very violent disputes. The reverend Van de Velde said in a sermon (which was published!):

Is there any difference between a Committee of Church Robbers and the Committee of Prebendaries (meaning: of the 'Elected')? Or does the Reformed religion turn thieving into something other than it is? Or are we to condone sacrilege and church robbery? Shame on those who would dare say so, nay think so!

Professor Nethenus, having got involved in a controversy with the Groningen Professor Maresius, 'defamed' before all the world (as the States of Groningen complained) *their* forefathers, too, as church robbers. But the defenders of the existing system found no difficulty in charging the attackers with ulterior motives. A few years previously someone had published a project, pretending that it came from the pen of Voetius and his friends, according to which the ministers were to appropriate the whole of the spiritual power that had once belonged to the sovereign Bishop of Utrecht. 'The Pope of Utrecht' became the current nickname for Voetius. His system was looked upon as designed to subject the temporal power to the spiritual, with the abuse of ecclesiastical discipline as its tool. At the same time the commonalty was beginning to get excited about the prebends, and while the Utrecht town government, after the example of the Amsterdam council thirty years before, decided to have the consistory meetings attended by 'political commissaries', the States of the province prepared themselves to take yet more vigorous action to maintain their prerogatives. After

[1] See Part One, pp. 192–3.

having borrowed troops from Holland (those States were more than willing to lend them), and in co-operation with the town authorities, they ordered two ministers, Van de Velde and Johannes Teellinck, to leave the town and province within twenty-four hours.

The consistory now meekly abandoned its resistance to the introduction of 'political commissaries', a measure which, indeed, the decrees of the Synod of Dort clearly acknowledged the town authorities to be entitled to pass. The consistory now also had to accept regulations by which the Dort decrees were made binding upon it in the matter of relations with the secular power as well as of doctrine, and by which in particular it was ordered to refrain from criticising the town government and the disposal of chapter property.

It seemed as if the days of Oldenbarnevelt had returned. Once again the orthodox ministers beheld the States of Holland and Utrecht united against them.[1] De Witt had become caught in an antagonism which was certainly not of his own seeking, but for him and his equals the zealots were 'mutineers', lunatics—he honestly believed himself to be acting under a compelling obligation to protect law and society. The ministers on their side regarded themselves as the martyrs of a godless abuse of power. Their submission was only apparent, but that very fact inspired Lodenstein to bitter reproaches:

If there were but faith in the hearts of the leaders of our Church, they would realise that our mighty King Jesus by no more than the raising of his finger would be able to destroy all those petty lords and rulers like so many ants, and they would not then fear to uphold the rights of the Church.

In their bitterness the ministers now turned to Orange in earnest. A pamphlet writer later said of Voetius:

I have heard it said that Voetius, the father of you all, in the time of Cromwell was not much of a Prince-man.

Puritanism, as long as it reigned supreme in England, had indeed had an influence on the Utrecht movement, and there had undeniably been contacts. But with the events now under review there happened to coincide the restoration of Charles II, by which the position of the Orange party was so much affected in other ways. We have seen how the States' government was

[1] See Part One, p. 61.

H

nevertheless able to draw strength from the political circumstances. The writings of De la Court and De Mist, which I mentioned before,[1] encouraged the supporters of the régime in power, but at the same time embittered the opponents, particularly the church people. De Witt had not shown much inclination to help De la Court, who after all had been in close correspondence with him, in the difficulties with the Leyden consistory in which the latter's *Interest* had landed him. But the régime did dare to erect a partition between the Church and Orange in the form of a resolution, the form in which from its very nature it put so much trust. In 1663 the States of Holland prescribed a specific formula for the prayer to be used in all church services in their province, and in it they themselves as sovereign were mentioned first, the States-General as being the assembly of representatives of the 'allies' second, and the Prince of Orange not at all. This was the logical sequel of the system instituted twelve years previously, yet the States of several of the provinces protested against the slight to the States-General implied, and a number of pamphlets appeared in which the omission of Orange was bitterly censured. The Holland Synods, restrained by the 'political commissaries', did not even discuss the matter.

In their hearts the orthodox had not of course given up any of their claims. Lodenstein had to be reprimanded more than once for his sermons. The fight against the fundamental tenets of Cocceius' theology was only now opened in real earnest by Voetius, with a disputation in 1665. Cocceianism and Cartesianism were damned in one breath, and faction, after smouldering for so long, now set the church ablaze anew. But even at his own university—'Academia Voetiana' an adversary had once written sarcastically—the enemy had been introduced by the authorities now roused against him.

As successor to Nethenus, who had been removed from his chair on account of his having insulted Maresius and the States of Groningen, the Town Council in 1662 appointed Franciscus Burman, son-in-law of Heidanus and as positive a Cartesian. In 1666 another heated dispute arose, over a student of Burman's this time, who, because he had defended an unmistakably Cocceian thesis when standing for his degree, could not obtain

[1] See above, p. 57.

the consistory's testimony needed for admission to the ministry until he had expressed regret. But even if Voetius still dominated the consistory (and there too the Town Council had succeeded in getting Burman in), in the Academic Senate the majority now sided with Burman as a result of a whole series of anti-orthodox appointments (of the classical scholar Graevius, of Wolzogen, minister to the Walloon congregation, and others). So, just as had happened at Leyden, the university protested to the authorities against the consistory's presumption in nullifying the efficacy of the academic degree, whereupon the Town Council ordered all reference to the incident to be struck out of the consistory's minute-book by a sheriff's officer.

A lengthy pen-and-ink war, in the shape of memoranda to the Town Council, was conducted by the consistory, from 1669 on, with the alderman Van Velthuysen, one of the political commissaries it had to suffer in its midst. Originally trained for the ministry, Velthuysen had later become a physician. He was of one mind with Burman and the others, 'the Committee of Savants', as people said. While Wolzogen and Graevius had given offence by describing as superstition the belief in an ominous significance of comets, Velthuysen went so far as to argue in a *Tractaet van afgoderye en superstitie* (*Tract on idolatry and superstition*) that all ecclesiastical rule or punishment should be done away with, that a binding confession of faith was a papist institution, and that the suppression of Catholic worship could be defended on political grounds only. He declared that as regards the latter he

had always perceived a general feeling of dissatisfaction among sensible people at their having never succeeded in finding an expedient by which the public exercise of the Roman Catholic religion might be combined with the order and security of our state.

Such a statement (however Platonic it may have been) again reminds us that side by side with characteristically oligarchic self-righteousness and self-interest there still persisted in the mentality of the States authorities a more liberal conviction of being called to safeguard the welfare of *all* the different groups in the population. De la Court, too, pleads emphatically for as much religious freedom as possible, even if only on purely materialistic grounds. Not only the Catholics, but the Protestant Dissenters also, and even many members of the State Church who had no great liking for consistorial discipline, looked to the regents for protection. No regent could put the authority of the State higher than did the lonely Jew, Spinoza, in whose *Tractatus theologico-politicus*, which appeared in 1670, we read:

It is beyond all doubt that religious worship in our day rests solely on the competence of the high authorities and that no one, unless with their authority and their approval, is entitled or has the capacity to regulate religion, to select its servants, to determine the basic principles and doctrine of the Church, to pronounce on morals and acts of piety, to excommunicate a person or to admit him to the church, or finally to care for the poor. . . . Whoever wishes to deprive the authorities of this power is trying to push his way to supreme power.

It would be very wrong to think (which is nevertheless a view often presented by historians) that the oligarchy was bound together by nothing but interest and that it stood isolated from the 'people' led by the ministers. If that had been so, it would be inexplicable how the Stadholderless régime managed to maintain itself for over twenty years, while indeed even after the Orangist Restoration, as we shall presently see, the oligarchy was in essentials left as it had been.

And yet, when it came to a crisis, the States could not expect much support from the groups outside the State Church. The Catholics, after all, were under their rule still treated in a way that could hardly inspire them with any enthusiasm for 'the gentlemen'. As for the Protestant sects, they were too much divided among themselves, the Baptists too unworldly, the Collegiants too individualistic and undisciplined, for their political influence to be on a par with their cultural contribution. Spinoza's book, which I mentioned above and which set out a theory concerning the relationship between Church and State that was so agreeable to the Holland authorities, they felt nevertheless obliged to ban on account of its theological implications. For the first time here was presented a rational and historical examination of Scripture, which left Cocceius' exegesis, both so timid and at the same time so bizarre, far behind. Indeed, this approach to Scripture was at variance with all the prevailing ideas accepted even by the States.

Thus the only well organised and politically conscious group was that of the Reformed. And their numbers were still on the increase, recruits flowing in from the masses which, cut adrift from their Catholic anchorage, had been for generations floating about rudderless. At Utrecht, for instance, Voetius during the period of his activity, between about 1640 and 1670, beheld the number of ministers increase from five to twelve. Torn by dissensions as the Reformed Church may have been, and burdened with many lukewarm members, and even though the regents themselves belonged to it and protected it that it might grow, yet at moments of crisis its power could be mobilised only by its ministers. Now these, feeling wronged and tyrannised over by the States of Holland and of Utrecht, since 1660 especially, saw at the same time the young Prince growing up apace and gaining in power (or so at least it seemed) on account of the Restoration of his uncle in England. The relationship of the first William to the religious problems of his day had been forgotten; Frederick Henry's Arminianism and his and William II's relations with the so definitely anti-Presbyterian Stuarts no less so; the Orange tradition as revered and propagated by the ministers was that of Maurice. By selecting Domine Trigland and after him Domine Bondius for the education of the young Prince, the Court showed how well it understood the importance of that connection. In the hour of crisis the States' government was to see zealous Reformed Church members rise up against it everywhere.

The safeguards De Witt and his supporters put up against this safeguarded nothing but their own circle, and that is as much as to say that they were of any avail only as long as they themselves were in power. For that reason those endless discussions and negotiations about how far exactly it would be possible to go in favour of the Prince, the mutual concessions, compromises, and expedients, in fact the whole attempt at trying to pin down the future on paper and with oath upon oath, show De Witt at his weakest as a statesman.

In the Union

THE worst of it was that during these years the system of loose confederation, too, the system of multiple authority which had carried the day at the Great Assembly and which Holland had proclaimed so triumphantly in the prayer formulary, began to reveal its weaknesses. The inherent dangers were to a certain extent met by Holland's ascendancy in the Union and by the Grand Pensionary's personal prestige. But his power was beginning to irk many of his own Hollanders. The towns became restless under a statesman who demanded subjection to the greater unit of the province. Amsterdam was beginning to sulk under the presumption of an all-powerful minister. De Graeff van Zuid-Polsbroek, the uncle of De Witt's wife, had died in 1664. It was now Gillis Valckenier, whom we have already come across, who rose head and shoulders above the other Burgomasters. Originally an even more vehement anti-Orangist than De Witt himself, he later caused him difficulties by thwarting his policy of exclusion of the Prince who was then growing from boyhood to adolescence. Through his arrogance and insolence Valckenier made himself hated in his own town, and it was a success for De Witt when in 1671 he was thrown out of power and politely banished to The Hague to become a member of the Standing Committee of the States of Holland. But apart from such weaknesses at the centre of the ruling group, it was gradually becoming clear that the ascendency of even an undivided Holland did not suffice to produce a truly coherent and positive Union policy. With respect to foreign affairs this could be managed, although in fits and starts, but where it proved particularly impracticable was in questions relating to the army.

There the Dutch people, who had brought forth naval heroes by the dozen and who in the Indies had not needed foreigners to lead their military operations on land either, showed a curious helplessness. It seems as if the aristocratic tradition, to which the armies throughout Europe were subject, kept men's minds paralysed. The numerous landed gentry of the Eastern provinces did supply officers to all the Dutch regiments. But for the leading posts men of higher birth were sought, men of near princely position and connections, such as were not really to be found in the Republic outside the House of Orange. De Witt, who when necessary had dared take the affairs of the fleet into his own hands, could only think of German mercenary troops and foreign commanders for the small-scale Münster war. Old John Maurice had had another German and a Scot under him. When after the war it was attempted to restore the deteriorated condition of the army, there was talk first of inviting Turenne to come over; behind this there was the political intention to have the young Prince of Orange orientated towards France by the guidance of his famous cousin. Finally (early in 1668) another German, Wirtz by name, had been appointed by the side of John Maurice as second Field Marshal; not a man of high birth it is true, but who had made a great name for himself in Sweden.

De Witt remained conscious of the need to have something done about the army; Wirtz, moreover, showed himself diligent and capable. Yet it cannot be said that the lesson of the Münster war had really been taken to heart. The attention of Holland, whence all the motive power had to come, was bound to be confined mainly to the fleet. The provincialist disintegration of the army, which had become worse in consequence of the arrangements of 1650, continued to be an obstacle. It was precisely for the army and the fortified towns—the most important of which were situated in the territory of needy provinces like Overijsel and Gelderland—that the immediate co-operation of all the provinces in the payment of their quotas was necessary. Now here local interests were deeply involved in connection with appointments of officers and garrison affairs. The States-General were certainly not alto-gether lacking in Union sentiment nor in Union prestige; nevertheless in the face of provincial particularism they, who were in a way also the sum of provincial particularisms, generally found it difficult to assert their power. In the smaller provinces, where the educative influence of The Hague was not felt so immediately as it was in Holland and where the whole of political life was confined within more restricted dimensions, particularist self-interest and narrow-mindedness expressed themselves with the least restraint.

With what blind zeal, for instance, did not the oligarchy in Friesland, which had now managed to get all power into its own hands, devote itself to the consolidation of its position and the distribution among its members of remunerative provincial and Generality offices! The democratic institution of the franchise for freeholders had been entirely overgrown by corruption and intrigue, and in the thirty 'grietenyen' (districts) and in the States assembly itself the noble 'grietmen' (heads of districts) maintained their rule with the help of bought-up 'hornlegers'[1] and dependent assessors.

[1] See Part One, p. 79.

All these unlawful oligarchic practices (*as the eminent jurist Ulric Huber, Professor at Franeker, wrote some time later in his 'Spiegel van doleantie en reformatie'*—'*Mirror of Grievances and Reform*'), which place the common government in the hands and reserve it to the enjoyment of a few, as if it were their paternal inheritance and patrimony, must inevitably give rise to pride, covetousness and intolerance. The Almanachs (*as the rosters were called in accordance with which the 'ambulatory offices' circulated among the gentlemen*) do, it is true, obviate disturbances, but nevertheless they are in fact the very means to stifle the original right of the inhabitants and to turn the government into a hereditary tenure.

The Stadholderly power of the Nassau family had never been of much consequence in Friesland; at this moment moreover it was paralysed by its being held by a minor: so these tendencies could not be counterbalanced by any strong court influence. The public, nevertheless, expected everything from that quarter, and in the meanwhile the authorities were mistrusted even more than they were in Holland: when the hour of crisis came this was to prove no small hindrance to an effective defence.

Bad also was the feud which kept divided, from 1668 on, the Knighthood and the Towns of Overijsel—Zwolle and Van Haersolte against Kampen and Deventer and Van Raesvelt—so much so in fact that at one time two self-styled States Assemblies sent representatives to The Hague. Vehement feelings and confusion in the finances of the province were the result. Not until 1671, when the threat of war brought the importance of Overijsel as a frontier province into evidence, was a committee from the States-General able to settle the conflict—but when the crisis came, Overijsel was to put up as bad a show as Friesland.

In Utrecht things were little better.

Here, so I am told by Mr. Van Sandenburgh and Mr. Van Zuylen, nought is being done for the common affairs of our dear fatherland. I shall be glad when all this jobbery will be over; I hope things will then improve. (*Thus on 22 December 1671, when the international situation already wore a threatening look, wrote the lady of Amerongen to her husband, G. A. van Reede, who was abroad on a diplomatic mission, and to whom she had previously sent extensive reports concerning the fights for office among the Utrecht noblemen and city gentlemen.*)

And then finally there was Brabant[1]. The régime established there had been unable to convert the population to Protestantism and thus had been all the less able to inspire the Brabanters with

---

[1] That is to say North Brabant, a Generality Land.

feelings of loyalty towards the States-General. The principle accepted in 1648 and confirmed in 1650,[1] only led to attempts which every time came up against the stubborn facts. Again and again in the following years, measures, fundamentally always the same, were proclaimed and tried unsuccessfully. The School Regulations of 1655, which admitted only such school teachers as were approved by The Hague, did not prevent the prohibited Catholic school system from surviving. In spite of the Administrative Regulations of 1660, which were at long last to put the 'political reformation' on a firm footing, Protestant 'quarter sheriffs' continued to make shift with Catholic Aldermen—with 'extreme Papists' even, as the ministers complained. The state was not, for all that, so impotent but that a ruling class of Protestant intruders was being formed in the Generality lands, the population (which proved impervious to the attempts at Protestantisation) harassed, and the natural structure of its society distorted. When the possibility of an invasion appeared on the political horizon, several Protestant officials became seriously alarmed. Actually, the Catholic clergy, although they could not feel much sympathy for The Hague, still took their cue from Spain rather than from France, and Spain was now on the same side as their persecutors.

E. THE REPUBLIC STANDS THE SHOCK

I. GELDERLAND, UTRECHT, AND OVERIJSEL LOST

EVEN though his system might be showing cracks, De Witt faced, undaunted, the danger threatening from abroad. Not only had there been an exchange of opinions with the Emperor; even the need of an alliance with Spain he could no longer disregard: no less a personage than Van Beverning had been sent to Madrid in 1671. What mattered most to the Grand Pensionary, however, were the preparations for a 'spirited defence'. When the English made a surprise attack on a Dutch return fleet in March, and the two Kings sent their declarations of war in April, he was ready, with the same unyielding courage

[1] See Part One, p. 155, and above, p. 23.

as in the dark days of 1653 and 1665, to urge the States to pay up their 'consents', to get the fleet at Texel ready to sail, and to provide the army at the frontier with all that was necessary. Unfortunately a great deal was left to be desired with regard to the latter. Through the negligence of Friesland and Zealand, Gelderland and Overijsel, the Union Exchequer found itself acutely short of funds. The fleet, too, was held up by the dila-toriness of the Zealand Admiralty until it was too late to prevent the French and English fleets from uniting.

De Ruyter and Cornelis De Witt, who again accompanied the fleet as deputy of the States-General, did not allow themselves to be intimidated by the numerical superiority of the combined French and English men-of-war, and off Solebay (immediately to the south of Lowestoft) launched an attack on 7 June. De Ruyter's masterly handling of the situation compelled the enemy to give way—the English fleet particularly was heavily damaged—and although he himself had to fall back as well, the danger of a landing had for the time being been averted.

How differently did things go on land! In May the mighty French army advanced through the territory of Liège. Louis led it in person, his two great commanders, Condé and Turenne, assisting him, and he was accompanied by his chief ministers. Maastricht was encircled and left in the rear, the army marching through Cologne territory to the Rhine, from where the route led through Cleves country. Here the States' outposts—Orsoy, Rheinberg, Burik, Wesel, Rees, and Emmerich—should have been able to stave off the invasion for a time, but they hardly succeeded even in slowing down the advance of the French, who took Doetinchem on 9 June, and on the 12th forced the Rhine under the eye of the King himself near the toll-house at Lobith, whench they rapidly deployed through the Betuwe.

The States' army was posted behind the river IJsel. In spite of the new reinforcements—mostly German mercenary troops, while from Holland *waardgelders* (troops in the pay of town governments) and conscripted farmers were also sent—it was much too weak to occupy so long a line: much more than half of the army was shut up in garrison towns and the field army amounted to no more than 15,000 men. The morale was ex-tremely low, the untoward news from the country round Cologne and Cleves having a paralysing effect. Amid all the confusion and the reverses, however, headquarters retained their composure. The young Captain-General did not lose his head, and it proved extremely useful that he was able to co-operate harmoniously with the chief deputy of the States-General—who himself kept in constant touch with De Witt—none other than Van Beverning, the man who eighteen years previously had arranged with Cromwell for William's exclusion. After the French had forced the Rhine, nothing remained but to fall back on Utrecht with all imaginable speed in order not to be taken in the rear. The weakness of the federation was revealed in the exertions of the Field Deputies to secure, each for his own province, the regiments in the pay of that province. It was clear that Holland and Zealand formed the natural strategic base for the whole Union, but for the occupation of Nijmegen, Arnhem, and the IJsel towns, all really admitted to be indefensible, particularly if attacked on the Western side, 13,000 men were left behind, while only 9,000 fell back. Near Utrecht there arose a heated and confused dispute as to whether an attempt should be made to save the town, but on the 18th it was abandoned, and the army retreated to Holland. Meanwhile hard work was already being done to put into effect the inundations that were to constitute the Water Line protecting the province of Holland—the farmers had to be forcibly restrained from preventing this; in fact there were also towns which caused trouble, Gouda in particular. If the French had advanced straight upon their goal, the disaster would have been complete, but they suffered just as much as did the other party from the delusion of the importance of fortified towns, and however disgracefully quickly Arnhem, Doesburg, Nijmegen, and Zutphen may have surrendered, the enemy was delayed sufficiently for Holland to be put in a state of defence. On 3 July Louis made his entry into Utrecht. By that time a wide strip of water running from the Zuyder Zee to the river Lek already stretched between him and the demoralised Dutch army. The bulk of the troops was stationed where the inundated strip was perilously narrow, north and south of Bodegraven.

The Bishop of Münster meanwhile (this time accompanied by the Archbishop of Cologne) had attacked Overijsel anew. Grol only delayed them for a few days. Soon after, the three big

towns of the province, Deventer, Zwolle, and Kampen, capitu-
tated in ways which each time caused military commanders and
town authorities to throw charges of cowardice or even treachery
at each other. In these capitulations, before peace had been
concluded or the States-General even consulted, the sovereignty
of the Holy Roman Empire was recognised. The Nobility of
Overijsel surrendered to Münster at the beginning of July by a
document in which the dissolution of the Union was accepted
as an established fact.

In connection with the first Münster War I pointed[1] to signs
that the boundary-line traced by political developments—the
growth of the Burgundian State, the stability of the North
Netherlands Republic—right through the Saxon area was still
somewhat indeterminate. The leading classes of the Saxon
population in the Gelderland 'Achterhoek' (the part of the
province behind the IJsel), Overijsel, and Groningen had
undoubtedly to a large extent adapted themselves to the
Frankish West under the influence of the political life of the
Union. The Eastern form of the Dutch language, which we saw
was still used in the sixteenth century in political correspondence[1]—and two generations later even by a Geldersman[2] like
Van den Bergh, who had remained under the authority of
Brussels—had in the meetings of the States and the Town
Councils of the Eastern provinces of the Union given way to the
Dutch of The Hague. But the nobility still had many connections with their fellow Saxons on the German side of the
frontier, and then there were always the Catholics, who in the
crisis at once rose out of their quiescent obscurity. Wherever the
French, as well as where the men of Cologne or Münster, took
control, churches again had to be placed at the disposal of the
Catholics. Would not, under the shock of events, all the
floating elements on the other side of the IJsel be drawn east
instead of, as had been the case so far, westward, and would not
a development of a century and a half be wiped out?

Later in the summer, however, the episcopal army, advancing further north, was checked before the town of Groningen.
The Groningers did not listen to Schulemborg, who was again
present. They offered stout resistance, led by the old warrior,

---

[1] See *The Revolt of the Netherlands*, p. 159.
[2] See Part One, p. 98.

Rabenhaupt, a German, who had learnt the art of war under Frederick Henry; inundations to the east and west prevented their being encircled. Friesland lay fairly safe behind its lakes and peat-bogs, just as in the time of Parma,[1] although, understandably enough, panic reigned in the province. Meanwhile the delay before Groningen revealed the weakness of the Bishop, of 'Bommenberend' (Bernard of the Bombs), as the Groningers called their besieger; the discontent among his own subjects did not fit him very well for the role of conqueror.

Nevertheless, the future of the eastern periphery of the North Netherlands territory was actually decided, as always, in the strategic, economic, and political centre, namely in Holland.

There, just as in Friesland, the population had been thrown into wild panic when in the second half of June the reports came in of the surrender of the fortresses in the Cologne and Cleves areas and in Gelderland and Overijsel. What was really the revelation of the weakness in the Union system was at once in the general excitement taken for evidence of the government's treachery. The most preposterous suspicions were voiced against the man who had tried to make that system work, De Witt. Under the double threat from without and from below many regents lost their heads, and no longer saw any way out except through peace, or rather surrender. On 15 June the States-General decided to send to England and to Louis' army camp envoys with humble requests to be allowed to know the conditions for peace. De Witt had no faith in these attempts. He was already preparing to hold on in Holland, if necessary by falling back, with States assemblies and government boards, upon Amsterdam and from there

to dispute every inch of the land with the enemy to the last man with a Batavian constancy; if matters should prove untenable outside (*that is, if the other provinces should be overrun*), even then every effort should be made to save ourselves; the only way of re-establishing the allies (*the other provinces*) in so sorrowful an event would be through the preservation of Holland and through the strength which it might still be possible for Holland later on to contribute towards their rescue.

But on 21 June De Witt was assaulted by four pro-Orangist young men and seriously wounded (the son of the Councillor Van der Graeff, who was executed on account of the crime, was regarded as a martyr by the misguided public, just as Buat had

[1] See *The Revolt of the Netherlands*, p. 201.

been). When one of the States' envoys came home from the
French headquarters—it was Pieter de Groot—to report in the
States of Holland on 25 June, the Grand Pensionary was not
there to stem the stream of cowardice. De Groot assured his
anxious audience that peace could be obtained by sacrificing
Maastricht and the Generality Lands. Led by the Nobility one
town after another advised that the Province's delegates should
be instructed to move in the States-General for acceptance of
that policy.

We know not what to do about our defence.—We are on the point of falling
into the utmost confusion.—The posts (*at the narrow parts of the Water Line*
—'*the passes*') are impossible to defend.—The matter can suffer no delay.

Thus wailed Haarlem, Delft, Schiedam, and Edam; Leyden
and Gouda even, situated as they were behind the 'passes' in
the inundated area, and for that reason immediately threatened,
wished to grant De Groot *unlimited* authority. But Amsterdam,
a prominent member, the most powerful of all, flanked by
Alkmaar, raised its voice against this pusillanimous policy of
fear which wanted to relinquish without a blow the position
built up by generations. For the time being the deputies of the
town insisted that Holland should not propose anything in the
Generality unless by a unanimous vote in the provincial assembly, and demanded time to go and obtain orders from their
principals. When the Amsterdammers and a few other North-
Hollanders had not returned by the evening of the 26th, the
rest no longer let the objection that the assembly was incomplete
stand in their way, and that same night the proposal was—in the
name of the States of Holland therefore—carried to the States-
General on the other side of the Binnenhof. Here Groningen,
which was proving by its actions that it was in favour of
resistance, was not present; Friesland and Zealand protested;
as for the Utrechters and Geldersmen and Overijselers, who
supported the Holland proposal, were they entitled to vote at
all now that their provinces were in the hands of the enemy? The
Greffier of the Assembly, Fagel, refused to sign the resolution,
but in spite of all these irregularities Pieter de Groot, urged and
beseeched by the pensionaries of Leyden and Gouda, set out on
his mission. The French King and his ministers, however, were
not content with the offers he was entitled to make: in addition
to the Generality Lands they wished to have part of Gelderland

as well; and also liberty of public worship for the Dutch Catholics. But 'Union' (that is to say, the seven provinces to remain intact), 'government' (that is to say, no Stadholder or sovereign to be forced upon the country), 'religion' (that is to say, no change in the monopolist position of the Reformed Church) were the restrictions which even the panic party had put on De Groot's plenary power. He had to return therefore to fetch fresh instructions, and how changed did he find the situation!

The Amsterdammers had come back on the 27th, strengthened with their principals' order to stand fast, and they had vehemently protested, supported this time by various towns in North Holland, against the resolution adopted in their absence.

Mr. Pensionary Hop (*thus did his deeply offended Leyden colleague report home from the Hague*) yesterday and to-day (*28 and 29 June*) used very vehement language, making imputations against members of the assembly as if they had been sellers of the common sovereignty and liberty, concluding that *they* (*the Amsterdammers*) would not allow themselves to be delivered up by the other members nor yet ever have to do with so base a negotiation. That *they* would be able to justify themselves before the citizenry, but that those have cause to fear who, without patent necessity and before having received one canon-shot, are so prodigal in handing over the liberty of their subjects.

The citizenry! That word was heard repeatedly in the assembly of the gentlemen during those hectic days. One deputy from Alkmaar had said, bluntly:

That *they* (*the regents of Alkmaar*) would rather be killed by the enemy than by the citizens.

2. THE FALL OF THE STATES' RÉGIME

In one month you spill the forefathers' glory
Bought in the course of a hundred years at the price of much blood. . . .

THUS the Hague minister, Domine Vollenhove, addressed the 'degenerate Batavians' in a sonnet. The commonalty did not want to surrender to France, but how could they contribute constructively to a bolder policy? The wild rumours they assisted in circulating, their attacks on the barges in which the rich tried to carry their property to the comparative security of Amsterdam, were increasing the general confusion. There was only the Orangist restoration that could be clamoured for, and through their wretched faint-heartedness the majority of the States of Holland did indeed draw that event down upon themselves. The discussions about Pieter de Groot's mission could not of course remain secret. They almost seemed to confirm the accusations of treachery launched against the regent régime. The States' government was badly discredited, although in fact defeatists were to be found among the Orangist as among the Loevestein regents: the Pensionary of Leyden, for instance, belonged to the first-named party. And the greatest Loevesteiner of them all, De Witt, as we have seen, had never wavered in his determination to stand fast. He and his supporters imputed the chaos, and with a relative amount of justice, to the 'disobedience', to the panic mingled with party spirit, prevailing among the citizens. Nevertheless, whichever way one looked at it, there was but one alternative: Orange.

In Zealand, at the end of June, a popular movement started to which the States of that province gave in at once. It spread to Holland without delay, and in one town after another the dismayed authorities, in order to pacify their citizens, promised that their deputies in the States of Holland would receive instructions to appoint the Prince of Orange as Stadholder. The oaths taken on the Perpetual Edict counted for nothing any more. On 4 July, the Prince became Stadholder of Holland; on 2 July, he had already been appointed Stadholder of Zealand; and on 8 July, the States-General appointed him to the Captain- and Admiral-Generalship with all the old powers attached. The next day the young man came from army headquarters to The Hague in order to be invested in the various governing bodies.

De Groot had brought out his report in the Holland Assembly on 1 July, right in the middle of the turmoil caused by the revolution. But the word revolution may carry a wrong suggestion. It should be remembered that the Prince was raised by the various States assemblies, with all due formality, to offices which in no way detracted from their sovereign authority. It was still the States of Holland—for another two months with the same personnel even—who had to decide about any proposal to be made to the States-General, and the new Stadholder came in only in so far as he was requested to give his advice in the matter. That advice carried a great deal of weight it is true, especially because, in case it was disregarded and matters were to go wrong, an outburst of fury on the part of the citizenry might be expected.

Turmoil at any rate was the order of the day. Holland was full of refugees: Utrecht notables for instance, tormented by uncertainty as to whether they had been wise to fly; because suppose the French were there to stay, would not their property in that case be lost to them for ever? Even a nobleman like Van Ginkel, whose father, the Baron Van Reede van Amerongen, was at that moment serving his country with devotion on a mission to the Elector of Brandenburg (although, since the eagerly looked for mercenaries from that quarter did not turn up, the public were already vociferously charging him with having appropriated the money)—Van Ginkel, himself colonel of a Utrecht regiment, with which he had retreated behind the Water Line, was wondering whether he could still go on serving without the risk of his estates being confiscated now that the States of Utrecht, his sovereign and paymaster, had capitulated. Such considerations, and he was not the only one to revolve them in his mind, go to show how the very existence of the Union was at stake.

And yet, entirely apart from the change in the régime, circumstances were no longer the same as when De Groot had been sent out so hurriedly the week before. The Water Line held. It was possible to breathe again. It was possible to reflect, not only how much the commonalty abominated the policy that had been followed, but also how much the single ally, Spain, had been made 'unhappy' by the offer of the Generality lands to France. That the conquest of the Spanish Netherlands would have followed as a matter of course must indeed be plain to every observer, and the new, energetic Governor, the Count de Monterey, sent auxiliary troops without delay, which in part were used behind the Water Line, but more particularly in 's Hertogenbosch, Breda, and Bergen-op-Zoom; it was an ironical dispensation of fate that Spain now felt its own hold on Antwerp to depend on the States' keeping those places. Meanwhile, the right of Gelderland, Utrecht, and Overijsel to continue in session in the States-General had become even more questionable now that those provinces had been occupied still more completely, and Friesland, Groningen, and Zealand indeed continued to protest. It became clear that De Groot had been allowed to offer more than it was possible to deliver, unless the break-up of the Union were envisaged as part of the bargain. Leyden and Gouda did not shrink even from that

I

possibility, but a very large majority in the assembly considered Louis' counter-terms unacceptable. Even though there were still some who wished to continue the negotiations, Amsterdam was now by no means alone in its opinion that the sooner they were broken off the better. After some days of confused talking the latter course was decided upon on 7 July. Van Beuningen had said, speaking for Amsterdam:

that the members had resolved in consternation and fear and now ought to return to sanity.

Van Beuningen acted as the Prince's chief diplomatic adviser in these days, and he attached a great deal of weight to yet another factor in the situation, namely England. On 4 July English ambassadors had stepped ashore at Maaslandsluis in order to go via William's army headquarters to that of their ally Louis; no less important personages than Arlington and Buckingham, two of Charles's leading ministers, headed the mission. Van Beuningen regarded it as so obvious that France's conquests in the Republic constituted a danger to England that sooner or later he counted on finding the English willing to come to a separate settlement.

But what was the Prince of Orange's attitude in these circumstances? That he urged resistance to France was what the public expected of him; it was also what in these days brought him and Amsterdam so close together. But was not De Witt's fear confirmed that he would bring the country under English subjection? That this fear was no mere chimera appeared only too clearly. On stepping ashore Arlington and Buckingham had been greeted with loud cheers by the people whom they were plotting with France to subjugate. The crowd shouted:

Long live the King of England and the Prince of Orange! Down with the States!

When they met the Prince at Bodegraven, the two ambassadors had represented to him how easily he could find his own advantage in agreeing to cede the cautionary towns and by accepting the sovereignty out of the hands of his uncle and the latter's ally. They fully expected William to see matters in that light, they even hoped he would deliver up the States' fleet to the Duke of York. To an unprincipled man like Nassau-Odijk, Van Beverweert's son (and thus a brother-in-law of Arlington)

and the representative of the Prince as First Nobleman in
Zealand, a policy on these lines seemed quite acceptable. Some
time later he even gave it as his opinion to Sylvius, the man of
the Buat intrigue, and who was now feeling very much in his
element, that Zealand would do best to place itself under the
King of England. Arlington and Buckingham found the youthful
noblemen surrounding the Prince ardently in favour of their
proposals; these young bloods ranted:

that a dozen of the States party ought to swing, so that the country might have
peace and the Prince become its sovereign.

So deeply had faction corroded the popular mind that if
William had so wished, he could have sold the country amid the
enthusiastic applause of his noble supporters and of the
unthinking mob. But now for the first time he showed the world
of what stuff he was made. Charles II, it is true, had had an
inkling of this on that visit the previous year about which De
Witt had been so uneasy. Originally he had thought of initiating
his nephew into the Dover secret, but he found him 'so ardent a
Dutchman and Protestant' that he had wisely refrained from
doing so. William now indignantly rejected the temptation.

He answered (*the ambassadors wrote*) that he preferred the position of
Stadholder, to which the States had raised him (*to that of sovereign*), and that
he felt himself bound in honour and conscience not to put interest before
duty.

There is something truly great in the strength of character of
this young man of twenty-one, going right against the evil
tradition which had all too thoroughly governed his party and
his supporters and still did. In the seemingly desperate situation
of the moment William repudiated his royal uncle's protection
and chose to stand on his own feet and by his own country. He
let his courtiers rant and decided on the policy to be followed as
between England and France in consultation with the States.

Van Beuningen's idea that an attempt should be made to
detach England from France, and not the other way round as
Pieter de Groot had wished to do in an evil moment, tallied with
his own view. It did not at once succeed. Arlington and
Buckingham proceeded on their way to the French camp, and
at Heeswijk the allies confirmed their concord. England's
demands, territorial and other, were added to those of France
and the total claim, with as a free gift William's elevation to the

sovereignty over what remained, was sent to the Prince—not to the States. But the Prince at once submitted these proposals to the States and vehemently declared them to be unacceptable. Not he, but the States answered to that effect, yet now he made an attempt to come to a direct understanding with the English alone. In the distressing situation his action can certainly be excused, even though William in the end was tempted to make offers which it is fortunate for his reputation that the English rejected, just as Louis had rejected the offers of Pieter de Groot; and the country too benefited by the over-sanguine attitude of its assailants.

In July the worst danger seemed to come from the sea. After Solebay the fleet had had to be partly laid up so that the guns and the men could be used in the Water Line and on the Zuyder Zee. As a matter of fact the Anglo-French fleet now made a serious attempt at landing a small French army, but it was beaten back by a heavy storm. The relief felt was unspeakable; it was looked upon as direct intervention of the hand of God. Moreover Spain was no longer the only ally. The Emperor sent a small army to the Rhine, in co-operation with the Elector of Brandenburg, William's uncle. Before the end of August the Bishop of Münster was forced to raise the siege of Groningen, and the French began to turn their minds to their elongated lines of communication with France—Louis had by then returned home.

The danger was certainly far from having been overcome, and in the besieged province of Holland the elevation of the Prince had not succeeded in calming down the public's mood. The 'commonalty' were still liable to wild outbursts of nervousness and excitement as a result of rumours, idle talk, incidents. The 'gentlemen' who had compromised themselves with De Groot's mission had given themselves a Stadholder certainly, but in both town and country they were still at the helm, and it is no wonder that the spectacle caused alarm. As for De Groot personally, William III had openly spoken out against him. Requested by the States-General to attend their assembly and express his views about the Heeswijk terms, he made it a condition that De Groot should not be admitted. For safety's sake the latter had hurriedly taken himself out of the country. But the state's disasters and the people's infatuation demanded a nobler and more innocent victim.

After his recovery from the attempt on his life six weeks before, De Witt on 4 August laid down his office in the States of Holland, with the correct and dignified motivation that in view of the prevailing public feeling his services could no longer be of use. At that moment his brother Cornelis was already in the Gevangenpoort prison under the manifestly trumped-up and villainous charge of having planned a murderous attack on the Prince's life. Absurd lies were spread about his conduct as deputy on De Ruyter's fleet. Quite as bad as any falsehood was the publication and distribution on 15 August of a genuine letter of Charles II to the Prince, in which the King, making much of his feelings of friendship for his nephew, laid all the blame for the war on the shameless Loevestein faction, enemies both to the King and to Orange. Nothing is more saddening in the tragedy of De Witt's end than to see how the transparent hypocrisy of the false monarch against whom he had defended the country's honour and interests was used to fan party hatred against him. On 20 August the Court of Holland pronounced sentence on Cornelis De Witt—a sentence that was both unjust and cowardly, because he was banished without any grounds being advanced, whereas if his guilt had actually been proved he should have been sentenced to death. In fact an outcry was raised that the traitor would get his deserts nevertheless, and a crowd assembled in front of the Gevangenpoort, where Johan was visiting his brother. The civic guard turned out and it was under their leadership really that, after long hours of excitement, during which the various authorities behaved with pitiful weakness, the two brothers were dragged outside and hideously murdered. Fingers and other parts of the body were hacked off and sold at high prices, the hearts were cut out and, as the general rumour had it, sent to England. The whole evening the bodies were left to hang on the gallows in the Plaats (the main square), while The Hague, in triumphant mood, brought ovations to Cornelis Tromp, who had been an onlooker at the evening's doings together with his brother-in-law Kievit, the traitor of 1666, come back from England. Two days later the Prince received those two men, while neglecting, in his capacity of Stadholder, to institute any legal proceedings on account of the outrage.

The massacre of the De Witts was the work of the Britons.

Thus wrote a Frisian schoolmaster. But it was only too plainly
the work of Dutchmen, and there were those who openly gloried
in it, like The Hague cleric, Simonides, who spoke from the
pulpit of 'God's vengeance'. But we have heard England mentioned repeatedly, and undoubtedly the people's powers of
discrimination had become so confused that they considered
they owed it to Orange to abhor England's enemy. This was an
inheritance left over by dynasticism and faction that one would
gladly have seen William III reject, true patriot that he had
shown himself in his negotiations with Charles II. But William
III was a good hater, and he did not have it in him to be mag-
nanimous towards De Witt.

It would not be right to describe the murder as the direct
outcome of the publication of Charles II's letter, and this had
certainly not been the intention of the originator of that
publication, to wit of Caspar Fagel, the Prince's trusted man in
the States of Holland, where he had got him appointed Grand
Pensionary after De Witt's resignation. But that the intention
had been to incite the citizens against the Loevestein faction is
beyond dispute, and indeed after the Hague atrocity unrest
continued, or became even more vehement, in most towns in the
province of Holland. It was a deliberate system of intimidation
which William III and his adviser applied, and with a definite
end in view, namely the changing of the regents' personnel.
Made pliant by the fate of their great leader in happier days, the
States of Holland at last took Fagel's advice and requested the
Stadholder, 'so that the citizenry should not take it upon itself to
restore order', that he should 'change the government',[1] for this
time only and without prejudice to the privileges, and leaving
the reputation of the victims untouched. In practically all the
towns of Holland the members of the town Councils placed their
seats at the disposal of the Stadholder, who—either personally
or through two commissaries acting in his name—replaced
those 'who were the subject of most adverse talk' by more
acceptable persons.

This looked more like a revolution than the Prince's elevation had done, yet it, too, was an extremely conservative one.

---

[1] This was the traditional term for what always remained a highly exceptional measure resorted to only in times of crisis. The authorisation of the
Stadholder was always (1618, 1748) hedged round by the safeguard mentioned in the text (cf. Part One, pp. 61, 62).

Out of approximately 500 life members of the councils in the eighteen voting towns not many more than 140 were replaced. Loevestein principles or connections counted more heavily in leading to a regent's discharge than having given way to panic in June: the pensionaries of Leyden and Gouda for instance, the most zealous promoters of De Groot's mission, were continued in office. In Rotterdam Kievit was restored to his seat in the Council. In Amsterdam the changes were largely directed by Valckenier, who had made use of his residence in The Hague to obtain a hearing from the new rulers, and who now took revenge for his defeat of the previous year. Here, too, the attitude taken with regard to the menace of the French invasion a few weeks ago was not the decisive factor in the conduct of the purge. One man was continued who had opposed the courageous resolution instructing the town deputies to vote against De Groot's mission; several who had supported it were dismissed. Nowhere did the newly appointed men belong to a different social circle from those who had been discharged. Often the wishes of the remaining members were consulted. There was not, on the contrary, any question of consulting guilds or civic guards.

Yet in Amsterdam and in numerous other Holland towns there had been something stirring among the citizens beneath the regent class. Pamphlets had appeared and meetings had been held at the civic guard halls. Restoration of old privileges was the current slogan. In practice what caused most discontent were the abuses that had crept in in the distribution, among lower middle-class citizens, of the numerous offices in the gift of the magistrates; there was also a general desire that the civic guard should be freed from the dominating influence of the magistrates so that their officers might form a 'free council of war' which could serve as mouthpiece of the citizenry with respect to the town government. The wish for a system of popular election to be applied to the town government itself had hardly as yet presented itself to people's minds, and in general these movements give an impression of weakness and fumbling, and, when it came to taking decisions, of divided counsels. In Amsterdam, for instance, a meeting of citizens was held in the Civic Guard Hall, where a petition to the Burgomasters in twelve points was put up for discussion in a somewhat diffident manner. According to the lively description in a pamphlet, it suddenly lay on the

table—a printed document and a written memorandum—
without anybody seeming responsible for it.

'Come, let me have a light, I shall read it out', so said a quiet-mannered
man, and climbed on to the table. Everyone who could clutched a candle—
there were many there, all lighted up—a circle was formed and those who
had a candle stood in front: it made a fine spectacle. Some stamped their feet
and bade everyone stand still, so he began to read. The jostling and the
noise made it impossible to hear more than half of what he said. In any case
he read one of the printed papers and also the handwritten piece. After he
had finished the question was asked of the crowd whether it was not right
and well put, and whether it was not the opinion of the citizens that they
should have their privileges as of old. There was a general shout of 'Yes, yes,
yes!' Thereupon the reader jumped, or was helped, from the table, and
people began signing the petition. 'Come on, I am ready to sign first', so
said one of the most forward ones. 'Hand me the pen', said another, 'I am
also willing to head the list. What do I care!' And so on, until the most
zealous ones had put their names down. When things began to slow down,
you could hear: 'Now *you* sign!'—'I shall', said the man addressed, 'after
he has signed'. But that one in his turn: 'I must wait and take thought and
first see who will be signing'. (*The writer of the pamphlet excuses himself by
saying that he does not know enough about the privileges:*) 'If we don't understand the matter', I was told in reply, 'the gentlemen do and they will explain
to the Burgomasters, leave it to them, and you sign!' But some of the most
respectable men there refused. Those who had signed asked why then had
they come, and the reply was: 'In order to see what goes on and what will be
proposed.' Then a shout went up: 'Deceivers! Spies! Jan De Witt's men is
what they are. If you are faithful and well-meaning citizens, then sign!'
And a raging and scolding arose as if the crowd were an assembly of wild
beasts, and all that one could hear was: 'draw, wine, beer, to your health, my
turn, pour out, thank you, empty your mug, and we want our privileges, yes,
we do want them, and we want to be masters of the Guard Houses, yes they
belong to us even though everything went to the devil.'

But the 'gentlemen' who seem to have been the instigators of
the whole movement, did not, after a meeting which had been
far from being an unqualified success, show any very great
daring towards the Burgomasters either. If the Prince had not
had his own ends in view, the Amsterdam government might
easily have stayed in power. And the Prince only *used* the citizens' movement. Out of a list with thirty-four names which the
pro-Orangist citizens later drew up in the Civic Guard Hall and
presented to the Stadholder to guide him in filling the seventeen
vacancies, he appointed only one, to the great glee of the
regents' friends. William III was not accessible to ideas of
democracy. Just as at his elevation, so he now, like most of his
contemporaries, accepted the constitutional traditions of the
Republic as immutable wisdom. Like Maurice after his *coup*

Legend:
- Frontiers of the Republic.
- Provincial boundaries within the Republic.
- Other state frontiers.
- Linguistic boundary.
- France's allies and territory of the Republic occupied by them.
- Territory occupied by the French.
- Inundated area.
- Movements of the armies of France and her allies.
- Towns in German territory occupied by the States-General.
- Ditto, lost in 1672.

THE REPUBLIC IN 1672

137

d'état in 1618, he left the oligarchy essentially untouched; for him it was enough to have it filled with more tractable men.

3. EVACUATION OF THE TERRITORY AND PEACE WITH ENGLAND

The War in 1672 and 1673

IN ITS hour of trial the state found in the position of the Stadholder-Captain-General a source of strength. The crisis was far from being overcome. It still required an enormous amount of effort and courage on the part of the community. In the hands of a born leader, a character of steel, a man who did not serve self but an idea—for William *was* all those things— the Orange tradition, which had threatened to lead the people astray with respect to relations with England, proved to be a precious possession. Above the confusion of particularism and even of faction, that slight young man suddenly embodied authority and the national will in a way De Witt with all his gifts and all his devotion had never been able to do. Here and there feelings of rancour naturally persisted, and also of suspicion, particularly with regard to the delicate relations with England. Vicious rumours were spread by the defeated Wittians about the Prince's treacherous intentions. But in the States nobody dared dispute his leadership, because open resistance might drive him to make an appeal to the people. As a result, indeed, of his relative moderation and co-operating as he did with Van Beuningen and Fagel, his relationship to the oligarchy, upon whom he imposed his will, was on the whole tolerably good during those early days.

On the other side of the Water Line area the French were at the same time lording it over Utrecht. Louis XIV had only driven through the town. The Cardinal de Bouillon had conse- crated the old cathedral for Catholic worship again. Neercassel had come rushing up and preached in it repeatedly. It was a yet more bitter humiliation for 'the new Zion' when on Corpus Christi (22 May 1673) the procession, which had not taken place for nearly a hundred years, wended its way through the streets in all its ancient pomp—the same procession which at the time of the Revolt had caused disturbances in so many towns (at Haarlem and Antwerp for instance).[1] With bitter feelings

[1] See *The Revolt of the Netherlands*, p. 173.

did the Utrecht Reformed see the Governor Stoupa drive past in his state coach behind Neercassel, carrying the Sacrament under the purple canopy. But a large crowd followed the procession, and everywhere the houses of the papists were decorated. The proportions in which the deputation of citizens was made up, whose assistance the town council enlisted for the thankless task of raising the levies for the benefit of the French, probably give an idea of the strength of the denominations in the town: by the side of eight Reformed members there were seven Catholics (squires and lawyers), four Remonstrants, three Baptists, and two Lutherans. The Town Council and the provincial States did not scruple to seek Neercassel's aid in persuading the French to lighten the intolerable burdens of billeting and levies. The Bishop must have been well aware of the awkward nature of his position. The French were unlikely to stay. Nor was it for the Catholic religion that they were making war. Was not Spain still the Catholic power *par excellence*?—and Spain was coming to the aid of the Republic. But the reaction to the régime of Reformed monopoly was too natural to be prevented.

On the Holland side of the Water Line meanwhile great efforts were being made at strengthening the army. At home as well as in Germany recruiting for the States went on on a large scale. By the side of John Maurice, who was getting old, and of Wirtz, with whom the Prince had never been able to work together very well, there were now added to the supreme command the Count of Königsmarck, a Swedish subject, and particularly the Prince of Waldeck, a man already in his fifties, in whom William came to repose great confidence. He was also inclined to value the opinions of de Louvignies, the commander of the Spanish auxiliary troops. It is curious to notice once more how little Dutch was the composition not only of the army but also of the supreme command. Even more remarkable is the immense financial strength of Holland, which almost alone had to bear the expenditure entailed by the increase of the army, which moreover was able, with the sole help of Zeeland, to get the fleet ready for the next year's operations, and which, finally, found the subsidies needed to enable the Emperor to maintain an army on the Rhine. The East India Company assisted with an advance of 2,000,000 guilders. But four times in 1672 and 1673 a special levy on property of one-half per cent was raised—a sensational measure at a time in which, apart from the land tax, indirect taxation was all that was usually practised; and excise duties were staggeringly high in Holland. The credit of the province proved equal to the occasion; the Amsterdam Exchange Bank rendered invaluable services in that respect.

If Groningen and Friesland failed to contribute their Generality taxes, this was not only because these provinces were taken up with their own defence against the Münster-Cologne troops. In Friesland a popular movement not unlike the one in Holland had had quite different consequences; it is an affair which makes one realise how in spite of all the slogans and interests they had in common, yet each of the provinces still led its own life.

In Friesland the corrupt and oligarchic States were more unpopular even than in Holland, and in July the example of Holland and Zeeland had been followed and the States of the province forced to invest the young Henry Casimir with the Stadholdership without waiting for his majority. The grievances of the citizenry were made known to the States by the ministers of religion in a body, 150 in all. But the fifteen-year-old Henry Casimir could not possibly play the part of his cousin of Orange. A movement was set on foot for reforming the oligarchic abuses, but it did not trouble much about the Stadholder or his mother (a daughter of Frederick Henry); it received its impetus largely from the towns. In October the States gave in and adopted a comprehensive constitutional programme by which the hated 'grietmen'[1] were barred from membership of their assembly. The States thus purged, however, proved incapable of controlling affairs, and presently the excluded 'grietmen' came together at Sneek, declaring that despite their enforced resignation they still were the lawful States, so that right in the middle of the war Friesland, like Overijsel one or two years previously, presented the spectacle of two States Assemblies each claiming authority. Mediation on the part of the States-General had no effect. Not until the end of March 1673 did a settlement come about whereby the 'grietmen' in fact retained their old position. The reform movement had come to nothing, but during critical months Friesland had counted for nothing in the Union.

[1] See above, p. 119.

Already in the autumn of 1672 William III had considered that the moment had come to proceed to the offensive. Attacks on Naarden and Woerden, just east of the Water Line, failed, however. In November William took the whole cavalry on a bold expedition straight across Brabant with the idea of joining the Brandenburg-Imperial troops and capturing Bonn in the Cologne area, which would have cut the French lines of communication and greatly endangered the army of occupation. The combination failed to take place and a severe frost necessitated a return. That same frost gave the French commander in Utrecht, Marshal Luxembourg, the opportunity to invade Holland across the ice north of Bodegraven. The posts there were abandoned, so that the French, when the thaw suddenly set in, could make an unhindered retreat. In the villages of Zwammerdam and Bodegraven they committed atrocities which made so profound an impression on the Hollanders, unused as they had become to invasion, that the memory did service for an entire generation to rouse popular hatred against the new national enemy. On his return William III made an example of Colonel Pain-et-Vin, who bore the chief guilt for the desertion of the posts (though Königsmarck was not free from blame either); twice he quashed the Court Martial's sentence, reminding them of the article imposing the death sentence on desertion, and for the third time, judging the affair himself with civil assessors, he carried through the sentence he desired: Pain-et-Vin was beheaded.

So when the new year began, the same circumstances were still prevailing, and the hope of liberation receded even further into the background when the Grand Elector concluded peace with France. The fortresses of Wesel and Rees, which the French army had captured on its advance towards the Republic, had been used by French diplomacy as a bait; their being garrisoned by the States had always annoyed the Elector, the lawful owner. In England the King obtained subsidies from Parliament by concealing his leanings towards Catholicism, and the speech of his Chancellor, Shaftesbury, who applied the *Delenda est Carthago* to Holland, 'through interest and inclination the eternal enemy', had a sobering effect upon all those who had not wished to believe in the seriousness of Stuart England's enmity.

De Ruyter in 1673

AGAIN that summer, the great danger threatened on the side of the coast, and the way it was met was most impressive. 'With hearts greatly moved' the sailors listened to De Ruyter reading a letter from His Highness, in which the latter, after expressing his regret at not being able to visit the fleet,

and of having the pleasure of seeing so many honest patriots gathered together for taking the work in hand of protecting the fatherland against the onslaught of the enemy; (*went on to assure them:*) the eyes and hearts of all the inhabitants of the country, nay of the Christian world, are directed on our fleet. (*After a promise of reward for those who gave a good account of themselves, there followed a threatening reference to the full rigour of the articles of war, and after the fate of Pain-et-Vin everyone was aware how seriously this was meant.*) So that to him who shows cowardice and behaves otherwise than befits a good warrior, nothing will be so dangerous as the harbours of the Republic, where he will find it impossible to escape the strong hand of justice and the hatred of his fellow-citizens.

Some time earlier the Prince had succeeded in bringing about a reconciliation between De Ruyter and Cornelis Tromp. Never did he rise above party strife in a more striking manner. De Ruyter, the friend of the De Witts, had suffered the outrage of having his house attacked by the Amsterdam mob while he himself was at sea. But the Prince never wavered in maintaining him in the supreme command, and he now induced the hot-tempered Tromp to give his hand upon it that he would whole-heartedly serve under him.

In June, off Schoneveld, the renewed comradeship in arms of the two naval heroes was sealed. There De Ruyter had awaited the Anglo-French fleet with his own much smaller one (fifty-two actual warships as against eighty or ninety) and a week after the undecisive battle attacked once more and drove the enemy back. Glorious days, but arduous, and the work was not done even yet. At the beginning of August the Anglo-French fleets appeared off the Maas and sailed along the coast of Holland. The event caused a renewal of dismay. The prince energetically saw to it that the coastal defence was brought into readiness; to get this done ample use was made of the compulsory services of citizens and farmers. When De Ruyter was summoned from Schoneveld to deliver battle once more, it was not so much to ward off a landing—against this eventuality the measures taken were thought to be sufficient—but to liberate the sea for trade, for a return fleet from the Indies more especially. First the new Grand Pensionary and the States' chief naval expert, Van Lode-steyn, came to consult with De Ruyter and his council off Scheveningen, the point to which the fleet had sailed. But when the Admiral proved unwilling to take the responsibility of an action which might cost the country its fleet, the Admiral-General (that is, the Prince) had himself rowed aboard the *Seven Provinces* with a number of members of his staff, and after a council of war furnished De Ruyter at the latter's request with written orders made out in the name of their High Mightinesses. Great enthusiasm fired the crew when in the presence of the Prince the old Admiral addressed them with a stimulating and admonitory little speech. The fleet set sail at once and encountered the enemy off Kijkduin on 21 August. There now started the most murderous of the three great battles of the war (the French only took a slight part in it). An anxious crowd kept watch from the dunes, whilst in the country prayers went up in packed churches for the success of the fleet. The battle ended with the retreat of the badly damaged English fleet. On the Dutch side two Vice-Admirals and four captains had been killed, among them De Ruyter's son-in-law. Mausoleums, chains of honour, and annuities were evidence of the gratitude of the States. At an earlier date a French minister had already said of De Ruyter:

The greatest commander the sea has ever known.

The sea had been opened. There could now no longer be any question of a landing. When in one of the battles some French ships scattered before the approach of his flagship, De Ruyter said, punning on the ship's name:

The enemy still stands in awe of the Seven Provinces.

The Hague Alliance and the Evacuation of the States' Territory

THIS was indeed the significance of that epic conflict. The English became deeply discouraged. Attempts on the part of Dutch diplomacy to persuade the Emperor and Spain to co-operate more closely were, on the contrary, furthered by the event. The alliance that was concluded in The Hague aimed widely beyond the liberation of the States' territory. Spain was now willing to declare war upon France (up till then it had only rendered assistance as an ally, without, in accordance with the international law of the time, abandoning the status of a neutral), provided a promise were given that France would be pushed back to the frontiers of 1659; in addition Spain stipulated for the restitution of Maastricht, which Frederick Henry had wrested from her in 1632 and which was now in the hands of the French. The importance of this Hague alliance was that it again united the two branches of the House of Habsburg, and with them the Republic, in a determined resistance against France. Van Beuningen and Fagel were the real authors of that policy, which meant that the possibility of a return to De Witt's system of an equilibrium between France and England was given up for a whole generation to come, and that for the same period of time a struggle set in with France for the preservation of the Southern Netherlands. Or was it not rather circumstances which had decided for the North-Netherlands people in this sense the choice that De Witt had tried to avoid? The struggle for their own existence had been one with the struggle for the Southern Netherlands from the moment that the Count of Monterey had moved to protect 's Hertogenbosch and sent de Louvignies to the Water Line, some fifteen months earlier.

The new policy was fixed before the two conditions which it could not do without had materialised; but at that moment, in November 1673, the evacuation of the territory and peace with England were only a question of time.

In September William III had attempted another attack on Naarden, and this time he succeeded. In November he repeated his cavalry expedition to the German Rhine and, in conjunction with troops of the Emperor's, succeeded in taking Bonn; it was an exploit evincing strategic vision coupled with daring. Luxembourg had already received orders to leave his precarious position. If the Emperor's men had co-operated, William would have been able to cut off his retreat. Actually he had to be content with winning back almost the whole of his native country's soil. Utrecht was evacuated by the French before the year 1673 was out, not without their having levied a last tribute and carrying off hostages. Part of the French troops continued to occupy Arnhem and Nijmegen, but in the spring of 1674 those forces, too, drew off again after having extracted a heavy tribute. Cologne and Münster could now no longer keep their hold on the eastern provinces either and concluded peace. Cologne indeed retained the full possession of the fortresses on its territory, out of which the States' garrisons had been thrown in 1672. With regard to Brandenburg, too, the Republic could not in the circumstances think of re-establishing its old usurpation: the garrisoning of Emmerich, Rees and Wesel was a thing of the past, as was that of Rheinberg and Orsoy. Almost unnoticed, the eastward expansion was given up in the face of the threat from the South. For the time being only Grave and Maastricht remained in French hands.

Peace with England

THE peace with England had been signed as early as February 1674. Spain's coming into action had helped to bring this about, because the economically passive Spanish realm formed an important market for English trade, and the English would not allow their Dutch competitors the privileged position that would have resulted from an Anglo-Spanish war. Carthage was far from being destroyed! Having proved superior in staying-power in the North Sea, the Dutch Republic also maintained its supremacy in the colonial world. The Dutch East India Company had seriously hampered English trade in the East, and an expedition sent out by Louis XIV in 1671 came to a sorry end. His Admiral, De la Haye, had taken Trincomalee in the north of Ceylon, but the Governor of the island, the redoubtable Van Goens, had driven him off and subsequently chased him to the coast of Coromandel. After having been blockaded there for a year, De la Haye had to surrender—it was then September 1674—and the 900 men who remained out of his 2,000 returned to Europe in Dutch ships.

In the West a Zeeland squadron under a young member of the Evertsen family had reconquered St. Eustace, which had been taken by the French, and after that, joined by a number of Amsterdam men-of-war under Binckes, he appeared before New York. The English Governor, Lovelack, capitulated after having offered little more resistance than Stuyvesant had done nine years before. Evertsen and Binckes took possession of the whole of New Netherland. New York, the former New Amsterdam, they now called New Orange. They made the inhabitants swear allegiance to Their High Mightinesses and to His Highness; they established a government after the Dutch manner and formed a civic militia from the Dutch population. After that they returned home with their prizes. In 1674 the Burgomaster, sheriff, and aldermen of New Orange sent an urgent request to the States-General for assistance, calling themselves their loyal subjects. But in the peace negotiations England demanded restitution (the basis this time was to be not the *uti possidetis* but the *status quo ante*). Peace was so urgently needed that the States had to concede that demand as well as a war tribute of 2,000,000 guilders. New Orange therefore once more became New York. The English Governor to whom it was delivered up demanded an oath in which no regard was taken of the promises of free worship and preservation of the privileges stipulated by the capitulation of 1664. Eight Dutch citizens protested—among whom were some of the former aldermen of the short-lived New Orange—but a threat of confiscation of their property brought them to submission. The West India Company, still saddled with its old Brazilian debt, could now carry on no longer. It went bankrupt. The States-General saw to it that its possessions passed into the hands of a new Company, freed from the burdens of the disastrous past.

In addition, the second Peace of Westminster contained strict regulations about the flag. Charles II did not owe all these advantages to any superiority shown in conducting the war, but to the complete absorption of the Republic in its struggle against France. The preoccupation with what was happening in the Southern Netherlands had been partly responsible for the moderation shown by the States-General at the Peace of Breda, and the neglect in fostering settlements in New Netherland could in part be ascribed to the war with Spain. Yet it now appears clearly for the first time how serious an impediment its situation on the continent meant to the Republic in its colonial struggle with England. As regards the old English ambitions, however, like a levy on fishing rights, inspection at sea, regulations for the Indian trade, these were not conceded even now. In the matter of dealing with contraband at sea, regulations were even laid down which seemed to satisfy the old Dutch desire for a large measure of trading freedom in time of war. This was due to the fact that the English saw a period of advantageous neutrality open up before them as long as the Republic was to continue its war with France; much later, in the Seven Years War and again in the war with France over the rebellion of the American colonies, in very different circumstances, when indeed the boot was on the other foot, the Dutch were to try in vain to make their rivals observe those regulations. In any case now, after three wars, the Republic was still able to maintain its position with regard to the other Sea Power.

f. WAITING FOR ENGLAND

1. THE FIRST COALITION WAR AGAINST FRANCE, 1674–78

William III's Power

THE war with France was continued, and to conduct that war and to make the Republic carry on with it, William III had more power at his disposal than any of his forefathers had had.

We have seen how he left the oligarchy in Holland fundamentally untouched, but that he filled it with his supporters. In 1674, after Grave too had been retaken, the States of Holland expressed their gratitude for the liberation of the territory by passing a resolution making the Stadholdership hereditary. William meanwhile systematically used the rights of his office in filling vacancies in the Town Councils and in the annual appointment of magistrates in order to form a party for himself among the town authorities. If Frederick Henry had still adhered to the recommendations which the town authorities themselves indicated by 'dots' on the 'double lists' of candidates, his grandson scorned to let the Stadholderly selection thus become a formality. And in addition, he was far from particular in the means he used for exercising influence.

He who was able to serve a political idea disinterestedly, appealed, in order to make the oligarchy subservient to himself, quite recklessly to their lowest instincts. He cared for nothing but that they should support his foreign policy. His tactics were bound to sap the character of the governing class, but this he did not notice or did not mind. Although he succeeded in making a number of towns even in Holland toe the line, that province—thanks chiefly to Amsterdam—remained relatively independent, and he gained a much more complete hold on the States Assemblies of his other provinces.

In Zealand he appointed his cousin Nassau-Odijk, Beverweert's son, to represent him as First Nobleman of that province. This man had long been the black sheep of the family, and now, socially saved by his new position, he continued to employ practices that were morally most reprehensible. Odijk bound the Orangist regents there among themselves and to him by means of a 'contract of correspondence'—the term will be explained later—but when Middelburg continued to assume a certain amount of independence, the Stadholder came in person angrily to bring it to reason. The immediate occasion was a religious dispute. Since the days of Maurice most orthodox ministers had consistently exalted Orange above the States. For the first time since Maurice a Prince of Orange now wholeheartedly answered to those leanings. From the lessons given him by Domine Trigland and Professor Bondius William III retained a firm belief in predestination; but the Voetians were political supporters into the bargain, and the Cocceians not only disturbers of the peace within the church, but political adversaries. In 1677 a Cocceian minister, Momma, received a call to Middelburg. Rushing up from the army camp William III not only exacted Momma's dismissal but that of another minister, Van der Wayen, as well, and then went on to purge the magistracy of their supporters. This impetuousness is characteristic. There was no question here of his protecting an oppressed majority; the town authorities were backed by the civic guard officers in their 'Council of War' and to all appearance by public opinion. The Stadholder simply used his position to favour his own party.

Of all the provinces it was in Utrecht, Gelderland, and Overijsel that he had obtained the most extensive powers. In the town of Utrecht the departure of the French had been the signal for a petition on the part of the Voetian party against the government then sitting. 'Sound churchman means sound Princeman', and the gentlemen who had just had to cope with the thankless task of living with the occupying power were pushed aside without further ado. Resistance was of course out of the question. The 'papists' themselves, who were at once dispossessed of the cathedral again, and fairly roughly too, tried to be among the most zealous in erecting a triumphal arch to welcome the Prince; 'with Shimei', as the Reformed church-man, Booth, well versed in Scripture, noted down in his diary.[1] Voetius—who had held the thanksgiving service in the recovered cathedral with Psalm 126, verses 1 and 2, for his text—Voetius and his party triumphed.

But the matter did not end with the changing of the personnel of the States and town governments. An arrangement was intro-duced, not only in Utrecht but in Gelderland and Overijsel also, whereby all political bodies came to be dependent on the Stadholder in a way hitherto unheard of. When in 1673–74 the French and their allies evacuated those three provinces, the other four were in two minds as to whether they would allow them to rejoin the Union on the old footing. William III then granted them his powerful protection, but in exchange he obtained for himself the so-called Government Regulations, by which he became absolute master of almost all the political appointments in the three provinces in question. By this means their States and their deputies in the States-General became the creatures of the Stadholder even more unconditionally than had been the case in the later years of Frederick Henry and William II. Even as it was, the nobility of those provinces used to wait on his every glance, of him who as Commander-in-Chief had the disposal of advancement in the army. The towns too were now reduced to submission. Not the slightest independ-ence with respect to the Stadholder was left in being. But even though the Prince had not disdained the aid of petitions from the citizens, democracy was advanced here as little as at Amster-dam. The regents, though they came to be dependent on him, could still play the lord and master over the citizenry. This made the system of the Government Regulations doubly unfortunate.

Nevertheless, together with this extension of his power, William was given a reminder of the limits imposed by Dutch tradition. The States of Gelderland, anxious to show him their devotion, offered him the sovereignty—in their province, the ducal rank. The Prince, who had been unwilling to accept this elevation at the hands of the enemy, did desire it in itself. But he first turned to the other provinces for their opinion. Utrecht,

[1] See II Samuel, xix, 16.

finding itself in a similar plight to that of Gelderland, expressed itself in favour, but Holland and Zealand were definitely against, and the oligarchy did not now have to protect the republican principle against the 'eminent head' supported by the multitude whose darling he was; they were able to plead the attachment felt by the people for the traditional form of government. The Prince therefore rejected the offer, but how much he felt galled by republican sensitiveness appears from the answer he gave publicly to the States of Zealand. These had pointed out to him

the praiseworthy example of Gideon, the judge of Israel: when a similar offer was made to him, in his days, by God's people, out of gratitude for his having so successfully delivered them from the Midianites and from slavery, just as now so much good has come to the fatherland through the hand of your Highness, (*he, Gideon, had rejected the offer*).

The Prince questioned the applicability of the comparison by remarking scornfully (and very unfairly) that in 1672 the nation had forfeited the right to be called 'God's people' by its willingness to surrender to an enemy who would have suppressed the reformed religion. The exclusion to which he himself had been subjected before the war he still bitterly described as an injustice. The men who were then in power, he said, with a clear allusion to the present case:

did not scruple to baptize with the name of Liberty and Defence of the Privileges those measures taken to humiliate and oppress our person, just as if we ought to be regarded as oppressors of those very same Liberty and Privileges, while the promoters of Liberty and Privileges were not in fact anything but promoters of their own greatness and prestige.

In writing like this William III does not show himself at his best, not the national leader but the violent party man. The whole picture presented by his domestic policy is unattractive. The old regent oligarchy was left in being unchanged, but its best qualities, its sense of responsibility and of self-respect, were undermined by a system in which it was necessary before everything else to show submissiveness to the Prince or to the far from admirable favourites by whom he allowed himself to be represented in the various provinces. Real opposition, opposition of political intent as distinct from purely personal intrigues, was now possible only for Amsterdam, which, for the time being co-operating with William III, had still managed to preserve its independence intact.

As to the realisation of the Voetian-Orangist idea, the
clearest sign of it one can discern is that orthodoxy was now
imposed upon the church and the universities much more
forcibly than it had been before. At Leyden the Board of
Curators repeatedly and sharply reminded the professorial body
of the resolution of 1656 against Cartesianism. In 1675 various
'classes' (district councils of ministers) urged them to take
measures against the 'shocking novelties' and 'offensive doctrines' with which 'many wanton minds' were leading youth
astray and jeopardising religion—

religion, the true safeguard and the precious treasure which the great
God has so providentially deposited in the bosom of this state for its
salvation.

Fagel and William III himself were consulted and an order
on the part of the Board of Curators prohibiting the discussion
in the University of some twenty theses was the result. When
old Heidanus—under his own name and in Dutch!—published
outspoken *Consideratiën* on the matter (he called it 'a dastardly
inquisition, smelling more of the breath of Rome and Spain
than of the Dutch soil'), he was dismissed from office, a decision
of which the Board of Curators immediately informed the
Stadholder, recalling the letter in which he had admonished
them to act energetically.

As a result of using coercion in this way the best tendencies in
the Orangist movement which it had manifested during the
period of the Prince's exclusion, those of a soundly democratic
and idealistically religious nature, went to the wall. When I
spoke above of the triumph of the Voetian party, the statement
should be qualified by remarking that its best representatives
were soon themselves bitterly disappointed. Lodenstein had
been back but a short time from France, where he had been
taken as a hostage (one of several) for the last tribute imposed on
Utrecht, when he found just as much reason for complaints and
angry protests as before. For all that there were now men in
office who passed for men of religion, nothing had changed at
bottom. Church property was used, or abused, in exactly the
same way as under the Wittians; the new gentlemen arrogated
to themselves the same right of interference in consistorial
matters. And when Lodenstein in one of his sermons threatened

to apply ecclesiastical discipline, as he had been accustomed to do before:

> (*Proposition:*) The authorities have no say in church matters.
> (*Objection:*) But the authorities cannot be opposed.
> (*Answer:*) Can they not be excluded from the Sacrament?,

—the States of Utrecht decided, as in days gone by, to request the 'gentlemen' of the town to summon the preacher before them, and to demand that he account for 'the aforesaid scornful expressions and unseemly licentiousness of speech'.

What brought the orthodox and William III most closely together was the war. Their faith, combative and wholly permeated with the idea of the state, embraced the war with complete sincerity. It was now the French who had become the enemies of God, just as it used to be the Spaniards (or to Van Goens the Portuguese) and to make war on them became one's Christian duty. In the same way that the ministers, in Flanders' need almost a century previously, had taught 'that God promises his aid to Kings and Lords who shall walk in fear of Him',[1] so Lodenstein and the consistories and synods now believed that disasters and defeats had to be combated by a more thorough 'reformation' of religious life. William III supported the orthodox because they were so zealous for war no less than because he was orthodox himself. But he felt he could rely on dependence even more safely than on orthodoxy, and no wonder, for after 1674 the war became so unpopular that even the orthodox wavered.

The War and the Peace (of Nijmegen, 1678)

IN FACT the war had in 1674 changed its character completely. France, left in the lurch by her allies England, Münster and Cologne, so far from being able to complete an easy conquest of the Republic, found herself surrounded by a European coalition. This coalition was contemplating vast plans for invasion and reconquest: all the territories incorporated into France by the Peace Treaties of Aix (1668), the Pyrenees (1659), and Münster (1648) were aimed at, that is to say Courtrai, Oudenarde, Thielt (Flanders), Lille (Walloon Flanders), Ath, Le Quesnoy, and Avesnes (Hainault), the whole of Artois, as

[1] See *The Revolt of the Netherlands,* p. 190.

well as Roussillon in the south and Alsace in the east. But French powers of expansion were not so easily arrested. French diplomacy found new allies (partly old ones as a matter of fact!) in a still wider circle round the attackers of the Kingdom: Sweden, Poland, the Hungarian rebels against Viennese despotism, Turkey. In 1675 Louis aided a rebellion in Messina against Spanish rule; a Dutch fleet had to go to the Mediterranean to help the Spanish fleet repulse the French; here De Ruyter was killed in a battle in 1676. At his funeral at Amsterdam splendid homage was paid to the naval hero who had become so outstanding a national figure. Similarly, Cornelis Tromp had to go and support Denmark against Sweden. The movements of the coalition were thus not a little impeded, but already in 1674, when these diversions had not yet made themselves felt, it became evident that the power of attack of a coalition is naturally weaker than is the defence of a closely co-ordinated unit.

Louis forestalled his enemies in that dangerous year by again conquering Franche Comté which he had restored in 1668; after that, Turenne kept the Imperial army and the Brandenburgers engaged, while Condé defended the northern frontier. There William III hoped to break through at the head of a threefold army, Dutch, Imperial, and Spanish. Out of the 70,000 men in the States' service at that time, some 30,000 were released for the field army. The Count de Monterey had not been able to raise much more than one third of that number, but nevertheless he submitted reluctantly to the orders of a young and untried Prince, whom he did not consider his superior in rank. Even more irritating was the attitude of the Imperial commander, De Souches, who refused to cross the river Maas with his 24,000 men to join the main army. The campaigning season had thus largely gone by before William could do what he was yearning to do, namely force Condé to give battle.

The self-assurance of the young man's conduct—he was after all no more than twenty-three, slightly built and of a feeble constitution—was amazing, and the contrast of his passionate energy with the hesitating caution of his grandfather Frederick Henry is very striking. The campaign of 1674 was the first of a long series he was to conduct in the Southern Netherlands—in co-operation with the Spaniards whereas Frederick Henry had conducted his against the Spaniards—and just as much as Frederick was all for sieges and avoided encounters in the open field, so William III sought out the enemy, even in the face of obstruction from allies. On 11 August 1674, it came to a battle near Seneffe. It was a murderous day, the young commander won laurels, but no victory was gained. William III wished to risk the invasion all the same; a siege (of Oudenarde) was the most that he could induce De Souches to undertake, and Condé soon compelled that to be raised. Furious with the Imperial commander, the Prince had to march his army homewards, yet before the troops had to go into winter quarters he was able to take Grave.

In 1675 the chances of an offensive against France were already much less favourable. On the contrary the French were able to take, in the bishopric of Liège (neutral territory really), Huy and the citadel near Liège, seriously hampering thereby the allies' lines of communication. From the advanced posts of Oudenarde and Thielt, which since 1668 had been in their possession, they lay the whole of East and West Flanders under contribution, until in 1676 regular contribution treaties were concluded with the Waesland, the Lordship (*Kasselry*) of Oudenburg, and other districts. Louvois, Louis' implacable Minister for War, saw to it that these treaties were carried out without mercy.

You must let no opportunity go by (*so he wrote on 7 September 1676, to the general on the spot, after receiving a report about 'executions' through setting villages on fire in the Waesland*) to harass those districts until the inhabitants have raised the whole sum due. The King does not doubt your having made use of the Duke of Villahermosa's[1] long halt on the great highroad (*of Brussels*) to have villages burnt and prisoners made in the districts of Waas, Termonde, and Oudenburg.

It goes without saying that these terrorised areas could produce but little for their lawful master, and the new Governor was in even worse financial straits than his predecessor had been. The dream of pushing back French expansion had vanished. On the contrary, Spain, which had already lost Franche Comté in 1674, now saw in the Southern Netherlands, too, its own possessions crumble away. In 1676 the French captured the towns of Condé and Bouchain, rendering Valenciennes and Cambrai, hedged in on all sides as they already were through

---

[1] Villahermosa had succeeded Monterey as Governor in 1674.

the annexations of 1659 and 1668, quite untenable. The former indeed was lost as early as 1677; whereupon the French threatened not only Cambrai but St. Omer as well. But William III, who to his chagrin had every summer had to march up and down with too weak or too slow an army (in 1676 he had fruitlessly tried to retake Maastricht), now forced a battle near Cassel (11 April) with practically the Dutch army alone. It resulted in a serious defeat. The commander's readiness to attack began to look like recklessness even to Waldeck, and all his strength of mind was now required to save the States' army. Bold attempts which he ventured upon later in the year came to nothing: the French had a decided superiority and the war was approaching nearer to its crisis.

In the Republic it had long been unpopular. Four campaigns had been conducted since the liberation of the territory. The finances were cracking under the heavy pressure, and at the same time the Dutch merchant class saw with envious eyes how the English—who had foreseen this only too well when they concluded peace in 1674—were working their way in wherever their competitors found access blocked against them. And in addition there were the losses inflicted upon Dutch trade by the Dunkirk pirates, now in the service of France as formerly they had been in that of Spain. Jan Bart (whose Flemish name is generally given in French translation) became a well-known figure:

> A pious and kindly man, not so bitterly popish as the rest (*the young lady from North Holland, who thus described him, had been a prisoner on his ship, and had met a priest there, whose church had been closed down by her father in his function of bailiff of Hoogwoude*).

If only from all this effort and sacrifice some effect could have been shown! But the helplessness of the Spaniard and the indifference of the Austrian appeared ever more glaring; the defence of the Southern Netherlands depended on the States army alone and it proved unable to prevent the French from pushing on step by step. And how attractive did Louis make it for the States to detach themselves from their unsatisfactory allies!

As early as 1675 English mediation had paved the way for a general Peace Conference and in the beginning of 1676 delegates from the King of France and from the States-General met each other at Nijmegen; towards the end of the year representatives of the allies, too, reluctantly made their way thither. For sadly deficient as were their achievements in the field, they would not hear of peace, and what drew them to Nijmegen was only the fear that the States might proceed to conclude a separate peace with France. And indeed the French diplomats—there was old d'Estrades and a new man, d'Avaux[1]—used all their artifice to induce the States—represented by Van Beverning—to do this very thing. What a change since 1672, when the overthrow of the Republic had been seen as the indispensable preliminary to the conquest of the Southern Netherlands. Louis was still pursuing that aim, but he found himself compelled to return to his former tactics and to win back the Republic to the old friendship—this was the favourite phrase. To that end he offered a favourable trade treaty (Colbert's economic policy was sacrificed to the policy of expansion) and even the return of Maastricht, which William III had failed, in 1676, to retake by force of arms. And he did not even demand that for his part he should be allowed to take the whole of the Southern Netherlands away from Spain at one go. He even declared himself willing to return part of what he already occupied.

How tempting those offers must have seemed to the Dutch statesmen! If they persisted for so long in declining it was chiefly owing to the influence of the Stadholder.

To defend the war policy which William III embodied in the face of a growing opposition, just as Maurice and Frederick Henry had done in their day, much was made of the debt of gratitude owed to the allies who had saved the Republic from destruction in 1672–73, and of the obligations which it had engaged in with respect to them by the Hague Alliance. But these were not the considerations that really determined William III's attitude; for that, the memories left by his personal experience in the field with the Imperial armies and the Spaniards rankled too much: he had suffered too badly from their neglect to carry out their own obligations. When during the siege of Maastricht in 1676 the Spaniards were already cherishing hopes that after its capture (which as a matter of fact never took place) that town would be delivered up to them, in accordance with what had been

[1] Son of the d'Avaux mentioned in Part One, pp. 143, 145.

agreed upon in 1673, the Prince wrote to Fagel from his army camp:

I must confess to Your Honour that the Spaniards do not deserve anything from us, and there is a great deal to be said on this subject. I do not believe that we should allow that precious bit to be wrung from us like that.

But William III was ever mindful that the only way to call a halt to the danger of France's advance in the Southern Netherlands was by united action of the European powers. Even though the existing coalition might still prove too weak, he wished at all costs to prevent its being broken up by a separate withdrawal on the part of the Republic; and especially so, as long as there seemed to be a chance that England might depart from her neutrality in order to strengthen it. All the time he kept his eyes fixed on England, as indeed did everybody who understood the European situation. English political opinion itself realised as much as did Dutch opinion that the Republic would fall into dependence upon France if the latter were to become master of the intermediate territory of the Netherlands. Would not that opinion, would not Parliament, be able to force Charles II to call a halt to Louis? That was what William III was hoping for, and that was why he preferred to persevere from year to year in his prospectless campaigns rather than to agree to an untimely peace.

The French danger since 1672 had been a reality to him governing the whole of his political thinking; freedom and Protestantism he saw threatened, and he saw it all in its wider European setting. To him it seemed a natural policy, it seemed the policy of duty, that the Republic should exhaust itself for an indefinite period standing in the breach of the general situation. Even political friends who shared his view, and who were no less familiar than he was with large-scale political calculations and with European considerations, at times found that demand too heavy. Fagel, and particularly Van Beuningen, were after all in too close touch with the practical needs and limitations of Holland society to be able to regard dogged persistence under all circumstances as the highest form of statesmanship. To the public at large William's policy was wholly incomprehensible. As they saw it, the danger had been overcome in 1673–74. Since then the exacting struggle was being carried on for goals of too distant and too speculative a nature, and even though the

Ministers of the Word might preach against France as they had used to do against Spain, there was not yet a tradition of enmity, and it was not until later that Louis was to appear not only as the insatiable conqueror but also as the destroyer of Protestantism. The immediate issue concerning a few fortresses on the southern frontier of the Southern Netherlands could not touch people's imagination as had done, in Frederick Henry's time, the war on their own frontiers to reconquer Netherlandish provinces. Moreover, the cost was becoming almost too heavy to bear. In Amsterdam there occurred a riot against a tax. William III, who had been welcomed back in Holland with exuberant honour after the campaign resulting in the reconquest of Grave in 1674 ('the Hollanders' great idol', as the religious fanatic Rothe had already, true to his Amsterdam patrician descent, scoffed at the time), was now with increasing impatience being blamed for the insatiable ambition and the blind passion with which he was holding up the peace. Those who revered the memory of De Witt were speaking out ever more loudly.

The young Stadholder was not lacking in the strength of mind required to defy this widespread grumbling, nor did he fail to make full use of the power we know he now possessed. But it was a serious matter that he could no longer count on Amsterdam. Anxiety about the republican régime and, simply, class pride joined with doubt about the Prince's war policy to cause so serious an estrangement that in political circles it was whispered that William II's coup might come to be repeated. In 1677 Valckenier and Hendrik Hooft, the leader of what remained of opposition since the change of the town government, concluded a formal reconciliation. Van Beuningen, who had in 1672 co-operated so wholeheartedly with the Prince, was now inclining to resistance. Given the popular mood, the energetic lead of a powerful 'member' of Holland (i.e. Amsterdam) might be able to push the peace through even in defiance of the Prince.

But at that very moment matters took a turn, hopeful for William's policy. The English Parliament vigorously expressed the view that the preservation of Flanders constituted an English interest. Under the pressure of his minister Danby, Charles II seemed to be resolving in favour of a change of course. William was invited to England to marry the eldest daughter of the Duke of York, the King's brother and heir apparent. What Charles was hoping to achieve was to bind more closely to him this nephew, whose prestige among the English as a Protestant hero he had come to regard with misgiving. William on the contrary saw in the marriage a pledge of the King's anti-French intentions. An alliance between England and the Republic was actually brought about. English troops landed at Ostend (not without raising suspicions in Spain) and the English intervention assumed a somewhat threatening tone towards France.

But Charles was no more a reliable ally for his nephew than he had been for De Witt. Soon he allowed himself to be bought off by Louis and it is a moot point whether all his preparations had had any other purpose than to push up his price on the French market. To William III this was a bitter disappointment. It also seriously weakened his position at home, because the English marriage, which would meet with applause so long as it could be thought to guarantee English aid against France, must otherwise be a source of unpopularity. The Holland regents remembered William II's marriage only too well. The opposition in England, too, now saw the Prince as affiliated to the Stuart interest, which was exactly what Charles had intended. The French meanwhile had opened their campaign of 1678 by conquering Ypres and Ghent, so that the whole of the county of Flanders lay within their grasp. Betrayed by England and not supported by Spain, the Republic no longer had any choice, and Van Beverning, who went in person to Louis' army camp at Wetteren, was only too happy when the great King persisted in his moderate peace terms, even with regard to the Southern Netherlands.

Before the truce which thus came about was turned into peace, everything was again thrown into uncertainty, because Louis announced his intention to postpone the promised return of territory in the Netherlands until his ally Sweden had received Pomerania back from the Grand Elector. Fury flared up in England as well as in the Republic, and a new rapprochement between the two seemed to introduce a fresh war effort. But Charles II once again played the same double game. The States did not dare jeopardise what had been attained by Van Beverning. When the French gave up their chicanery the States eagerly caught at the chance. The alliance with England remained an empty form; on 10 August peace was signed at

Nijmegen between the States and France. William III, who when the war seemed to be reviving had again eagerly taken the field, gave battle a few days later near St. Denis in the hope of relieving Mons (in Hainault); still more perhaps in the hope of definitely upsetting the separate Franco-Dutch peace; officially he had not yet been advised of its having been concluded. But the peace survived the shock. It was soon followed by a peace between France and Spain on the terms stipulated by the States. The other allies, Brandenburg and Austria particularly, were left to settle their own affairs, and complained vociferously about the selfishness and ingratitude of the Republic.

Spain herself, who had to foot a large part of the bill with the cession of Franche Comté, was but moderately satisfied; she was particularly aggrieved at the Republic for recovering Maastricht and not delivering it up to her. As against this the States maintained that they had fully made good that obligation by means of the areas elsewhere in the Netherlands they had recovered for Spain from France.

Indeed, besides the recently conquered town of Ghent, the French evacuated also their most advanced outposts under the impossible settlement of 1668, namely Courtrai, Thielt, Oudenarde, and Ath. However, they retained considerable areas of freshly conquered territory: St. Omer and a large bit of Dutch-speaking Flanders, from Cassel and Bailleul to Ypres and Roulers; as well as Cambrai and considerable parts of Hainault, with Valenciennes and Maubeuge. From the point of view of the political future of the Dutch linguistic area it is important to note that France's conquests finally resulting from the three peace treaties of 1659, 1668,[1] and 1678 (half Hainault, the whole of Walloon Flanders, and the whole of Artois) reduced the Walloon population of the Spanish Netherlands to less than half. Inroads had been made into the Dutch-speaking region, it is true, but, as we shall see later, this was largely undone again after the War of the Spanish Succession, whilst France retained almost the whole of its French-speaking acquisitions. For the future of the Dutch element in what was one day to become Belgium, that alteration in the ethnic proportions was of incalculable importance.

[1] Peace of the Pyrenees, see p. 46; of Aix, see p. 99.

While everywhere in the Republic there was great rejoicing, William sulkily withdrew to his estate at Dieren to find distraction in solitary hunting. Dutch historians have more than once described the Peace of Nijmegen as a monument to the short-sightedness of merchant rulers. Mistakenly; for although the French commercial treaty may have proved an irresistible temptation to many, the interest the State had in the South-Netherlands barrier (the term coming into use round about this time) had not been forgotten. Seeing Charles II's untrustworthiness, the alternative of carrying on the war could only have led to a further crumbling away of Spain's possessions in the Netherlands. Fagel, Van Beverning, and the Amsterdammers showed wise judgment in bringing about the peace of 1678.

2. AMSTERDAM CHECKS 'UNTIMELY WAR'

The Luxembourg Question

THIS does not alter the fact that the European situation created by the peace was highly favourable to Louis XIV and fraught with danger for the future of the Netherlands. Concerned as they were about the northward expansion of France, the States had not troubled about her pushing on across her eastern frontier; and the anti-French coalition lay in pieces. Particularly Brandenburg, left in the lurch in the war against Sweden, was so incensed as to go over to the French camp. In England the King and his Parliament came to loggerheads about Oates' 'no Popery' campaign and the attempt to exclude the now openly Catholic Duke of York from the succession, so that support from that quarter was less than ever to be expected. Charles did continue his pose as the protector of Spain, but secretly he let himself again be bribed by French subsidies to promote Louis' undertakings.

For Louis XIV the Peace of Nijmegen was nothing but a springboard for fresh conquests. Sure of the impotence of his enemies, he presumed so far as to base a right to fresh annexations upon the pronouncements of his own courts of justice (*parlements*) interpreting the articles of the various peace treaties concluded during his reign. He put these one-sided decrees into effect without bothering even to declare war; and the injured parties, amid a great deal of diplomatic cackling, let him do as he pleased. The chief of these 'réunions' was Strasbourg, in October 1681. Meanwhile he went on and on negotiating with helpless Spain about an indemnification which he asserted he was entitled to in return for the evacuation of Courtrai (which in fact had been stipulated by the peace of Nijmegen!). He demanded Luxembourg, the fortress which ensured the communication between the Spanish Netherlands and Germany, and in 1682, tired of Spain's refusals, he had the town blockaded. Soon, however, he abandoned that enterprise, but in the following year a French army again marched into Flanders and occupied Courtrai itself and Dixmude; once more the wretched land of Flanders was laid under contribution, and when the Governor of the Netherlands, the Marquess de Grana, marched across the French frontier, terrible reprisals were announced and Luxembourg was bombarded. The Emperor could not think of sending help: he was involved in a serious war with the Turks—Vienna was besieged in 1683. Brandenburg, in alliance with Denmark and Münster, now talked of maintaining the peace, the peace as understood by Louis XIV! Charles II, who had been proposed as umpire by Louis, acted as if aggrieved when Spain proved unwilling to submit the dispute to him, although he was secretly drawing money from Louis on condition that he should help him retain Luxembourg.

And the Republic?

In 1681 the Dutch statesmen had made a highly remarkable attempt at organising Europe against French aggression. Towards that end William III once more co-operated whole-heartedly not only with Fagel but also with Van Beuningen. The only opposition came from Friesland and Groningen, and it was in the end ignored by the States-General. So in October 1681 the Association Treaty with Sweden was concluded, to which it was hoped that all the other Christian powers would accede, and which aimed at maintaining the territorial situation created by the peace treaties of the last generation. Van Beuningen travelled to England to invite Charles II, and here at once disappointment began. Fine words were not wanting, but the Amsterdammer soon understood that deeds were not to be counted upon.

It was under far from favourable circumstances, therefore, that the Republic had to face the Luxembourg problem.

In 1682 Spain had immediately addressed a request to the
Republic for the aid of 8,000 men laid down by the Treaty of
1673. Compliance did not, according to the law of nations of
those days, necessarily mean war with France, but it was of
course a serious step. For William III, personally still deeply
offended by the 'reunion' of his principality of Orange, there
could be no doubt about the matter. The Amsterdammers and
the Frisians (the latter were not amenable to his influence on
account of the separate Stadholderate of Henry Casimir, who
was profoundly envious of his famous cousin) pointed to the
impossibility of effecting anything without England and
Brandenburg. William III, feeling bitter enough against those
two powers, yet maintained that the treaty should be honoured.
He persuaded the States to give a conditional promise, and that
proved effective: Louis' raising of the first blockade was the
result.

But next year came the invasion of Flanders, and Spain's
need became more pressing. The 8,000 men were now actually
sent, but Amsterdam obstinately opposed a proposal to take
16,000 new troops into service. As had been the case in 1650, it
was not the augmentation in itself, it was the policy they
believed it was to serve that moved the Amsterdam regents to
their attitude: they did not wish to be dragged into another war.
A Frisian deputy said to the Amsterdam Burgomaster, Witsen:

rotundis verbis: (that) war is being sought here (*in The Hague*) and a number of
courtiers, dining together, had shouted *vive la guerre* with tipsy voices.

The Prince heatedly disclaimed seeking or desiring war; but
that his policy must lead to it was difficult to deny. And the
international situation being as it was, the Amsterdammers
regarded this as really too reckless a line to take. Van Beuningen,
having come back from his English mission in open disagree-
ment with the Stadholder, but all the more a powerful man in
his native town, spoke most pessimistically (and rightly so)
about the prospects of English aid. That the alliance of Denmark, Brandenburg, and Münster for keeping the peace
implied a warning to the Republic could not be overlooked.
Relations with Brandenburg were somewhat endangered anyhow, for the Elector had begun interfering in the affairs of
East Friesland (Emden), where the Republic had kept a

garrison for almost a century and exercised an influence that had very much the appearance of a protectorate.

And now in November 1683, Louis, who even in these years of intoxicating pride of power did not disdain the weapon of moderation, announced, through his ambassador to the States, d'Avaux, that he would content himself with other places than Luxembourg—again an arrangement, it is true, that would have to be extorted from defenceless Spain. In the States of Holland Van Beuningen, speaking for Amsterdam, contended that, seeing the state of affairs in Europe, this proposal deserved preference above a provocative recruitment of troops. Whereupon His Highness, who attended the meeting, burst out:

that the Count d'Avaux could not have spoken differently, had he been present in person; that Van Beuningen might lose his head if everything were sharply investigated; that he, Prince of Orange, was as much interested in the country's welfare as was Amsterdam; that he would not allow himself to be tyrannised over by that town and much less dance to the tune set by Van Beuningen.

A 'visit'[1] followed, under the personal leadership of the Stadholder and with the Grand Pensionary as the chief spokesman, to persuade Amsterdam to join the rest of the States and to approve the recruitment. It was just as unwise a step as when the Prince's father had undertaken it in 1650, and, as had been the case then, it only led to an increase of bitterness on both sides. Spain, driven beyond the limits of patience, now declared war on France, but Amsterdam refused to allow itself to be dragged along in the policy of despair of an impotent ally. The town continued to set up a policy of its own over against that of the Stadholder. Feeling was inflamed still more when the Burgomasters of the town were observed to be continually consulting with the French ambassador.

It has now come to this (*so the Prince exclaimed at another meeting of the States of Holland*): shall we allow ourselves to be induced by Amsterdam to submit to France; which I mean to oppose as long as I can. . . . April will not perhaps have come before the street will be in an uproar and matters take on the shape they wore in 1672. Then it will appear who carry their heads more securely on their shoulders and which regents have and which have not acted in accordance with their oath and obligation. The Amsterdam Corporation is simply repeating what the French Ambassador has been telling them.

---

[1] See footnote on p. 16.

Amsterdam meanwhile, supported only by Schiedam, persisted for months in holding up the resolution for recruitment. When Fagel at last wanted to carry through a majority decision, Delft also ranged itself on the side of Amsterdam. In money matters outvoting had never been allowed. When the majority stuck to its intention, therefore, Amsterdam protested and declared that in no case would it contribute its share in the costs of the contemplated recruitment.

William III's vehemence with respect to Amsterdam

THE conflict became even more threatening when the Stadholder suddenly (in February 1684) laid before the assembly of the States of Holland a letter from d'Avaux to his master which had been intercepted in the Spanish Netherlands, deciphered, and now passed on to him by de Grana. In that letter d'Avaux reported on his conferences with the Amsterdammers.

Individual 'members' (towns and nobility) of the States had never been debarred from having intercourse with foreign diplomats, and if on this occasion remarks were made about it to the Amsterdammers, they answered by referring to negotiations sometimes conducted by high officials on their own initiative. The practice was after all inseparable from the constitution of the State, and if in the long run it was to prove to have a disintegrating effect—as was to appear only too clearly in the eighteenth century—both parties had on occasion applied it. One need but call to mind the negotiations of William II with Mazarin and the relations entertained by Downing. What the Amsterdammers now alluded to were the activities of Waldeck, who at that very time was performing for William III the thankless task of trying to unite the divided German princes against France; a man who, as the Amsterdammers saw it, 'abused' his field marshal's salary to 'seek war'. But William wanted to use the intercepted letter to overthrow the opposition against his policy and interpreted it as treason. Two Amsterdam delegates, Gerrit Hooft and the Pensionary Hop, were practically indicted by him, but he failed to carry the assembly along in these extreme courses. The papers of the Amsterdam deputation were sealed, it is true, but the two gentlemen could return to their town unhindered. There the governing circle were thrown into alarm. A coup similar to that of 1650 now seemed to be imminent in real earnest. But no more than on that occasion did the town government give way. While keeping its deputies from attending the meetings of the States, it vigorously protested against the treatment they had received. Abroad, a civil war was expected, and a break-up of the Republic.

William III's unbending and passionate personality again comes out sharply in this conflict. He is governed by one idea: that it is his mission at the head of the Republic to offer resistance to Louis XIV and to save both the European states system and Protestantism from 'a general monarchy and a general religion'. Misgivings, attempts at evading the issue, considerations concerning the smallness of the state compared to the power of France, he despised as so many manifestations of faint-heartedness. The miraculous escape of 1672 made him think that God had destined him for great things still to come.

But admiration for the truly heroic in his personality must not lead us to despise his opponents. The criticism from common sense and caution had its rights. Nor were those who exercised it either traitors nor cowards. The difference was not really one of principle, except perhaps that the regents did not like the citizenry to be stirred up by allusions to the danger of Protestantism; Hop, so it is told,

when a certain gentleman represented to him how dangerous it would be for religion too if they did not arm themselves in time against French ambition, answered: 'What, religion? Tut tut, religion!'

But as regards the Southern Netherlands, the Amsterdam leaders were no less convinced than were the Stadholder and the Grand Pensionary that its preservation was needed for the very life of the Northern Republic. They only considered the moment ill chosen for fighting it out. To an ambassador of the Grand Elector, now allied to France, who supported Amsterdam in its attitude, Van Beuningen tried to explain that the Prince had let his head be turned by the specious representations of the impotent Spaniards.

Not that (*so he added*) the Amsterdammers are so bereft of sense as to want to augment France's power and forge their own shackles. No two things could be more opposed than France's interest and the Republic's. But it was now the fashion to regard those who voted against an untimely and disastrous war as having been won over or bribed by France.

William III did indeed misjudge and underestimate his opponents. Thus it was that he and Fagel came to make that great mistake of thinking that a town like Amsterdam would be cowed by their methods of intimidation and that all this vehemence could be the way to get the Republic to face its dangers with a united and determined front. On the contrary what they brought about was that offended pride and party feeling came to strengthen the resistance of purely objective considerations. The Burgomasters of Amsterdam, who had the ice in the canals broken up out of fear of a surprise attack, could in this conflict count on their citizens as much as their predecessors had been able to do in the conflict with the Prince's father. Amsterdam pride was a sentiment not confined to the regents.

What would all the other towns in our country be worth (*so the Amsterdam interlocutor in a pamphlet 'conversation' exclaims*) if they had no share in our trade and all sorts of foreign and domestic wares! You (*so he addresses the man from The Hague*) may say what you like and you can readily consent to a recruitment of so many thousands of men, but who is to furnish the money? Is it not our widely-famed metropolis which will have to serve for that purpose like a fertile milch cow? Remember that we alone must contribute to the expenditure of the general country (*of the Union*) a larger quota than all the other towns of the province of Holland together and as much as one third of all that the seven provinces together have to raise.

And especially there manifested itself, just as under the preceding Stadholders so in these circumstances, a stirring of burgher aversion to the court nobility, who were represented by the other side, with the Captain-General himself, as naturally inclining to war.

Nothing is more deplorable (*so wrote another pamphleteer*) than that so many of the nobility, for which the state has annually to spend so many millions for so little, if any, service, dare to indulge in vituperation and abuse against the government of Amsterdam, and show so little respect to the merchant that it is intolerable. . . . And these are the men who in the times of Liberty (*meaning the 'Stadholderless' period, 1650–72*), before Liberty was fettered, were not sufficiently well off to keep a horse or a lackey at their own expense. . . . Look, these are the men, my faithful fellow citizens, who are now exhausting the country's finances and trying to reduce us to beggary.

In the whole of the province of Holland the Burgomasters of Amsterdam thus appeared to large numbers of its inhabitants as the mainstay of republican independence, threatened by the unquenchable lust for power of a Stadholder whom most of the other regents simply did not dare to resist. Yet there were other centres of resistance in the Republic, apart even from Groningen and Friesland, whose opposition in the States-General constituted a great stumbling-block to William III. In Zealand, Middelburg refused as obstinately as did Amsterdam in Holland to agree to the recruitment. A personal visit of the Stadholder had no effect, except that he forced the States to pass a resolution by a majority of their seven 'members' instead of waiting for unanimity to be achieved; but afterwards Zierikzee protested against this. Even in the provinces under 'government regulations'[1] there appeared great reluctance to follow the Stadholder's instructions.

The constitutional machinery of the Republic could only function when oiled by a spirit of readiness to parley and to give and take. Trying to force it, William brought it to a standstill. The States-General offered a spectacle of confusion such as had never been witnessed in the Stadholderless period. Time meanwhile was passing. The campaigning season had opened and the Republic was powerless. Luxembourg was taken by the French and the States of Holland came over to the Amsterdam standpoint that negotiations should be started with d'Avaux about a settlement at the expense of Spain. In the affair of the asserted high treason no legal proceedings were taken; the papers of the Amsterdam delegates were unsealed without having been examined. Louis meanwhile made a change of policy easier by contenting himself with a truce instead of a peace. In the States-General this policy was supported by Holland, Friesland, and Groningen; Overijsel, freeing itself from the Prince's authority, joined them, so that the three provinces which still followed his orders were outvoted. Spain had to agree to a truce on the basis of the surrender of Luxembourg; the Emperor associated himself with the arrangement, which meant that for the time being he gave up Strasbourg. It took another year before the French, after collecting the arrears of contribution, evacuated Courtrai and Dixmude.

The whole business had brought deep humiliation to the Prince.

It is all the fault of those scoundrels of Amsterdam.

Thus he wrote to Waldeck. But that it was much rather the fault of his own impatience appears from what followed. In the

[1] See above, p. 149.

European situation a change was taking place which caused the differences in the Republic automatically to vanish.

Immediately after their victory indeed, the Burgomasters of Amsterdam had evinced a desire to be reconciled to the Prince. They felt the truth of what their colleague, Witsen, cousin of the powerful Hudde, wrote from The Hague:

Everyone here is crying out that the Republic is lost as long as there are these dissensions.

But it was not reconciliation that William III desired. It was submission. He chose to have nothing more to do with Van Beuningen. At Utrecht, at Dort he used his Stadholderly rights to the full—according to many he exceeded them—to exclude from office the regents who had thwarted him. In the Dort case he had the support of the Court of Justice of Holland and of a group of regents in the town itself, whose leader, Teresteÿn van Halewijn, stood high in his favour. The conflict with Amsterdam flared up again for a moment over what that town considered to be the Prince's illegal actions at Dort. Amsterdam was thinking of pushing through a reduction of the army. But meanwhile the need for unity made itself felt more and more.

Persecution of the Huguenots; Reconciliation in the Republic

LOUIS XIV destroyed the whole effect of his diplomacy of moderation by his persecution of the Huguenots. In October 1685 this culminated in the Revocation of the Edict of Nantes. Already, from 1681 onwards, groups of fugitives had come and settled in the Republic. Everywhere they were encouraged to feel themselves at home. There was the strong feeling of community of faith, that is to say also of belonging to one and the same European party. There was moreover the practical view that these people, many of them well-to-do, manufacturers on a scale almost unknown in the Republic, and skilled in many profitable trades, might prove useful to the country's economic life; in Amsterdam and Haarlem, to name only these two towns, new branches of the textile industry sprang up. After the Revocation in a number of places French Reformed congregations were founded, which often merged with the old Walloon ones; 200 ministers of religion settled in the North, there were fifty French-speaking congregations to be found at the end of the influx. Everywhere these immigrants spread fear and hatred against their persecutor. At the same time, early in 1685, Charles II of England died and a Catholic mounted the throne. In the whole of Northern Europe these events roused among the Protestants a consciousness of danger. The religious motive, which from 1672 onwards had counted for so much in William III's policy of resistance to Louis XIV, now made itself more powerfully felt with others too. D'Avaux noticed at once that his relations with the Frisian delegates in the States-General were adversely affected. The attitude of the public in Friesland and Groningen was not without influence on their Stadholder Henry Casimir's decision to seek a reconciliation with the Prince of Orange; a formal treaty was concluded, in which Henry Casimir promised to do what lay in his power to make his provinces adopt the Prince's leadership in matters appertaining to foreign policy. Notably also the Grand Elector, deeply distressed by the threat to Protestantism, now sought a rapprochement with the Republic, which before he had threatened.

All this did not fail to produce its effect in Amsterdam. Just as before 1672, there was the added annoyance about French protectionism: the so-called tonnage dues that were levied in French ports on foreign ships injured Dutch trade considerably. Witsen initiated fresh attempts at reconciliation with the Stadholder; they were furthered by the circumstance that Van Beuningen was not in 1685 among the Burgomasters (soon after this he became a prey to religious mania and ceased to count for anything in politics). Naturally Amsterdam did not give up its independence in regard to foreign policy, as the Stadholder of Friesland had done, but 'harmony' was restored in a way that greatly benefited William III's prestige. There was now no longer any question of reducing the army.

3. ENGLAND DRAWN INTO THE ANTI-FRENCH ALLIANCE

WHILE the religious factor worked so strongly to unite the Protestant States and peoples in distrust and hostility against Louis, he at the same time, by his presumption and high-handed interpretations of international law, managed to antagonise his Catholic neighbours and even the Pope himself. His ambitions were for the moment directed more towards Germany, but there too the inclination to withstand him was growing, and nobody could doubt any longer that the Republic would be among his enemies when the hour came.

The most unpredictable factor in the situation was still England. As ever the Dutch East India Company was trying to brush aside all European competition in the Malay Archipelago (we shall relate the subjugation of Bantam in 1682 later), and it was only natural that this should have aroused annoyance in England. This again contributed to the decision taken by the States-General to start at last in earnest on the long neglected strengthening of the navy, even though Holland and Zealand had to bear the expense more exclusively than ever.

At the same time the private relations between the Prince of Orange and his father-in-law were in an extremely delicate state. It had been avowed now as between William and Mary that in the case of the succession becoming vacant she did not wish to have him beneath her as Prince Consort, but by her side as King. In England meanwhile, James's attempts at raising his fellow-religionists out of their seclusion were already causing his Protestant subjects to look out for the heirs across the Channel as deliverers. As conditions became more strained, the Prince himself began to cultivate his connections with the malcontents. This was the purpose for which in 1687 his Utrecht confidant Van Weede van Dijkvelt went over to England: Van Weede's credentials from the States-General were little more than outward form, in actual fact he was to sound the leading members of the English aristocracy on behalf of the Prince. Somewhat later Fagel himself acted as mouthpiece to proclaim to the English people what were the Prince's views on the burning question of the dispensation from restrictive ordinances with which James was benefiting Catholics and Dissenters and distressing the intolerant Established Church. Through Fagel the Prince reassured the Dissenters, with whom as a member of the Dutch Reformed Church he felt akin, but whom his marriage had made suspicious. Even the Catholics cannot have been disappointed when, in accordance with North-Netherland tradition, although holding out no hope of public employment, he could promise them free worship—and all this without alienating the Established Church, so badly harassed by the King. In June 1688 a son was born from James's second marriage, and the

English people saw a Catholic dynasty established. All the more eager acceptance did the rumour find that the child had been substituted. At that very time there also happened to be great excitement about the prosecution and acquittal of the seven bishops. A number of people of rank from all over the country now signed a petition to the Prince of Orange to come over with an army to help the nation rise against the King; it was handed to him (in great secrecy of course) on 16 July 1688.

For William III there could be no doubt: his hour had sounded, he must act. He was free from vain ambition, but the call to action ever found him ready. The opportunity was offered him to preserve the English people for Protestantism, and at the same time and above all to deliver it at long last from the dependence upon Louis XIV in which his uncle and father-in-law had kept it to the detriment of Europe.

But it was not a decision that lay with the Prince alone. The States-General were faced with a fateful choice. It was *their* fleet and *their* army that would be needed by the Stadholder-Captain-General to comply with the request of the English malcontents. Should they put them at his disposal for that purpose?

To approach the States-General directly with a proposal such as William III now had to make was not the way things were managed in the Republic. While already taking such preparatory measures as lay within his competence as Commander-in-Chief, he first had the Burgomasters of Amsterdam sounded, by Fagel, Dijkvelt, and Bentinck, the latter his most confidential friend. For a considerable time the Burgomasters evaded replying. They feared that the Catholic rulers, whose support was indispensable, would be put off by an undertaking which it would be so easy to represent as an attack on Catholicism. Nevertheless after a time Witsen expressed himself fairly favourably. Then—it was already September—James II's ambassador and d'Avaux directed a request to the States-General for an explanation of the preparations for war which their Captain-General was making. Not only did this joint step embarrass James, because he did not wish to appear as the protégé of Louis in the eyes of his people: the effect in the Republic too was the opposite of what had been intended. Instead of intimidating, it alarmed and provoked the States: so James was indeed Louis' man!

The threat caused quite a stir in public opinion and while the impression was still fresh, Fagel revealed the great plan to the States of Holland. His Highness, so he said, had decided

to come to the aid of the English nation for the preservation of their Reformed religion and of their liberties and laws; . . . His Highness therefore requested that the State (*that is, the Republic*) will lend a helping hand to their Highnesses (*that is, William and Mary*) in so righteous a cause, in which the State's interest is so deeply involved, and will assist with their troops and navy.

For the politicians there was much to be said for and much against the matter. Who would not wish to deliver England from its long servitude to France! As a result, so Fagel expressed it, that country would once again be able to do something for its friends, in particular for 'this State'. But what 'if the enterprise miscarried'? Was it possible to imagine a more alarming situation than to be involved in an English civil war and at the same time be exposed to Louis XIV's anger? But then, would it be possible to stand aside now that this civil war was not in any case to be prevented and James in case of victory must be expected to join Louis, while his defeat might result in a republic, which was not likely to prove an easy-going neighbour? In that same summer of 1688 the tension between France and the German States had also come to a head. The immediate occasion was a dispute about the election of an Archbishop for Cologne. It was to be foreseen that the Republic would not be able to keep out of a quarrel to be fought out so close to its frontiers. But, so urged Witsen, if we proceed to intervene, let us at least stipulate for conditions with the English people who need our help so badly.

But while the town corporations were deliberating, public opinion was unambiguously expressing itself in favour of the undertaking. Fear of France and zeal for the cause of Protestantism combined in men's minds. The ministers from the pulpits extolled the God-pleasing work.

At the end of September the States of Holland passed a resolution in favour of granting aid to the Prince, and some ten days later it was unanimously adopted by the States-General. Round about the same time Louis declared war on the Emperor, and there began a Franco-German war over the Cologne and the Palatinate questions. Could not the King have added force to his ambassador's threat and by directing his arms northward instead of eastward have compelled the Republic to let James be? Probably enough,—but actually Louis was not sorry to see his most formidable enemy start out on an adventure which he hoped would engross ·the attention of both England and the Republic for a long time. A calculation which failed, but which makes us realise that the States, in that late summer of 1688, when the outcome was still hidden from them as much as it was from Louis, did indeed need courage for their decision.

As matters fell out, William's boldest expectations were fulfilled. On 15 November he landed with his army at Torbay. James, deserted by everybody, failed to put up any serious resistance. In January 1689 he fled to France. William, in London, took the temporary government of England upon himself and summoned a Convention which, when William declined to act as Regent, on 23 February offered the royal dignity jointly to himself and his wife.

The news of this event was greeted with exuberant joy by the North Netherland people. But King William was still for a considerable time prevented by an accumulation of other cares from applying to the French danger that curb which people hoped his elevation would result in. Rather did the English Revolution open up a fresh period of severe trial for the Republic. War with France was now inevitable. In the long run the united efforts of the Naval Powers were to preserve the menaced Southern Netherlands; but it was to take nearly a generation.

g. THE DUTCH EAST INDIA COMPANY

1. EXPANSION OF ITS DOMINION IN THE MALAY ARCHIPELAGO

WE LAST considered the Dutch East India Company in the episode of the conquest of Ceylon and Malabar.[1] Cinnamon had tempted it to Ceylon, and pepper to Malabar. But Van Goens, who had driven the Company on step by step, now developed a policy differing sharply from that of thriftily enjoying the new trading possibilities. As Governor of Ceylon, and after 1672 (when his son succeeded him in that post) as Superintendent

---

[1] See above, p. 67.

of Ceylon and Coromandel, then as Director-General, this remarkable man fought for a grandiose plan of building up an Empire in which the Malay Archipelago, the centre of Coen's field of vision, would eventually lie on the periphery. Maetsuycker and his Council at Batavia were averse to the idea. Towards the end of his life (1671–81, he had been born in 1619) Van Goens was himself to rule at the Castle of Batavia, but the Directors who had appointed him were not sufficiently convinced to give him their full support.

'A colony of our people', that is what Van Goens wanted to make not only of Cochin[1] but particularly of Ceylon. 10 to 12,000 families from home he wanted to settle there. Strongly fortified and intensively cultivated, Ceylon would not only make the Company's fortune, but, much better and more centrally situated than Batavia, it was the natural capital for a trading power whose connections reached as far as Japan on the one hand and Persia on the other. To become master of the island Van Goens wanted to subject Rajah Singha, and while in Batavia the view prevailed that the latter's friendship was needed, and was sufficient, for the cinnamon picking, the unmanageable Governor went on to isolate the 'Emperor' in his mountains, infuriating him in the process. Van Goens was blamed for wasting huge sums on strengthening the fortresses of the harbour towns. It was also held against him that neither Ceylon nor Malabar yielded the profits he had predicted. The pearling proved disappointing, the pepper monopoly could hardly be enforced in so vast an area, split up among a number of independent princes. Van Goens naturally answered that his policy could not be fairly judged from results affected by the obstruction he had met with. With passionate conviction and proud eloquence he defended his views.

The task of a great and ambitious king, not of merchants who are only out for gain;

thus Pieter van Dam, the Company's able lawyer and fierce opponent of Van Goens, describes the latter's plans in his voluminous *Beschrijvinge van de Oost-Indische Compagnie* (*Description of the East India Company*; the work was meant for private circulation only, but has been published in our time).

[1] See above, p. 70.

Shall we conclude that Van Goens's view was that of the statesman as against his opponents' commercial programme? The statement would be an undue simplification. To me it seems that he was pursuing a plan which was bound to over-strain the already severely tested powers of the Company. Even though for the concern in whose service after all he was working, the standard of profit *must* prevail, the establishment of power was not, in spite of the costs it necessarily involved, rejected on principle. Maetsuycker, however, kept his eyes fixed on the Archipelago, where so much had already been done and so much still remained. However attractive Van Goens's ideas about settlements on Ceylon may sound, the reality was different. By the end of the century the island had come to weigh on the Company like 'a troublesome burden', the more difficult to bear because the unavoidable expansion in the Archipelago was also entailing heavy expenditure upon the Company.

There continual exertions had to be made to drive competitors out, and just as before, only more exclusively so, the method followed consisted in breaking up the native powers that still retained some independence.

The first important action taken was the complete subjugation of Macassar, the initial step towards which as we have seen[1] was taken in 1660. The execution of the treaty then concluded was far from following a smooth course. The great Portuguese merchant Vieira kept on inventing excuses for postponing his departure. The new Dutch 'factory' met with all sorts of opposition until in 1665 the officials, faced by worse eventualities, took ship for Batavia. The Sultan resumed his policy of hostile independence. In all the 'Eastern Quarters'—that is to say the islands round the Moluccan Sea—as far as Ternate and Tidore, he sought contact with the Company's more restive vassals. And yet his position was vulnerable enough, for his own vassals nearer by, particularly the Prince of Boni, Rajah Palakka, were so tired of his rule that they did not scruple to seek the aid of the Dutch. And when at the end of 1666 a fleet was sent from Batavia to settle matters in the Eastern Quarters once and for all, Palakka and many of his followers accompanied it, and the expedition found active support against Macassar on the spot, in Buton and Boni.

[1] See above, p. 72.

The commander of the expedition was Cornelis Speelman, who soon showed himself a second Van Goens. After cruising all round the Eastern island area in order to make the power of the Company felt, he finally, reinforced by an ever greater accession of native enemies of Macassar, came to grips with the central position. For weeks bitter fighting raged against successive fortifications. The alliance with Palakka and his 'Bugis' (inhabitants of Boni) presented problems of its own. As Speelman wrote to Batavia:

> The job has to be done by the Dutch military mainly. . . . The Bugis are reasonably reliable for the moment, but at the first reverse, especially when they haven't their bellies filled with food, this may change. Rajah (Palakka) himself is greatly concerned about this possibility, fearing that, unless we make a successful end of the business shortly, the bulk of his men may take themselves off and especially that there would be no holding them if they came to hear any ill tidings from the back country.

The mutual animosities of groups of natives added a quality of atrocity to the warfare. Speelman was less callous than Coen, and his sincerity must not be questioned when he asserts that his sentiment as a Christian was revolted by the Rajah of Buton's suggestion that 5,000 Macassar prisoners should be killed. But when he found he could not turn them over to either the Butonners or the Bugis and their numbers proved too large to sell them as slaves, he knew no other solution than to maroon them on an uninhabited island where he himself foresaw that they would wretchedly perish of hunger.

The so-called Boni Treaty, to which the Sultan of Macassar was finally forced to accede, not only obliged him to expel the Portuguese but also the English (the news of the Peace of Breda had not yet reached the Indies). The Company received the exclusive right to trade, all the native peoples too being strictly barred. And to provide for the eventuality that the Sultan might prove unmanageable in the future, his power was weakened by making him give up explicitly his rights to the neighbouring districts of Celebes. As early as 1669 an attempt was made to overthrow the settlement, but it only led to still more complete subjection. For a time, indeed, things looked very grim for Speelman and his troops. His small army was afflicted by sickness; but the Admiral carried on with inflexible strength of mind and inspired his men to almost superhuman efforts. In the end he received a complete surrender and proceeded in triumph

M

to Batavia with 'a large train of kings and other great ones'. In the presence of Governor-General Maetsuycker and before Admiral Speelman there was now enacted, amid stately ceremony, a scene of confessions of guilt and submission, followed by gracious forgiveness. The Dutch understood very well that this 'deep humiliation' must be a bitter experience for the Macassar lords, with their 'proud and obstinate character', and afterwards they did not stint civilities. But in any case the Boni Treaty now governed the situation. The Lords Seventeen praised Speelman and appointed him to the Council of India. At home these warlike feats and the personality of the new hero attracted great attention.

All the time, however, Macassar nobles who had left their subjugated fatherland were still preaching hatred and war against the white intruders. There was one power left after the fall of Macassar which might in the Archipelago form a point d'appui against Batavia, namely Bantam, to which place, it will be remembered, the English had withdrawn when their position at Batavia under Coen had become untenable.[1] On the other side of Batavia, in the central part of the island of Java, lay the realm of Mataram, whose ruler (the Susuhunan), Amangku-Rat, deeply impressed by the Company's display of power against Macassar, looked for strength in its support. A popular hero now rose against him, Taruno Djojo by name, who, with the eager support of Macassar exiles and the help of Bantam, pressed the Susuhunan so hard that the latter, in accordance with a treaty of 1646, called in the protection of the Company. As the ally of the greatest ruler on Java, therefore, the High Government, at the end of 1676, reluctantly embarked upon a war which was to carry it much further than had initially been intended, and which laid the foundations for direct authority by the Company over Central and East Java. Speelman, again entrusted with the conduct of the war, was more than the executive of that policy; he was its motive force. His powerful personality governed the scene in the Indies and he possessed what all the Dutch Empire-builders in those parts always needed: the knack and the courage to overrule the objections of the Directors. His policy followed the familiar trend. From his helpless protégé—all the more helpless because Amangku-Rat

[1] See Part One, p. 180.

investigating and suspending or sending back home, but behind his back the evil immediately sprang up again and he died in the middle of his task without having brought about any lasting improvement. If I point out that Dutch national history owes to the Company powerful and interesting personalities, that it developed special capacities and furthered the search after knowledge, I do not therefore overlook that at the same time it allowed to spring up (to its own detriment!) a system of fraudulent practices which lowered the moral tone of the whole of its system.

Generally speaking, the spirit of what was growing up there in the East in the way of a Dutch society—at bottom an unfree society of hierarchically-bound officials, diluted here and there with dependent free Burghers—was distressingly materialistic and gross. Making money, but also spending it in ostentatious display; taking pride in high rank in the Company's service, exciting the envy of less fortunate colleagues by profusion, gold parasols, carriages and four, numbers of slaves—these are the features characteristic of the way of life of the Dutch in the East. A state of affairs somewhat different from what had been in Coen's mind! He had not foreseen what a corrupting element slavery would prove. On the Banda islands, the nutmeg planters had become slave-owners on a large scale. Most of these estates were worked with some hundred slaves, dozens of whom at a time sometimes ran away to the mountains. But it was the domestic slaves who affected family life with a pervading influence. A contemporary gives a telling picture of what grew out of Dutch women and mothers under these unfamiliar circumstances.

These little women, generally speaking, both Dutch and half-castes, are most of them, especially at Batavia, so fond of finery, so proud, so wanton and frolicsome, that they hardly know for exuberance what follies to commit. They let themselves be served like princesses, some of them having numerous men and women slaves in their service, who have to attend to them night and day like watch-dogs and to look out for their slightest sign. They themselves are so lazy that they won't stir a finger for anything, nay they won't lift a straw from the floor even though it lay within their reach, but they will at once call one of their slaves to do it, and if these are not quick about it, they will scold them for a *pute rastade, pute de nègre,* or *fils de pute* or *fili di chachor*[1] and sometimes worse. And for the slightest mistake on the part of the slaves they have them tied to a pole or on a ladder and beaten and whipped with

---

[1] Note the Portuguese terms: *puta* = whore; *cachorra* = bitch.

split canes cutting their naked bodies so that the blood will run and the flesh
be rent to pieces, which they then have rubbed with mixed pepper and salt
that the loose flesh may not come to rot or stink. . . . These East-Indian
women . . . especially those that were born out there, are unable, or speaking
frankly they are too lazy, to raise their own children, but they leave them,
almost as soon as they are born, to the care of a black nurse or slave-whore, or
of one of their inferior slaves, who will nurse and look after them, so that the
white mothers have little to do with their own children. The result is that the
children prefer to be with their black nurse and with the slaves generally than
with their parents, and have taken on the manners and ways of thinking of
those who have really educated them. In fact they speak Malabar, Singhalese,
Bengal and Tiolese, or bastard Portuguese, as well as the slaves do themselves, and when they come to maturity they can hardly utter an honest
Dutch word, much less speak Dutch fluently and decently, but mix it up
with grating Tiolese or bastard Portuguese language.

We saw above how Van Goens warned against this language
danger at the Cape,[1] even though the Dutch there had settled
upon virgin soil, where no Portuguese occupation or penetration
had preceded them, and where it was only the slaves from the
Indies who introduced Portuguese or a mixed Portuguese-
Malay language. The men at the top were well aware that for
preserving national sentiment and prestige in the eyes of the
subjugated populations the maintenance of Dutch was essential.
That is why by the third quarter of the century various schools
had been started at Batavia where the young people were
grounded 'in Dutch literacy, morals, and religion'. Not everybody, however, instinctively considered the babbling of
Portuguese as an unworthy habit, as did the observer just
quoted. The powers of resistance of the large majority were
none too great. Very, very slowly the Portuguese influence
receded before ever fresh waves of the Dutch influx. In Ceylon
it was rooted more deeply than the new conquerors could
ever reach. It was no different on the Malabar coast; Cochin
was a Portuguese town and remained so. But even in Batavia
for generations it was considered necessary to have sermons
preached in Portuguese.

There was besides the language yet another means of binding
and building, the importance of which was clearly recognised
by the leading men—religion. But again, in spite of all protestations, heartfelt ardour was lacking here too. The influence of
'our ministers', on whom Van Goens counted for making
'popery' gradually disappear,[2] did not in actual practice go very

[1] See above, p. 65.   [2] See above, p. 72.

teachers to evangelise the East. Actually there were at one point of time (1681), not counting the 'comforters of the sick', no more than thirty-five ministers in the entire vast territory of the Company, and these had first and foremost to attend to the ordinary pastoral work among their compatriots and the native Christians in the Moluccas and elsewhere. The Company paid their salaries. There was never any serious question of a plan for collecting money from the faithful in the Netherlands for the more vigorous conduct of missionary work properly so called.

The ministers never exercised any considerable influence upon the servants of the Company. They were too much a part of the official machinery. They did not as a rule dare utter protests against the higher officials' sins. Many of them were wordlings themselves. And yet I have had occasion to mention various names from which it appears that there were some among them who represented a higher state of culture. Ther were but few who sincerely exerted themselves to penetrate into Asiatic life or thought, as did Rogerius; but many, all through the period, learnt the native languages, in India and Ceylon as well as in the Archipelago.

H. SOCIETY AND CULTURAL LIFE

THE story of the political activities and overseas adventures of the Netherlandish people—and at that period this could only mean almost exclusively the North-Netherlandish people—has long engaged our attention. Impressive as was the spectacle these offered, we should be missing the deepest essence of the life of that generation if we did not investigate, more deliberately than was possible in immediate connection with those events, what cultural and social treasures it defended with such perseverance now against the English, now the French; what it contributed to the world; what inspired it in its existence so often disturbed by war. We shall soon come across a strange phenomenon. Halfway through this period, long before political energy had spent itself—for even at the end of it the State once more prepared itself for an enormous effort—fecundity in the domains of art and literature seems to become exhausted. In Flanders and Brabant cultural impotence corresponds to the uninspiring political circumstances, but in the North we are struck by a discrepancy. Strangest of all is it to note the supineness of Dutch culture as well as Dutch social life in the face of that superior power of France against which politically the nation held out so firmly.

But to confine our survey to art and literature and social life would mean being very incomplete. When we first turn to social conditions and religious life we shall find enough that is distinctive, enough of spiritual riches and originality, to prove the independence of Dutch society and culture. Yet there perhaps lie, at the same time, some of the causes of that withering of the artistic and literary creativity which but a short while before had seemed so full of vigour.

I. THE DUTCH REGENT CLASS

I SHALL discuss economic relations only in so far as the Netherlandish people or parts of it manifest themselves in peculiar or significant ways, or were deeply affected by them. A good deal of course could be mentioned in the way of changes and of ups and downs for the period we are now discussing. The wars and the tariff policies of other countries keep trade and export in a continual state of flux. In the Southern Netherlands economic life is languishing more than ever under the influence of the French invasions and of Colbert's protectionist policy. Nevertheless the picture remains essentially the same. In the Netherlands as a whole it is still Holland that strikes the attention as the province of the flourishing trading towns. Industry has not been able to keep up with the development of trade. Not until the end of this period do Huguenot refugees introduce industries of a clearly capitalistic character for the sake of which guild restrictions at Amsterdam and elsewhere are suspended.

Altogether there is an increase in prosperity, comfort, and luxury. The expansive energy of the first half of the century has calmed down, wealth becomes older and more dignified. Gentlemen's town mansions have become statelier, country residences become more numerous and have a more aristocratic air. Strangers visit them, and notes are made in diaries about good Orangist and like the most ardent legitimist hail the Restoration of Charles II and abhor Cromwell, while at the same time, in tones that one will not come across in French or German writers of that period, ascribing the never-ending wars to

> . . . a gang of crowned fools,
> Who cry nothing but fire and blood, and destruction.

Through family ties, through interests and community of thinking, the oligarchy was much more deeply rooted in that society than is often represented. The events of 1672 are instructive in that respect. The burgher movement is a manifestation of a great deal of irritation and vague aspirations. But even though it could force the régime to give itself an outstanding head once more, it did not for a moment in any essential way jeopardise the local supremacy of regent rule. But at the same time this close inter-connectedness with a wider class made the oligarchy very sensitive to criticism and in general to public opinion, which used to express itself with what to foreigners appeared a surprising amount of freedom. Indeed the regents always justified their rule by emphatic protestations that its aim was the promotion of the general welfare.

And when one studies the actual practice of the régime and compares it with the conditions prevailing in the surrounding countries there is certainly much to appreciate. The regents' achievement in the sphere of general government has been noticed above. Never had the Republic been so powerful or enjoyed such prestige as at various times under De Witt. And as regards the management of provincial affairs, there were so far no signs of deterioration. On the whole the regents acted with a sense of responsibility in their posts, which, in accordance with the system, they held in turn. The elimination by the Revolt of the ruler's central power and its supervising effect had its great disadvantages, and this was especially noticeable in the administration of justice. The provincial Courts could not exert much authority over the sovereign town governments, and we have seen how the latter sometimes permitted themselves action of an absolutely arbitrary character with respect to their citizens. And yet on the whole the Aldermen's Courts did their work seriously and with discernment. The best picture of what that administration of justice meant in practice can be gathered from

N

the notes of the Amsterdam alderman, Bontemantel, which indeed introduce us into the whole of the political life of his town. True, there are an uncertainty regarding legal norms and a confusion of personal and public interests which astound and even appal the modern reader. But one should not measure the conditions of those days by our own more stereotyped practice. Whoever is able to judge historically will see that in the class of which Bontemantel was a not very distinguished but an industrious and useful member there existed, along with a good deal of group and personal self-interest, a strong sense of public duty. It is worth while to hear on this subject Sir William Temple, who wrote down the impressions he had received during his ambassadorship in The Hague at the moment when the Republic seemed to be going to pieces in the disaster of 1672. In order to understand him one should remember that the history of an entire generation in England had been dominated by the unwillingness of Parliament (no more initiated in State affairs through responsibility than were the States Assemblies of the Southern Netherlands) to furnish money to a government it distrusted and whose servants it saw acquire fortunes in office. To Temple's mind the population of the Republic suffered 'the most cruel hardship and variety of taxes that was ever known under any government' with exemplary patience, and here is his explanation:

but all this, whilst the way to office and authority lies through those qualities which acquire the general esteem of the people; whilst no man is exempted from the danger and current of laws; whilst soldiers are confined to frontier garrisons (the guard of inland or trading towns being left to the burghers themselves); and whilst no great riches are seen to enter by public payments into private purses, either to raise families, or to feed the prodigal expenses of vain, extravagant, and luxurious men—all public monies are applied to the safety, greatness, or honour of the State, and the Magistrates themselves bear an equal share in all the burdens they impose.

The sober style of living observed by De Witt, the powerful statesman, or De Ruyter, the renowned naval hero, was unique in the world of that time. A papal nuncio was struck by the modest state in which the Governor of the Spanish Netherlands, the Conde de Monterey, lived in 1676, during the blackest days of the war with France:

I believe he does this to win the hearts of the people, who, burdened to the utmost limits, will bear the charges more readily when they are given no

It was fortunate for the future of the Dutch people that the real power in the North Netherlandish State rested with a broader, less easily denationalised class.

Signs of Oligarchic Degeneration

BUT the picture of the Dutch regent class as I have sketched it so far gives too flattering an impression, because it is incomplete. It is not untrue to life, and the additions it needs cannot touch the essence; but I already hinted that the reality showed ugly shadows, and they too must be put in. An oligarchy, a government made up of a closed body of a few, can for a time produce great power and true idealism. But, as I have observed above, it is exposed continually to the danger of a progressive narrowing of its ranks, which will in the long run squeeze out its political capacity and imagination. The theory of the ancient charters to which every regent on entering upon his functions took an oath, the theory of a government of the best men, chosen for their fitness, not by the people it is true, but certainly for the people's good, was still professed, while in reality a family-government, a clique, was being formed; and to 'the subjects' no other function was left than obedience, no higher virtue than that of 'quietness' or 'submissiveness'. It must again be said that in this development other provinces led the way, particularly Zealand and Friesland, but ominous signs were unmistakable in Holland as well.

In Zealand the notorious 'contracts of correspondence' were already flourishing, those formal agreements made by groups of regents to divide among themselves the municipal posts, or the provincial posts that were left to be filled by the towns in rotation. The actual purpose was at times—and this became more and more the true significance—to exclude a minority, so that each member's share in the spoils should be the greater. For many families government had by now become a career. They had retired from business, their sons went to the University to take a law degree. The emoluments of office were not on the whole excessive, although some posts were 'fatter' than others; in Zealand the coveted bailiwicks in rural districts were extremely numerous and, particularly for small town regents, the offices, whether great or small, had become a matter of vital importance, and 'sitting still' meant having to reduce. But in the contracts (although carefully kept secret) the justification regularly advanced was: the promotion of order and harmony.

Since it is highly necessary and pleasing to God that public quiet should be promoted and everything directed in such a way as to bar all *brigues*, intriguing for office, and evil practices (by which the commonweal is greatly disturbed, damaged and set back) and on the contrary to maintain peace, friendship and mutual correspondence by devising and establishing a firm footing on which this town may be governed by honest persons suitable and qualified for office, to the benefit of the country's untroubled harmony in general and of the inhabitants of this town in particular. . . .

Such was the hypocritical preamble of an 'alliance' that was concluded in 1652 between two groups of Zierikzee regents, to which excluded gentlemen could be admitted only by a unanimous vote of the 'friends'; but it did not in fact prevent violent quarrels from occurring. The passage was quoted above in which Ulricus Huber pointed out so strikingly how the Frisian oligarchs violated the general interest by bartering public offices as if they were private property. Public opinion was very emphatic on this point, hence the secrecy as well as the hypocrisy on the part of the intriguers—but the evil custom spread none the less. In fact the word 'hypocritical' should not, perhaps, be used too unreservedly. When unbridled, the intriguing for office could blind the contestants completely to the public interest (the Lady Van Amerongen's complaint in December 1672 will be remembered[1]). The seemingly ineradicable nature of the evil made it possible to regard the contracts as a means of at least preserving peace among the regents, thus increasing their capacity for taking decisions on larger issues. But that the method was in itself objectionable and in its own way undermined the public spirit of the regents remains a fact for all that.

There do not seem to have been any formal contracts in Holland before 1672. The intrigues about which Bontemantel tells us in such detail were not wholly devoid of political intentions; on the contrary, the conflict round Valckenier between 1666 and 1672 was at bottom concerned with the great questions: for or against De Witt; libertinist or reformed. But they were accompanied by calculations and 'arrangements', votes were won by promises of Directors' posts in the East India Company or other advantageous appointments, nephews

[1] See above, p. 120.

were roped in to strengthen a party, opponents silenced with threats—in short the means were of such a nature that one might almost come to regard the contracts, the 'harmonies', the 'drafts of unity', the *instrumenta pacis*', as the beneficial solution for which their authors so unctuously passed them off. One need but lay the accents a little differently, and from Bontemantel's story the struggle among the cliques in the Town Council will appear as intended to secure offices quite as much as to uphold the principles of 'Freedom'.

Indeed that impressive word was sometimes scoffed at by outsiders. Thus the Hague lawyer, Van der Goes, a Catholic, wrote to his brother in 1672, just before the fall of the régime, after mentioning the bestowal of companies on captains who did not come up to requirements ('that is, on relatives'):

> Not long ago the son of the Secretary to the Council of State, eight years of age, was given a receivership in the Meiery of 's Hertogenbosch, carrying a salary of 1,200 guilders. You will now see how stupid are the commonalty and what is the effect of Freedom. The duties of the office will be fulfilled until his twentieth year by somebody else, who will get the emoluments (*that is to say, who would have to be content with the levies and bribes going with the office*). So now the stupid ask: Why then give a salary?

The officers' posts in question were in the gift of the States of Holland; the receivership was a Generality office, but Holland co-operated in this favouring of a regent's child. That not everyone in Holland had such complete confidence in the financial administration of his own States, as was asserted by Temple, appears from the grumblings of Jan Zoet on the occasion of the 200th penny raised in connection with the States' intervention in the Northern War:

> Peace, farmer, give and be silent. The gentlemen must live.
> Carriages are expensive, and the more heavily the burgher
> (Note this well) is taxed, the better will the town fare!...

Zoet, peculiar among the 'freethinkers' on account of his Orangist sentiments, was altogether too odd a figure for us to count him as typical. But listen to Aitzema:

> 'Orangists', 'States' friends'? (*he says somewhere*). Let us have a good laugh: I can only see lovers of self.

The great chronicler loved to affect a cynical scepticism and his utterances should not be taken as objective observations. When he derides the attempts at a clean-up on the part of the

Grand Assembly: 'They want to wash the hide without wetting it', he is being definitely unfair: those attempts did prove that the true view of the regents' task still held sway over men's minds. Nevertheless, the sketch with which he continues has an unmistakable air of being true to life:

> Decent people now don't mind indulging in reflections like the following: 'I must help my children into offices while I live. *Here* I haven't much opportunity for advancing my children. There are few vacancies. There may be gaping, but it does not bite. I must go and live where there are more posts going'. Just as if it had been written that none but these or those families should govern! . . . And if they were only content with one office! As a rule they get too much, but think it too little. This must in course of time create an impatient citizenry.

Dissatisfaction was indeed in the air. Orangist as well as Church sentiment fed it. In 1672 it burst forth against the System of Freedom with hurricane force.

We have seen how in that crisis many of the town gentlemen fell miserably short of the ideal conception, held by the best of them, of their duty and dignity. De Witt himself, Van Beuningen, Van Beverning, and quite a number of others, bore out this conception by their deeds. Three sons of Amsterdam patricians went to serve on the fleet, each of them at the head of a number of sailors recruited and paid by themselves. Others again assumed command of Companies of *Waardgelders*. But as against this the defeatists should be remembered, who in their fear and alarm pushed through Pieter de Groot's mission, and who shortly after panicked quite as much before the fury of their own people. The satirical portrait, too, drawn by the political opponents of the bumptious town boss, thinking of nothing but his own interests and revealing the abject depth of his hateful pettiness and cowardice in its nakedness when dealing with national affairs, was not untrue to reality.

The Government under William III

IT IS one of the saddest disappointments presented by the history of the Republic when we see how the tremendous popular rebellion against the oligarchy brought about by the disaster of 1672 did not lead to a reform of its most objectionable peculiarities. On the contrary, with William III's régime a lowering of its spirit sets in. The regents' seizure of undivided power in 1650

understand *honest man*, then the prophecy of the young men[1] who observed him in his wild Paris days was not fulfilled; but *a man of note* Odijck *had* become: his house in The Hague was a society centre, and William III remained wilfully blind to the practices by which his representative in Zealand obtained the money to live in so high a state. No more than a year after the prohibition of 1673 Odijck put his name to a contract concluded by some Flushing party leaders (Dirk Buysero, son of the Prince's Greffier, was one of them and owed to it his appointment as a member of the Admiralty of the Maas), a contract that could easily hold its own with the one of Messrs. Groeninx mentioned above. Thereupon, in 1676, all the 'well-intentioned' regents of the province concluded, among themselves and with Odijck, a correspondence ('the honour of God' and 'the service of His Highness the Prince of Orange' being their professed aim), in which they promised Odijck to help continue him 'in all his dignities' in the event of the Prince's decease. Revealing, too, is a contract of 1684, concluded at Odijck's house in The Hague by two gentlemen (this time from Zierikzee), leaders of two up till that time opposing cliques, with each other and with him; they had just been with His Highness at Soestdijk, and it was at the latter's 'serious desire and recommendation' that the renewal of the correspondence was agreed upon. This document opens with the remark that nothing so commonly disturbs concord as divergent interests regarding offices, and therefore

we contracting parties undertake not only to maintain each other in those offices that we at this moment fill or shall fill in future, but also to favour each other's families, children and friends and help them obtain whatever is possible; promising to help in the promotion of the children not only in their parents' lifetime but also after their demise.

Hypocrisy can here no longer be imputed. Offices are unblushingly represented as family property!

In the three provinces under 'government regulations' the situation was still less edifying, and even now, in spite of the Rotterdam scandals, and of the subjection of some other towns and of the nobility and the high Courts of Justice to the Stadholder's arbitrary orders, Holland still distinguished itself by a loftier conception of the regents' dignity and duty. That was chiefly owing to the independence which the Amsterdam

[1] See above, p. 195.

Burgomasters had been able to retain. There, under Van
Beuningen, and, after his fall, under Witsen and Hudde, some-
thing of the pride and the public spirit, which had been the best
product of the System of Freedom, still lived on. The anti-
Orangist tendency characterising that attitude of mind some-
times, it is true, assumed very unpleasant features. De Witt's
Deductie, De la Court's and Uytenhaghe de Mist's writings,
ushered in an entire literature to which the experiences with
William's régime added an especial bitterness. The whole
Orange tradition was systematically maligned.

> Ever remember, oh Lion of Holland, the year Nineteen!

And hammering in unpleasant memories was not all. Worse
than the slandering of Oldenbarnevelt in the old days was the
way in which the Republicans now systematically distorted
everything the Princes of Orange had ever done. The death of
William the Silent was described as a happy event, because
otherwise he would have been proclaimed Count. The disasters
of 1672 were the fault of William III, who should have made a
stand on the river IJsel. And so on. During the next century the
whole of this historical system can be seen obtaining ever wider
authority. But meanwhile, although popular enthusiasm for
Orange had cooled considerably after the disappointment of
democratic aspirations and under the bad impression made by
the scandals of correspondences and corruption, any real
confidence between the citizenry and the oligarchy was equally
unattainable.

All too often States party regents answered criticism levelled
at them from below with scornful disdain and admonitions to
obedience. If they wanted to keep the clergy under control, it
was not only in order to safeguard spiritual freedom against
them, but because they feared them as possible leaders of the
commonalty against themselves. Characteristic are the satirical
utterances elicited by the attempt to introduce fresh blood into
the Town Council at Amsterdam when the Prince came to
'change the government'.

> Here's wonder, here is news! John Nobody plays the master.
> A lime-burner or a cashier would fain be an alderman.
> Ambitious shopkeepers now will forge laws.
> A needy broker is out to establish himself in office.
> And every man shouts: "Tis for the Prince'.

The isolation of the regent class continued to grow also in the towns that had managed to remain independent, and the regents' whole position was too seriously undermined for Amsterdam to be able to arrest the deterioration of public life in the Republic. As a matter of fact the entire civilisation of the Northern Netherlands is marked by a certain loss of character in the last quarter of the century. Sober simplicity became puffed-up pomposity, and the counterpart to the heavy wigs aped from the French is to be found in the unnaturally stilted style of the literature and official language of the day. And underneath these trappings widespread materialism made itself felt. In religious life we shall see side by side with a certain stiffening a good deal of spiritual unrest manifesting itself.

The picture painted in his diary of Hague political and court life by Constantine Huygens the younger, secretary to the Prince as his father had been before him to the Prince's father and grandfather, is indeed far from edifying. It would undoubtedly be unwise to derive an estimate of William III and some of his best collaborators and servants (such as the Grand Pensionaries Fagel and Heinsius, or Bentinck and Dyckvelt) from the notes of a man who had obviously no eye for the wider perspectives of the politics of his day. The Stadholder and those few supporters of his lived in accordance with a genuine political faith, and so there was undoubtedly an inspiring idea behind the political life of the State as such. The pity is only that they were unable to link it up more efficaciously with what was after all one of the most distinguishing features of North Netherland society—the attachment of all groups to their particular rights, the free co-operation in the government of a numerous group of regents not too far removed from their citizens. Not that these characteristics could be obliterated or all of a sudden suppressed. They remained strong enough to lend an ideological basis to the resistance against the most powerful absolutism of that age. Freedom as against unlimited State authority—that was and continued to be the contrast between the Republic and France, and of that conception the regent class was and remained the bearer. But at the same time that much-vaunted Dutch freedom was unmistakably in a bad way—certainly not solely owing to the Stadholderly dictatorship now imposed upon it—and this is one factor that worked adversely on cultural life as a whole.

2. RELIGION

WHEN I spoke of spiritual riches and originality in religious life, I was thinking of religious life in its widest sense. I did not mean, as we heard the South Holland Synod assert above,[1] that the Reformed religion was the palladium which God had deposited in the State to ensure its preservation; although through both its spirit and its organisation the Reformed Church was undoubtedly a State-preserving element of the greatest importance. Freedom was one slogan employed against Louis XIV, but religion was another, perhaps a more powerful one, and it was notably the slogan voiced by the Reformed Church. Yet that church was far from being in sole possession of the country's religious life. It did continually expand its domain, but, even apart from Catholicism, Protestant sects, solitary eccentrics, and 'freethinkers' obstinately challenged its monopolist claim. That too is what I mean by religious life. I mean the struggle and the multiformity, I mean the searching and the seething. Thereby Dutch society afforded no less eloquent a testimony to its peculiarity and vitality.

Jesuits and Jansenists in the Flemish Netherlands

THIS holds good even for the history of Catholicism. At a first glance one does not *see* Catholicism in the North, and one gets the impression that North and South have lost all contact. But if one penetrates into the hidden depths in which the history of Northern Catholicism is enacted, one finds a full life there too, which was not, it is true, one with the religious development in the South, but which was yet closely and indissolubly linked up with it.

It is curious to observe how the Counter-Reformation, dreaming of a system of grandiose unity, should yet at the very moment of its triumph clash with the irrepressible diversity of the human mind. For indeed the central fact of the history of Catholicism at this time, in the Spanish provinces as well as under the States-General, is the dogged resistance put up against every attempt at suppression of the Jansenist deviation (whose origins I mentioned above).

[1] See p. 151.

Something remained unsatisfied in men's minds by that brilliance and that success, of which the Jesuits were the chief exponents. Round the memory of Jansenius an opposition was formed against what to many serious spirits and conscientious souls seemed superficial and frivolous in the system by means of which Rome had recovered by storm so large a part of the world. Mariolatry and the fraternities devoted to it, the newly proclaimed dogma of Mary's immaculate conception, the ostentatious splendour of church decoration, the interdiction to the laity of Bible reading—towards all these matters part of the secular clergy maintained the greatest reserve. The main point where all the discussions converged was that of the cure of souls in confession. In their zeal to save mankind, the Jesuits stressed the fact that Christ had died for all men, and they wished to distribute grace liberally. They saw spiritual pride as the motive of those who, valuing their personal experience of religion above all things, in consequence wanted stricter standards to be applied. The Archbishop of Mechlin (still Boonen), on the contrary, regarded the Jesuit mentality as charged with fearful consequences. With the support of his suffragans in Bruges, Ypres, and Ghent he persisted in refusing to publish the papal bull by which Jansenius' *Augustinus* had been condemned as early as 1642. At the end of 1648 he turned to Philip IV for assistance.

The insolence with which they (*the Jesuits*) go about their matters is so excessive and the liberty they arrogate to themselves in order to introduce new and pernicious doctrines, particularly in cases of conscience and the cure of souls, so great; and they are on the other hand so deficient in the respect due to prelates and superiors, that I am beginning to believe my predecessor Matthias Hovius, in his day the pattern of bishops, was right in predicting as he did to me shortly before his death: that I should live to see the Jesuits bringing the Church into trouble.

But in appealing to the King the Archbishop had come to the wrong address. It was out of the question for Philip to go counter to his representative, the Archduke Leopold William, who (so Boonen complained) favoured the Jesuits. How little freedom was left to the Southern Netherlands in their cultural and social development here appears anew. The Jesuits were relying on Italy and Spain, on the powers based on which Parma had forcibly withdrawn Flanders and Brabant from Protestantism and from spiritual intercourse with their Northern brethren. It is from there that the Jesuits now received assistance to suppress those old Netherlands tendencies so strongly represented in the clergy of both South and North. In 1651, when the Governor and the Internuncio, using all means of pressure, have still failed to persuade the Archbishop, the Pope summons him to Rome. He refuses on the plea of his health, on the strength of the old Netherland privilege *de non evocando;* the Council of Brabant, acting directly against the King's Governor, backs him on the latter point. Innocent X then issues an interdict against him. By order of the Internuncio a notice is posted up at the church of St. Gudula in Brussels to the effect that the Archbishop shall abstain from all church services. The Council of Brabant has it pulled down and promises an award to informers should anybody post it up again. Leopold William annuls the Council's notice. But now the old Archbishop and the last remaining of the recalcitrant Bishops (the bishop of Ghent, Antonie Triest) submit. After assurances and promises on their part, the interdict against them is lifted and the bull is at last promulgated.

What Boonen feared was that the declarations required by the bull would make impossible the promotion of those very ecclesiastics who to his mind were the most deserving, the most serious and the strictest. New forms of oath and condemnations were just being issued from Rome to bar any evasions. It is certain that in this way the higher ranks in the church were gradually occupied by adherents of Jesuitism, yet the other tendency was able to maintain its resistance for a considerable time, obstinately standing fast or using subterfuges as the case might require. It gave some relief when in 1668 a Pope of less actively anti-Jansenist sentiments, Clement IX, came to occupy the Holy See. How sharp the contrasts still were, and this on the capital issue itself, can be gathered from the clash between eight Ghent priests and the Jesuits of their town. A Jesuit had published a small book *Nieuw onderwijs voor de jonckheid om wel te biechten ende te communiceeren* (*New Teaching for the Young on how to Confess and to Communicate Properly*). There the priests to their indignation (and 'in our Dutch language' too!) found the doctrine expressed that

repentance inspired by nothing but the fear of hell or of such punishments as God may inflict, without even the slightest movement of an imperfect affection towards God (*typical Jansenist terminology*), is sufficient for obtaining justification and grace in the Sacrament of Penance.

Their protests against this pronouncement elicited the 'slanderous' reply that they were not shepherds for their flocks but wolves. Failing to obtain support from their Bishop, the priests turned to the Theological Faculty of Louvain and received a unanimous declaration to the effect that their view of the matter was the orthodox one, and even at Rome this was now acknowledged.

The same Contest among the North Netherland Catholics

JUST as in the preceding period, these relationships in the South Netherland Church were reproduced in the Northern Netherlands, and both the Dutch secular clergy, with their Jansenist leanings, and the Dutch Jesuits sought support in the Spanish provinces. Rovenius, the personal friend of Jansenius, was succeeded in 1651 as archbishop of Utrecht (by now a somewhat problematical title) by a man of quite different sentiments. De la Torre, born of a Spanish noble family, had withdrawn from the North after the disturbances in North Holland[1] and had thereupon been appointed by William Leopold as his Grand Almoner. No sooner had he been made Archbishop than, still at Brussels, he granted privileges to the Jesuits which caused their numbers to grow by leaps and bounds, to the profound alarm of the chapters of Haarlem and Utrecht. Neercassel, the man who was called to the archbishopric in 1661 after de la Torre's not very successful administration, this time in complete agreement with the wishes of the chapters, was on the contrary imbued with the Jansenist spirit: he was intimately connected, not so much with Brussels and the Jesuits, as with the Louvain faculty: Professor Gomarus Huygens was his particular friend. A book, *Bevestiging in 't geloof en troost in vervolging* (*Confirmation of Faith and Comfort in Persecution*), in which he pointed out to the faithful in the North the eternal profit which their exclusion from the soul-confusing temporary benefits of participation in the government might bring (a typically unworldly attitude of mind), was published in the South in 1670. He too had to withdraw to the Spanish Netherlands after his behaviour

[1] See above, p. 24.

at Utrecht in 1672 during the French occupation, and at Antwerp he now preached on mariolatry in a typically anti-Jesuit spirit. Later still, in 1683, there appeared at Emmerich his *Amor penitens*, one of the classic expositions of Jansenist thought, on which Jansenius' French disciples had been consulted. His relations with the French were always very close. From 1679 until his death in 1694 Antoine Arnauld himself lived at Brussels, with a short interruption at Delft. From 1685 onwards Pierre Quesnel lived there too, the man whose own chief work was to make the theological controversy with the Jesuits flare up again before the century was out. One should not over-estimate the influence of these French exiles, however. Neercassel did not need to learn his fundamental ideas from them: those they all found in Jansenius, and as regards the Jesuits, in his eyes they were exactly what they had been for Boonen: destroyers of souls and disturbers of the peace. During his lifetime the Jesuits were powerless to storm the position defended under his leadership by the chapters at Utrecht and Haarlem in the Louvain spirit entirely. Clement IX had been succeeded by Innocent XI, who was even less well-disposed towards the order. But the contrast was there, and in the following generation it was to lead to a crisis in both North and South, and to the destruction of the Netherlands variety of Catholicism.

The national Netherlands character of the resistance, in both North and South, against the Jesuit movement, which at bottom was un- or supra-national, drawing its strength from Southern Europe, becomes especially evident when attention is given to the fact that it was supported not only by the secular clergy, the chapters, the theologians from Louvain, but also by bodies such as the Council of Brabant, and that in the struggle it constantly appealed to old rights and customs—just as formerly the resistance against the centralising absolutism imposed from without had done. In that case, it is true, the lawyers had often supported the side of the King, and their anti-ultramontanism now can be seen as a way of championing the cause of the modern State as against papal presumption—the King's own cause indeed, as they often put it themselves. But the King and his Spaniards at Brussels, wholly under Jesuit influence, were not willing to look at matters in that light. This contrast, then, revived, in a class of men who had for many years been monarchic jurists above all else, both in the Louvain faculty and in the Councils, the feeling for national rights, or rather for particularist rights.

In the next generation the dispute was to become even more bitter, first under a violently anti-Jansenist Archbishop of Mechlin, de Precipiano (like Granvelle a Burgundian; he filled the primateship from 1689 to 1711), and then when Rome herself began to take determined action. The opposition was stiffened by Van Espen's juridical arguments, which were already adding lustre to the otherwise somewhat sleepy University of Louvain.

Reformed and 'Erring Spirits'

WE HAVE often had to concern ourselves with the Reformed Church in relating the fortunes of the people of the Northern Netherlands during these years. Her internal dissensions, and particularly her conflicts with the secular authority, have an immediate effect on the history of the State. Voetius and Lodenstein, Cocceius and Heidanus are public figures of moment.

The resistance offered by the Church to secular interference was always important, but her internal struggles did not in the end prove very fruitful for cultural life in general. Cocceianism lost itself in odd, fantastic interpretations of the Bible, while the Voetians on the other hand swore by the 'States translation', as if through that 'faithful rendering' the whole meaning of the Scriptures had been unambiguously rendered once and for all. A spirit of literalism became manifest, quite as unedifying as was the zeal for persecuting Papists, Dissenters, and 'erring spirits', animating the same men who so boldly and proudly defended their own spiritual freedom against secular presumption. Consistories, classes, and synods were continually engaged in examining questionable sentiments among their members and moreover kept on importuning town governments and States assemblies with requests to show a strong hand when heterodoxy was found among their own Reformed ministers or professors, or to resort at long last to measures against the Romish magistrates in rural districts, or to put an end to 'licentious printing'.

After 1672 they also frequently turned to William III, who responded only too readily by recommending vigorous measures. We saw something of this in the cases of Heidanus and of Momma-Van der Waeyen.[1] During his Stadholdership one 'case' followed another (and I am now referring particularly to cases of discipline within the Church). It is true that the threatening rupture between Cocceians and Voetians was averted by a compromise to which the Amsterdam government was able to persuade its ministers and which was imitated elsewhere. But great commotion was occasioned in Friesland, where William's cousin and enemy, Henry Casimir, had had Van der Waeyen called to the University of Franeker. Hardly had it died down when a fresh sensation was originated at that same University by Roëll's doctrine about the true significance of Christ's being the son of God. Even after the pen-and-ink controversy over this question between Roëll and Vitringa had been 'calmed down' by the States of Friesland, the Synods in other provinces decided to take care that such 'pernicious principles' should not penetrate into their resorts and that graduates from Franeker

should be very closely examined regarding these theses and not admitted to the public ministry unless they first affirmed that they reject with all sincerity and are determined to combat the aforesaid theses all and every one.

Dragging on through the whole of that period was the case of Koelman. In 1675 this man had received his dismissal as minister at Sluis from the States-General (rulers of the Generality lands in which the little town was situated) on account of his refusal to use the regulation forms for church ceremonies and to observe the holidays of the Church. Besides these personal and somewhat stiff-necked peculiarities, Koelman, a writer of pious and sometimes orthodox works, was a zealot for the freedom of the Church and for personal religious experience, entirely in the Utrecht manner. After his dismissal he tried, now here now there, to hold 'conventicles', Bible readings, and prayer-meetings, but everywhere the consistories and synods put the authorities on his track to have him expelled, until the protection of Van Beuningen secured him accommodation in Amsterdam. In 1691 (when Van Beuningen could no longer

[1] See above, p. 148.

help him) the consistory again managed to get him expelled and he ended his days in Utrecht.

The case of Balthasar Bekker went deeper. There the Church encountered in one of its own servants the rationalism which since Descartes had developed so powerfully. Even less than Descartes was Bekker minded to use that weapon against Church or religion: it was only superstition that he meant to attack. The Church nevertheless chose to consider herself the offended party. In 1674, at forty years of age, Bekker, having had enough of the difficulties raised over his catechismal writings, said farewell to his Franeker congregation, and in 1679 he became a minister at Amsterdam. Some years later, when comets spread fear of the wrath of God all over the country, he wrote his *Onderzoek van de betekeninge der kometen* (*Inquiry into the Meaning of Comets*). According to him it was not possible to divine God's intentions from such natural phenomena. When years ago that same view had been proclaimed by the Utrecht savants[1], it had filled Voetius with horror; lately it had also been put forward by the Huguenot refugee minister, Pierre Bayle. In 1691 Bekker produced a more original and important work with his *Betoverde Wereld* (*Bewitched World*), in which, on the strength of systematic research patiently carried on through a number of years, he combats the view that the devil or evil spirits play a role in human life. Witch-hunting had never caught on to any extent in the critical Northern Netherlands. Nevertheless epileptics and the insane were still popularly believed to be, in the most literal sense of the word, 'possessed'. Great was the excitement among Bekker's colleagues about his dismissal of this superstition, particularly about his explanations (often indeed forced) of awkward passages from the Bible. The North Holland Synod declared him deposed, although the Amsterdam government, without heeding this, continued paying him his salary right up to his death. The South Holland Synod found that the book

is cordially detested by all the classes (*district assemblies of ministers*) and by every one of their members individually, being full of offensive, detrimental and soul-destroying theses, going right against God's Holy Word and the formularies of Unity underwritten by all the ministers, bulging with horrible mockeries and disgraceful distortions of Holy Writ—

---

[1] See above, p. 115.

on which grounds the Synod decided to urge the competent authorities to prohibit the book (which as a matter of fact they never did) and to be on their guard against Bekker's apologists. In this connection the Synod made particular mention of a certain Ericus Walten, a pamphleteer by profession, who had been currently employed by William III's favourites. In 1694, at the request of the Synods, Walten was arrested and shut up in the Gevangenpoort by order of the Court of Holland; he was charged with blasphemy; William III gave his personal attention to the case, just as he had done in the case of Van Zuylen. Walten's sentence was delayed, but he was not released, and died in 1697 in prison.

It is infinitely easier to prohibit someone's books than to refute them.

Thus Bekker said pointedly enough in one of the memorials he published in his defence. And indeed it proved beyond the power of the Synods to stifle the new perception. The book attracted widespread attention; it was translated into French and German; and contributed a great deal to the cessation of witch-hunting in Germany. The part played by the Reformed Church in this affair does not redound to its credit.

No doubt it would be unfair to perceive in the Church nothing but literalism and zeal for persecution. I need but mention Lodenstein, and we are reminded of quite a different trend, of the ardent search for communion with God, in which the old leader, Voetius, also had his share. Lodenstein deplored the prosecution set on foot against Koelman, and never concealed his affinity with him. No more did the man who, after Lodenstein, best represented this Reformed mysticism, namely Willem à Brakel, a minister in Friesland until 1683, and later at Rotterdam, where in 1688 he came into conflict with the town government by taking exception to its presuming to cancel the call of a minister. In 1700 à Brakel, from the hand of whose father there is a publication bearing the characteristic title *De trappen des geestelijken levens* (*The Stages of Spiritual Life*), published a book on dogmatics and morality, called *Redelijke godsdienst* (*Rational Religion*), written so as to be understood by the layman. Throughout the whole of the eighteenth century this book was continually reprinted as the devotional book *par excellence.* Those who believe in the world, so we read there, can also live virtuously and love virtue. Yet:

> In the saintly there is something besides; and ask you what it is—It is *spirit*, it is *life.*

It remained a moot point whether in the atmosphere surrounding the State Church, bound as it was to its articles of confession, inclined to subtle disputations and to calling in the strong arm of the law, such life and spirit could flourish. One cannot avoid the impression that the Church was suffering from the consequences of the insurmountable inconsistency between the ideal and the real. According to the principle that had triumphed at Dort, it was to be a community of the elect, a Gideon's band, fighting the good fight for the great body of the 'nominal Christians'. But at the same time it wished to be the State Church, and through the privileges enjoyed by its members, it was indeed able by degrees to win over the majority of Catholics set adrift, of indifferent worldlings, and of waverers. But as a result its character imperceptibly and inevitably underwent a change.

The dry cerebral doctrinalism, by which the sermons of the time were often marked, is a sign of this. But it can still more clearly be seen in the fact that disciplinary jurisdiction over its members fell more and more into disuse. In the heroic early days this had been stubbornly defended when libertinist authorities had tried to curb it. It did indeed belong to the essential attributes of a Church which wanted to be a community of tried men of piety. But when that same Church came to be a State Church also, the secular power could not unconditionally allow it a right by means of which it could cut off what it regarded as rotten members not only of the Church, but, in effect, of the State as well. The way matters had now developed, with all respectable people members, but not for that reason intending to live differently from the way in which respectable people are accustomed to live anywhere in the world, excommunication following upon a public confession of guilt had simply become unthinkable in most congregations. Individual ministers at times complained bitterly about this state of affairs.

> It is clear that among the causes of our decay we must count the weakening and neglect of ecclesiastical discipline. (*So wrote a Leeuwarden minister in*

1669.) One has only to look through the old church registers, they will reproach us a thousandfold for our present remissness.

Lodenstein and Koelman too believed that the evil lay there, but that it was incurable and inseparable from the way in which the Church had been developing they would not admit.

There were some who gave up the Church, mostly for differences in doctrine it is true, but not without discouragement about the prevailing spirit contributing to their decision. A man of whom Voetius and Lodenstein had at first expected great things, the French pastor de Labadie, who had been invited to the Republic in 1666 (first via Utrecht to Middelburg), but who was soon deposed by his Walloon Synod for heterodoxy, came straight away to the conclusion that nothing could be hoped for from the Church. Voetius, Lodenstein, à Brakel, Koelman even, all deplored the course de Labadie adopted, the course of secession and group-formation. First in Amsterdam, then in Germany, and finally under the protection of the three sisters Aerssens van Sommelsdijk at Wiewerd in Friesland, he led a colony of 'God-seekers'. Anna Maria van Schuurman, a patrician lady renowned for her learning, left Voetius and Lodenstein in order to follow 'the man of God' not only to Middelburg, but in all his wanderings. How difficult it was to experience religion intensely and personally within the Church appears also from the tribulations of the Zealand minister Van Hattem, who was deposed in 1683 as 'a soul-tainting heretic'. Van Hattem (who was followed by many in his banishment) found all his happiness in sinking his whole personality in the merciful omnipotence of God, which after all had been glorified by the Synod of Dort.

The Labadists and Hattemists—by those names did they go—were orthodox believers who somehow came to find themselves outside the Church. There they found a bustle of groups and individuals seeking religious experience in many different ways, but agreeing in this that they regarded churches and confessions as human institutions which they held in little esteem, if they did not actually abhor them. They measured the reality of religious belief by different, much more personal, standards. Many in their sensitive individualism still allowed themselves to be loosely bound by Collegiantism.

This was a movement of 'free speaking' that had had its

origin at Rijnsburg (near Leyden) among the Remonstrants who had in 1619 been bereft of their minister. Camphuysen had spent the last years of his life there, without any attachment to the Remonstrant community, to the great annoyance of his one-time brethren. The young regent's son Van Beuningen came to live there in the forties to fortify himself with the religious conversations and exercises in that remarkable group. Shortly afterwards the movement found a new centre among the Baptists at Amsterdam. Its spiritual father there was a Zealander of good family, Adam Boreel, who wrote theological works in Latin and whose leading inspiration was the profound awareness of the deterioration of the churches: those who felt religion in their hearts could only gather together in 'a church hidden from the world', where nobody would rule over another with arbitrary formulas or commandments. A young and talented Baptist teacher, Galenus Abrahamsz., introduced the 'College' into his congregation (in the Meeting-hall of the Lamb) and thus brought in a crowd of recruits—but not without opposition on the part of the older Baptists, who wished to keep their religion pure in its historic forms just as much as did the Reformed. For years there raged what a pamphleteer called mockingly 'the War of the Lambs'. Galenus held his own, and in numerous other places the Baptists started to 'hold College' with believers of different backgrounds. Rotterdam particularly became an important centre. The poet Oudaen was a leading personality here, and the distinguished regent, Paets, an ardent Wittian, attended the meetings; his fellow-regent, Hartingveld, even renounced the world altogether, living solely for the faith.

On the whole the Collegiants were people of a certain education. Like the Labadists, and like yet another group under French leadership, that of Antoinette Bourignon, who had been resident in the Northern Netherlands since 1668, they were able to attract the upper middle class. In the fifties there also came a number of Quakers from England, who as a rule appealed to the lower classes, less by means of arguments, explanations, or reflections, than by sensational warnings and admonitions. There was something in the spiritual atmosphere that made men receptive to all such movements; right and left there were audiences to be found for quite different preachers again, calling

to penitence or prophesying the millenium. Was it disillusionment with the ever more doctrinal and intolerant churches? So
much is certain, that all those various seekers had one thing in
common: for all of them ecclesiastical unity meant spiritual
death.

> Never confide your soul and salvation to any priest,
> But by your own exertions move through the narrow gate.

This was the counsel of the Amsterdam publican, Jan Zoet,
who was at the same time an admirer of

> Galenus, who does not want to tie anybody to his views
> And readily confesses his own imperfections.

Real hatred against the ministers sometimes manifested itself
in those circles, and not only in the poetry of Zoet, sometimes
witty, but in the main boorish, gritty, and singular. All preaching and disputation was passionately rejected. Yet their cult of
toleration did not always safeguard the brothers from dissensions
among themselves. The very problem of the limits of toleration
occasioned a bitter quarrel among the Rotterdam Collegiants
when, in 1681, Jan Bredenburg, having been accused of
atheism by Frans Kuyper, a troublesome and unaccountable
man, defended himself by appealing to the principle of freedom
and the unlawfulness of censure. Also a question arose as to
whether toleration was to be extended to the Catholics. Oudaen
denied this, whereupon Bredenburg's friend Geel remarked:

> that it was a sad sight when an aged man, who had for fifty years been heard
> speaking of tolerance and love, now himself halted before the temple of love.

The spiritual ecstasy of the early years was not preserved in
its purity either. At that time the faithful had been used to pray
so 'ardently', 'gaspingly and sobbingly in broken words', that
they had fancied themselves 'drawn up almost into Heaven'.
Now that same Frans Kuyper uttered a warning that a great
deal of 'pretence' came into the matter, that people 'pressed
their bodies into stiff attitudes, moving their heads droning and
moaning out words the while' in order to act as if 'shattered'.
The plain living, the contempt for fine clothes and objects of art,
did not last either. Asselyn in a famous comedy sketches the
Collegiants as consummate hypocrites. But the figure of Luyken, whose 'conversion' caused him to write spiritual poetry
from about 1680 onwards, is there to show that the movement

could still inspire. And what signs of palpitating life are apparent in the very quarrelling, what personalities have come down to us from the beginning to the end of the movement, what excellent prose was written there without any literary intention! Those 'erring spirits' needed the protection of the secular power against the ministers, but in their contempt for the world they sometimes behaved to those in authority with an almost provocative pride. The Baptist tradition of ignoring society—their 'defencelessness' before everything—sometimes assumed almost tempestuous forms. When in 1662 by a strict edict the States of Friesland forbade all 'Socinians, Quakers, or Immersers' (so the Rijnsburgers were called because they had introduced baptism by immersion) to enter their province, a Quaker answered:

Alas, it is not your jail nor your gallows that will make God's faithful servants afraid to set foot in the province which you presumptuously call *your* province. For we know that it and all other provinces are the Lord's and that only He and no one else rules with an unlimited power.

Nothing was safe from the questioning and probing on the part of the anti-Church people. The institution of marriage was spared by some no more than was that of the sword. They sometimes make one feel how indispensable a social function was fulfilled by the severe restraint exercised by the Church. But so much is certain that this Church did not control the whole of life, that the essential character of that age lay in the contrast between the Church and the 'free spirits'.

The deep personal religiosity of these last, their strong feeling of communion with God, sometimes expressed itself in the very language of the medieval mystics.

Oh that my soul might break through these ties of the flesh into the origin of my soul and life of my life, without which I cannot live. You know, my soul's beloved, I know You know, that there is nothing in the world that can give me pleasure. But if You once show your visage all my suffering is forgotten, my soul cannot find rest without You, You are its one and only aim, oh treasure above all treasures, oh most excellent part of the soul, sweet kindly Jesu.

Thus wrote Maaike Hendriks, who certainly did not know Hadewijch.[1] But Thomas à Kempis *was* read and enjoyed, as well as the old and new German mystics, like Tauler and Boehme.

[1] The great mystical poetess of the thirteenth century; a native of Brabant.

That strong mystical trait was the characteristic of but one trend in non-Church thinking. In addition there was a bold, at times audacious, rationalism. The current of ideas which had received such momentum from Socinus and Descartes and which we saw penetrate into the Church with Cocceius and with Bekker, made itself powerfully felt outside the Church as well. We have already heard Bredenburg being accused of atheism. It was a word that was in the air. At times it moved the authorities to drastic action. This became apparent in 1668 in connection with Adriaan Koerbagh, an Amsterdam jurist and physician, who had already given the consistory cause for offence with his *Bloemhof van allerlei lieflijkheid* (*Flower-garden of all Kinds of Sweetness*), and who was now lured out of his hiding-place and seized on account of a book that had not yet even appeared, *Een licht schijnende in duistere plaatsen* (*A Light Shining in Dark Places*). The Amsterdam aldermen sentenced him to ten years in the house of correction, where he died before a year had gone by. Almost thirty years later there was, in The Hague, the case of Walten, which has already been mentioned. Indeed Walten deserves to be mentioned in the same breath as Koerbagh only because of the treatment he received. For Koerbagh was a man of real conviction, and how little he himself considered his daring assertions to be irreligious, appears for instance from his passage about heaven, no 'diverting place or pleasure garden', because:

> In this consist our salvation and blessedness: in knowing and being in community with God, through which our souls shall experience the greatest enjoyment in all things, which enjoyment no mortal being has so far attained or can attain even in the imagination.

The knowledge of God. Here reason is not meant to act destructively but is called in to build up the union that others sought by means of emotional ecstasy. In 1660 there appeared *Philosophia Interpres S. Scripturae* (*de Philosophie d'Uitlegster der Heilige Schrifture*, i.e. *Philosophy as the Expositor of Holy Scripture*), written by Dr. Lodewijk Meyer. This work was almost pure Cartesianism and as free from mysticism as was for instance Domine Bekker's work. We shall presently get to know Meyer still better as a matter-of-fact man of intellect in his efforts to reform the stage. His philosophic book caused a great sensation and only missed landing him in difficulties because he took good care to keep his authorship secret. In the history of Bible criticism the book has its importance, although it is in that respect not on a level with Spinoza's *Treatise* mentioned in connection with the constitutional theories of the Wittian period.[1] To see rationalism serve real religious sentiment one must turn to a figure like Jarich Jelles, a Baptist grocer in Amsterdam. Of him Jan Riewertsz, who acted as publisher to the whole of that circle of seekers, wrote:

Seeing that the scraping together of money and possessions could not make him happy in the soul, he made his flourishing and profitable shop over to an honest man and said a sudden farewell to that life. Without ever taking wife, he betook himself outside all the world's bustle to the acquisition of the knowledge of truth and of wisdom in accordance with godliness. About thirty years did he spend in this investigation of truth, sparing neither time nor money to obtain it. . . . (*Then he died*) in great joy and happiness of soul, fully assured that he would live eternally with God.

Like Meyer, Jelles proceeded from Descartes. And like Meyer he was on friendly terms with Spinoza.

Interesting in itself, this ferment of thinking and striving becomes doubly so because the great figure of the Jewish philosopher rises above it, because Spinoza breathed that atmosphere and found food in it for his inmost being. After his expulsion from the Synagogue (1656), Spinoza lived for a time in the house of the Antwerper Van den Ende, a one-time Jesuit, but at that time married and the head of a greatly esteemed Latin school at Amsterdam; he had intercourse with Collegiants and afterwards even lived at Rijnsburg for a time. A stranger not only by origin, but brought up at Amsterdam, his birthplace, to speak Spanish and in the traditions of his people, he became a Dutchman through his relations with this circle which was so palpitatingly alive and so open in many directions. Such a development was possible in the Netherlands not only because of the toleration shown by the authorities, but through certain humane qualities of the Dutch way of life. 'The sentiment that one may treat the Jews with all manner of indignity' was in the eyes of the Dutch a sentiment 'that was current in Germany', an alien sentiment. Spinoza, one of the greatest minds known to the history of Dutch culture, is undoubtedly an integral part of it.

His greatness lies in harmonising reason and inner experience, in the serene courage of his philosophy of life, which did not,

[1] See above, p. 192.

like that of Descartes, build up a system of logic by the side of religion, but which dared to identify God and Nature. His *Ethica*, his chief work, edited by Dr. Meyer, and provided with a preface by Jarich Jelles, was published by Jan Riewertsz in 1678, a year after Spinoza's early death. The book was forthwith prohibited as 'profane, atheistic, and blasphemous'. It took a long time to penetrate beyond the circle of friends. And it met with sharp opposition from Collegiants also.

The scene we have observed in the previous pages is characteristic of a society that has broken loose from Catholic unity. In the North we have seen patterns of cultural life for which the South had nothing similar to point to. The interplay of the unleashed forces of individualism is highly interesting and entirely peculiar to the North. How little these same forces were able to achieve in the South is proved by a case such as that of Arnout Geulincx (1624–69). This Antwerper became Professor of Philosophy at Louvain in 1646, at a very early age. His was a lively mind, and he took up an individual attitude towards life. So it was not long before he clashed with the prevailing Aristotelian scholasticism. Little is known about the crisis, but the spirit of his teaching must have been the chief cause of his dismissal in 1658. Having come to Leyden, Geulincx soon embraced Protestantism, became vice-regent of the States College and received the title of 'extraordinarius professor'. Leyden too, as we know, remained officially wedded to the Aristotelian philosophy. Nevertheless at Leyden Geulincx met with no difficulties in developing his system which, though proceeding from Descartes, was in many ways original.

But it would be to lose sight of proportion if one were to believe that during this time the idea of spiritual authority, of conformity, was not gaining ground in the North. Not of course that the peculiar character of Dutch society was lost. Even William III's trusty Fagel appealed to it when in 1677 he pointed out to the South-Holland Synod, in answer to one of its requests for censorship,

that in so free a country as we live in every evil cannot be remedied so readily as one would wish; and that books of that nature can be best overcome by contempt.

That does not alter the fact that since the Synod of Dort Reformed Orthodoxy had with the help of quiet official pressure steadily expanded—more in breadth than in depth certainly; but that meant that home-grown and spontaneous spiritual movements sometimes came to be entangled in the resistance offered by the conventional thinking imposed upon society.

3. SCIENCE

Philology and History

WITH Spinoza and Geulincx we have already made a transition from religious to scientific thinking. With respect to the latter, the seventeenth century is a great period in the history of Europe. What was the share of the Netherlanders in the general movement? The Latinists J. F. Gronovius (a German from Hamburg, 1611–71) and, though to a lesser degree, his son (1645–1715), and Jacobus Perizonius (1651–1715), continued the great Leyden traditions; outside the University Daniel's son Nicolaas Heinsius (1620–81) combined Latin poetry and erudition with diplomatic activities. Classic philology was no longer so fundamentally connected with life as it had been in the preceding generations, yet on ceremonial occasions the classicists still had their say on public affairs and received a respectful hearing. Speeches of Gronovius and Perizonius on the occasion of victories or of royal deaths were thought by the States-General to deserve rewards. In such matters, however, Louis XIV was more liberal: he rated the influence of the humanists on educated opinion high enough to grant annuities (this was before 1672) to Gronovius and Heinsius, as also to old Gevartius at Antwerp.

Law and history flourished by the side of philology, and in this the Southern Netherlands had some share. I have already mentioned the great figure of Van Espen; in one peculiar field of history, the Bollandists did notable work. But here again it appears how much stronger the position of the mother tongue had become in the North. In the South it is hardly possible any longer to point to Dutch publications of any scholarly pretensions. In the North on the contrary not only a regent like Simon van Leeuwen (1628–82) contributed important juridico-historical work in Dutch (for example his *Batavia Illustrata*, of which only the title speaks Latin), but so did even an academic jurist

P

like Ulricus Huber (1636–94), at Franeker. I mentioned above[1] his remarkable controversial work *De Spiegel van Doleantie* (*The Mirror of Grievances*), but he also published his chief work, *Hedendaagse Rechtsgeleerdheid* (*Contemporary Jurisprudence*) in Dutch. Even a classical philologist like Schotanus (1603–71), also professor at Franeker, wrote about the history of Friesland, under the patronage of the States of the province, in Dutch.

These were not isolated or merely accidental achievements. They should be seen in connection with an entire literature which perhaps can hardly be placed under the heading 'science', but which did help create the intellectual atmosphere in which those other works could come into being.

I am not thinking only of the large chronicles of Aitzema: *Saken van Staet en Oorloch* (*Affairs of State and War*), fourteen quarto volumes published between 1655 and 1671 and covering the period 1621–69, and their continuation by Sylvius, or Valkenier's work dealing with 1672 and the following years, nor of the town descriptions, of which Velius had already given a foretaste at the beginning of the century in his *Kroniek van Hoorn* (*Chronicle of Hoorn*), and which were appearing in ever greater numbers (for Amsterdam I mention only Dapper, Commelyn, and Van Domselaar). Those works show how widespread was the interest in history. A man like Aitzema, who in no sense aimed at any kind of composition or literary style, had still a view of his own upon events and did not shrink from bluntly expressing it in a way that could not fail to have a stimulating effect. History was indeed treated in a more truly historical fashion as well and at the same time with greater attention to literary form. Hooft's example was not lost sight of.[2] There was Gerard Brandt in particular, whose lives of Hooft and Vondel, and of De Ruyter, are works of real importance. His *Historie van de Reformatie* (*History of the Reformation*), which gives the Remonstrant view on the disputes during the Truce culminating in the Synod of Dort, loses itself, in its four heavy volumes, in too much detail to be called readable.

But what I am chiefly thinking of is the party writings, to which allusion has repeatedly been made in my earlier chapters[3]: in them ample use was frequently made of historical and juridical arguments. Pieter de la Court was a strong party man,

[1] See p. 120.   [2] See Part One, p. 153.   [3] See above, p. 57, 115, 120.

but he was also a shrewd and original thinker. Above all, his expositions of economic and social conditions demonstrate this, and also the downright way in which he championed the right of criticism in his historical reflections and dared to put tradition to the test of reason, make the Leyden cloth manufacturer an important figure in the intellectual life of his day. The popular view of the War of Liberation—even though an intellectual aristocrat like Hooft had already departed from it on several points—was still either that of the school book *Spieghel der jeught, of Spaanse Tyrannie* (*Mirror of Youth, or Spanish Tyranny*), which dated from 1614 and in which generation after generation was treated to one long series of Spanish atrocities, or that of the Reverend Van de Velde (the same who had been expelled from Utrecht in 1660), the title of whose work gives a clear idea of its trend: *De wonderen des Allerhoogste, ofte Aanwijzinge van de oorzaken, wegen en middelen, waardoor de Geunieerde Provinciën uyt hare vorige onderdrukkinge zoo wonderbaarlijk zijn verheven* (*The Miracles of the Almighty, or Indications of the Causes, Ways and Means by which the United Provinces were raised so miraculously out of their previous Oppression;* 1668). Many historical disquisitions were written in this vein, but the more rationalist view was quite as strongly represented. The Party strife in itself had a stimulating effect on historical awareness. Years after his attack on the Orange tradition (mentioned in another connection above[1]), Uytenhage de Mist published a book that counts for something in the earliest studies of the Middle Ages. The past was continually being appealed to, for and against, *haec religionis ergo* versus *haec libertatis ergo*, Oldenbarnevelt against Maurice, the States of Holland against Frederick Henry and William II, and in that way facts were brought to light and problems posed which were to prove significant for later historical discussion.

The Natural Sciences

BUT the real importance of the seventeenth century, differing in this from the sixteenth, lies in the advance made by the natural sciences. In the second half the rate was speeded up by the stimulating force of Cartesianism, but in spite of the difference from the South which we noted, the Universities in the North,

[1] See p. 57.

too, were still too firmly bound to the traditional system of thought to be able to keep the lead in this movement. The truly important figures are found outside them. Not that the three chief personalities of whom I am thinking here, all three renowned in the general history of science—Christiaan Huygens, (1628–95), Jan Swammerdam (1637–80), and Anthonie Leeuwenhoek (1632–1723)—came into any violent collision with the ruling theology; but the atmosphere of the Universities did not apparently arouse originality, nor did it attract it. In the course these men's lives took one can once more find an illustration of both the strength and the weakness of North Netherlands society. What remarkable personalities were produced by that small community, what a high level of education was to be found in a wide circle, what a thirst after research and knowledge! But if one asks what was done to help those personalities to develop to the full, to make their work contribute to the building up of the national community, then there is less reason to admire.

Christiaan Huygens, whose mathematical and mechanical ingenuity had been noticed at an early date by his father, the poet and secretary to the Orange Stadholder, discovered, when he was no more than twenty-six, a new moon near Saturn with a telescope constructed by himself. The next year he proved the existence of a ring round that planet, and the year following invented the pendulum-clock. After which he was induced to go to Paris (in 1665) to become a member of the new Académie Royale des Sciences; he had already been in personal touch with that circle for years, as well as with the Royal Society founded by Charles II. Thus between 1665 and 1681 Huygens helped to raise the prestige of Louis' foundation. The War of 1672 did not disturb him. What finally drove him back was the progressive exclusion of Protestants. One need not blame the savant absorbed in his mathematical reflections for considering the war as none of his business. Father Constantijn was perhaps more at fault when he, who might have known better, had had his sons given so thoroughly French an education that they corresponded among themselves in French; although the eldest brother, also called Constantijn, whom we have already met in his capacity of secretary to William III, almost always wrote the notes for his diary in Dutch; as a matter of fact Christiaan himself in his youth gave 'the gentlemen of Amsterdam' the advice, in good

Dutch, to have the lessons in mathematics at the Athenaeum 'given in our own language, as is done at Leyden'. In any case, of course, it was not a matter here of personal shortcomings, but of social conditions. Not only is there in Huygens's *Oeuvres* scarcely a word in Dutch to be found, but there is the fact that the Republic had nothing at all equivalent to the Académie des Sciences or the Royal Society to offer.

The tragedy of Swammerdam's life lay deep down in his own nature. The son of an apothecary, he had become a doctor of medicine at Leyden, where he devoted himself entirely to anatomical research, particularly on insects. In his lifetime a few works appeared from his hand in Dutch with wonderfully precise and accurate descriptions of what he oddly called 'bloodless little animals'. To investigate and record without allowing himself to be confused by pre-conceived ideas was his consciously Cartesian attitude. At the same time, however, he perceived analogies in animal and vegetable evolution which were of far-reaching significance. But the longing for a personal religion brought him under the influence of Antoinette Bourignon: in his last work, on the anatomy of the heart, he continually wanders off into pious reflections; after that he says farewell to science and gets immersed in ever more profound religious solicitude. Meanwhile there was no buyer to be found in the Netherlands for his wonderful scientific collection. Even his manuscripts fell into the hands of Thévenot, the Frenchman who had already acted as his patron during his life. Not until half a century after his death did Boerhave edit a *de luxe* edition of his works under the title *de Bijbel der Nature* (*the Bible of Nature*).

Leeuwenhoek's long life was not diverted from his studies on the microscope by any cares or spiritual agonies. A lower middle-class citizen of Delft, without any university training, he was enabled to devote himself to his hobby by being invested with a small municipal office. In 1676 and 1677 he discovered the microbe and the spermatozoön, and he continued his researches with inexhaustible patience almost up to his death. He too was more than merely the observer or describer of his observations. He dispelled the delusion, for the support of which Aristotle's authority was still generally appealed to, that life could arise out of anything but life.

God does not call any new creatures into being. He, the Lord, has from the beginning so ordered things that in all perfect or full-grown seeds He has already created so as to make them carry within themselves—albeit forever hidden from our eyes—the matter which is the origin of the body that in the fulness of time will spring therefrom and that will be in all respects similar to the body from which it proceeds. This being the way it goes in the vegetable world, I conclude that it must of necessity go likewise in the male seed of all animals.

Thus wrote Leeuwenhoek in 1688 in his sixty-fourth letter to . . . the Royal Society! Since 1673 (again in the middle of the war!) he had been regularly sending his reports to that body, in Dutch (because he knew no other language); there they were translated into English and aroused the greatest interest. Not until 1684 did the first collection appear in the original version.

To assert that in the Northern Netherlands no interest was evinced in natural science would be wide of the mark. Christiaan Huygens' posthumous papers were excellently edited through the care of Leyden professors. In 1737 Boerhave largely made amends for the neglect from which Swammerdam had undoubtedly suffered. Leeuwenhoek was in touch with Huygens and many other scholars and became a celebrity at Delft; later he circulated epistles to the Grand Pensionary, Heinsius (his old fellow-townsman), Mr. Van Reede, and other 'persons of high standing'. But the interest remained poorly organised. Leeuwenhoek's career proved in fact that it was possible to serve science in the mother tongue and yet to take part in the world movement and to become world-famous. Over against his example, even in his own day, could be put that of Huygens with its opposite tendency—as could indeed those of many other Latin-writers and collaborators of the *Journal des Sçavans*! In any case no tradition was built up sufficiently strongly to prevent future practitioners of the natural and the exact sciences from neglecting their national cultural task.

In the South, where Jan Baptist van Helmont had met with so much difficulty and obstruction[1], his son Franciscus Mercurius, a more imaginative mind than his father had been, but less really original, had found it impossible to stay. It was at Amsterdam that he got his father's work published, both in Latin and in Dutch, and he himself ended up in Germany. Very little scientific life was left in the Spanish Netherlands.

[1] See above, p. 48.

4. ART

IN ART too—certainly for us who review that period in retro-spect—the North had the lead in the third quarter of the seventeenth century.

The figure of Rembrandt rises mightily above all the rest, just as the previous period had been dominated by that of Rubens. Rembrandt lived and worked until 1669, all the time at Amster-dam, and during the whole of those last twenty years his art continued to develop, fathoming, with unflagging intensity of participation, ever fresh domains of the human heart and of the human mind. The brilliance of his youthful period, the vehe-ment contrasts in which there had been an admixture of mere Baroque convention, all lose themselves in an increasingly grave and relentless struggle with life, and yet this steadfastly unembittered soul retains its freedom for quiet reflection, and for sharing, sometimes with profound sympathy, sometimes with a touch of playfulness, in the human experiences of others. There is no more tragic illustration of Christ's sufferings than those produced by Rembrandt in this period of the 'fifties, no more melancholy rendering of the nostalgia for unattainable beauty and perfection than in his man in armour with a lance; but neither is there any nobler or more profoundly settled peace than in his portrait of Burgomaster Six, his friend and patron, nor any more direct or heartfelt warmth than in the portrayals of the faithful Hendrikje Stoffels. In the end it seems as if peace had descended into his own soul too, and in the works of his later years one finds that moving serenity which comes only after much struggle. The tragedy of Saul is dissolved in David's harp-playing and whatever there may be of pain in the bridegroom's tenderness for his young bride in the warm glow of love and colour.

Right up to the last Rembrandt's art was in communication with cultural world currents of his day. He continued to study the Italians, and likewise the Flemings, and everywhere he took what suited him. At the same time numerous painters, not always to their advantage, underwent his influence, because the greatness of his genius irresistibly impressed most artists of his circle. And yet the personality which permeated his art and made it participate in eternity kept him lonely. The official world had deserted him long ago. Commissions for the new Town Hall or for the Orange Room in the House in the Wood (*Huis ten Bos*) were not for him. In 1658 he went bankrupt and his art collection was sold. I compared his dominating position to that of Rubens thirty years previously. But apparently it was of a different nature. If Rembrandt and Rubens are to be contrasted as the typical Hollander against the typical Fleming (it is done frequently enough!), it should not be forgotten (apart from numerous other objections) that Rembrandt was never able to conquer Holland society as Rubens had that of Flanders.

We have a phenomenon here that was not confined to Rembrandt. In 1662 Hals in his old age—he was well over eighty by that time—received a small annuity from the town of Haarlem, because the fame of his middle years was remembered; but the unadorned directness of his way of painting at that time, going straight for the human quality, left contemporaries cold, while we of to-day, in almost his last work, the Lady Regents of the Old Women's Home, of 1664, recognise a culminating point in his achievement.

The decades following the Peace of Münster, however, do not owe their splendour to that older generation only. A whole band of painters born between 1620 and 1640 flourished. Out of that abundance I shall name only the most outstanding and distinctive: the landscape painters, Philips de Koninck (1620–91), Jacob van Ruisdael (1628–82), Meindert Hobbema (1638–1709); and the painters of interiors and middle-class scenes, Jan Steen (1626–79), Pieter de Hooch (1626–79), Johannes Vermeer (1632–75).

There is no North Netherlander to-day who will not recognise in those painters, together with the great ones of the preceding generation, with Seghers, Van Goyen, Salomon van Ruysdael, Hals, Rembrandt, Terborch, Fabricius, representatives of what is most valuable, because most characteristic, in seventeenth century Dutch painting. What is it they all have in common? It is easier to point to the amazing diversity in temperament and style which they display. Yet there are two main elements, akin and yet different, which one will observe in all of them, although mingled in varying proportions: intimate intercourse with the surrounding reality, and an intent and absorbed listening to the inner voice.

The great landscape painters I mentioned do not just give body to dreams as did Rembrandt in his landscapes, but how much more than faithful reproducers of their town or region did they show themselves! In the work of De Koninck, who was Rembrandt's pupil, the influence of Seghers lives on most clearly. Cuyp, who never tired of portraying Dort and its river and church, bathed them in the golden evening tints of his imagination. Ruisdael, who was able to catch the wide spaces of the Dutch landscape even in a small canvas like the famous view of Haarlem, participated in those cloudy skies and far horizons not only with his painter's eye, but with his soul. By his side the clarity and cheerfulness of Hobbema strike the beholder as almost matter-of-fact.

Of the others Steen showed the keenest, and at the same time coolest and most impersonal, interest in the people of the lower middle classes. He is the merry, witty story-teller, whose psychological insight, subtle and unsentimental, never cruel and never moving, hits off children and shy young women just as well as jolly fellows and ne'er-do-weels. De Hooch is tenderer and more intimate; for him the sentimental value of the family is more important, but at the same time he had a passion for the homely interior itself, for the cool flagstones, the fall of light through half-open windows, the outlook on to passages or courtyards. Differently from Steen, both these qualities link him up with numerous other painters, masters among them. The patient and precise portrayal of daily surroundings, ennobled in him by a classic equilibrium and feeling for space, becomes in the older Dou and in his contemporary Gabriel Metsu already that (often charming) art of the meticulous detail that was to prevail in the end, and to which still-life and townscape painters also became enslaved. But in the meantime Vermeer, of Delft, was creating out of these same elements his incomparable work, so transparent and passionless, and yet, in the clear light, shed over the familiar objects and materials, so mysterious—reality transformed into a silent, pure eternity.

What riches that society has left us in the realistic or imaginative rendering of its outward appearance and inner nature! And what a disturbing thought that at the time so little attention was paid to what was to survive as its finest achievement. Rembrandt was not spared his bankruptcy, the landscape painters could not make even a bare living out of their art, Steen had to keep an inn because he could not sell his canvases, Vermeer had to pawn his paintings to the baker. And in the seventies and eighties a style made its way in from abroad, which irretrievably swept away all this that was so peculiarly Dutch.

What I have here singled out from the overwhelming production of the numberless Brethren of St. Luke in the Dutch towns, to us seems to spring from the most real, the most profoundly Dutch artistic capacities, but their contemporaries never considered it so highly. They were still swayed by that predilection for what was foreign, still, and indeed increasingly, disregarding the beauties lying within their reach in order to gaze in wonderment at a style and form which in their imitation generally lost its essential quality.

Immediately after the peace of Münster a veritable artistic invasion had taken place from Antwerp. The greatest of the painters living there at that time, Jacob Jordaens, was summoned to The Hague by Amalia of Solms to decorate the Orange Room in the House in the Wood in honour of the late Prince. Van Thulden too worked by his side, as did a number of North Netherlands painters, not only old Honthorst but also Jan Lievens, a man of Rembrandt's generation who was once strongly under his influence, but who after a stay in Antwerp had become a follower of that city's school. Jordaens triumphed over them all with his 'Triumph of Frederick Henry', the high light in the whole of that gamut of colours, and a wonder of skill. Pompous show-pieces, is what the modern spectator is nevertheless inclined to call this work and all the rest flanking it. We know that Jordaens could do different and better work. But what was wanted of him and his school was precisely that. The Hollanders admired the ease with which, with the tradition of Rubens and the whole of the Counter-reformation society of the South behind him, he moved in that manner. The Amsterdammers did their best to do likewise. I have already mentioned Lievens. Nicolaas Maes, of Dort, who also had originally been under Rembrandt's spell, soon learnt as a portrait painter that the 'young ladies' preferred (so Houbraken put it) being portrayed in light tones rather than in darkling; he too went to Flanders and changed his style. Bol and Flinck were not able to shake off Rembrandt so easily, but their paintings in the Town

Hall at Amsterdam prove how they too (who after all had only been able to follow the master's flight on faltering wings) were beginning to strive after glamour and elegance—of which they made still worse a job.

So the Town Hall of the proud republicans gives as little idea of the true art of Holland as does the showy palace of the Oranges. It shows, certainly, that Van Kampen, the architect, was able to apply the new European style in a masterly way. Nevertheless it stands there on the Dam more as the manifesto of that foreign trend and as an expression of the determination to be in the swim than as an organic part of a Dutch town. The most beautiful portion by far of the rich ornamentation, within and without, is the sculpture by the Antwerp artist, Artus Quellin.

In this period likewise, sculpture was in Flanders still maintaining the high standard it had reached under the influence of the political and social conditions there prevailing. The impoverished country still found money for building churches on the grand scale. At least two great masters grew to fame shortly after the middle of the century, namely Father Hesius, whose Jesuit church at Louvain has remained famous, and Rubens's beloved pupil, Lucas Faid'herbe (1617–1697), who in spite of his French name came from Mechlin, and who was before all else a sculptor. The sepulchral monuments which bishops and archbishops sometimes had erected for themselves during their lifetime offered an opportunity for the development of a style sometimes mainly ornate, often truly moving, but which in any case kept on the whole within the Italianate conventions. The younger brother of the Frans Duquesnoy mentioned above, Jerome (1602–54), was engaged at Ghent in making a mausoleum for Bishop Triest, when he was arrested and executed for his Italian morals; the noble, recumbent figure of the bishop is his work. Altars, halls, choir-stalls—the zest for ornamentation on the part of ecclesiastics and of laymen gave work of all kinds to sculptors and wood-carvers, and the Gothic churches became ever more crowded with works, which were often very beautiful in themselves but did not go so well with the surrounding architecture. In the churches that were built at the time, or in secular buildings, one can admire the decorative works without that reserve which did not indeed trouble that generation, disdainful as it was of the Gothic style.

Quellin's famous marble reliefs in the Amsterdam Town Hall fit in perfectly with Van Kampen's classic style. At the same time there is in the balance of the composition and the purity of the lines so much truth and life that one cannot for a moment entertain any idea of constraint or of soulless imitation. Once more the South Netherlander moves with perfect freedom in a style which the Protestant burgher society of the North never properly learnt to master. If on account of this one should imagine that the Fleming by his very nature inclines to outward form and embellishment and the Hollander to character and sincerity, then one should compare Quellin's bust of De Witt, in which the sitter's rugged, steady seriousness has been so strikingly caught, with Bol's loud and empty portrait of Quellin himself—or with the forced elegance of the portraits of De Witt by Hanneman or De Baan.

After Quellin, Rombout Verhulst (1616–98) from Mechlin became the most sought-after sculptor in the North. He too had first worked at the Amsterdam Town Hall, and from his hand moreover are some of the best-known works of the whole of that period, as for instance the mausoleums of naval heroes—of Tromp at Delft, of De Ruyter at Amsterdam, of the Evertsens at Middelburg.

In certain fields, however, there were also North Netherlanders who developed great mastery in *genres* learnt from the Italians and the French. That after all was what the patrons wanted. In that way one could gain admission to the drawing-rooms of patricians' houses and to the cabinets of connoisseurs instead of exhibiting at fairs and finding customers among small townspeople or farmers. As a model of style Italy for a long time continued to take first place:

> To Rome! the school of numerous liberal arts.
> For he who never saw Rome will never obtain the favour of Pictura.

So says, in 1662, in his *Gulden Cabinet*, the well-meaning versifier De Bie, the notary of Lierre, who was not, however, by any means exclusive in his multifarious admirations. France is now indeed starting to rise by the side of Italy. Some time before the Peace of Münster we saw the French example beginning to extend its influence over literature and classical studies; it can now be seen at work also in the field of art.

Utrecht was still a centre of italianising, and at Amsterdam too, famous artists of the Utrecht school were now much in fashion. The Italian landscape as painted in endless variations by Nicolaas Berchem (1620–83) and Adam Pijnacker (1622–73), mainly for the houses of rich Amsterdammers, was completely detached from reality: it was an ingenious and graceful game according to rules laid down chiefly by a great French master, Claude Lorrain. Instead of seeking an intensely personal contact with what their own eyes had seen, these painters (there were a great many more) breathed an atmosphere of romantic nostalgia for southern or classic beauty, and compared to the visions of Seghers or Rembrandt their work seems to be lacking in genuine individual feeling. It was not only in landscape painting that the tendency which put convention and form above reality and the distinctively personal made itself felt. In 1665 a young painter from Liège settled at Amsterdam, Gerard de Lairesse by name (1640–1711), whose lifeless academic work pleased the well-to-do Amsterdam connoisseurs more than that of the passionate and profound Rembrandt, of Steen, the roguish observer of our kind, or of any other of the truly national painters. Elegant sharp outlines and harsh, clear light, that is Lairesse: nothing but noble personages, Achilles and Apollo and Jupiter and Neptune, not modelled on living beings, but portrayed in accordance with the recipes of the masters— Poussin and Lebrun—who were now setting the fashion in the dazzlingly brilliant France of Louis XIV.

The State of the Northern Netherlands was loosely organised. Without any strong centralised government it gave free play to local and group interests and suffered a number of organs of power to exist, keeping each other in equilibrium. Its society was middle-class. It lacked a strong centre whence taste and style could have radiated. Protestantism had broken up the old Catholic unity without replacing it by any new cohesion that might have become the growing ground for an artistic manifestation of the community. Determined by those three negations, a culture that was all the more fresh and distinctive had sprung up, richly fed by untrammelled individualism. But individualism was already showing its weakness.

In France, under the leadership of an absolute monarch, the embodiment of the State, there was imposed, in cultural life also, the standard of regularity, the subordination to law and reason, the strict observation of an all-embracing unity. Nothing could be less adapted—I do not say to the nature, but—to the circumstances and traditions of the North Netherlands people; and although in the Southern Netherlands the Counter-Reformation had laid a foundation for unity while at the same time maintaining a natural connection with the whole of Romance civilisation, yet there too particularism was still so prevalent, there was so pronounced a chasm between the people and the Court, that the French standards could not really apply. Nevertheless, no more in the North than in the South could the leading classes and the intellectuals, made ready to capitulate as they had been by generations of classical education, put up an effective resistance to that example made attractive by the radiation of kingship and nobility. When I deplore the French influence, it is not because I cannot admire the French ideal. But it could only bear fruit in the France of Louis XIV; in the Netherlands, where society and religion were maintaining their own character, it had the effect of a freezing breath sweeping over the field of culture.

Andries Pels, whom we shall presently meet as a literary leader, and who was a great friend of Lairesse's, shook his head doubtfully and as it were pityingly when he remembered Rembrandt some twelve years after the latter's death. He complains that the great man took 'no Greek Venus' for a model when he wanted to paint a nude woman, but rather a washerwoman or a bog-trotter—and all in the name of nature! And he concludes:

> A woeful damage did art suffer when so capable a hand
> Did not make better use of the gift it had received.
> Who would have surpassed him in painting!
> But alas, the greater the mind, the worse it will run wild
> If it does not stick to a foundation or bridle of rules
> But presumes to know everything by its own light.

Rules—that was to be the catch-word of the new era; and the first rule was that one should portray beauty and avoid what was common. In the whole way of life of that generation one finds this view reflected: 'the wig' which came to replace 'the hair that nature gave to everyone' is as it were symbolical of this development. Samuel van Hoogstraten (1627–78), who had once been one of Rembrandt's pupils, expounded the new doctrine in his well-written and well-thought-out *Inleiding tot de Hoogeschool der Schilderkonst (Introduction to the High School of Painting)*, which appeared in the year of his death. First and foremost he assured his readers:

that the art of painting, no less than any other liberal art, consists in fixed and certain rules. And although it may seem more difficult of execution than any other, it can be completely analysed and by submitting to tuition be mastered from the first to the last point.

His final warning is:

The art of painting is in my opinion such a noble one that one comes near to disgracing it if one makes it serve to picture an object that is not in itself worth contemplating. Nothing but what is charming and elegant should be placed before our eyes by it.

Away with Brouwer, Ostade, Teniers, Steen! And indeed had not Louis XIV said: 'Otez-moi ces magots!' in order that the canvases of those all too 'natural' Northern and Southern Netherlanders might make way for the new stately or graceful school which was always at two removes from nature. The Netherlanders now echoed that cry. Away with Rembrandt, Ruysdael Vermeer—what remained? For was not Rubens also far too full of tempestuous life to be accepted as a master any longer? Not only realism, but everything that dared be personal, everything that had character, must be planed down to the prevailing taste. Strikingly original manifestations, such as in the period just past had come from dozens of painters whom I have not even mentioned, must not in future be tolerated any longer. The theories of art which Hoogstraten, Pels, Lairesse, had imported from France cancelled everything that in Dutch art had been most characteristic, and for that very reason most valuable. Several of the painters still living of the generation of the twenties and thirties adapted themselves; others laid down their brushes. There was no future except for the academic or drawing-room manner. France, whose armies had been arrested by the Water Line, saw its spirit overrun the field of art in the unvanquished land of Holland.

5. LITERATURE

In the North

THE contrast between the rich, distinctive character of religious life and the decline of originality in painting, strikes us as strange in the picture presented by culture in the North. Now that we have come to literature we shall once more find originality on the wane. But is it after all so strange? The religious movement preserved its own particular domain from dispossession through Frenchification. Its attitude towards art and literature, however, was so negative, antagonistic even, that these could not look for support from that quarter; on the contrary its spread would rather block access to remaining sources of vitality. Calvinism indeed, however intensely experienced, did not offer inspiration to the painters, and to the poets only a strictly limited one. The fresh and varied culture of the first half of the century had still been in close contact with the old humanistic and Renaissance traditions, imbued as they were with Catholicism, and responsive to life and nature. In proportion as society in the North became more set in the Dort mould, this contact became more difficult to maintain. As for the Protestant individualists and mystics, they did bring life and movement into religious thinking and feeling as such, but this was limited to a plane where culture in a wider sense, where the feeling for beauty and cultural refinement, could find little encouragement; only purely religious, preferably mystic, poetry benefited. For the rest all this was too Protestant, too peculiar, too unworldly.

The after-effects of the great figures

IN THE fifties and sixties the drying up of real literary inspiration was not yet so obvious, because the few great figures whose time of birth went back to the sixteenth century still dominated the scene. Even the nestor, Cats, who died in 1660 at the age of 83, was after Münster still writing tens of thousands of alexandrines, and the autobiographical works of his old age strikingly round off our picture of him. At Zorgvliet, his country-house near The Hague, resting from the cares of his statesman's career, he liked to entertain ministers of religion and discuss the dangers of the world and how to avoid them. Huygens at the time resided in his country-house of Hofwijk, on the other side of The Hague. Always gallantly engaged in various activities, he continued— until much later in fact, because he lived to a greater age even than Cats, and did not die until 1686—to give pointed shape to anything that met his eye or happened to cross his mind, commenting on it all with worldly-wise and devout reflections. Here was a man who, just as he had remained himself at the court of Frederick Henry, now took no notice of the increasing tyranny of French classicism. His work remained as personal in spirit and form as ever. But as a result he hardly counted as far as influence went. His only follower was a little younger than he: Jacob Westerbaen (1599–1670), a Remonstrant while Huygens was a Contra-Remonstrant, but like him and like Cats the owner of a country house near The Hague (Ockenburg), and on friendly terms with both.

Vondel, finally, born some years after Cats and before Huygens, lived on till 1679. During the last twenty years of his life, bankrupted by the debts incurred by his son, he eked out a living in a modest post in the Amsterdam Loan Bank. Until the end of the sixties, in other words until he was well over eighty, true poetry kept flowing from his pen. In 1654 his *Lucifer* appeared, and in 1665 his *Adam in Ballingschap* (*Adam in Exile*). In between he wrote some singularly beautiful funeral poems and a long rhymed exegesis of Catholic doctrine, which, although the modern reader does not get much pleasure out of them, yet nowhere impress him as being either feeble or hollow.

In this later work of Vondel's his personality appears as if purified from the last remaining passions and egotisms. It was a development in the natural direction of his life, but at the same time it kept him from clashing with the self-confident style conceptions coming in from France. Living in a world of the imagination disfigured by no stain or crack of the commonplace or mean, consorting with the idea of things, disturbed by no inner storms, full of respect for the rules laid down by the ancients, Vondel in his old age, having outgrown the passions of his polemical poems and the over-ornate splendour of his Renaissance period, became an object of reverence and a model for the younger generation.

Q

But that generation growing up in his shadow proved deficient in native poetic power. While in the fifties and sixties a host of painters of the first rank were still coming on, there was a dearth of newcomers in the field of literature. Jeremias de Decker (1609–64), a grocer at Amsterdam, and Joachim Oudaen (1628–92), proprietor of a tile-works at Rotterdam, were both, although mutually differing in style, akin to Vondel in religious feeling and in the ardour with which they followed public affairs, yet both lacked the master's imposing flight of imagination and power of form. Lodenstein, whom we saw at work in Utrecht, was a true religious poet, but limited in scope. Subtler, and with an exceptional gift of beautiful versification, but no wider in scope, was Heiman Dullaert (1636–84). Johannes Vollenhove (1631–1708), Arnold Moonen (1644–1711), Joan Broekhuizen (1649–1708), and Johannes Antonides van der Goes (1647–86) were all typical epigones, capable workers in a cut-and-dried tradition, to which they added nothing personal. Vollenhove and Moonen were clerics, both from Overijsel, but the former lived in The Hague for the largest part of his life. With the classicist formality learnt from Vondel they combined a somewhat solemn unction, the tone of the new period, which sometimes makes one wish for the hammering, combative directness of the preceding generation. Captain Broekhuizen, who fought in William III's wars, wrote melodious verse after the manner of Hooft's lighter love poetry, keeping up the while an extensive Latin correspondence.

Antonides, a pupil of the Latin school at Amsterdam, later a clerk in the Admiralty at Rotterdam, was the child prodigy of the period, in whom Vondel believed himself to be reborn. It was Vondel from the outside, because the young man had wrapped himself in Vondel's cloak and wore it with quite an air. But except for his talent for writing swelling alexandrines and his mastery over the stereotyped classical turns of phrase beneath which the whole of base reality had now to be concealed, Antonides did not have much. One poet there was who stood somewhat apart from literary life, but it was from him that came the truest poetry. This was Jan Luyken (1649–1712), etcher of Amsterdam, whose youthful volume named the *Duitsche Lier* (*Dutch Lyre*) met with general applause. But fresh and pure as is the voice heard in those love songs, the poems he subsequently published, after his conversion to a mystical faith bound to no church, came from profounder depths and reached greater heights. All his volumes were charmingly illustrated by himself.

Most of the poets who counted in the literary world showed a veneration for Vondel and Hooft. The works of these great ones began to be diligently studied with a view to deducing from them laws for the use of language and of verse form. This is apt to make the modern observer somewhat impatient. But thus at least was formed a national tradition which was of the greater importance as in that and in the period immediately following there was such a dearth of strong, original talents, and imitation after the French threatened more and more to overlie everything.

In the Southern Netherlands

IN THE South the work of the great Northern poets—it was more particularly Vondel and Cats who counted there—was performing that same service. Even De Bie introduces his poems (*Faems Weergalm der Nederduytsche Poëzie—The Echo of Dutch Poetry's Fame;* 1670) with the announcement that they have been written 'after the Holland manner', apparently considering this to be a recommendation. In actual fact this industrious man, who it must be said imitated Poirters[1] quite as much as Cats, was totally devoid of poetic talent: I mention him only because in the general dearth not only of poets, but even of reasonably cultivated publicists, everyone who was at all a figure deserves our attention. Poirters lived until 1674; down to the end he kept writing, and his work bore a more and more devotional character. The superiors of the Society of Jesus had come to realise the value of his books from their special point of view. The Jesuit scholars, Bollandus, the compiler of that awe-inspiring series of historically documented Lives of the Saints, and Papebrochius (Van Papebroeck), his younger collaborator and successor, both appreciated Poirters. The number of his imitators, among both the clergy and the laity, is considerable, but all their work remained colourless. As of old, poetry in the South was industriously practised by the Chambers of Rhetoric, who arranged festivals and competitions and devoted themselves

[1] See Part One, p. 244.

especially to the theatre. But even more so than in the previous century these manifestations were now essentially a lower-middle-class pastime. Even religious zeal was no longer able to express itself in original forms. Medieval plays were still put on the stage, at Brussels for instance the fourteenth century *Seven Vrouden van Maria* (*the Seven Joys of Mary*), but of newly written material there was hardly anything except bombastic melodramas, often after Spanish and sometimes after English models, and popular farces: two *genres* which similarly flourished at Amsterdam, but which produced nothing really outstanding either here or there. No doubt the coarse-voiced comedy can raise a laugh, and the manners of the day are displayed true to life, though only on life's basest side. After the Antwerper Ogier, the Brusseler Johan de Grieck is at times amusing.

But to this general low-life triteness there is one remarkable exception. At Dunkirk, as subject of Louis XIV (the town was conquered in 1658), there lived a surgeon, Michiel de Swaen (1654–1707), a member of the Chamber of Rhetoric *Verblijdt u in den tijd* (*Rejoice in the day*). This Chamber not only kept in regular touch with other Chambers in towns annexed by France, like Furnes and Ypres[1], but also with those in towns that were still under Spain, like Dixmude and Bruges. The 'literature' produced by the Rhetoricians was most of it wretchedly insignificant, but the members yet possessed enough discernment warmly to admire De Swaen, who was himself rightly aware of his intellectual superiority. Indeed, here, in this out-of-the-way corner, so dangerously exposed to gallicisation, a man made himself heard in moribund Flanders who had ideas to express and was a poet. In 1686 he wrote *De Menschwording The Incarnation*), which no doubt was a true offshoot of the Rhetoric tradition and a real mystery play, but yet was couched in a form that was inconceivable without Vondel, and especially without *Lucifer*. Indeed, the spirit and the voice of the great Amsterdammer came to life in De Swaen infinitely more truly than in Antonides or any other North Netherlander. Vondel's influence could the more easily bear fruit here on account of his Catholicism. In the North the attacks of the Reformed ministers had driven the religious drama off the stage: none of Vondel's

---

[1] These towns reverted to the main body of Flanders—to Spain—in 1715.

imitators ventured to try anything like it. De Swaen also wrote lyric poetry of genuinely religious inspiration and with an accent of its own. Besides (a thing Vondel never attempted) he wrote an amusing comedy, *De gekroonde leerse* (*The Crowned Boot*) (1688), in which Molière's influence is unmistakable, although it attains its chief effect through the truly Netherland portrayal of everyday people. How little the French annexation had yet affected the spirit of the annexed part of Flanders appears here strikingly: the scene is laid in Brussels and the monarch who plays the Haroun al-Rashid part is the Emperor Charles V of glorious memory. But the fact is also demonstrated by the treatise on *Nederduitsche dichtkunde* (*Netherland Poetry*), which De Swaen wrote probably towards the end of his life. He does quote the French poets by the side of the ancient ones, but only when mentioning Cats and Vondel does he give his admiration free rein, obviously taking pride in their achievements: Cats was in his opinion the first famous Dutch poet by whom 'our language and national character were glorified', but to Vondel's qualities, so widely differing, he also does justice, distinguishing between the two with excellent perception.

De Swaen, as I have already said, was much admired in Flanders. It is therefore an all the more depressing proof of the weakness that had already overtaken Dutch culture in the South that practically none of his works were printed in his lifetime. The manuscript of the *Menschwording* was not found until 1886, at Bilsen (between Maastricht and Hasselt), where it had probably belonged to the archives of the Chamber of Rhetoric; forty years later, the finder, Camille Huysmans,[1] was able to establish De Swaen's authorship. Here indeed was poverty, which could no longer even profit by a treasure. De Swaen's work could no longer help towards rebuilding a Dutch literature in Flanders; with so much of earlier production it fell into oblivion.

That De Grieck's dramatic works should be able to save the mortally sick Dutch language from its decline was indeed too optimistic a thought. Nevertheless it was expressed in all seriousness by a eulogist—Godin, in 1660—and I quote some of his lines to show that there were those who at least

---

[1] The well-known Flemish Socialist, who was in his younger days Burgomaster of Antwerp and on several occasions a Cabinet Minister.

recognised the weaknesses from which native culture was suffering:

> Your noble Dutch
> will reduce to silence all those rascals
> who with their foreign caprioles
> are spoiling our language.

In the North: the new Spirit

IN THE North, no doubt, a national literary tradition was, as we saw, created which could offer some resistance against the overpowering flood of French influence. But it is necessary to distinguish carefully. The bearers of that tradition were themselves to a large extent imbued with it.

There was one group of intellectuals who made themselves the special propagators of French conceptions. These were Dr. Lodewijk Meyer, the lawyer Andries Pels (both already known to us), and a number of others, who together founded the society *Nil Volentibus Arduum* in Amsterdam in 1668. Their chief ambition was to reform the theatre, and it must be admitted that the theatre urgently needed reform. Under the leadership of Jan Vos the true drama had been more and more replaced by spectacle; for a time Meyer had indulged in that fashion himself. Exactly as in Flanders, Spanish and English examples were followed, but most of the plays performed in the Town Theatre were mere roaring bombast, and ever more horrible and sanguinary at that.

> *One* tramples on the bellies of pregnant women
> Until they belch forth their last breath together with the child.
> Another drags the daughter on to the dead body of
> Her mother and rapes her within the view of the husband;
> Yet another tears out the heart of the bride who had taken
> Refuge in the bridegroom's arms; the latter's bowels
> Serve to link up the couple. . . .

This is a sample of the delicacies to which a dramatic poet in 1655 promised to treat his audience. The farces and comedies for their part were, with all their amusing lifelike quality, unbelievably coarse, even foul. The urgency with which the ministers kept admonishing the Burgomasters to close down the theatre becomes understandable in the light of such outrageous licence. It is true that they reserved their bitterest vehemence

for the denunciation of a play like Vondel's *Lucifer*, because
there

the high matter of God's profundities is represented in a carnal manner and
with many offensive and irregular fancies.

And indeed, the performance of *Lucifer* was prohibited. As
has already been remarked, that genre became extinct in its
entirety. On the whole, however, the town government remained
favourably disposed towards the Theatre. In 1664 even, a new
building was inaugurated, soon closed on account of the second
Anglo-Dutch war, but opened again before peace was concluded
in spite of the remonstrances of the consistory:

that this is a time of anxiety, such as caused even the pagans to close down
their comedies, and, indeed, that Christians in the circumstances we are now
living in take pleasure in entertainments foregone even by the pagans cannot
be regarded otherwise than as designing to spit into God's face.

These objurgations brought about no improvement in the
standard of what the stage had to offer, and Meyer and his
friends deserve some appreciation for setting themselves the
task not of suppressing but of refining. Unfortunately, they
sought improvement in a strict application of the French stage
laws and, worse, they believed they could save themselves the
effort of original work, and confined themselves to translating
French plays. Their literary gifts were in fact but meagre—the
stress they laid on the will (expressed in the very name of their
'Chamber': 'Nothing is hard for those who will'), on study, on
'polishing' and improving, was not wholly due to the spirit of
the times. Nevertheless both Meyer and Pels were interesting
personalities. The latter formulated the theories of the society
in his treatises: *Q. Horatius Flaccus' 'Ars Poetica' Applied to
our Manners and Times* (1677) and *Use and Abuse of the Stage*
(1681). We have already seen that in the eyes of this consistent
classicist even Rembrandt found no favour, and that same
uninspired sense of order and regularity he also applied to the
entire field of literature. And indeed this doctrine held a
fascination for that generation of intellectuals, especially if it
presented itself accompanied by an appeal to the French, to
Racine, Molière, or Boileau. Pels's poems on literary theory
gained great authority; they governed the views prevailing in
the near future. In 1677 the 'Nil' men had obtained a share in

the practical control over the Theatre, which did not indeed mean that it was set for good on the course they pointed.

Their activities were continually accompanied by violent quarrels. And sometimes their criticism, even when it was not undeserved, was parried by telling blows. 'One's own invention', that was what mattered according to Asselyn, at that time still only a writer of noisy historical dramas, but who was later to produce the best and truest comedy of the period with his *Jan Klaaszen or the Pretended Maidservant* (1682); and he ridiculed the everlasting translations from the French—'because he knows only his mother tongue': even that argument the other party did not scruple to use. The inquisitorial scrutiny after what might not conform to the artistic canon, the team-work without inspiration but with industry and will—all those concomitants of the principle were observed and called forth protests.

The members of the society considered themselves good patriots (after 1672 Pels no longer took French wine), and they themselves professed the cultivation of the Dutch language to be one of their chief aims. Yet the opposition against their pretentions found support in a reaction of national self-esteem. It grouped itself round the memory of Vondel, of whom Pels and his friends had said that he too had not been quite true to the doctrine. Antonides, who at first had consorted with the group, with great vehemence stood up for his revered master. Oudaen too, in his funeral poem, spoke scornfully of 'the envy of the Literary Society'.

At bottom, however, the attitude of Antonides, Oudaen, and Vollenhoven did not really differ from that of 'Nil Volentibus Arduum'. They too believed in immutable laws of art, which were only then being properly established; to them too what mattered was delicacy and neatness; they too wanted to serve rationality and understood ecstasy in no other guise than that of bombastic appeals to 'the Goddesses of Song', and quiet meditation not at all. In the eyes of Oudaen, Vondel surpassed Homer and Virgil because he never departed from nature and refrained from exaggeration—one would almost be inclined to say, because he had no imagination, and so the conclusion would inescapably present itself that Oudaen understood no more of the man he admired than he did of Homer or Virgil.

Anyhow, Vondel's poetry, such as it appeared to him, he boldly declared to be the imperishable standard for language and poetry. Just as Latin had been established—'unshakable, eternally fixed and immovable'—by the writers of Caesar's era,

> So will the power of Netherland's various dialects
> Be defined in the changeless state of Vondel's Dutch,
> And his poetry, despite the frown of whomsoever,
> Will constitute, to the benefit of us all, the polestar of our art.

And even more directly did Vollenhove put it in *his* funeral poem:

> You poets, are you desirous of gaining honour
> By metrical art designed for enjoyment or edification?
> Learn to speak Vondel's language, the language of Parnassus.

All this was inspired by the same principle as was the doctrine of Pels. De Swaen's treatise on *Dutch Poetry*, too, although excelling in subtle power of discrimination, personal judgment, and commonsense, is a piece of classicist thinking, is intended as a manual, stating examples and laws, and before everything else demanding clarity. When one sees how general was that attitude of mind, one realises that literature could not escape a period of devitalisation and desiccation. But, once more, it was not without importance that a reconciliation was attempted between that irresistible style and a national tradition. The literature of the future was to be overmastered by French influence, but it managed to retain a modicum of self-respect by the cult of Vondel and Hooft—of Vondel and Cats in the case of De Swaen.

Vondel especially, then, was during his lifetime and later proclaimed to be the greatest Dutch poet. What does that mean? Certainly not that his plays drew full houses: it leaps to the eye that for that purpose they made too large demands on the imagination, and even on the patience, of the audience. In addition there was the enmity of the churchmen. But this made the secular-minded intellectuals closely connected with the regent class esteem him all the more; even his Catholicism, about which he was far from keeping discreetly silent, was readily made allowance for. In the case of *Lucifer* the Burgomasters gave in to the consistory, but they nevertheless continued to protect Vondel and at the end of his life gave him a small pension, just as the Burgomasters of Haarlem had done for

Hals. The intellectuals—it was on them that Vondel's fame really rested. In the South a man like De Swaen stood alone. The Rhetoricians there kept versifying in Dutch, but to them the higher spheres of intellectual life remained closed. The leaders in traditional culture and in society had, speaking generally, turned away from the national language. But in the North Dutch-reading and Dutch-writing intellectuals were a force along with the ministers and regents. There were many links between them and the latter. Important literary figures such as Cats, Hooft, and Huygens had been in the previous generation were now no longer to be found among the leading class. Not that there were not many regents who dabbled in poetry. I mention Pieter de Groot, although he had spent so many years abroad as a result of his father's exile; Jan Six, the Amsterdam Burgomaster, whose name has remained linked with that of Rembrandt; and Adriaan Paets, who has already been referred to as a Collegiant. And there were also those who were genuinely interested in the literary movement and who did not merely 'protect' but liked having their say about problems concerning poetry and drama—Van Beuningen for instance, or Dirk Buysero (whom we have also already come across[1]); the latter procured a post for Antonides in the Rotterdam Admiralty. Nor did the orthodox ministers form a closed group in opposition to the literary movement; the case of Vollenhove was not singular.

One hardly meets the nobility in Dutch cultural history. It had either retained its rural complexion intact, or, mixing in Hague society life, had become Frenchified. It was only in the burgher regent class that the Dutch-writing intellectuals found support from above against the social gallicisation which (as we know) received so strong an impetus from the influx of the Huguenot *refugiés*. In this way Netherland culture, notwithstanding all its weaknesses, was strong enough to develop the Dutch prose style yet further. The language as used by politicians and officials—and its importance should not be underestimated in this connection—continued to be larded with words of foreign extraction—an abuse of long standing. In De Witt's style, of which I have quoted a few samples,[2] this was certainly due more to his Latin schooling than to French influence.

[1] See above, p. 205.   [2] See above, p. 32.

That powerful if cumbersome prose, masterly in its way, is clearly distinguishable from that of Oldenbarnevelt or even Grotius. De Witt's command of it enabled him to make it serve sarcasm or passion, but it was a heavy instrument and difficult to handle; the directness, which had characterised the preceding generation, seems lost. It is as if the prose writers of the mid-seventeenth century imposed a constraint upon themselves, which in the case of some very few may have directed the inner force with greater point, but which cost most of them an effort detrimental to their naturalness.

But towards the end of the period it was again French influence which caused this style to drop into disuse. When one goes through the letters of the later politicians from this point of view one will hardly come across a stylist of De Witt's calibre; at most one finds that the style becomes less complicated while French words appear much more frequently, without even having been turned into a Dutch form. But in the literary prose, which like the poetry, curiously enough, continued to eschew words of foreign extraction, the change is also discernible. However little fruitful this period in literature may have been, and however threateningly the gallicisation was beginning to affect intellectual life, there was something like a leap forward in the development of modern narrative or argumentative prose. The modern spirit could not express itself either in the colourful liveliness of the popular language, which had all the time maintained itself in pamphlets or books of travel, or in the cumbersome or compact constructions of the language of the humanistically educated. If one wishes to see how clumsily, owing to the absence of a useful standard in style, people could write in the latter half of the seventeenth century, then one should read the chronicle in many volumes of the clever, worldly-wise Aitzema. Neither in contemporary France nor in contemporary England could a man of so much ingenuity and of such good birth (Aitzema was diplomatic representative in The Hague for some Hansa towns) have perpetrated such a formless book; the half-French Dutchman, De Wicquefort, who had been commissioned by De Witt to deal with the same period in his *Histoire des Provinces Unies*, ridiculed it. And indeed only a little later so crude a compilation would be unthinkable in Dutch as well.

Prose literature might have been much richer had not the Universities been so enslaved to Latin. French—as we saw— deprived the national language of Constantyn's son, Christiaan Huygens. Nevertheless Dutch works did extend over ever wider fields. In addition to a wealth of theological and devotional works, such as had not been lacking at an earlier date, I mention the well-turned-out books of travel by Joan Nieuhof (1618–72), born in the Bentheim district (outside the seven provinces), the politico-economic disquisitions of Pieter de la Court (1618–85), Simon van Middelgeest's plea in favour of Pieter de Groot (1676), the historical and biographical works of Gerard Brandt (1626–85), Samuel Hoogstraten's treatise on the art of painting mentioned above, Jan Zwammerdam's (1637–80) *Bible of Nature* (not published by Boerhave until later, it is true), and Balthazar Bekker's (1634–98) *Bewitched World*.

Of them all it was only Gerard Brandt, Remonstrant minister, poet, and playwright, who was conscious of adding to Dutch literature. He indeed was one of the chief builders of the new prose style. One will not find Hooft's (admirable though often exacting) individual treatment of the language in Brandt's *History of the Reformation* or in his *Life of Vondel* and *Life of De Ruyter*. But for that very reason his influence could reach more widely.

In the South this field presents a void. Except for small devotional works, hardly any Dutch prose appears there at all. De Swaen's *Art of Poetry* was not published until our own day. Nothing brings out more clearly the stagnation in South Netherland civilisation. And while North Netherland poetry of the first half of the seventeenth century, as we saw, still met with some response in the South, prose-writing there was hardly affected by the development taking place in Holland.

But in the North too we have noticed signs of deterioration in the picture presented by literary life for which the spectacle of political events had hardly prepared us. It is true that Antonides in a poem written in that same year brought the disaster of 1672 into the closest possible connection with the general passiveness in the face of French influence. He spoke bitterly of 'the bastardy' fallen into our own domain—'the monster',

Which insolently raises its head with the air of a ruler
And expelling Netherland's language intrudes France

With its bastard tongue and lascivious manners.
Are we really degenerating from the old Batavians?
. . .
Wake up, it is time, rub the fog out of your eyes
And do not look outside yourselves, with disgraceful suspicion,
For the cause of the defeat that has overtaken us.
The French Weathercock has for a long time been crowing its law to us.
Its voice pleased us only too much, now we are cowering under the blows
Of its wings and terrible spurs,
And even now there are fools who take pleasure in listening to its voice.

A sombre note on which to close the chapters in which the most glorious period of the North Netherland Republic has been treated! But truly, the poet who recognised a danger in the inclination towards French culture, at a time when the State was to display so formidable a capacity for resistance against France for another generation to come, was gifted with prophetic insight; this was to appear all too clearly in the next century. And yet the matter should not be taken too tragically. The loss of originality remained confined to certain fields of intellectual life. Even the South, where no State tradition could spring up which might have given some support to national Netherland culture, retained, under a foreign superstructure, its peculiar character. Netherland civilisation, in the North as well, had weaknesses which were to make themselves felt more seriously as time went on. But even after a much more profound decline, after catastrophes and humiliations, it retained the capacity for recovery. The Netherland tradition was never wholly extinguished.

VII
With England Against Louis XIV
(1688–1715)

A. UNDER THE STADHOLDER-KING

ON 15 November 1688, the Prince of Orange had landed at Torbay. On 23 February 1689, he and his wife were raised to the throne by a Convention.

1. THE SECOND COALITION WAR AGAINST FRANCE: 1688–97

BEFORE November 1688 was out, Louis XIV had declared war on the Republic. The attempts he made to convince the Emperor that the interests of Catholicism demanded co-operation against William III failed: the German War which he had started in an evil hour went on, and the alliance between the Emperor and the States-General was restored. One German prince after another joined them; Spain presently followed suit and—which was of importance for the Italian theatre of war—Savoy also. The aim of the so-called Grand Alliance was to drive France back to the territorial situation of 1648 and 1659. England at first took part only by virtue of the alliance of 1678, that is to say in the Southern Netherlands and with no more than 5,000 men (under Marlborough)—there were more Dutch troops in England at that time! Later in the year 1689 she got involved in the war on her own account and entered into fresh undertakings. But William's position in England was still extremely difficult. Many of the gentlemen serving him had their doubts. Catholic Ireland remained faithful to James, who was assisted by the French to go there in person. In 1690 William himself had to cross over to that island and it was not until the victorious battle of the Boyne that he gained greater freedom of action. Even so a strong army (part of which were States troops under Van Reede van Ginkel) was needed until the end of the following year to break the last resistance in Ireland. At the beginning of

1691, at all events, the Stadholder-King was able to go to The Hague and to take upon himself the command of the new summer campaign in the Southern Netherlands.

Twice, in 1689 and 1690, he had had to leave the conduct of affairs there to Waldeck, and, just before he himself had established his position in the three kingdoms by the battle of the Boyne, Luxembourg had administered, near Fleurus, a serious defeat to Waldeck and his army largely composed of Dutch troops. The French fleet had simultaneously been able, off Beachy Head, to defeat the States' fleet because the English had remained idle; the English Admiral, Torrington, was court-martialled but found not guilty, although William roundly criticised his behaviour in a letter to the States.

In spite of these disappointments the Stadholder-King was welcomed exuberantly on his entry into The Hague in February 1691. And indeed at the illustrious Congress that collected around him there he was able to announce a more vigorous English participation in the continental war. The Imperial ambassador, the Spanish Governor of the Southern Netherlands, the Electors of Bavaria and Brandenburg, the Duke of Brunswick, the Landgrave of Hesse, and a number of other German princes, had all come to The Hague in person. William cut a greater figure than any of his predecessors had done, not so much because of the royal crown he now wore, but rather because more than ever he had become the soul of European resistance against Louis XIV. It was a right instinct that moved public opinion in the Northern Netherlands to acclaim him as such.

True, the natural tendency was still to appreciate the situation in religious terms; nothing moved a large part of the public so deeply as an appeal to the interests of Protestantism. In reality, nevertheless, just like after 1672, the alliance with the Emperor and with Spain prevented the war on the Continent from assuming the character of a religious war: the fears of the Amsterdam regents did not materialise.[1] William himself fully recognised the importance of this fact, and however much Protestant sentiment came into play, it remained chiefly defensive. The Voetian ministers might again vehemently urge that measures be taken against the Catholics among their own

[1] See above, p. 172.

people, whose position indeed had not been strengthened by the short-lived emancipation of 1672, but the States of Holland and of most of the other provinces would not hear of anything that smacked of reprisals. The North Netherland Catholics did not in fact think of conspiring with the enemy. After all, the Pope himself seemed plainly to be on the side of the coalition. In Ireland alone the Protestant slogan found a practical and only too offensive an application. In the Northern Netherlands, such national energy as it aroused served mainly—curiously enough! —to help keep the Catholic southern provinces out of the hands of France. The kinship with Flanders and Brabant was now hardly remembered any longer, but that the independence of the North Netherland State and its Protestant culture demanded that barrier between itself and France was universally recognised.

But the policy of which William III was the embodiment, and which he maintained with inflexible strength of mind, demanded heavy sacrifices on the part of the Republic, and the heaviest were perhaps not those of the almost unbearable burdens of war, but those consequent upon the close association with England following upon the revolution that the Republic had itself helped to bring about. Public opinion did not as yet give much attention to the dangers that lay concealed in that situation. The regents of Amsterdam and of other trading towns had indeed discerned them at once, but for the time being they saw no remedy.

Witsen's suggestion[1] that the Republic should exact conditions from the English people before lending assistance had been impossible of achievement; and later, in the negotiations with the newly established régime, in which he himself took part as member of a special mission, the situation in which the Republic found itself between England and France had still made this impossible. The Republic was already at war with France; the French menace was for her much more direct than for England, which, as Fagel had once expressed it, 'was separated from France by so wide a moat of water'. The English now even presumed to speak as if they were making war on France for the Republic's sake, and however little they might be able as yet to contribute towards that end, they therefore considered themselves entitled to stand stubbornly upon their

[1] See above, p. 172.

own views, especially as regards the way the war was to be waged
at sea.

That the Republic should furnish a smaller number of ships
for joint fleet operations was no more than natural, seeing that
the troops it had to maintain for the war in the Southern
Netherlands were such a drain on its finances already, and there
England's contribution was the smaller. The proportions for
maritime contributions were stipulated to be five to three; as
regards operations on land, in 1691 William III as King of
England promised 20,000 men as against 35,000 from the
States for the campaign in the Netherlands; in both contingents
the German princes furnished a considerable share, the men
being paid for by the Naval Powers. Implied in this arrangement was the recognition by the Republic of England's superiority in the two countries' competition from now on in the field
of trading and colonising. The naval battles of the past generation had not been able to bring the Republic to that recognition;
the effort needed for the struggle against France now left it no
choice. Coupled to this arrangement there was the provision
that in any joint action the English admiral should always be in
command, and the Dutch were even forced to submit to rules
for the order of precedence in courts martial which deeply
offended Witsen.

Witsen also vainly opposed the demand that the two powers
should bind themselves jointly to put an embargo on all trade
with France, on the part both of their own subjects and of those
of neutral countries. This went right against the cherished
principle of 'free ship, free goods', which the Dutch Republic,
so largely dependent on commerce, had been trying for generations to get everywhere adopted; and indeed, later it had again
to exert all its strength—and against England—to maintain it.

In all those differences the Amsterdammer had had to do
without the support of the Stadholder become King. William
III's new quality was seen at once to have gained the upper hand
over the old. It would be unfair on account of this to reproach
him with forgetfulness of his Dutch origin. William III was not
blinded by the brilliance of his new position. He never felt at
home in England. Dijckvelt soon told Huygens the diarist:

that the King had often said to him, I can see that this people was not made
for me nor I for them.

R

And no more characteristically Dutch utterance is imaginable than the one William permitted himself to make to Witsen after his coronation:

Whether he had seen that farce of the coronation, and what he thought of those silly old papist ceremonies?

But William III had always interpreted the interests of the North Netherland State, both before and after his elevation to the English throne, in a very one-sided manner. He could only see them in connection with the menace from France. That was why any opposition to what he considered the realities of the international situation only roused his impatience. He was right in so far as resistance to France must indeed be recognised to be the dominating factor. But it was not the only one, and thus it was not only inevitable, but it was right, that criticism should make itself heard. The Amsterdam aversion to the exhausting land war and to this playing second fiddle to England was a sound national reaction, and there was a real danger in the circumstance that, now that William had become King, the Stadholderly policy attained to almost a monopoly of power in the Republic. The other members of the mission representing the States-General in the negotiations of 1689, Dijckvelt and Odijck, followed in everything the wishes of the master.

An attempt made by Amsterdam the next year to resist William III in a matter of domestic policy only proved how greatly the latter's power had waxed since 1684. Now that the Stadholder was absent abroad, the town refused to present to him a double list of nominations for the annual election of seven aldermen. In so acting the leading men landed themselves in a constitutional impasse, and dissension arose in their own town government. Hudde and Witsen, who were in favour of giving in, won against Hendrik Hooft and Bors van Waveren, who wanted to hold firm. In such matters William III took the advice not only of the new Grand Pensionary, Anthony Heinsius—Gaspar Fagel had died at the end of 1688—but also of Bentinck, who now bore the title of Earl of Portland. On account of this, Amsterdam wished to bar William's favourite, now become an Englishman, from the Knighthood of Holland, of which William had made him a member in 1676 (and in that capacity he sat in the States of Holland); but here too the town failed.

In Bentinck's view Heinsius was too much inclined towards mild courses—it is true that the new Pensionary was less vehement than his predecessor. Bentinck himself usually counselled the absent Stadholder in the most radical sense. He wrote to William that the inhabitants of Amsterdam were this time far from unanimously behind the regents. Complaints were again heard about the infringement of the citizens' privileges; there were calls for 'a free court martial', that is to say that the civic guard companies should be allowed to choose their officers, who could then face the oligarchic town government as the spokesmen of the citizenry. Bentinck openly encouraged such ideas. The Stadholderly court more discreetly put pamphlet-writers at work who added fuel to the flames. That William III and his counsellors only saw their own tactical advantage in the popular slogans appears at once from the choice of their henchmen. 'A trio of ruffians', an indignant Amsterdammer called the writers of the most biting of the pamphlets, all three of them non-Amsterdammers, Romein de Hooghe, a brilliant engraver, Govert Bidloo, an able surgeon, and Ericus Walten, an indefatigable hack. The unflattering description fitted at least the first of them, although, as I have already related,[1] the last mentioned was to prove the most unlucky of the lot.

A truer offshoot of the popular mind, no doubt, was a pamphlet in which Groothans, representing the regents, instead of standing by the genuine book of old privileges, fobs the citizens off with ten commandments, of which the following will give an idea:

4. Your guilds will be nought,
   Nor ever will a citizen be made a captain.
8. Next, when you marry our cast-off whores
   You will get a job without fail.
9. Provided that you will be ready to risk your lives,
   Let it be understood: against Nassau's offspring.
10. And whosoever ventures to say a word against this,
    Within twenty-four hours he shall make his exit through the gate.

But William III and Bentinck certainly did not give a thought to reform or construction with the aid of the vague aspirations stirring in the minds of the multitude. Everything that has been related above[2] about the Prince's governing methods goes to show the contrary. It is significant that in the three provinces

[1] See above, p. 227.   [2] See p. 147 ff.

under 'Regulations', in order to be able to rule all the more absolutely with his dependents, he never heard the 'Commonalty Committees' which had there of old represented a certain amount of popular influence; he did not even fill up vacancies in these survivals of medieval democracy. In Rotterdam, where as we know his influence was unlimited, the magistracy had gone so far, in 1686, as to remove six civil guard captains, replacing them by town councillors: the 'Court Martial' was evidently far from 'free' at Rotterdam. And how little William troubled his head about the privileges or the wishes of the citizenry, when he felt his authority was being infringed, is proved by his blunt intervention in a regents' quarrel at Goes, when the ruling party had disregarded his Stadholderly orders to postpone an election. Immediately, without notifying the States of Zealand, he despatched troops to the little town, and the Burgomasters, who had begun by closing the gates to them, were subsequently sentenced to heavy punishments by their opponents now brought into office. There is no doubt that the large majority of the inhabitants were in sympathy with the men thus overthrown, and were angered by the roughness of the treatment meted out to them. Outside Goes too, the case made a bad impression. A lampoon entitled *The Conquest of Goes* exhorted the postmaster to send messengers to every quarter with the report that

> Goes has been conquered, Goes, Goes, that mighty town,
> That excellent fortress, that indomitable hamlet.

But Odijck had the States of Zealand well under control and no other town lifted a finger on behalf of the Goes regents.

Yet William III had never shown any hostility on principle towards the regents' régime. During these years he even co-operated with them in order to impose restraints upon the Church. True to his Voetian sentiments he had as we know[1] helped in one case after another, on complaints addressed to him by Reformed ministers, to suppress heterodoxy. It was the magistrates he had just forced upon Rotterdam who in 1693 removed the Huguenot minister Bayle from the Illustrious School, where Paets had got him appointed; in fact the Synod had been stirred up against Bayle for a considerable time by another Frenchman, Jurieu. But these eternal quarrels bored a

[1] See above, p. 148.

man who, however punctilious he might be about dogma, was so deeply involved in the affairs of the world. What he desired was unity, quiet, submission. Apparently that could not be realised by carrying disputes to extremes; and so at the end of 1694 he gave his moral support to the resolution by means of which the States of Holland sought to make an end of the great quarrel between Voetians and Cocceians. The States laid down in that resolution that, concerning points which the Synod of Dort had left undecided (the whole controversy that had since cropped up naturally fell under that head),

no minister should represent those points to be of such importance that without them Holy Writ could not be understood in a sense sufficient unto salvation.

Had Trigland still been alive he might have blamed the authors of this State document, as he had done those of the notorious resolution of 1614, for their presumption in 'making themselves masters of the word of God'.[1] The resolution of 1694 went further still: it ordained that all authorities and private individuals who had any say in the calling of ministers of religion should only take into consideration 'persons of a moderate and peaceable nature'. It was no small triumph for the States to be able to proclaim such a measure with the concurrence of the Stadholder; the States of Utrecht made haste to follow the example of Holland.

Working with all means at his disposal, now driving the oligarchy hard, then again slackening the reins, stronger than ever through his imposing position abroad, William III had the situation sufficiently under control for the end that mattered most to him, the continuation of the war.

The only unfortunate thing was that the cause he represented remained so very unlucky in the field that in the long run even his authority was not proof against the resulting disillusionment and exhaustion, indeed he was himself affected by these feelings. After the two first, another seven campaigns were conducted under William's personal command in the Southern Netherlands. They again provide a monotonous tale. The taking and retaking of a few strategically important fortresses (particularly Namur, Huy, Mons in Hainault) usually determines the movements of the armies for months on end. A few times

[1] See Part One, p. 49.

William is able to force a battle, but each time he suffers a defeat (near Steenkerke in 1692, near Neerwinden in 1693)—not that anything decisive resulted. The French too, may be getting exhausted by the exertion demanded of them year after year, but there is no question of breaking through their defences so that, in accordance with the plans of the Grand Alliance, their conquests since 1659 might be undone.

The power of the coalition was again weakened by the envy and squabbling prevalent among the allies. They differed about the relative importance of the various fighting areas. While the Naval Powers always wanted to concentrate as much of their forces as possible in the Southern Netherlands, the Emperor felt more for the upper Rhine and was moreover deeply involved in a war with Turkey, which produced great successes, but which did not for that reason demand less of his resources. The German princes would only fight for subsidies which the Naval Powers had to furnish.

Soon Spain was no longer in a condition to exert herself in any way at all. Her unlucky Netherlands provinces were hit in this war by the misfortune of a lengthy interruption in the contribution system,[1] which at other times had made the situation at least bearable for the population of the country that was the theatre of war. At various times various districts had been occupied by the French: these were not the worst off: they had one master to reckon with, who, it is true, was wont to make heavy demands in the way of money tributes, supply of waggons, horses, corn, and so on, but whose interest it was not to disturb economic life and who also left the political order in being, the administration of the country districts and of the towns, seeing that he needed it for his requisitioning. It was worse when a district only fell *within reach* of the enemy armies: because then, while still liable to taxation on behalf of its lawful sovereign, it had to meet the enemy's demands on pain of being 'executed'. It was best off in such a case when the lawful master allowed it to come to an understanding with the enemy. Such contribution treaties came increasingly into vogue in proportion as people became accustomed to that method of conducting war. But woe to the husbandman when the high lords started quarrelling about the carrying out of them. Then came the retaliatory

[1] See Part One, p. 117.

measures, the reprisals, the 'rupture of the contribution'; then there was a reversion to the absolute lawlessness of former times; all the safeguards of passports were at an end, all measure was lost sight of in the requisitioning, fields were laid waste, villages burnt, and well-to-do citizens carried off as hostages. That was what happened in the Nine Years' War when at the end of 1689 the French announced reprisals for the raids undertaken in their territory, not by the Spaniards, but by the Dutch and Brandenburgers with the Spanish Netherlands as springboard: a dispute that led to the complete suspension of the contribution arrangements and right up to 1694 exposed Flanders especially to the most terrible ordeals.

In the field meanwhile the generals of the various allied powers were quarrelling and, each supported by public opinion in his own country, blamed the other for reverses that had been suffered. It is remarkable that under such circumstances William III was able to retain his great moral authority with the soldiers as well as with the diplomats. But, for all that, these were exacting years for him, and there is no doubt that they did tire him.

The only big success of those seven campaigns was the capture of Namur in 1695. It had been lost in 1692 and since then had been fortified by Louis' great fortification expert, Vauban. Now his Dutch rival, Menno, Baron van Coehoorn, directed the engineering work needed for the counter-attack. But while the allied armies were detained here, the French had it all their own way in the Southern Netherlands, and from 13–15 August Marshal Villeroi subjected the open city of Brussels to a devastating bombardment, which was yet another heavy blow to the prosperity of the Southern Netherlands, just when (the year before) the contribution system had been re-established.

The shooting with red-hot ball from cannon and mortar continues (*so wrote on the 15th a Hollander from Schaerbeek to the Grand Pensionary Heinsius*) and there is such misery as has not been seen for centuries. I much regret having to transmit these sad tidings. . . . The terrible destruction is largely due to the poor direction given by the town authorities for the immediate quenching of the fire. The sufferings of the townspeople are indescribable. The inhabitants of the lower town began by transporting their possessions to the upper town, but the fire, fanned by the wind, has already come up dangerously high: not only round the market place, but far up Bergstraat have the houses been reduced to ashes, nay even in the Corn

Market; the churches of St. Nicolas, of the Dominicans, of the Franciscans, of Our Lady, the Exchange, the Meat Hall, several monasteries and the béguinage, the Church of Our Lady . . ., built only some years ago, the Fish Market. . . . In short there is so extensive a destruction that I cannot enumerate all the places damaged.

Even at sea things did not go too well for the Dutch. In the battle off La Hogue in 1692, which put an end to the danger of a French maritime ascendancy, only the English had been in action—not that this was the fault of the Dutch Admiral, Van Almonde. But after that the Dutch naval forces repeatedly suffered serious reverses at the hands of the old Dunkirk enemy. Jean Bart in particular proved a formidable opponent, even against regular men-of-war. The Admiralties still left the building of ships to master carpenters ignorant of the theory as by that time applied in England, but especially in France; and this now began to tell.

From 1693 onwards serious negotiations about peace had been going on. How tired people in the Republic were of the war after so many disappointments appeared from the case of Simon van Halewijn, one-time Burgomaster of Dort, whose wife had been a daughter of the late Grand Pensionary De Witt, but whose brother was the man who in 1684–85 had urged the Stadholder on in the Dort dispute[1] and who was considered one of the latter's chief supporters. After Steenkerke Simon van Halewijn had started secret negotiations with the French about peace. In 1693 he was suddenly seized, as was also a Frenchman who had come to Holland for these discussions, and brought before the Court of Holland. Halewijn's action was of a much more serious nature than that of the Amsterdam regents who in 1683–84, in peace-time, and by order of their government, had been in contact with d'Avaux,[2] and his conviction was inevitable and just. But that he had been moved by an honest conviction of more than personal purport is beyond question. He expressed himself bitterly to his judges about a policy which was turning Holland into the dupe of England: that apparently rankled most with him.

He would rather be dead (*so he flared out*) than look on any longer at our people being made to sacrifice their money and their blood in order to play the assiduous servants to the King of England.

---

[1] See above, p. 196.   [2] See above, p. 172.

But William III, who had attended a meeting of the States of Holland to induce them to have Halewijn tried before the Court of the province instead of before his own town's magistracy, reminded the assembly that his position in England was only tenable so long as the English could believe in his prestige with the Dutch. A fresh revolution in England was a nightmare to the Dutch. However much grumbling there might be against the relationship—and the English grumbled no less—the tie was in fact an indissoluble one. Halewijn was sentenced to imprisonment for life—a milder punishment than that of Buat almost thirty years previously. A few years later he escaped from Loevestein.

The tension nevertheless remained. In Amsterdam, so the Swedish ambassador reported from The Hague, everyone is of Halewijn's way of thinking, and in many towns in Holland a peace party was coming into existence. That same summer a certain Mollo, resident of Poland at Amsterdam, where he was connected by marriage to families of importance, spent some time at Versailles and established contact between the French government and the great city. Dangerous possibilities arose when a dispute broke out between Henry Casimir, the Stadholder of Friesland, and his powerful cousin. The vain and insignificant man was greatly offended when after the death of Waldeck the post of first Field Marshal was not bestowed on him but on a German princeling, namely the Duke of Holstein-Plöhn. Henry Casimir left his army in the field in a passion, and his Frisians, who felt slighted in the person of their Stadholder, now refused to furnish their 'consent' and were in a mood to take part in any peace intrigues that might be going.

In these circumstances, the danger of which he realised to the full, William III had tried to remain master of the situation by opening peace negotiations himself. While Mollo was at Versailles, Dijckvelt met a Frenchman in Brussels. What mattered was now how to prevent Louis from playing off against each other those two negotiators, Amsterdam and the Stadholder-King. Heinsius managed this with great skill. He induced the Amsterdammers to be entirely frank about the doings of Mollo by assuring them that their special trade interests—especially the abolition of the 'tonnage dues'—were a matter of great concern to himself and William III; and when

Burgomaster Boreel grumbled that the official negotiations were in the hands of a man from Utrecht, whose province was not interested in navigation and commerce, so that for those interests he was not likely to 'put on armour', the Grand Pensionary persuaded William to let Dijckvelt go to Amsterdam in person. His instructions were to propose in the King's name mutual 'confidence' to the Burgomasters, reassuring them the while on the point of trading interests. His mission succeeded beyond expectation. From that time on relations between Amsterdam, where Boreel was still left in charge of these affairs, and William III and his political friends were indeed characterised by 'confidence'.

The town now supported a policy of negotiating for a general peace only. As regards terms: in particular were Spain and the Empire to be helped to get back the unlawful 'reunions', which had never been ratified except by the twenty years' truce of 1684: above all Luxembourg and Strasbourg. Dijckvelt, however, had already given the French to understand that they might have Luxembourg in exchange for an equivalent, that is, for the restoration of three (or two even, William sighed) out of the five towns of Ypres, Menin, Tournai, Condé, and Maubeuge (all of which had been in the possession of the French since the Peace of Nijmegen—1678—or even of Aix—1668).

A conclusion was almost reached on these terms as early as 1694. And yet the war kept dragging on from year to year. On either side it was a game of patience and endurance. However little either side was able to take from the other by force of arms, the allies knew that in France the stress had almost reached breaking-point, and Louis on the other hand was confident that sooner or later discord among his enemies would offer him a way out. And indeed that is what happened at long last, although harmony between William III and the Republic remained intact: it was between the Naval Powers and their impotent protégé Spain on the one hand and the Emperor on the other that the breach occurred. On the Amsterdam Exchange murmurings could be heard early in 1696 to the effect that the Republic should not continue the war for the sake of Strasbourg, which afterwards might be bartered away to France any moment by its own magistracy, just as indeed German rulers and ministers were ready to sell, if it must be, the whole Empire. A short while before, a popular riot at Amsterdam—the so-called undertakers' revolt, directed against a tax on funerals—had revealed how irritable the general mood was; it can hardly have been a matter of chance that the house of Burgomaster Boreel, the close collaborator of Heinsius, had been ransacked with particular violence.

And how much more menacing did the outlook become when in the summer of that year Savoy concluded a separate peace! The Emperor and Spain as a result let themselves be persuaded to consent to a declaration of neutrality for Italy, so that by the time that 1697 came round much larger French military forces would be available for a campaign in the Netherlands.

Nevertheless the Grand Pensionary remained inflexible, still more so than the Stadholder, who in his quality of King was exposed to the attacks of the English peace party, and the French actually seemed to give up hope of intimidating the Republic and to start thinking seriously of peace. But when the Emperor might have won Strasbourg by a settlement, it appeared that he cared more about the continuation of the war than about the town. At the Peace Congress that gathered at Rijswijk in 1697 the imperial ambassadors resorted obviously to obstructive methods. The explanation was to be found in the state of health of the unfortunate Carlos II of Spain, whose death at last seemed at hand. A much wider prospect than that of a small shift in territory was thus opened up: the struggle between Habsburg and Bourbon for the heritage of the whole Spanish monarchy, the seeds of which had been sown forty years previously by the marriages of Louis and of Leopold, might any moment have to be fought in real earnest. At the Grand Alliance of 1689 the Naval Powers had recognised the Emperor's claims, so he thought it would serve his interests if the coalition against France were still in arms at the moment that the question of the succession was raised.

When in March 1697 the drift of Imperial diplomacy became clear to him, William III burst out, in a letter to Heinsius, about the 'intolerable conduct' of that Court; and to the Austrian ambassador in London he exclaimed:

What likelihood is there at this moment that we should succeed in making France renounce a succession for which alone she would be prepared to wage

war, if need be for twenty years? Indeed we are in no condition—God knows
—to prescribe the law to France.

Indeed, so it proved soon enough! That same summer the
French armies advanced still further, taking Ath in the Netherlands, and in the southern theatre of war, just as they had done
fifty-seven years before, Barcelona. But if Leopold hoped for
the Spanish king to die while the war was still on, Louis was no
less anxious that the death might occur in peace time; and if
when it happened the cordial understanding between the
Emperor and the Naval Powers should be troubled, so much the
better! For that reason and in spite of his military successes
against Spain, he still offered favourable terms, favourable
especially for Spain and the Republic: all his conquests, such
as Mons and Ath and Barcelona, and even Luxembourg, he was
ready to restore; the Republic was tempted with extra favourable trade tariffs—but the offer of Strasbourg he withdrew.

It was impossible to hold on. Amsterdam warned that delay
might result in the loss of a unique opportunity; English public
opinion expressed itself unequivocally for peace. William III
decided to act quickly. In his name Bentinck had an interview
with the French Marshal Boufflers at Hal south of Brussels. The
idea was to remove all Louis' mistrust in William III as the
irreconcilable war-monger, and to make it clear to Europe also
that he desired peace. The Stadholder-King even let it be
known that, if necessary, he was willing to conclude peace
for the Republic and England alone. Spain had no choice,
but the Emperor had to be presented with the accomplished
fact and did not indeed join the peace until after it had been
concluded.

At the peace treaty of Rijswijk, therefore, Strasbourg remained in French hands, but everything the French had
conquered in the Netherlands they evacuated, including
Luxembourg. The States placed troops in a row of fortresses
along the southern frontier of the Spanish Netherlands, in
Luxembourg, Namur, Charleroi, Mons, Oudenarde, Courtrai,
and Nieuport. Spain, which for a generation already had had to
rely on the Northern Netherlands for the defence of those
provinces, readily agreed to that arrangement. The peace
inspired so little confidence that the Republic did not dare leave
its 'barrier' unprotected for a single moment. Meanwhile it

obtained another favourable commercial treaty with France, by which moreover the tonnage dues were abolished.

2. CONTINUED ECONOMIC PROSPERITY OF HOLLAND

IT IS necessary to dwell for a moment on the economic situation of the Republic. Two wars of such magnitude against France—involuntarily one sympathises with the lamentations about the unbearable burdens which accompanied their prosecution, and one is surprised that presently there will appear to be courage and strength left for a third on a larger scale than ever.

Taxation had indeed been forced up ever higher. Shortly before the outbreak of the Nine Years' War a pamphleteer had already lamented that

of taxes, God save us, there are in this republic so many and of such variety as has hardly been the case in all the world in any empire or land.

These taxes lay heavily on everything, on luxury articles and on primary necessities; for that reason prices were nowhere so high as in the Republic, and especially in Holland. But that only resulted in a tension which heightened the resilience of that society. A lively and resourceful activity continued to prevail, which overcame every difficulty. If perhaps there was a decline in some fields, then it was more than made up for by fresh rises elsewhere.

The old textile industry at Leyden and other towns in Holland, for instance, was in a bad way. Competition with England and with adjoining German districts became increasingly difficult. The high wages made indispensible by the cost of foodstuffs and the high standard of living were in large part the cause of this, and the protection of the home market, which the States, departing from their free trade principles, were wont to grant in the interests of that one privileged industry, could not save it. The manufacturers found a way out by setting an ever increasing number of looms in Brabant, especially in Tilburg, to work on their account. There, in the Generality Lands, wages were lower, while the restrictive regulations of the guilds and the irksome supervision of the drapers' hall did not operate there either. Those advantages might have been found nearer home, had not the towns of the province of Holland persistently prevented the rise of any kind of manufactures in the surrounding rural districts. Apart from that, the Holland countryside was a great deal more prosperous than that of Brabant, systematically over-taxed as it was. Thus, in the rising Tilburg industry the misery of the Generality Lands actually served the prosperity of Leyden, where not only the employers lived, but where, protected by the guild regulations, the dyeing was still carried out.

In a number of places in Holland and Utrecht the new industries introduced by the French refugees were now making their appearance, and these remained outside the guild organisation. Everywhere the town authorities tried to attract them by tempting offers of relief from taxation, of loans even, and of exemption from the guild restrictions. This last-mentioned favour especially very soon aroused the annoyance of the citizenries, and it is indeed a fact that there were serious social drawbacks attaching to the manufacturing system which thus sprang up by the side of the indigenous small-scale industry. The labour of children and women was used on a large scale, town orphans were set to work in numbers. But for a short space of time the wealth of the country increased considerably through the manufacture of costly materials such as silk, taffeta, brocade, and velvet, which had previously been the monopoly of France. A start was also made with home-distilled cognac, as also with gin; the great vogue of this new drink became a serious menace to the national health. If, however, beer-brewing was on the decline, then it was not only on this account, but also because tea became ever more popular as a beverage, and soon coffee too made its appearance, with which the East India Company was starting to earn a mint of money.

As regards European trade, the English and North Germans, especially the Hamburgers, were now beginning to push their way in, right and left, where once the Hollanders had been in almost sole possession of the field. But Dutch trade was not therefore declining. Contemporaries were inclined to consider world trade and world wealth as a constant quantity: according to them one could therefore gain only at the expense of another. Actually the world found itself in an era of economic expansion. The confirmation of internal order created the conditions needed for this. Even the endless wars among the new strong States by which the development was accompanied did not interfere in economic life so fundamentally as had the previous confusion. As a matter of fact the Dutch were still far ahead of the English in the Baltic. With France the English hardly traded at all, while the Dutch traders had not only always devoted much of their energies to that country, but in peace treaties time and again, as we know, the States-General had obtained from France terms favouring their trade. During the wars, it is true, this trade used to meet with difficulties, but the States, as was their regular custom, would not hear of discontinuing it on account of war between the Governments.

The Mediterranean countries, especially the Levant, were the regions in which the English were ahead of the Dutch; not that Dutch trade was in a bad way even there. In these mutual trading relations, too, 'the balance' (which was anxiously watched by the economists and politicians of the day) was distinctly favourable for England—a result of the Navigation Laws. But in the vast Spanish empire, after the Peace of Münster, and especially during the last decades, the Dutch made tremendous strides. Not only was the trade of the Spanish Netherlands largely in their hands, but that of Spanish America as well: and this notwithstanding the Spanish 'Navigation Laws', which from the early days of Spanish colonisation were meant—no less than the English—to keep the intercourse between the colonies and the mother country in the hands of the latter's merchants. But the economic indolence of the Spaniards had increasingly made them lose their hold on this trade. Dutch smuggling to the various ports in South and Central America reached large dimensions. It was among other things the need of the Spanish colonies for ever fresh cargoes of slaves which made this inevitable: the supply of slaves was controlled by the Dutch and the English. To the horror of the clerical party at the Spanish Court, the government had even granted the notorious importation contract, the *asiento*, to a Dutch group—the Amsterdam Coymans family. Even when this arrangement came to an end in 1689, Curaçao yet remained one of the chief markets of negroes for Spanish American use. And under cover of this trade, profitable in itself as it was, the Dutch kept up extremely important connections. They continually came up against the English here, but undoubtedly were still retaining a lead in these parts of the world.

In short, the economic resilience of the country was unbroken and in a world where other countries were making headway in catching up their arrears, the Republic was still capable of absorbing heavy shocks.

3. BETWEEN TWO WARS (1697–1702)

The Barrier Arrangements

THE Peace of Rijswijk was not so very different from that of Nijmegen, which William III had so wholeheartedly branded as a betrayal. In point of fact the attitude of the allies in both cases had made separate action inevitable. They were lucky in that this time Louis' obsession with the possibilities of the Spanish succession did more than all their years of persistent effort to obtain such favourable terms for Spain and its Netherlands. But a feeling of irritation remained between the Naval Powers and the Emperor. In England war-weariness and mistrust of William and his favourites found expression in violent Tory opposition, determined to economise on the army. International circumstances were hardly less favourable for Louis than after Nijmegen, and in that state of affairs he and all his neighbours were now faced with this one fateful question, that of the Spanish succession; courier upon courier came from Madrid with reports of Carlos II's poor state of health.

But Louis was not in the mood to make use of the state of affairs for a policy of aggression as he had done after 1678. The impoverishment of the French people made him shrink from a fresh war. William III was assured by Heinsius that the States would unflinchingly draw the sword anew if the Spanish inheritance should threaten to fall into French hands, but he could not count on England. Thus it was that the two great opponents came quite naturally to consult together about a compromise whereby European peace might be maintained. This meant that the Naval Powers attempted to come to an agreement with Louis for a partition of the Spanish monarchy, whereby the other pretender, the Emperor, would get his share. In all the various plans which were successively taken into consideration, Spain's Italian possessions were offered for the satisfaction of Louis; William and Heinsius were willing to see him add a good bit to his own country rather than allow the

Spanish Empire in its entirety to fall to one of his grandsons, who would (it is true) set up a dynasty of his own but would nevertheless, so they feared, be in fact dependent upon France. What they wanted above all was to keep out of the hands of the French the Southern Netherlands and the American colonies, the one being 'the barrier' of the Republic, while in the other their trading interests feared French competition. There was no doubt also a great deal to be said against allowing the French to extend their power in the Mediterranean, and the States were certainly not indifferent on that point, although it was especially the English, with their large trade interests in the Levant, who were sensitive about it. But if war was to be avoided they would have to allow France *something*.

In this way then the treaty of 1698 came about between the Kings of France and England and the States-General, whereby in the case of Carlos II's death it was laid down that Spain itself, together with the Netherlands and America, should fall to the small son of the Elector of Bavaria, Governor of the Netherlands; this child, chosen because his own hereditary dominions would not endanger the equilibrium of Europe, had indeed quite as good a claim as the more powerful pretenders, being the grandson of the Emperor and the great-grandson of Philip IV of Spain. The Dauphin of France was to get Naples and Sicily as well as some scattered places in Italy and North Spain. Milan was assigned to the Emperor's second son, Charles. In 1699, however, the young Electoral prince of Bavaria died before the sickly Carlos II, and everything had to be done anew, and this time, in the absence of a harmless third party, with less chance of success. The second Partition Treaty stipulated that the Dauphin was to receive the same compensation as had been stipulated in the first treaty, with the addition of Lorraine, whose Duke was removed to Milan. The remainder, Spain, the Netherlands, and America, were now to be the share of the Emperor's second son.

But these partitions, which the Naval Powers had presumed to arrange for with only one of the Pretenders, aroused the greatest irritation at the Viennese court, and no less at Madrid. There, amid all the confusion, incompetence, and impoverishment, Spanish pride clung to one passionate determination: that the empire should remain in its entirety. When the small

s

Bavarian Prince was still alive Carlos II had therefore appointed him his universal heir. Now the struggle carried on around the King's death-bed between an Austrian and a French party resolved itself in the conviction that Louis would be best able to maintain that unity. On 2 October 1700, Carlos II put his name to a will in which he left the whole of his empire to the French King's second grandson, Philip of Anjou. On 1 November he died. The Spanish envoy who went to Versailles to offer Philip the crown had been given instructions to travel on to Vienna if the French wished to stand by the partition treaty, and to offer the undivided inheritance to Archduke Charles. The Emperor had not let himself be persuaded by William and the States to become a party to the partition treaty, on the contrary he protested against it with might and main. Upholding the treaty was bound therefore also to lead to war—a war in which it seemed uncertain whether William would be able to carry out his undertakings, for in England vehement criticism made itself heard against the cession to France of Italian territory as provided in the treaty. So it is not to be wondered at that Louis decided to ignore the partition treaty and to accept the entire monarchy for his grandson.

For William III it was a mortifying experience to be duped by Louis, because that was how he saw it.

If (*so he wrote angrily to Heinsius*) one is prepared to break all promises and oaths, it is easy to deceive the other party.

Worst of all was that in England a general feeling of relief manifested itself—'the blindness of people is incomprehensible', the King grumbled—so violent was the aversion to the partition plan. During the last few years William had needed in England all his patience and self-control. In 1698 a new Parliament had been elected in which the Tories, with their dislike of a standing army and their distrust of foreigners and of this policy of meddling with the continent, possessed a majority. Never had the lack of understanding between William and the English been so complete as it was now.

At one moment, when the Parliament decided to discharge his Dutch regiments still in English service, he thought of relinquishing the crown and going back to Holland. But he had not, on his part, shown much regard for the national susceptibilities of the English: of necessity perhaps—but in any case he had kept his English ministers completely in the dark about the secrets of his foreign policy. He worked confidentially only with Dutchmen: Heinsius was his associate, not his servant. The confidence and understanding between those two was complete. It should be noted that their correspondence, in which Heinsius does not by any means await orders but gives his own views in detail, was conducted in Dutch: none of William's English ministers need have access to letters in which the fate of England and of Europe was disposed of. The chief negotiations for the Peace of Rijswijk had been conducted by Dijckvelt and Boreel, then by Bentinck. The latter, Earl of Portland as he now was, although at the same time a member of the Knighthood in the States of Holland, had been sent to the French Court as first English ambassador after the peace. It was he who had set on foot and concluded in great secrecy the negotiations for the first partition treaty, always, of course, in close consultation with Heinsius; Lord Somers, the Chancellor, had affixed the great seal to discretionary powers given to Portland. The second treaty also had been concluded without letting the English ministers into the secret. As soon as the matter became public, English opinion had turned sharply against it. Although William had consented to the cession of Naples and Sicily to France only because he realised his weakness as a result of the paralysing opposition of Parliament and the reduction of the English military forces, he was nevertheless blamed for these concessions as implying a betrayal of the highest English trade interests: an abandonment of the Mediterranean! Feeling against William ran so high that Louis could imagine himself back in the days when Charles II had been reduced to impotence by his Parliament. But William was not the man to abandon the game. The idea of retiring from England was no more than a momentary reaction of anger. To Heinsius he wrote:

I am entirely convinced that should this will (*of Carlos II of Spain*) be carried into effect, England and the Republic will find themselves in the utmost danger of being totally lost or ruined. I still hope that this will be realised in the Republic and that all exertions will be made to prevent, if possible, so great an evil. To me it is most mortifying to find myself unable to act in this important affair with the vigour it demands and to set an example by going ahead, but it is up to the Republic, and as regards people here (*the English*) I hope to conduct myself with such circumspection as will carry them along gradually without their noticing it.

Heinsius saw the matter in the same light as William III, and was much less isolated in his attitude of mind than the King was in England. It is true that in Holland also there were many who listened to the French when (as William expressed it) they used 'that sweet word *peace*'. Peace in the present, and troubles in the uncertain future? At the news of the acceptance of Charles II's testamentary disposition stocks and shares rose on the Amsterdam Exchange:

> Your Majesty knows (*so Heinsius wrote*) how unreliable is that foundation, yet what powerful an attraction it exercises. (*Indeed, soon the burgomasters and young pensionary Buys were trying to make him see:*) that the Exchange is composed of numerous experienced men, who have a sound knowledge of the affairs of the world, and they are all of them unanimous in the opinion that no mischief can result from the acceptance (*in France*) of the late Spanish King's will.

Nevertheless Heinsius succeeded in gradually getting Amsterdam on his side, but to that end he had to assume as 'careful a conduct' as William III in England, and there was no question of the Republic 'setting an example by going ahead'.

Philip V had already been invested as King in every part of the Spanish Empire, and still the States were negotiating with France about guarantees for the 'security' which they considered to be menaced by the new state of affairs. Heinsius wanted to obtain the guarantees before recognising Philip V; Amsterdam was inclined to recognise him first, as the French wished. One of the motives for that line of conduct was the anxiety felt about the States troops in the barrier fortresses, whose position would become untenable as soon as the Elector-Governor came to an understanding with the French. Both sides tugged hard at Maximilian Emanuel. In February he resolutely went over to Louis' side. French troops (not Spanish!), to the alarm of the States, and also of the English, marched into the Southern Netherlands. In The Hague relief was felt when it proved possible to fetch the encircled garrison troops safely home, but with the Southern Netherlands wholly in French hands the Republic's own frontiers were now immediately exposed.

The fears of a lifetime had suddenly been realised. Everybody could now see—even though the plenary powers which Philip, before his departure for Spain, had granted to his grandfather, remained a secret—that the Southern Netherlands had in fact become a French possession. In their danger, and still uncertain about England, the States now recognised Philip V, but at the same time the negotiations in The Hague about guarantees were continued; d'Avaux arrived there on behalf of Louis XIV. William III was already able to act a little more energetically. In addition to the alarm about the Southern Netherlands, there was now in England the annoyance about the attempts which the French at once made to get control of the Spanish American trade. Louis' megalomania was leading him to act in such a way, both in Europe and America, as must put William III and Heinsius in the right as against the credulous, the appeasers. Amsterdam continued to urge moderation, reminding the Dutch public of the expenditure a war would entail while the country was still burdened with the debts left by the last one. Yet the town agreed with what might be called the truly national policy of William III and Heinsius.

So now the States' terms were communicated to d'Avaux: the Southern Netherlands to be evacuated by the French troops and the States to be allowed to maintain garrisons in barrier fortresses—fortresses situated in the North of the Southern Netherlands this time of course!—and in the East: the line of defence had in any case come closer! Trade, moreover, was to be safeguarded in all the Spanish dominions; and the Emperor (whose troops were already fighting in Italy) to be given 'satisfaction' for his claims. That last-mentioned point shows that the necessity for renewed association with the old ally was already felt. And indeed, Louis was not willing to agree to any of the demands made to him. The negotiations with France consequently came to nothing and those with Austria assumed vital importance. The terms which had proved to be unobtainable by agreement with Louis XIV became the basis for a renewal of the Grand Alliance, which would have to try and exact them by force of arms.

The Alliance was signed in The Hague in September; Marlborough was the representative of the King of England. The embarrassments caused him by the partition treaties (that same summer Somers and Portland were indicted for trial by the Tory Parliament) had taught William III to employ Englishmen for the conclusion of treaties. The object was to obtain 'satisfaction' for the Emperor. Even now William and

Heinsius did not wish to promise him that Philip V would be deprived of the whole of the monarchy. Furthermore, it was stipulated that the trade interests of the Naval Powers should be guaranteed; and as regards the Netherlands, that they should be reconquered,

in order that they should serve for a dyke, rampart and 'barrier', as had been the case in the past, so as to separate and keep France at a distance from the United Provinces.

A few days later James II died in his French exile and Louis, who at Rijswijk had recognised William III as King of England, now greeted as such the child whose birth in 1688 had been the sign for the Revolution. If there could still be any doubt as to whether the English people would support William in his war policy, it was removed by this insult. A new Parliament was elected, which showed all zeal in taking the necessary measures.

That same spring of 1702, in which his preparations for the great war to disturb Louis XIV's dreams of power were crowned with such success, witnessed the death of William III. Having been sickly for years, he died as the result of a fall from his horse in Hampton Court. England continued his work under Anne, his deceased wife's sister, who most opportunely found a commander and diplomat of unusual gifts in Marlborough, long her confidential friend. But in the Republic, too, there was, in spite of the general dismay, no hesitation—much to the disappointment of the French, who had imagined that 'the republicans' and 'Messieurs d'Amsterdam', once escaped from the grip of the Stadholder's powerful influence, would prove ready for peace intrigues. A gross misconception! William III's régime of favourites had indeed been felt to be oppressive, and in several places violent reactions broke out against the men or the bodies associated with it. But the danger of French domination in the Southern Netherlands was very generally envisaged as it had been by the Stadholder-King. In addition to that, the fear that France would make itself master of Spanish-American trade, made a profound impression at Amsterdam; and now that England and Austria, and together with them once more a number of German princes (although not Bavaria this time, nor as yet Savoy) were ready to march against France, Heinsius had no difficulty in persuading the States to make a unanimous effort.

4. LATTER DAYS OF THE SPANISH RÉGIME IN THE NETHERLANDS

AN ASTONISHING spectacle, that presented by the history of the North Netherlands people under the Stadholdership of William III! Earlier we saw it establish its independence in the face of the world power of Spain; we saw it maintain its carrying trade, its naval supremacy, its colonial expansion in spite of England. Now after all that effort it had strength and courage enough to give Europe a lead in resisting the imperialism of Louis XIV, a task nevertheless which demanded more of blood and treasure than any of the previous wars. Altogether the gigantic struggle, whose first skirmishings and whose first catastrophe had taken place under De Witt and which now, after William III's death, had to be continued by Heinsius with all the power at his disposal, was to cover a period of half a century. This last war, for which we have just seen the Republic bracing itself, was to attain the goal but was also to exhaust the Republic and reveal its intrinsic weakness compared with the great powers properly so called.

The goal? To the Republic what had mattered all along above everything was to keep France out of the Southern Netherlands. In a letter to Heinsius, written in the critical days of 1700, William III said so in so many words:

What has made us conclude the partition treaty was only to preserve the peace of Europe and in particular the Spanish Netherlands. (*And in the new situation created by Louis' acceptance of Carlos II's will, again:*) My concern above all other things is to prevent the Spanish Netherlands from falling into the hands of France.

This anxiety was not inspired by any feeling of community with the co-lingual people in Flanders and Brabant; no one gave a thought to the fact that their denationalisation, which might be the sequence of their being incorporated in France, would adversely affect Dutch culture as well. All that was perceived in the North was that the independence of their own North Netherlands State would be gravely compromised if the French managed to push up their power to its southern frontier. So, just as in the days of Frederick Henry, the Dutch wanted to keep France at a distance. We saw in what terms that was expressed in the Grand Alliance of 1701. In 1684 Fagel had summarised that article of the North Netherlands political creed thus:

It is better to meet the Frenchman at Brussels and Antwerp than at Breda or Dort.

That generation of North Netherlanders, accustomed as it had become to the split, and to the political impotence of the South, could not so much as play with the idea that it would be even better if Antwerp and Brussels had been able to combine their own untrammelled force with that of Breda and Dort in opposition to the French. It is true that in 1691 a pamphlet appeared (the writer was Ericus Walten, no doubt the mouthpiece, once again, of important personages in the entourage of the Stadholder-King) in which it was argued that since 'the horribly bad direction' of the Spanish Governors doomed to futility every effort to keep the Spanish Netherlands intact, it would be better if Spain ceded them to a more powerful enemy of France, namely to the King of England, or to the States-General, preferably to the latter. One would have thought that the community of language was bound, in this connection at least, to be mentioned (as was still done in political speculations of half a century earlier[1])'and that something would be said about the services which under a better direction the inhabitants themselves would be able to contribute. Neither the one nor the other. The argument confines itself exclusively to considerations of strategy, geography, and international politics.

We on the contrary are impressed and surprised by the contrast between the activity of the North and the passivity of the South in a struggle in which the fate of the South was much more immediately involved. To us it is clear that what gave France her opportunity was the destruction of the young Burgundian State as a consequence of which the southern half, including Flanders and Brabant, once imbued with such vigorous powers of resistance, had fallen into the saddest helplessness and intellectual and material decadence. The separation from their co-linguists in the North had in itself been a misfortune; the permanent coupling to the Spanish Empire in its moribund state completed the downfall.

In one respect all the Governors who succeeded each other in Brussels were similar: in their impotence. The weak government in Madrid never wholly trusted them. Not content with keeping in its own hands the appointment to numerous posts—military, as well as civilian and ecclesiastical—it also let itself be confidentially informed about what went on by agents within

[1] See Part One, p. 112.

the administration. These men all too often undermined the authority of the King's Governor by giving it to be understood that he did not possess Madrid's full confidence. In these late days of the Spanish régime even the three Councils, of which the Privy Council and the Council of Finance had long been the tools of absolutism, often disregarded the Governor's directives, sometimes indeed, as when they defended Jansenism against the Jesuits and the Pope, on behalf of what seemed to them the true interest of royal authority. Over the army and foreign policy, of course, these Councils had even now no influence whatever.

The provincial States' assemblies, that is to say the representatives of the privileged classes, did still have a say in the raising of taxes, but this does not mean that they were allowed— or even that they ever seriously attempted—to bring up for discussion any of the general problems of governmental policy. Had they been regularly convened in States-General, then this would have been difficult to prevent. But in fact the 'consents' were discussed separately, not only with the provinces, but within the provinces with the orders (clergy and nobility) and with every single town. In that way at most local interests were voiced—and, naturally, the indiscriminate aversion of a harassed and exhausted people to any sort of payment. No vigorous national feeling, no conviction that its own fate was at stake, could steel its powers of resistance, as was possible in the Republic. The chances of any constructive opposition against the government materialising were still further diminished by the social contrasts within the towns. In Louvain and Brussels particularly the relationship between the oligarchy ('the families') and the guilds was one of tension. In general it was the guilds in the three large Brabant towns[1] which caused the government the greatest trouble, but there were times when their anger directed itself with equal force against their own magistrates. At best the Burgomasters acted somewhat hesitatingly as their spokesmen; occasionally they tried in consultation with the government to coax them to do 'their duty'. The whole of this last stage of the Spanish régime is characterised by serious disturbances in Brussels, Antwerp, and Louvain.

Take for instance the short-lived governorship of the Prince of Parma, who between 1680 and 1682 went through difficult

[1] See Part One, p. 27.

moments, especially with Antwerp. In spite of the Peace of
Nijmegen (which did not in fact for a moment remove the
French menace), the financial position was desperate. Parma's
predecessor, Villahermosa, had been so hard pressed that in
order to get some money quickly he had contented himself with
a smaller contribution than customary from the States of
Flanders, a precedent that now caused Parma the greatest
difficulties in his attempts at getting the Brabanters to consent.
The new Governor had come to Brussels armed with promises
of ample subsidies from Spain. These soon appeared unlikely to
be realised. Plans for an army reform also suffered from the
delay of the necessary authorisations from Madrid. So wretched
did the condition of the army become that the soldiers were
begging in the streets in tatters and even infested the highways
with their robberies. And meanwhile Brabant's 'consent' was
held up while the Governor's plenipotentiaries, the Count
d'Arquinto (his influential minister) and Don Bernardo de
Salinas (note that both were Spaniards) were carrying on long-
drawn-out negotiations with Antwerp, where the guilds were in
a particularly intractable mood. This was occasioned in the first
place by an injudicious display of authority on the part of the
government, which had caused a Frenchman, a well-known
inciter of guild resistance, to be lured to the Castle, and was
now keeping him imprisoned at Brussels. The Antwerpers felt
this to be an infringement of a privilege especially dear to their
hearts, that *de non evocando*.[1] But other grievances combined to
rouse public feeling, and in the end Antwerp could only be
persuaded to agree to the new tax (which, as long as its refusal
was maintained, could not be obtained from the other towns
either) in return for a reduction in the scale of import and
export duties levied in the great seaport. Antwerp hoped this
would lead to a revival of her trade—an idle hope so long as the
Northerners kept up the closure of the Scheldt—but now
instantly a protest was raised by the States of Flanders, of old
chiefly an industrial province. Nor did the Antwerp guilds keep
quiet for long. Already in 1682, long smouldering disturbances
over a projected beer tax flared up there. The compliance of the
magistrates aroused the fury of the mob. Even a number of

---

[1] Laying down that no citizen was to be called before a court of justice
other than that of his own town.

guild 'deans' were inclining to vote in favour. The cry arose that they had been bribed; the Antwerpers dubbed them 'nodding masters' or 'nodders'. On the day when the decisive vote was to be taken a number of ring-leaders played a game of marbles in the market-place—the word for marbles in Dutch being identical with that nickname—and the demonstration was witnessed by thousands and caused the greatest excitement. The government, thus provoked, dragged some heroes of the mob to Brussels to have them put on trial there. In order to evade that same privilege which ruled out prosecution elsewhere than in a man's own town, the case had to be treated as one of treason. But it cost a great deal of trouble to find witnesses, and the magistrates of the central government were dismayed by the feeling evinced by this obstruction.

Indeed the government never dared to persist to the bitter end in cases of this nature. The intervention of the military at Antwerp in 1658[1] was remembered as an act of authority which had become impracticable in the greatly worsened circumstances. Parma might flaunt his title of Highness in the face of the Spaniards, who despised him as an Italian, and might (as scornfully described by a contemporary) 'drive through the streets, in a fine carriage resembling a triumphal car, followed by thirty or thirty-six lackeys on foot and twelve pages', but his weakness in the face of the intractable Antwerpers did the prestige of his office no good. Yet in a certain sense the foreign rulers made a virtue of necessity and consciously followed a policy which through its leniency and compliance contrasted with the harsh methods of the powerful French neighbour. Methods of force could avail no longer to maintain their position in the Netherlands against the ever impending menace from the South. That they could not make an appeal to national sentiment either goes without saying, and the principle which had sometimes enlisted the support of the population on their behalf in the struggle with the Northern Netherlands before 1648, the Catholic principle, was of course irrelevant where France was concerned. On the whole one may observe that in the wars with France the attitude of the inhabitants between the lawful ruler and the invader was determined by purely opportunist considerations.

[1] See above, p. 49.

Look for instance at the behaviour of the Council of Flanders, when the town of Ghent fell into the hands of the French in 1678. Eleven of the twenty-two members, headed by the President, Errembault, submitted to the demand of the conqueror that they should swear an oath of allegiance to him and administer justice in his name; the other eleven preferred to leave the town and at Bruges constituted the only Council of Flanders recognised by the Spanish government. The calculations of Errembault and his companions were sadly frustrated when Louis XIV presently, by the treaty of Nijmegen, restored his conquests in Flanders. But even so the King, to the bitter chagrin of the loyal councillors at Bruges, managed to protect those who had served him: the treaty contained a clause stipulating that no retaliatory measures were to be applied on account of services rendered to the other party during the war. President Errembault of his own accord sent in his resignation and went over to the French service for good, but the other gentlemen remained in office.

At the turn of fortune they had apologised to the Spanish Governor, arguing necessity, insinuating at the same time that their colleagues who had fled to Bruges had only done so because their estates lay outside the district of the town of Ghent. The public nevertheless did look upon the councillors who had remained at Ghent as 'traitors', and the others had on 'their long-desired return from voluntary exile' been enthusiastically cheered. The continuance in office of the 'traitors' meanwhile was not only creating false and unpleasant relations within the restored Council, it could not fail to weaken still further the feeling of loyalty and promote the inclination to watch the struggle between the Kings with an eye to chance and interest. That in 1690, when the war had broken out anew, the surviving 'traitors' were at length removed from office and superseded, cannot have done much to improve matters; particularly not when this measure was soon repealed again by orders from Spain.

The inhabitants of Ghent in any case had come to know French methods of administration by experience. As a matter of fact connections were still sufficiently close with those regions which had been detached from the Spanish Netherlands since 1659 and where these methods had since been in full working order. Several portions of the county of Flanders in particular had at various times been in that situation; after 1678 Dunkirk, Bergues St. Winox, Cassel, Hazebrouck, Bailleul, Furnes, and Ypres still were.

The French régime showed little patience with the ancient rights of that fragment of the Dutch-speaking area. As early as 1670 an ordinance on penal law had appeared, to which districts incorporated in later years were also subjected, and which considerably restricted the full competence over their citizens of the urban benches of magistrates: in itself a reform for which there was a great deal to be said, but which was undoubtedly highly objectionable to the town gentlemen's class. The right *de non evocando* was dear to their hearts; and there was too little of a conscious or consistent opposition between democracy and oligarchy for the citizenry as a whole not to share in this feeling (we have already seen an example of this): this privilege was still looked upon—and so it was all over the Netherlands, so indeed it had been intended in the Middle Ages—as a right not so much of the town government as of their like-minded citizens who much preferred to appear before their own magistrates than before the Count's judges.

For the Flemings fallen under French dominion this whittling down of their municipal independence brought along with it simultaneously an infringement of their linguistic freedom. Their benches of magistrates were placed under a newly established court in the Walloon town of Tournai. The Dunkirk magistrates had been ordered to use French as early as 1663; in 1684 the same injunction was issued for Ypres, incorporated in 1678, and other towns and bailiwicks of West Flanders.

Having been informed (*so ran the motivation of the royal decree*) that at Ypres (*etc. . . .*) pleadings are done in Flemish, so that Our subjects in the said towns and bailiwicks, when they are obliged to go and plead in Our court at Tournai, and this sometimes in cases of little importance (*consequence of the ordinance of* 1670), have to have all documents relating to their case translated into French, the which entails expenditure and is a source of confusions; therefore, wishing to guard over Our said subjects' well-being and to put an end to those inconveniences, We wish and it is Our pleasure that from now on in the town of Ypres (*etc. . . .*) no language shall be used before the bench but French, and We forbid all barristers and solicitors, and the judges equally, to make use any more of the Flemish language, on penalty of nullity.

We see here already this curious trait of the French feeling of linguistic superiority, which was to be consistently displayed in times to come: that the well-being of the inhabitants might have been served better by judges with a knowledge of Dutch at Tournai never so much as occurred to the men who composed this regulation. And yet it need hardly be pointed out that, even though some jurists and magistrates may have been able to carry out the order, it did not alter in the least the fact that the people at large continued to use their own language and that they remained completely ignorant of French for century after century. How essentially Dutch was the culture of that conquered region is shown by a figure such as that of Michiel de Swaen, the Dunkirk poet, brought up in the Dutch language at the Jesuit College of the town, physician and town councillor, and a member of an active Chamber of Rhetoric.[1]

But what undoubtedly most alarmed their fellow-countrymen still under Spanish rule when observing the French administration of the conquered Flemish area, was the complete abolition of their beloved right to be asked for their 'consent' before contributing to the exchequer. The Flemish towns now under France were no longer even consulted about their share in the Kingdom's expenditure. It was simply fixed every year by Royal Decree and levied without any supervision on the part of the taxpayers or their representatives. This, according to Netherlands ideas, was the worst kind of despotism.

No doubt, then, the mildness of the Spanish rule, wretched as it was, did win for it a certain attachment; but its financial embarrassment and incapacity to protect the country at the same time exposed it to the contempt of its subjects. The allies were roused to impatience no less, and it was partly owing to the urgings of William III that the Spanish government in 1691 proceeded to confer the Governorship on Maximilian Emanuel, Elector of Bavaria.

This brilliant figure, proud of his actions against the Turks, ambitious and enterprising, but at the same time frivolous and prodigal, hoped from the beginning that he might maintain himself in this new position for life, and even that, one day, at the great change which was likely to follow upon the extinction of the Spanish dynasty, he might obtain the full sovereignty

[1] See above, p. 244.

over that country, so much wealthier, even in its present deteriorated state, and of so much wider European importance, than his Electorate. For an instant, in 1698, the designation of his small son as successor to the Spanish throne opened up still grander prospects to his ambition, but after the boy's death in 1699 all his ambitions were once more centred on the Netherlands.

Although he had on his arrival, in 1692, been greeted (from Roermond on) with all the magniloquent demonstrations of joy with which the ever-hopeful people of the Southern Netherlands had so often in the past welcomed as saviours princes of the blood, the war for the time being created the worst conditions imaginable. The Elector met with but little opportunity of distinguishing himself in the field. Only during the bombardment of Brussels, by the zeal and courage with which he stood by the citizens in their ordeal, was he able to win some of the popularity he desired. But his governorship was not really put to the test until peace had come in 1697.

Public opinion in the Southern Netherlands was aware, more sharply than one would have expected considering the political dependence of the country, of a task to be fulfilled, a task of economic reform, of economic recovery. For years a few enthusiasts had been advocating particular plans: the Brussels lawyer Van der Meulen, appointed to a post in the central administration in 1687, and the Antwerp merchant, Cardon, roused public imagination with their plans for colonial trade (if only Spain would ease its monopoly somewhat for its loyal Netherlands); for new canal communications, from Antwerp viâ Bruges to the sea, from Brussels itself to Bruges, and in the other direction to the eastern coalfield (if only the Republic did not too severely interpret its rights under the Münster treaty); for a protectionist tariff. This last was a reaction against the free-trade policy upon which the Governor, the Prince of Parma, had decided under Antwerp influence in December 1680; industry was suffering too greatly under French competition not to wish to imitate the methods whereby Colbert had promoted it. The Provincial States of Flanders and of Brabant were actually starting to take cognisance of ideas so much above their competence; the turbulent 'nations'[1] of Brussels were

---

[1] As the guilds in that town were called.

letting themselves be instructed by Van der Meulen. Now under
Maximilian Emanuel a powerful personality came to the fore
out of the home-born ranks of the administration. Jan van
Brouchoven, Count of Bergeyck, was not in the first place a
lawyer such as had been those earlier servants of the central
government, Peckius or Roose, but—a sign of the new times—a
financier. The Treasurer-General (this was his office) became
the chief councillor of the Elector. Colbert, whose activities had
inspired Van der Meulen and Cardon also, was Bergeyck's
great example. But Colbert had had the support of a powerful
and self-assured absolute authority. Would the Elector be able
to give similar support to his minister?

Circumstances were not entirely unfavourable. The old
wealth, zest for work, and skill of the people of Flanders and
Brabant were well-nigh indestructible, and while in the Republic the tremendous military effort was laying a heavy burden on
economic life, in the Southern Netherlands, as we know, taxes
were light. The ravages caused by the wars were quickly
repaired. The rebuilding of Brussels was an impressive achievement—the famous guild-houses on the market-place date from
this time. The Elector's pleasure-loving Court, in whose cosmopolitan composition the native nobility was lost, might assort
strangely with the exhausted state of public finances, but it
nevertheless meant business for the Brussels tradesmen.

Without waiting for ever-evasive Madrid, Bergeyck in 1698
founded an East India and Guinea Company. The country
proved to be somewhat lacking in the capacities required for
overseas undertakings, however. Since the loss of Dunkirk it
had hardly any sailors left. The prohibition against taking
service in foreign companies, of which the Hague States-
General emphatically reminded their own subjects, need not
have formed a hindrance—there were Norwegians and Han-
seatics available in plenty—but in any case the charter was
never really carried into practice. When serious preparations
were made for digging the projected canals, the Northern
States-General again manifested uneasiness, and when the
scheme was suddenly abandoned, its disappointed advocates
suspected behind this an intervention on their part with
Maximilian. Here too, however, the true cause lay in the insufficient preparation. The condition of the soil involved an

expenditure to which the financial strength of the country was not equal.

But protection, was not that a method in any country's power? At the beginning of 1699 Bergeyck, at a conference convened at Brussels for the purpose, obtained the advice of representatives of the chief towns and of leading businessmen. The most extreme measures for keeping out foreign industrial products were suggested. However greatly convinced Bergeyck might be that protection was the essential condition for prosperity, he yet wanted to set to work a little more circumspectly. But a dangerous excitement manifesting itself at Brussels drove the government on.

The 'nations' had for a long time been in a state of turmoil. Out of the fire of 1695 the charters had been salved which contained the old privileges that, after the Burgundian Dukes had withdrawn them, had gradually been forgotten. They were now published by the nations under the title *Luyster van Brabant* (*Glory of Brabant*) with a respectful dedication (in Spanish!) to the King.[1] In the curious picture of medieval privilege that arose out of these documents the deans of the guilds (just as much as the civic guards at Amsterdam had done) recognised their ideal; thus not only the arrogance and corruption of the oligarchy were to be curbed (although *their* privileges too, those of the seven 'families', were considered to be sacrosanct!), but in this way the country's ancient greatness was to be regained. The preface addressed to 'the Honourable Good Men of the Nine Nations of this Town of Brussels', probably composed by Van der Meulen, treats chiefly of lost prosperity and the desirability of setting trade going once more (within the Spanish Empire, was what he had in mind).

The attention drawn to the privileges so suddenly was meanwhile bringing about a great deal of unrest. Difficulties followed upon difficulties; about consent for taxes, about the choice of magistrates, and so on. The Elector's government, just as before him the Spanish Governors, gave way every time before the demands of the guilds. The government did at last prohibit the book with the resurrected privileges, which an enthusiastic guild dean wanted to have prescribed to the young as their primer,

---

[1] The publication itself was of course couched in Dutch. At that time Brussels was as much a Dutch-speaking town as Antwerp or Amsterdam.

but it still sought the favour of a movement that was seen to control the man in the street. Thus in April 1699 it announced, by the so-called 'Perpetual Edicts', protection in full measure: the import of woven materials and the export of raw wool were prohibited outright, and heavy duties were imposed on numerous other articles. But the effect of these measures was unforeseen. A number of interests were fatally hit by that drastic interference. While requests for still more protection kept pouring in, protests also burst forth. A mob gathering before Bergeyck's house caused him to tender his resignation. The Elector, who had not supported him very firmly, did not completely repudiate him either, but in any case, since the danger of counter-measures on the part of the surrounding countries was manifesting itself as well, the 'perpetual' edicts were toned down.

The Elector's position in the face of the disturbances in Brussels, which continued throughout the year, was seriously weakened by the opposition he met with from the Spanish officials. The most important personage among them was the ambassador in The Hague, Don Bernardo de Quiros, who took it upon himself to interfere. These Spaniards saw a danger in Bergeyck's attempts at reform: would not the country in that way become more closely bound to the Elector and more completely subjected to his authority? And was the Elector to be trusted? There were rumours of his intending to establish himself in independence with the assistance of the Republic. That idea was no more than an echo, in the minds of a people yearning after change, of plans which had been discussed generations before. As for the States, however deeply they might be involved in the affairs of the Southern Netherlands (where since Nijmegen they were, as we know, maintaining garrisons in certain towns) ambitions of that kind no longer appealed to them. In their overriding fear of Louis XIV they wanted to perpetuate the connection of the Southern Netherlands with a great power in order to ensure themselves of an ally in case France were to attack the Netherlands. That the South Netherlands people, if placed in a more independent position, might exert themselves more in their own cause, that—as we saw already—did not yet occur to anyone. But if the Republic no longer contemplated any attempt upon Spain's sovereignty, was there not Louis XIV and might not Maximilian Emanuel let himself be persuaded by *him* to come to an arrangement redounding to his advantage? More than once the Elector had had the intentions of Versailles sounded. The best guarantee against any tricky moves on his part seemed to the Spaniards to be found in the continued weakness of the central authority in the territory rashly entrusted to him, discord between him and the population, and disunity among the provinces themselves.

The native nobility was on the whole but little pleased with the person of the Elector and the reforming schemes of Bergeyck. The conservatives—the Malcontents they called themselves—felt much more at ease with the old Spanish do-nothing policy. The democrats, who took their programme from the Middle Ages, were no less hostile than were the conservatives to the bureaucratic radicalism towards which Bergeyck's mind tended. When in 1697 De Grieck, in a play performed at Brussels, has the Peace of Rijswijk greeted with a hearty

Long live our King and all the friends of Spain,

one should not interpret that as showing a true inclination towards the once so bitterly hated nation: it is first and foremost this party feeling that is here expressing itself. And anyway, 'pro-Spanish'?—everyone knew that the time of the Spanish dynasty was almost up, and that soon the country would belong either to an Austrian or to a Frenchman. Or perhaps to a Bavarian, if not the Elector himself then at least his small son, as suggested in the Partition Treaty of 1698. When that son died at Brussels in the beginning of 1699, several people in the crowd come to watch the funeral service in St. Gudula's were heard to mutter:

What luck! What great good luck for this little country of ours!

According to the Count of Merode-Westerloo, who noted down the Dutch words in his French memoirs, what they rejoiced about was that thus the chances of an Austrian succession were revived. The Count himself was a zealous advocate of that cause: the Bavarian Governor and Bergeyck, his minister, might come to an understanding with the French King as the patron of the French pretender, the one on account of his personal ambitions and the other inspired by his admiration for that régime; both the Malcontents and the guild democrats knew full well, or at least imagined they did, that the old Spanish tradition of administration would be safest in the hands of an Austrian. Freedom and the privileges—those were the fine slogans in which people indulged. No doubt they covered a good deal that was less fine, in particular the abuses and the corruption that flourished all too luxuriantly in the local administration of many towns and bailiwicks, under the management of a closely interconnected privileged class.

As long as the question of the succession was in suspension, at any rate, the Spanish government and the ambitious Governor's native Netherland opponents supported each other. To the chagrin of Maximilian Emanuel, Quiros got into touch with the discontented guild leaders and encouraged them to appeal against the Elector to the Spanish court. At the end of 1699 Maximilian Emanuel, at his wits' end, decided to use the troops. As on earlier occasions, so now, resistance collapsed. Van der Meulen was arrested, other leaders fled. The Court of Brabant started legal proceedings which ended in numerous convictions, mostly by default. In August 1700 the Elector issued a decree curtailing the powers of the 'nations', particularly their right of having a say in the matter of taxation. But the 'nations' were far from quietly submitting, and while still raising all sorts of objections instead of meekly consenting to taxes, they demanded pardon for their convicted deans.

These were the circumstances in which the great moment of the change of dynasty arrived: an impotent government which had failed in all its constructive work and which, on account of this as well as of its sudden severity against the people of Brussels, had lost its popularity; a Governor, moreover, who thought of nothing but his own position; a people divided by a struggle of interests and of classes. So Louis XIV could carry out his ever-cherished project and overmaster the Southern Netherlands without striking a blow. We already know that this was the real situation behind what was nominally the succession of Philip V. Maximilian Emanuel, who could in the Habsburger see nothing but a rival, had begun by recognising the Bourbon, and soon, letting in the French troops, detached himself altogether from his erstwhile friends, the Emperor and William

III, and threw in his fortunes with those of Louis. In return he was able to secure no more than confirmation in his Governorship; only in the event of his losing his Bavarian possessions was he promised the sovereignty over the Netherlands.

B. THE THIRD COALITION WAR; THE WAR OF THE SPANISH SUCCESSION (1702–13/15)

1. THE SOUTHERN NETHERLANDS UNDER FRENCH RULE (1701–6)

WITH what kind of feelings did the population of the Southern Netherlands submit to the future thus settled for them? Nothing is more difficult than to determine the feelings of a community no longer able to take an independent part in the higher ranges of political life and hardly expressing itself on the subject. That the clergy regarded Franco-Spanish supremacy as a guarantee against any connections with Dutch and English heretics we know for certain. At Antwerp, they gave an impressive demonstration of this immediately after the occupation by French troops in May 1701: the chapter and clergy of the cathedral began to throw up with their own hands a fortification near the St. George Gate, on the side where a Dutch attack might be expected. One after another the Abbot of St. Michael's with his monks, the Dominican and Franciscan friars and other monastic communities, the canons and chaplains of St. Jacob's, the Jesuits and the Augustinians with their pupils, came to relieve each other at the work, until at last the eighty-four-year-old Bishop Cools himself arrived to wheel some barrow-loads of earth.

Even outside the ecclesiastical circle, and in that same Brussels that harboured such bitter memories of the French bombardment, there had been a moment of joy when Philip V started by exercising royal mercy and the banished guild deans were free to return. But this was mere empty show. The citizens were soon made to feel that the change of régime did indeed mean a change of system, but that in a sense very different. The fears of those, whether magistrates, nobility, or democrats, who had expected only from the Austrian a continuation of the

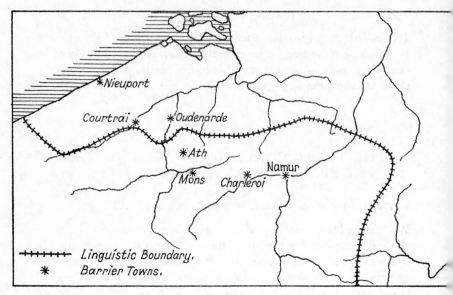

A. THE BARRIER OF 1678–1701

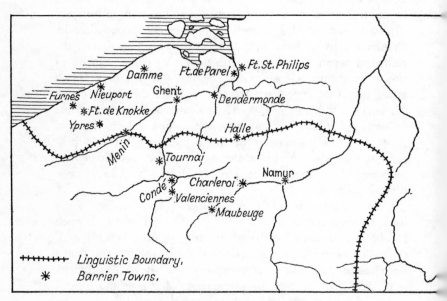

B. THE PROPOSED BARRIER OF 1709

294

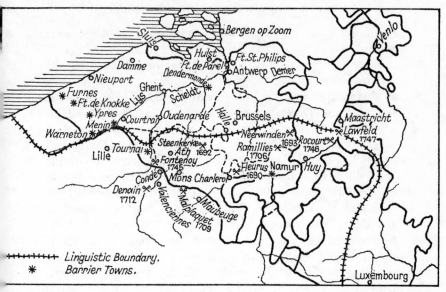

Map labels: Sluis, Bergen op Zoom, Venlo, Damme, Huist, Ft. de Parel, Ft. St. Philips, Nieuport, Dendermonde, Antwerp, Demer, Furnes, Ghent, Ft. de Knokke, Lijs, Scheldt, Ypres, Courtrai, Oudenarde, Halle, Brussels, Maastricht, Menin, Lawfeld, Warneton, Neerwinden, 1693, Rocourt, 1747, Steenkerke, Ramillies, 1746, Lille, Tournai, Ath 1692, 1706, Fleurus, Namur, Huy, Fontenoy, 1745, Condé, Mons, Charleroi, 1690, Denain, Valenciennes, Maubeuge, 1712, Malplaquet, 1709, Luxembourg

†††††††† Linguistic Boundary.
✳ Barrier Towns.

C. THE BARRIER OF 1715

EXPLANATION OF THE 'BARRIER' MAPS

THE BARRIER arrangements shown under A, B, and C differed in character. By the first the States-General were enpowered to place garrisons in towns side by side with Spanish garrisons. The second is the one laid down in the Townshend treaty which was never carried into effect; the towns mentioned in that scheme were to have been garrisoned by the States alone. This was also stipulated by the treaty of 1715, except for Dendermonde (Termonde), where the new Austrian overlord of the Southern Netherlands was also to have a garrison.

295

traditional Spanish lenience with regard to the privileges, were realised.

Firm government, that was what was now tried upon the South-Netherlanders, and there was nothing they had become so unaccustomed to as that. Before his departure from Versailles for Spain, in December 1700, Philip V had empowered his grandfather to take in his name all the measures deemed necessary in the Southern Netherlands. As soon as the French troops had occupied the country and the arrangement with the Elector had been made, the latter was persuaded to return to his hereditary principality of Bavaria, and the administration at Brussels was entrusted to the Marquess de Bedmar, a Spaniard and Philip V's representative, but an ardent advocate of the French connection and indeed assisted by Frenchmen, such as the Marquess de Puységur, the Marshal de Boufflers, and the intendant of the Flanders districts already annexed to France, Du Gué de Bagnols. There was one distinguished native official who gave his unconditional support, Bergeyck. He felt at last completely in his element. He now saw a master, ranking above the Elector, above Philip V, who knew what he wanted and who would not give way to popular discontent; that master he served with enthusiasm.

And yet, this centralisation and absolutism which he could now help to realise did not promote the economic recovery which had been his first concern; it was only intended to subserve the war into which France dragged the country against its allies and protectors of yesterday.

Peace—that might perhaps have reconciled the Southern Netherlanders to the French régime, inflexible efficiency and all. At first it might seem as if the succession of Philip V, which put an end to the Franco-Spanish feud, would indeed ensure peace. But even if the South-Netherlands people might allow themselves to be absorbed by France, the North Netherlanders —as we know—could not acquiesce in this fulfilment of Louis XIV's ambitions, and as early as 1702 an Anglo-Dutch army under Marlborough was operating on the Maas. Venlo, Roermond, Stevensweert, and Liège were taken that same year, and Gelder and Huy the next. States troops also pressed forward from Zealand-Flanders towards Antwerp and Bruges; there was fighting, with less success, near Calloo and Ekeren. The province of Upper Gelderland meanwhile was in the hands of the allies, firmly secured by the Maas fortifications of Liège, and communications with the German princes were as open as ever they had been in the days of Frederick Henry—for it is to his field of operation that we find ourselves transferred, and it is of his problems that we are reminded, now that the front of the Southern Netherlands is once more turned to the North instead of to the South. In 1704, however, Marlborough made use of those open communications in a way that would never have occurred to Frederick Henry: boldly advancing into the German Empire as far as and right into Bavaria, he annihilated Maximilian Emanuel's Franco-Bavarian army near Blenheim, thus saving Austria. In 1705 the war of positions in the Netherlands was resumed and with the Maas as base a beginning was made with the piecemeal reduction of Brabant: Tirlemont, Diest, and Zoutleeuw were taken. In 1706 there followed the great catastrophe of the French army at Ramillies in Walloon Brabant (in between those places conquered the previous year and Namur). Even after that battle on the Danube, which had revealed Marlborough's genius to the world, so sensational an event had not been expected. In all the campaigns that had been fought for a century and longer in the Southern Netherlands, and of which the possession of that country was the prize, no feat of arms had occurred that had such immediate and far-reaching consequences. The whole of Brabant, and even the whole of Flanders, was evacuated by the French. For five years they had ruled in those provinces as if they were there for ever.

From the very first the French officials had regarded the country as a new possession, and, conscious of representing a tradition of government of their own, which in their eyes was of a superior order, had set about making plans for reform. Maximilian, who had returned after the loss of his Bavaria, was kept out of the realities of government. The cumbersomeness and slowness of the administration, continually hampered as it was by the share that groups of subjects could claim under the old privileges, irritated the French. They considered preventing the confirmation of the privileges by Philip V's representative, but gave way when it was made clear to them how greatly this would have alarmed public opinion; after all, to override those parchment obstacles would not be so difficult. The spirit of the

new rulers appears from what Puységur wrote to Louis' minister
Torcy from Brussels in May 1701:

> We need have no fear of this people. If we want to, we are the masters.
> They are powerless to do anything against our wishes. The right line of
> action in this country is, never to propose anything. If one wants the thing to
> be done, simply order it to be done and it will be done.

Even so the old spirit of the Spanish administration was still
trying to make itself felt, not through Philip V or Bedmar, but
from the offices in Madrid and Brussels. But interference from
that quarter was pushed aside without ado. In 1702 an administrative reform was introduced in consequence of which the
Council of Flanders at Madrid and the Spanish offices at
Brussels were abolished; the three large boards of administration, too, instituted by Charles V, disappeared to make way for
one single Royal Council. The Procurator-General was given
admittance to all the central and local Courts of Justice. The
financial administration was centralised and an unprecedented
position of power thus created for Bergeyck, who became
Surintendant of Finance and Secretary of State. Another decree
robbed the provincial Governors of certain powers which were
transferred to the central government. The main tendency of
the reform, in short, was to strengthen central authority considerably. Nothing was of greater moment than that the judicial
power now penetrated local circles hitherto so carefully sealed
off by the privileges. Under the Spanish régime, so at least it
was asserted, the grossest irregularities had occurred with
impunity, particularly in the raising of taxes, and that was how
the money difficulties of the luckless Spanish government had
arisen: a part only of the taxpayers' contributions used to reach
the exchequer, the remainder adhering to the fingers of the local
magistrates.

The government had not waited for these reforms to undertake the most pressing matter, the expansion of the army and
the improvement of its efficiency. The abominable condition of
the troops under the Spanish régime could not be allowed to
last a moment longer. A new army was created by introducing a
system of conscription in which the inhabitants were made to
draw lots. Harsh interference indeed in the life of the community
did the intruder permit himself! Protests and complaints came
pouring in, yet the measure was carried out successfully. In the

Republic, as we have seen, farmers and citizens could in times of very exceptional danger—as in 1629, and in 1672—be forced into army service. In the Southern Netherlands the wars had always been considered as the foreign government's concern (how could it be otherwise?) and its badly paid and consequently unruly mercenaries were feared hardly less than the troops of the enemy. But now an end was made of irregular payment and with it of indiscipline. A reorganisation, devised by Puységur, was undertaken, which placed the army in the Southern Netherlands on exactly the same footing as the French army. But regularity of payment was the principal thing, and that was where the financial reforms came in which constituted Bergeyck's chief occupation.

It was a question of extracting as much money as possible out of the unwilling provinces by means of the new and awe-inspiring power at the centre. Not content with the hitherto unprecedented supervision exercised by the central judicial organs, Bergeyck resorted to the method of farming out taxation. In order to lease out the direct sources of royal income, he only had to overcome the opposition of old official bodies which were in any case soon done away with altogether; but the revenues from domains and import excises were not so large as to preclude the central government from having to depend mainly on the contributions of the provinces. To persuade the latter to lease their own revenues was a much more difficult undertaking. Bergeyck had his way in Flanders—where as a result the returns rose from 700,000 to 1,300,000 livres, a striking confirmation of the assertions about fraudulent practices under the system of imposition by the local authorities—but Brabant offered obstinate resistance. There was also a lengthy struggle about smaller measures, in which the minister was time and again able to get his own way, or at least to make money by allowing his decisions to be bought off. Thus a stamp tax was introduced for the whole country without previous consent from the States; offices which had always been in the bestowal of provincial or local authorities—of notaries and of a special class of notaries in Flanders called 'bâton-holders'— were abolished and new offices instituted by authority of the King; those offices (that was what mattered) were sold to the highest bidder. This was in itself a custom accepted in the code

of morals of the country; what aroused general indignation was
that the abolition of the old offices injured many in long-
acquired rights and that by the institution of the new ones a
source of income was transferred from the possession of the
local authorities to that of the central government.

The arbitrariness that characterised all these proceedings
shocked the public mind, and in a war to which no national
significance could be attached there could hardly grow up a
countervailing sentiment of solidarity with the French government that had so suddenly descended upon the country. Meanwhile, even in a sphere where its financial interest was not
involved, the government did not spare the sensibility of the
South-Netherlanders with respect to the old legal forms—I am
thinking of the contest over Jansenism.

It was still during the Spanish régime that this question had
again taken on a sharper character. In 1689 a Burgundian
nobleman, de Precipiano, had become Archbishop of Mechlin,
and during his long primacy he had opposed the spirit of independence in the Netherlands church with all the power at his
disposal.[1] The dogmatic aspect of the controversy is now overshadowed by the issue between the insistence on rights and the
demand for blind subjection. The famous Declaration of the
French clergy, of 1682, in which limits were set to the papal
authority over the national church, were far from being
Jansenist in origin, but the principles there propounded came
in most usefully for strengthening the cause of Jansenist resistance, and the University of Louvain obstinately refused to
condemn the Declaration. At first the Archbishop's methods
did not meet with undivided approval even in Rome. The
continual hunting down of unorthodox clergy by means of
Alexander VII's formula, the deposition of the holders of
benefices in the face of all privileges and forms of law, was
checked in 1694 by Innocent XII with a brief, which a Louvain
doctor (the Walloon Hennebel) had managed to elicit. But in
direct opposition to this, de Precipiano and the Jesuits obtained
from the Spanish government (from Madrid, because Maximilian Emanuel at Brussels did not trouble his head much about
these matters) that orders were to be issued to all authorities
that anyone who was only so much as suspected of Jansenism or

[1] See above, p. 213.

rigorism was to be excluded from benefices. 125 clergy and members of the University then empowered Willem van de Nesse, a priest of St. Catharine's at Brussels, to represent in their name to the sovereign, the ministers, and the States, that these orders should only be applicable:

with due regard taken to Clause I of the Edict called the Joyous Entry[1], to all divine and human rights, to the privileges attached to ecclesiastical immunity and to the dispositions of Innocent XII's brief, especially that one which lays it down that no one shall be excluded from any office except in conformity with the order of justice.

The Archbishop had Van de Nesse prosecuted for plotting against the sovereign authority. The Privy Council acquitted him. The majesty of the law could count for something under the feeble Spanish régime. But in 1700, with the succession of Louis' grandson, the Archbishop's hour struck. In France the theological dispute had at that very moment flared up again, first as a result of the book of Quesnel, who was still living at Brussels.[2] In Rome itself a change took place, even during Innocent XII's lifetime, but particularly under Clement XI, who succeeded him in 1700. We shall see how this Pope engaged in a renewed contest with the Jansenist spirit in the North-Netherlands Catholic Church also, or perhaps we should say with the national, or independent, spirit manifesting itself there. But what counted in the Southern Netherlands after the advent of Philip V was above all the disposition of his grandfather. And Louis XIV, as he grew older, detested the Jansenists ever more cordially, and in the latter part of his reign he exerted himself to the utmost, this time in close co-operation with Rome, to stamp out their self-righteous mentality. This must now be tried in the Netherlands too. In 1703, at the express order of the King, the Archbishop had Quesnel arrested and confined in the archiepiscopal prison. While the States of Brabant are still protesting against this violation of the security promised by law, the prisoner escapes, but the King now writes personally to his Governor ordering him to banish two other ecclesiastics from

---

[1] The charter granted to Brabant in 1355 under critical circumstances by the then Duke securing large powers to the States. The Blijde Inkomst (Joyeuse Entrée) was always regarded as a guarantee against arbitrary power. It had served as an inspiration to the men who in 1581 drew up the Placard of Dismissal (see *The Revolt of the Netherlands*, p. 184) by which the rebellious provinces (Brabant still among them) renounced their allegiance to Philip II.

[2] See above, p. 212.

the country 'for cogent reasons known to me'. One of these was the Walloon, Ruth d'Ans, and the other Van de Nesse. Banishments by means of a *lettre de cachet*, or in other words by administrative measure, were a familiar procedure under the system of French absolutism, but the method was wholly at variance with Netherland notions—although, as we know, town governments in the North did sometimes assume the right to banish citizens from their towns without assigning any reasons. In Brabant in any case the treatment of the priest Van de Nesse made so bad an impression—he was held in high esteem in Brussels—that Bedmar urged the King to allow him to return; without success, however. Indeed a few Louvain doctors were removed from the University at the order of Madrid (which really meant Versailles).

So, when on 23 May 1706, the French army was defeated at Ramillies, it was hardly to be expected that the towns and States assemblies of Brabant and Flanders should evince much zeal in keeping Philip V's régime on its feet. As early as 26 May, representatives of the States of Brabant appeared in the Anglo-Dutch army camp; the French were retreating everywhere; town after town opened its gates to the conquerors, the officials composing the government at Brussels were at their wits' end, Bergeyck and others who considered their fortunes indissolubly bound up with those of the French made off. And now Marlborough and the Northern States' Field Deputies received the Brabant delegation with marks of great respect, assuring them that they were in the war only to help their ally, Charles of Habsburg, to obtain his due share of the succession, and that the latter, Brabant's rightful ruler, would govern the country in accordance with the old privileges and without any distasteful innovations. How tempting must this have sounded to the Brabanters after their experience of French rule! And indeed, the French occupation already seemed no more than an evil dream. On 5 June the States of Brabant recognised Charles as their sovereign. Marlborough and the Dutch Field Deputies, having advanced in a westward direction, were by then already at Ghent, and there, on 6 June, the States of Flanders passed a similar resolution. The Elector of Bavaria, against whom, after the loss of his hereditary land, the Imperial ban had been pronounced, was now, as Governor too, left with only the Walloon provinces.

2. THE STADHOLDERLESS RÉGIME IN THE WAR

FOR the first time in its existence the Republic took part in a large-scale land war without a Prince of Orange. Immediately after William III's death the 'Republican' party took control in all his five provinces, firmly resolved to retain it. The Stadholder of Friesland was a minor; he could not even take possession of William III's personal estate, since the Elector of Brandenburg (who at that very time became King of Prussia) also laid claim to it on the strength of his own rights as a descendant of Frederick Henry. Nevertheless in the long run the Frisian Nassau might be expected to become a pretender to the Stadholdership in Holland, just as a generation earlier William III had been during the Grand Pensionaryship of De Witt.

Meanwhile those regents whom the great Stadholder had kept in the background or had shut out altogether during his administration came back into their various offices everywhere. In Holland this went off fairly smoothly. In the provinces where the Stadholder's hand had lain heaviest, the repercussions were more violent. In Zealand not only were the Goes exiles of 1692 reinstated, but the States of the province put an end to Odijck's domination; the First-Nobleship itself was abolished and Odijck was thrust from the representation of the province in the States-General; in several other towns popular fury broke out against his local tools. The magistrature of Middelburg was renewed by the guilds. In 1704 the men then ousted tried to get back into control by force. For three hours they were able to maintain themselves in the Town Hall. Finally, they were driven out again by the new men supported by all the citizens' companies except one. All this took place without any bloodshed, which did not prevent the magistrature, after their narrow escape, from writing to the States of Zealand as follows (an example of the sentimental and inflated style now coming into vogue):

Next to God it is due only to the extraordinary loyalty and zeal manifested for the maintenance of the lawful magistracy by our good citizenry that our good town has not been overturned and plunged into civic blood. Our hair stands on end, trembling assails our nerves, our eyes burst into tears, when we consider, on the one side the intentions of the men of violence, and on the other side God Almighty's blessing and the faithful ardour of the good citizens in helping to put down so awful a conspiracy.

In Gelderland and Overijsel too, the old democratic traditions, which just as in Brabant were possessed of so much more vitality than in Holland, but which the system of the Government Regulations had kept in abeyance, reasserted themselves. The Commonalty Committees, which had of old elected the magistrates there, but which William III had allowed to die out,[1] were filled up once more and in the town governments his favourites were replaced by new men. In various towns this change was accompanied by considerable disturbances. The struggle between 'the Old and the New Fold' (as it was put) kept Gelderland in commotion for quite a few years. The States of the province were divided, each party trying to use the military and requesting or opposing the intervention of the States-General or of the States of Holland. Just as at the time of the dissensions in Overijsel in the days of De Witt or in Friesland after 1672, Gelderland's contributions fell hopelessly behindhand. The different parts of that loosely knit province (a Republic of the United Provinces in miniature) were internally disturbed and mutually at cross purposes; in 1704 and 1705 it almost seemed as if a civil war were imminent; mediation on the part of Holland had little effect. At Nijmegen, after an unsuccessful attempt of the Old Fold to get into power again, a former Burgomaster, Roukens, was beheaded. It was only after the lapse of some time that conditions settled down under the new men in power.

The Commonalty Committees were restored, but that did not really signify a victory for democracy. In Gelderland, Zealand, and elsewhere, it was hardly more than another clique wanting to have its turn, and once it had got into power, maintaining itself in office by force and in accordance with the true oligarchic methods. The democratic idea was not yet able to make itself felt because—we saw that same phenomenon in the events in Brussels—it could only appeal to precedents, and never tried to express itself in any but historical forms which had lost all vitality since the Middle Ages.

Thus a new period of regent 'freedom' set in, much more exclusive, much more self-assured, than in the preceding period; for now there was no alternative. The disorders in Gelderland and Zealand

[1] See above, p. 149.

was not, on that account, less its own, sustained by its traditions, by the energies of its population, by the management of its statesmen. Nevertheless there was something unhealthy in the disproportion between the political and the military effort. This is reflected in the fact that the wars of this period made so little appeal to Dutch popular imagination, that no Dutch legend was created out of them and that barely any Dutch military tradition was formed. The cosmopolitan culture and style of life of the Dutch nobility and officer class had undoubtedly also to do with this. William III and his immediate entourage had, owing to his peculiar upbringing, been less deeply gallicised than had been the case with Frederick Henry or William II. Nonetheless the bulk of what we possess in the way of military correspondence of that period is written in French.

It is true that since 1672 quite a number of Dutch superior officers had been formed who might have seemed fit for the really leading commands. Van Reede van Ginkel—or Athlone: the Dutch, too, usually referred to him by the title he had won overseas—had made a great name for himself in Ireland; at the beginning of this new war he saved Nijmegen from a sudden French attack which had looked as if it might have disastrous results. Wassenaer van Obdam, Slangenburg (a Catholic nobleman from Overijsel), Nassau-Ouwerkerk[1] (a brother of Odijck's) —all had proved themselves to be able commanders. And yet, when the position of commander-in-chief, made vacant by the death of the Captain-General, had to be filled, it was again felt that recourse must be had to someone from abroad. It was regarded as indispensable to have a man excelling everyone by birth or position. The Stadholder of Friesland was too young; moreover most of the provinces did not want him in a position where he might win fresh glory for the name of Orange. With difficulty his supporters obtained for him in 1704 the rank of general; Nassau-Ouwerkerk was at the same time raised above all other Dutch officers by conferring the rank of Field Marshal upon him. But already in 1702 the States-General had appointed Marlborough Commander-in-Chief with the rank of Lieutenant-Captain-General. By this choice it was hoped, both to involve England more deeply in the war, and to secure unity in the leadership of the allied armed forces. Just as in the days of

[1] Known to the English as 'Overkirk'.

Frederick Henry and as on the occasion of William III's first campaign in 1672, however, the States appointed by the side of the foreigner Deputies in the Field without whose consent he was not free to dispose of the Republic's army.

A most unsatisfactory arrangement this was to prove in practice! Without knowing it the States had placed their army under the control of a bold and original strategist. The Dutch commanders, grown up in the war of fortresses and position, firm believers in the rules of the game, were inclined to look upon their new Captain-General as an amateur without experience, as a diplomat and courtier more than a military man. In reality he was a man possessed of sufficient imagination to perceive the chances for a decisive battle, and eager to take advantage of them. He soon felt intolerably restricted by the caution of the conservative Dutch gentlemen. One should not forget, it is true, in watching the struggle between his urge for action and their inclination to hold back, that an unsuccessful venture would have exposed their country to much more immediate danger than his. But the victory of Blenheim in 1704, coming after that daring expedition far from his base, for which the States had been unwilling to place any of their troops at his disposal, had given Marlborough an enormous prestige. This became evident in 1705, when he openly complained about the opposition he met with in the Netherlands on the part of the Deputies and still more of Slangenburg—the French, as he maintained, had narrowly escaped an annihilating defeat— public opinion not only in England (where people were always ready to scoff at the ally), but in the Republic itself, hotly took his side. Slangenburg, whose Catholicism counted heavily against him in any public dispute, was obliged to retire from the service. The Deputies received fresh instructions. Thereupon followed, in 1706, the offensive that led to Ramillies.

Nassau-Ouwerkerk won much praise on that occasion as Commander of the left wing and the Dutch troops no less. For once criticism in England was silenced. But the glory of the victory was Marlborough's.

3. THE REPUBLIC ECLIPSED BY ENGLAND

Diplomatic Miscalculations and Disappointment (1706-13)

THIS was only one sign of much that had changed as between the two Naval Powers since the last war. At that time England had still felt somewhat out of its element with regard to the continental policy into which her new King had dragged her, but now she took her part in it with views and convictions of her own. There was no longer any question of her needing Dutch agents for her European diplomacy. Particularly after his sensational victory at Blenheim the figure of Marlborough overshadowed, at Vienna, at Berlin, and throughout the whole of Germany, that of any Dutchman, and in between his summer campaigns he repeatedly went on diplomatic travels in the winter. The English kept in close touch with the States about their European plans, certainly, Marlborough in particular with Heinsius, but the initiative was now usually theirs. That is especially apparent in the southern areas of the ever more widely spreading war.

It was an English idea, to which the States allowed themselves to be persuaded half against their better judgment, to expand the aims of the Grand Alliance in the spirit of the Emperor, and to undertake to conquer for his younger son Charles not only the Italian possessions and the Netherlands, but Spain itself and the American colonies. An alliance with Portugal in 1703 was the first step towards the realisation of this plan, and presently Charles III (as the Habsburg prince now called himself) was introduced into Catalonia by an Anglo-Dutch army. Yet the attention of the States remained wholly engrossed by the Southern Netherlands. The enormous effort required of them there made this inevitable. The Amsterdam money market was still the financial mainstay of the whole coalition against France; not only did the Emperor and other German allies come to obtain loans there, but even at times the English government. Yet the Dutch State was finding it increasingly difficult to raise the funds needed for the military force of 100,000 men (in the end almost 120,000) which it had to maintain in the Southern Netherlands theatre of war. After a time, the Republic got England to provide two-thirds of the outlay in subsidy treaties concluded jointly instead of half. And in its view the war on the Southern frontier had to be given precedence over all other interests. For joint fleet enterprises the States were still liable to furnish two-fifths as against England three-fifths, but more and more they failed to make up even that share. The States fleet had never been in so sad a plight as now—under a Stadholderless régime, in which Amsterdam could set the tone!—but the burden of the army was already heavy enough. Only Zealand privateering flourished as much as ever, but that was an activity that cost the State nothing, although at times it caused it quite an amount of trouble on account of the unmanageableness of the privateers who would not spare the neutrals. The war in Spain, too, which dragged on for years with great successes alternating with heavy reverses, the States, after their initial participation, came to leave entirely to the English. The result was that the English conducted themselves as lords and masters in the jointly conquered strategic points of Gibraltar and Minorca, exercised exclusive control over the Mediterranean, and looked upon Charles III as their special protégé, who might be expected (in the case of his actually supplanting Philip V one day) to regulate the trade possibilities of Spain and America to their exclusive advantage. It was this prospect, indeed, which had inspired the English policy set on foot in 1703, and the reluctance of the Republic was only too understandable.

The events of 1706 at any rate bound it more closely than ever to the Southern Netherlands. In 1702 and 1703 the States-General had made the conquered towns of Upper Gelderland (Venlo, Roermond, Gelder) swear the oath of allegiance to them as their sovereign: Gelderland still considered that region as having been torn from its own territory, and as we know[1] the Peace Treaty of Münster contained a somewhat half-hearted recognition of the States' claim. The case was different with Limburg, which had been conquered in 1703, but there, while having to acquiesce in the transfer of sovereignty to Charles III, the States had first obtained a convention under which they were entitled to maintain a garrison in the small town of Limburg. As regards Flanders and Brabant, too, in 1706 they appealed to the Grand Alliance in order to keep the administration of those provinces in their own

[1] See Part One, p. 155.

hands, in the name of Charles III it is true, until an agreement should have been reached as to *how* that area was to serve them, according to that treaty, as a 'barrier'; and their ambitions with regard to that agreement now went a good deal further than the simple right of maintaining garrisons by the side of those of the sovereign in a chain of fortresses along the French frontier, such as they had exercised in practice, with the Spanish government's consent, after the Peace of Rijswijk.

It is customary to blame the States régime for not having perceived the importance of territorial expansion. The zeal, however, with which the States during these years aimed at the annexation of Upper Gelderland, and at an occupation differing but little from annexation of the remainder of the Southern Netherlands, could hardly have been exceeded. Their policy did not meet with success; nor were their methods always judicious; but that does not alter the fact that their participation in the war was largely governed by a burning interest in that region, the severance of which had been recognised in 1648, it is true, but without ever resulting in stable conditions.

Immediately after the expulsion of the French from Flanders and Brabant in 1706 it became apparent how jealous the States were of their position in those parts. In the eyes of the Austrians the 'barrier' ambitions of their ally rendered the possession of the Southern Netherlands almost worthless to themselves. So they were already seeking support for the negotiations on this matter which were to be expected at the end of the war, and offered Marlborough the Governorship. A princely position: one need only recall how highly the Elector of Bavaria had prized it. In The Hague, however, the idea aroused such an outburst of alarm and irritation that Marlborough felt obliged to refuse. But from that moment he was no longer so well disposed towards the Dutch designs in the Southern Netherlands, and actually the Austrian manoeuvre had served its purpose.

England's attitude was to be of central importance all through. Even after having affronted Marlborough (there were those who for that reason would rather have acquiesced in his appointment) the object of Dutch diplomacy must be to obtain a promise of English support at the final settlement for extracting a barrier-treaty from the new Austrian sovereign of the Netherlands in conformity with its desire. Negotiations were carried on all the time.

The Dutch thesis that England's safety was involved in that of the Republic, which latter could be secured only by giving it a predominant share in the defence of the Southern Netherlands—this thesis was now generally accepted in England. But in the minds of North Netherlands statesmen the barrier system had so developed and expanded as to embrace much more than only military aims. Not only were they no longer to be satisfied with the right, which they had enjoyed after Rijswijk, of maintaining occupation troops by the side of the sovereign's— the danger of this arrangement had appeared in 1701—they also wanted to control towns which were not so much of strategic as of economic importance. During the war the States had already made use of their occupation of all the most important places along the South Netherlands rivers to promote their own trade—at the expense of their English allies, as the latter complained. For that reason Ostend, where English imports would escape Dutch supervision, soon became a bone of contention between the two Naval Powers. The demand of the States that Ostend should be included in their barrier was by no means the least important factor whereby the negotiations between them and England came to nothing in 1706.

Despite the current phrases about their common struggle for Protestantism and the liberties of Europe, relations between the Republic and England were not much more cordial than between the Republic and Austria. While the Dutch could not observe the tremendous development of English trade without concern, the English were not yet free from the feelings of suspicion and envy conceived in the days when the Dutch economy was still in the full vigour of expansion. This added acrimony to the old dispute, which soon flamed up again, about the admissibility of trade with the enemy. In 1703 the States, giving in to English pressure, had enjoined upon their subjects a prohibition against trading with France. But already in the following year they omitted to reaffirm this prohibition, because —so said even so zealous a champion of the English alliance as Heinsius—experience had shown that only the neutrals (Hamburgers, Swedes) had profited, without France having suffered as a result. When, after that, Dutch ships again put in at French harbours, while the Dutch at the same time reduced their contributions to joint enterprises or even failed to fulfil obligations already entered into, scornful comments were heard in England to the effect that the war was a stroke of luck to the clever Dutch, and that it was only the English who made sacrifices for the common cause.

How was it possible that in spite of this the Dutch statesmen succeeded in making the English listen to their desires regarding the barrier? For although they had failed in this in 1706, in 1709 an Anglo-Dutch treaty was concluded in which the States obtained the most complete assurances. It was the general war situation which enabled them to extract these. Let us first see how that situation came to develop.

Already in 1706 Louis knew he was beaten and had made overtures for peace. In the Republic there were many, Buys in particular, who considered that on the basis of the French offers (indemnifications and guarantees in the sense of what the allies themselves had agreed upon in the Grand Alliance) a satisfactory conclusion was not impossible. The English, however, just as did the Imperials, held fast to the wider objective that had since been accepted, namely to wrest from Philip of Anjou the whole of the Spanish Empire. In 1707 the war dragged. In 1708 France suffered fresh heavy defeats: an initial success, the capture by surprise of Ghent and Bruges, which endangered the entire position of the allies in the Southern Netherlands, was undone by the battle of Oudenarde, after which the allies, right in the middle of the winter, took Lille after a famous siege. The misery and exhaustion of his people were such that the old King could no longer evade what he felt to be a bitter humiliation: he sent to The Hague no less a person than his minister Torcy to open negotiations on the basis of his enemies' most ambitious demands. England, Austria, and the Republic (Marlborough and Lord Townshend, a young man, the confidant of the Whig Party then in control of the government, Prince Eugene of Savoy and Zinzendorf, and Heinsius) submitted to Torcy the draft of a peace treaty in forty articles (the so-called Hague Preliminaries, in reality an ultimatum), which was accepted at Versailles with the exception of the notorious article 37 (and article 4, which went with it).

What seemed unacceptable to Louis even in the desperate emergency in which he found himself was not the demand that he should recognise Charles III as King of Spain. He was willing to concede that—in other words, completely to disown his grandson. He was also ready to acquiesce in the loss of a considerable portion of the conquests which in his own eyes constituted the glory of his reign: besides Strasbourg, which was to be returned to the German Empire, Furnes, Ypres, Lille, Valenciennes, Condé, Maubeuge, and other places (in his possession ever since the Peace Treaties of Aix—1659—and Nijmegen—1670), which (under Charles III's sovereignty of course) were to serve the States for their barrier. But article 37 stipulated that France was first to cede these places and that the peace would not take effect until she had likewise, within a brief period of time, seen to it that Spain was actually transferred to Charles III. Not only was the idea that he himself would have to force his grandson repugnant, but he declared that the impossible was being demanded of him. Philip V's position in Spain had become unassailable, and with the sacrifices laid down in the Preliminaries Louis, therefore, would not even be procuring peace for his people. Members of the States who had come to urge upon Heinsius not to carry things too far were assured by him that the financial and economic exhaustion of France was so great that Louis would sign anything that was submitted to him. This proved to be too optimistic, and the negotiations were broken off.

And now, in the new campaign, France's powers of resistance proved to be unexpectedly stubborn. It is true that in 1709 Ghent and Bruges had once more to be evacuated by the French troops, but not until September did a battle occur, near Malplaquet, and although the French had to quit the field the allies suffered heavy losses. The Dutch troops particularly suffered enormously. (They were no longer under the command of Nassau-Ouwerkerk, who had died, but under that of the young Stadholder of Friesland, who acquitted himself courageously, just as did the energetic Field Deputy Goslinga—also from Friesland—a man with strategic insight as well as character.) A cry of anguish went up in the Republic at the death of so many noblemen's and regents' sons from Friesland, Gelderland, and elsewhere.

But France's plight was not any the less serious for that. In the winter the negotiations were resumed and in the spring of 1710 two French delegates came to Geertruidenberg, on the south bank of the Moerdyk, to meet two members of the States-General. The basis for the discussion there was that, while the Preliminaries of the previous year were still considered accepted, an expedient was to be sought to mitigate article 37. Again and again messengers from Versailles brought fresh concessions from the King, whose greatness was on the verge of so miserable a collapse. Even now he stood by his contention that it was impossible for him to make everything dependent on the actual transfer of Spain, but he offered cautionary towns over and above the territory ceded in the Preliminaries; in the end he even brought himself to promise financial aid for the expedition the allies would still have to conduct against his grandson. It was all considered insufficient and denounced as being insincere and evasive, until the negotiations had to be broken off once more in July. The war (that had gone on for nine years by now) was again continued.

It is an astonishing spectacle to see the Republic supporting so reckless a course, by which, when the defeat of Louis' expansionist policy could have been accomplished by a nod, the task was once more entrusted to the uncertain chances of war and coalition diplomacy. Almost from the beginning the country had been weary of the war. Buys by no means reflected the opinion of Amsterdam only, when he argued how foolish it was to stake everything upon the conquest of Spain. Heinsius, no doubt, believed in the policy he was conducting in agreement with England and Austria, but among the regents doubts about its wisdom were rife. Yet even the sceptics allowed themselves to be dragged along. Buys himself was one of the two negotiators at Geertruidenberg; the word 'negotiators' flatters the position: he and Van der Dussen, his colleague, who belonged to the peace party quite as much, were no more than the messengers of the English and the Austrians, who together with Heinsius determined the course. How came it that they accepted so thankless a task?

The explanation is to be found first of all in that same barrier treaty which the States, as has been related, had managed to conclude with England. When we now look a little more closely at those inter-allied negotiations of 1709, the point that stands out will be how the zeal of the Whig government for the conquest of Spain had given the Dutch statesmen the opportunity to exercise pressure on it. If England fell in with Dutch ambitions concerning the Southern Netherlands, it was not because the arrangement for which she promised help was to her liking. First of all, the barrier as outlined in the treaty was not only to serve as a defence against the French but, as was hinted above, it was to subject the Southern Netherlands to the Dutch both financially and economically. Quite as painful to the English government was the promise to help the Republic get the full sovereignty over Upper Gelderland, because there the Prussian King now also had ambitions, and to displease him was a risky thing to do. And even worse from the English point of view was the promise, also obtained by the Republic under the treaty of 1709, that it was to share in all the trading facilities England might obtain for herself from the new claimant to the Spanish monarchy. Charles III in Barcelona was really no more than a puppet in English hands, and the English commander, Stanhope, had already extracted a secret treaty from him which would have given English trade a tremendous lead in America. The French cited this to the States as a proof of English double-dealing, and they, greatly indignant, had thereupon demanded the implementation of the stipulation for shared trade. Townshend, who conducted, for England, the negotiations (from which Marlborough kept strictly aloof), warned his government that the States would listen to the French offers of a separate peace if they were not humoured. Once it had been agreed upon, on the contrary, the 'Townshend Treaty' (the negotiator had foreseen this accurately enough) bound the Republic as if with golden chains to England. In the critical conferences with the French at Geertruidenberg Buys and Van der Dussen did not dare follow their own better judgment be-cause they wished at any price to go along with England: if at the end of the war the Republic was to realise the prospects held out by the Townshend Treaty, it must not now antagonise its ally.

The French, if they could thereby have drawn away the States from the coalition, would undoubtedly have abandoned the Southern Netherlands still more completely to them. But even the Amsterdammers no longer dared think of such an arrangement, not only out of fear of public opinion, swayed as much by anti-French feeling expressed in terms of principle and even of religion as it had previously been by anti-Spanish feeling, but because even if the States had been able in that way to secure the adjacent territory they would in the wider overseas world have been helpless before an England roused to anger. Trade with South America and in the Mediterranean could only be retained with the help of the other Naval Power, which did still actually deserve the name and which kept Charles III in leading-strings. How greatly the Dutch position in the colonial world had been weakened was to appear at the end of the war, when the French admiral of privateers, Cassart, was able to plunder with impunity one West Indian possession after another.

In outward appearance the proud, powerful Republic of the United Netherlands, whose statesmen for a whole generation had been leading Europe in the struggle against Louis XIV, had never been greater in strength and in prestige than when its representatives in 1710 at Geertruidenberg haughtily communicated to the French plenipotentiaries the coalition's negative answer. In reality they played the part of a subordinate. It was England that laid down this policy: England, which ruled the seas, while the Republic, wholly engrossed in the land war, had to be content with the guarantee that it should find its final reckoning in the ultimate treaty—a guarantee that was in fact no more than a piece of paper. As fate would have it that weakness was revealed almost at once.

The negotiations at Geertruidenberg had not yet come to their conclusion when in England a change of government was beginning. The Whigs, who through thick and thin had stuck to the conquest of Spain as the object of the war and who had bought the support of the States for that purpose by means of the Townshend Treaty, had to make way for the Tories, the party which had never cared for a continental policy and which represented in particular the national habit of considering England the victim of the selfishness of her grasping allies. Events themselves seemed to condemn the war policy of the Whigs when at the end of 1710 Philip V, in Spain, inflicted a serious defeat upon his assailants, and when at the beginning of 1711 Charles III, on the death of his brother, became ruler of the Austrian hereditary lands and Emperor under the name of Charles VI. Could it be considered sound policy to make him a present of Spain on top of that? But the new ministers (Harley,

later Lord Oxford, and St. John, later Lord Bolingbroke) did
not only want peace, they wanted peace at the expense of their
allies. In great secrecy they entered into negotiations with
France, declaring themselves willing to leave Philip V in Spain.
That the French fell in with this opening can well be imagined.
They promised England, still in secret, the special advantages it
desired—Gibraltar and Minorca, a privileged trading position
in the South American colonies, acquisitions in North America,
and the demolition of the fortifications of Dunkirk. Marlborough, fallen into disgrace when the new men came in, had in
the meanwhile been conducting a rather feeble campaign and
now, in the autumn, the Tory Government proposed to the
allies that a general Peace Congress should be held on the basis
of new preliminaries. These new preliminaries differed from
the Hague preliminaries of 1709 not only in that Philip V's
removal from Spain was no longer demanded; all the other
stipulations, too, concerning the interests of the Republic and of
Austria were left entirely vague.

Great was the anger in The Hague and Vienna, but it was
impotent anger. The States began by consenting to England's
desire for a peace conference, to assemble at Utrecht, hoping by
this complaisance to win the favour of the new men in power.
But a willingness to give up the established war aim, Spain, was
not enough to satisfy the Tories. They could only enter into
enjoyment of the special advantages they had been promised by
the French if the States relinquished the promises made them
in the Townshend Treaty. In England therefore a fierce press
campaign was started against this treaty, soon followed by
diplomatic action. Here was a predicament! A separate arrangement with France, which the States had declined in order to
obtain that treaty, was now no longer possible: the French would
be much better off under a separate arrangement with England.
Meekly to accept England's conditions, nevertheless, was more
than interest or self-respect could stomach. But the Tories did
not shrink from a total rupture. The treaty of 1709 was declared
void as being detrimental to England, and its English authors
were prosecuted, while at the same time masterly pamphleteers,
like Swift and Arbuthnot, were stirring up resentment against
the allies who, so it was now said, were trying to prolong the war
in order to squeeze England dry.

The outburst of fury and impatience against the Dutch was amazing. There now showed itself in full truculence a trend of English policy with respect to the Netherlands which we.1t back to the past quite as much as did the opposite one of cordial co-operation in which Temple and William III had continued the tradition of Elizabeth or even of Edward III. It will be remembered how decidedly Charles I had considered detrimental to his country the 1632–33 plans for reunion of the Low Countries, and how Charles II, too, when De Witt was planning a partition of the Southern Netherlands between the Republic and France, had been quite as much against an expansion of the former as of the latter.[1] So now St. John wrote (and Swift sounded an echo in his venomous pamphlet *The Conduct of the Allies*):

This is certain, we have given to the Dutch, by that infamous compact, extent of country, the only thing they wanted to enable them to be superior to us in trade.

The English government even went so far, when the Republic and Austria after a whole winter spent in negotiations were still refusing to give in, as to send orders to the new Commander-in-Chief, Ormonde, Marlborough's successor, to come to a secret agreement with the French Commander-in-Chief to avoid any encounter. At the cost of a tremendous financial effort (it was soon to prove an effort beyond their means) the States, when the English defection became clear in June 1712, took over for their own account the German troops in England's pay. Together with Austria they now undertook to try the chances of war. Before two months had passed, their own army received a heavy blow near Denain. That was the end of that policy of despair.

Those (*among the regents*) who were for the continuation of the war are under the greatest consternation imaginable. They apprehend violence themselves, and confusion and ruin in their country. Those for peace, who were kept under by the torrent before, now crow, blame the violence of the other party, and say, had they been believed, things had not come to this extremity.

Thus, with malicious satisfaction, the English ambassador, Lord Strafford, depicts the mood prevailing in The Hague. The explosion of feelings of fierce bitterness against the false ally did

[1] See Part One, p. 100, and above, p. 57.

X

not greatly disturb him. His windows were smashed, from the pulpits the Tories were denounced as disguised papists, the poets asserted that England's 'white cliffs for noble shame were blushing', or cried vengeance on the 'ungrateful one, in whose eyes can be perceived the glimmer of deceit'. But England was not therefore any the less master of the situation. The defeat of Denain seriously undermined the prestige of the States government with its own people. Keppel, the Earl of Albemarle, the compromised commander at Denain, had been a favourite of William III's during the last years of his reign, yet many cried that under the Stadholder such a thing would never have happened. The worst meanwhile was that the idea of having to raise still more money frightened even the old 'perseverer' Heinsius, who had always thought only of what the war was being fought for and never of the debt that kept piling up. All that had been obtained at the price of 'so much blood, sweat, and money' (to quote one of the many rhymers who hastened into print) had now been 'thrown away by the loss of one accursed night'. Harsh words were not spared old Heinsius, whose miscalculations were costing the country so dear, but nothing remained for the States but to 'submit' (the word used by Bolingbroke and Strafford) to what their powerful ally thought fit to allow them and to stipulate for them from France.

First of all they had to accept the fact that the Townshend Treaty must be considered annulled, and in January 1713 they might even be grateful that England granted them a new treaty in place of the one repudiated. And as for any share in the commercial treaty that England had secured for itself for South America (the *asiento*), or any equivalent for it or for England's acquisitions in the Mediterranean, there simply was no question of such a thing any longer. The promise of support for obtaining Upper Gelderland, too, lapsed, for England was not minded to offend Prussia, the rising Protestant power, which had already introduced its troops there, for the sake of the Republic, England's competitor in trade, which had showed itself so unmanageable into the bargain. As regards the barrier, the principle of having the Southern Netherlands serve the security of the Republic was saved out of the general shipwreck. A number of places, however, were dropped from the draft of 1709 because

England could not, under the altered circumstances, exact them from France (the chief being Lille and Valenciennes); economic-financial stipulations, from which Tory propaganda had taught the English to expect damage to their own interests, also had to be removed. But in the new treaty England still promised assistance in obtaining a barrier settlement, less far-reaching, but, even so, highly obnoxious to Austria and to the Southern Netherlands themselves.

The Peace of Utrecht

MEANWHILE, throughout the whole of the year 1712, the Peace Congress had been holding its sessions at Utrecht, but the realities lay elsewhere, namely in the separate negotiations taking place between the English and the French governments: at Utrecht the result of these was in the end, in April 1713, only registered. That peace treaty laid the foundations for the colonial and maritime greatness of England, which continued to rule the Mediterranean through Gibraltar and Minorca, which came to control the South American trade through the *asiento*, and which strengthened its position in North America at the expense of France. Austria did not at once resign itself to the inevitable: it did not conclude peace until 1714, after separate negotiations at Rastatt; Strasbourg, which the French had been prepared to cede in 1709 and 1710, remained in their hands. Nor was the French northern frontier pushed as far back as would have been possible in 1709 and 1710; nevertheless Louis did have to give up Ypres and Furnes, which had been in his hands since 1678. As regards the Republic, it had to suffer Prussia to remain in the larger part of Upper Gelderland; only Venlo was assigned to it. And for the rest the only positive advantage it acquired out of the war was the barrier in the Southern Netherlands. As a matter of fact years passed before this ambition was fulfilled in practice. Promises on the part of England were all very well, but the actual settlement had to be made with the new Austrian master of the Southern Netherlands. The strength of the States' position in the protracted negotiations lay in the fact that they were holding the country occupied—together with the English it is true; but in any case they refused to evacuate as long as Austria had not consented to a permanent arrangement.

In order to understand the composition and significance of the barrier as it was at last established in November 1715, it will be necessary first to give attention to the way in which the position of the States in the Southern Netherlands had developed since the expulsion of the French in 1706. Only then, too, shall we be able to draw up the balance and ask ourselves what was, after the great wars of the Louis XIV period, the position of the Netherlands in the world.

4. THE REPUBLIC IN THE SOUTHERN NETHERLANDS (1706–15/18)

IMMEDIATELY after the battle of Ramillies the States-General had instructed their Deputies in the Field to establish a temporary government in the provinces now liberated from the French, that is in Brabant and Flanders. After consultation with the States Assemblies of the two provinces the Deputies decided to institute a Council of State as well as a Council of Finance and two Chambers of Accounts; that is to say that the situation previous to the French reforms was not completely restored. The Hollanders, basing themselves on the Grand Alliance, which declared the Southern Netherlands to be their bulwark, believed themselves to be competent to make all the necessary settlements on their own authority, but although the initiative remained in their hands the English did not allow themselves to be eliminated, and in the end the new governing bodies were appointed by the two Powers jointly. From the beginning it was an odd situation that this Council of State, composed, as formerly, of a number of high officials together with the great ones of the land (the Archbishop of Mechlin, the Duke of Arenberg and Aerschot) had to act in the name of Charles III, but in obedience to the orders of the occupying Powers. The Count of Merode-Westerloo was the only one of the gentlemen approached who before giving his reply had consulted the new sovereign-in-name; and at the latter's request he had then refused to serve on the Council. The occupying Powers had their regular supervision exercised by the so-called Conference, composed of Marlborough and another Englishman (who generally had to act for the absent General), and two Dutch gentlemen; of these Johan van den Bergh, onetime Burgomaster of Leyden, remained in office from beginning to end, and since the other members were from time to time replaced that alone was enough, although he was no outstanding personality, to give him a predominating influence.

Although it did not present itself to the public as the country's government, yet it was this Conference in which in reality rested the supreme authority. The Council of State was bound to follow its 'requisitions'. For almost ten years therefore Flanders and Brabant (to which Hainault was soon added) were governed on the lines prescribed by the Naval Powers. That meant, chiefly by the States-General, whose troops were used before those of Queen Anne for the occupation of the South-Netherlands towns, a right to which they jealously clung and which inevitably gave them an ascendancy. In his report to the King about that ten years' régime, after the transfer of the country in 1716, the Austrian minister, von Königsegg, wrote:

Not without reason have the ministers of the Naval Powers after the surrender of these provinces acted in a contrary manner (*from the preceding French regime, when the Count of Bergeyck, with the French troops behind him, had exercised an absolute authority*). The intention was to win the affection of the population, which was therefore treated with much mildness. But since this alien and provisional administration did not trouble to look farther than the morrow, it did not greatly care how much difficulty its accommodating policy might create for the future. In order to get the provinces to supply what was needed for the moment, it did not therefore scruple to grant conditions which were sometimes highly detrimental to the sovereign authority.

This was how the servant of absolutism must look at things. But the main point has a more general validity: the most striking feature of the administration of the Conference was indeed its entirely negative character. While the French period, which had been cut short by Ramillies, was inspired by a faith, so that it had been able to find a convinced servant in Bergeyck, the occupation of the Naval Powers was devoid of any faith whatsoever. It was undoubtedly important for the development of Flanders and Brabant that the absolutist tendency was so suddenly interrupted and so radically. The fact alone that they had, after Ramillies, been able to enter into negotiations on their own account raised the prestige and the importance of the States Assemblies. How seriously their views had to be taken into consideration appears from the fate of the 'règlement' the occupying powers introduced as early as 1706 for the raising of taxes in Flanders. That 'règlement', drawn up by an official,

De Meulemeester, who hoped to play the rôle under the new rulers that Bergeyck had under the French, would have sub-jected the local authorities concerned with the levying of taxes to the supervision of central officials, just as had been customary under the French. Against this, and against the appointment of 'delegated judges', a veritable storm of indignation broke loose among the interested parties, that is to say the authorities in towns and in bailiwicks themselves, and their representatives, the States.

When His Highness (*the Duke of Marlborough*) and their Excellencies (*the Deputies of the States-General*), at the head of their victorious army, solemnly assured the deputies of the States and of the magistracies of Flanders, both by word of mouth and in writing, that they had come to reinstate the country in its ancient rights, liberties and privileges and to cast out despotism, they were received with open arms. These same States and magistracies are now hoping that these promises will be fulfilled and the said règlement conse-quently be withdrawn. (*So did the States of Flanders expostulate with the Conference.*)

And the allies had no choice but to drop De Meulemeester's plan. The most they could do was to protect him in the following years against the vengeance of the violently offended States and of the Court of the Province which was ready to back them up.

In spiritual life too it meant something that the ban on Jansenism was lifted once again when the French made their exit. The Austrian, on entering upon his heritage some years later, shuddered at the progress made by Jansenism while the heretics had looked on indifferently. Indeed, now and again, they had not shrunk from interfering in a startling manner. There was the case of Ruth d'Ans, who had been expelled by Louis XIV and whom the States-General's representatives, making use of the absence of the fugitive bishop of Tournai, had by virtue of royal prerogative thrust into the deanery of the chapter.

But that the policy of letting the provinces have their own way as much as possible did not prove enough for winning their 'affection' is not after all to be wondered at. Even so, the Conference still interfered deeply enough in social life. The appointment of magistrates in the towns, for instance, it kept carefully in its own hands. Cadogan, the English member, once complained that he could not appoint even a single alderman;

that was because he was no match for Van den Bergh's influence. The Hollanders were trying in this way to form a clientèle for themselves in the Flemish and Brabant town governments. And for another thing the Conference continually watched over the interests of military operations. One 'requisition' followed another with regard to financial contributions, levies of troops, and billeting. How unbearable such interference must have appeared, particularly to the Council of State, which was only allowed to be a tool in the hands of the intruders! Van den Bergh and the Deputies in the Field, travelling all over the country with the armies, were more closely related to the inhabitants, undoubtedly, than were the English lords, but for that very reason the population was perhaps even less willing to submit to them. The counts and barons of the South Nether-land administration could hardly be expected to like receiving orders from a Leyden Burgomaster! A nobleman like Goslinga certainly found it easier to get on with those gentlemen—and probably often spoke French with them. But even so there remained the insuperable difference, occasioning arrogance on the one side and irritation on the other: the relationship was still one of sovereign, or at least exponents of sovereignty, against subjects.[1]

How clearly does this appear in the complications following upon the recapture of Ghent and Bruges at the beginning of 1709. Had members of the Ghent magistracy neglected their duty or even committed treason on the occasion of the surprise of the town by the French six months earlier? When the French soldiers, led by the fugitive Chief Bailiff of the town, Della Faille, had made their way in by means of a ruse, the magistracy had at any rate offered little resistance and had presently for the second time sworn the oath of allegiance to Philip V. But these Flemish town regents had from long and repeated experience acquired a great proficiency in bowing to new masters. From 1701 to 1706 those of Ghent had dutifully regaled all the great lords of the Franco-Spanish party that passed through their town, and with no less zeal had they done the same between Ramillies and the capture of their town in 1708 for those of the Imperial-States-English Coalition; never forgetting, when they decided to bestow a complimentary gift, to vote themselves in

[1] See *The Revolt of the Netherlands*, p. 245.

accordance with time-honoured custom a small douceur as well. As late as July 1708, they prepared a brilliant reception for the Duke of Burgundy, a grandson of the great Louis and brother of their recovered (though never beheld) King Philip; the States of the province came to pay their respects in person. But in the same way they hastened to welcome Marlborough with a banquet in the Town Hall on the day following the capitulation of 2 September 1709. As a matter of fact there is no doubt that they were heartily sick of the French long before the year was up, and when the Anglo-Dutch troops set free by the fall of Lille began to prepare for a siege of Ghent the French Governor remarked at once that he could not count on the inhabitants; the guilds refused all help, and the magistracy was already entertaining secret relations with the besiegers.

Were there nevertheless among the town regents (apart from a man like Della Faille, who made common cause with the French quite as wholeheartedly as Bergeyck had done), secret sympathisers with the French? The restored rulers seemed to think so. Through members of the Council of State acting as 'delegated judges' (that is to say over the heads of the Council of Flanders, itself suspect) the allied authorities set a prosecution on foot against a number of persons belonging to the Ghent town administration; the Bailiff-in-Chief, Heer Rijm, lord of Rammelaere, the aldermen, Baron van Pottelsberghe and the lord of Pottelsberghe van Herlegem, the town secretary Frederick, and others, were arrested. Violent feeling was aroused in Ghent at so flagrant a violation of the privilege *de non evocando:* 'delegated judges' was a word abhorred in both South and North. But now listen to the humble tone in which the States of Flanders addressed The Hague States-General:

We pray Your High Mightinesses humbly that it please them to be good enough to grant the suppression of the aforesaid Junta or Chamber of Delegated Judges.

The humility, it is true, became less pronounced when it was discovered that the new rulers did not agree amongst themselves; the English shielded the men of Ghent, and the Hollanders in the end had to shelve the affair by means of an amnesty—a solution against which the people of Ghent, after having vociferously cheered the prisoners on their return, angrily protested; because amnesty implies guilt. Even more angrily than against the Hollanders, with respect to whom caution remained advisable, they turned against their neighbours of Bruges, whom they suspected of having suggested the amnesty and whom they wished to prosecute for defamation.

Königsegg later affirmed that there were only too many Francophiles in the provinces. Under the régime of the Naval Powers, and soon even under Austrian rule, the spirit of opposition easily tended to present itself in pro-French guise, but when the French were actually there, they had found but little sympathy on which to build. The fact is that the South-Netherlanders could not see their own interests clearly involved in the war, and on the whole the course of events was little calculated to strengthen their public spirit.

Could they forget that they had sworn allegiance to Philip V in 1700? The change of 1706 had been undertaken by both Brabant and Flanders independently, without their having given any thought to the Walloon provinces. In these latter the French remained for the time being, with Maximilian Emanuel as Governor, until in 1712 he succeeded in getting Philip V to bestow on him the sovereignty by virtue of the treaty of 1702: as we know, he had in fact lost Bavaria.[1] But the French had meanwhile been thrown out of Hainault too, and so he was inaugurated only in Namur and in Luxembourg. Upper Gelderland had by then been detached also, and the States-General and Prussia were quarrelling over its final disposition. In 1712 the Naval Powers, too, fell out, and the English, who had come to an understanding with the French, and who had for a long time been playing off the discontented elements in the magistracies of the South-Netherland towns and provinces against the Hollanders, secured their position against their allies-in-name by occupying Ghent, Bruges, and Ostend with the troops that now became available. The South Netherlands were a helpless puppet tossed about in the struggle between the Powers.

Nevertheless some towns did at times boldly repulse French attacks, Brussels for instance in December 1708, and Louvain in August 1710. On both occasions the citizenry readily mobilised; the town of Louvain received a key of honour from Charles III, and its Burgomaster, Van de Ven, was knighted.

---

[1] See above, p. 293.

'The French, of old our sworn enemies', thus Van de Ven expressed himself to his King. And at Brussels the States of Brabant even fraternised with the two North Netherland members of the Conference, Van den Bergh and Renswoude; in recognition of their vigorous assistance in the defence of the town they bestowed upon each of them a golden ewer with the arms of the province.

But of a positive *rapprochement* on the basis of a common war effort there is nevertheless little to be perceived. The part taken by the population remained only incidental. The anti-French feelings of the South, interwoven with medieval memories, partly local, and for the rest connected with the name of Habsburg, did not in any case harmonise too well with those of the North, where the purely political consideration of the European balance of power was supported by concern for Protestantism, where scoffing at 'papists' and monks was regarded as good style, and where 'the Brabanters' were generally looked upon as folk foolishly enslaved to 'the deceits of the Romish Church', and who moreover spoke an ugly caricature of the Dutch language.

Nor were there only these difficulties in mutual intercourse or understanding. The Protestant trait in the policy of the Republic came home from time to time to the people of the Southern Netherlands in a directly sensible manner when secret sympathisers with the Reformation, such as were still surviving here and there, found the support of zealous garrison commanders or army chaplains. And even if proselytising under the protection of States troops remained of sporadic occurrence— but which, even so, lent itself only too well to arousing ill-feeling against the Hollanders—there was yet one particular aim for which the States undoubtedly tried systematically to use their position in Flanders and Brabant: their own trade interest. Opportunities to that end offered themselves first of all in the occupied towns. Supplies for the States troops, indeed everything to do with the war, was allowed in free of duty, and that elastic regulation was given a very wide interpretation by the Dutch merchants, with the connivance of the Dutch rulers (and to the indignation of the English, as we know). When the allies pushed across the French frontier and captured such important trading towns as Lille and Valenciennes, the States took it upon themselves to establish custom-houses along the frontier, which levied special duties from everyone but their own traders (this too occasioned bitter conflicts with the English). Of a more general bearing was another measure taken by the Conference (here England and the States co-operated fraternally), to wit the re-introduction of the short-lived tariff of 21 December 1680; a veritable act of sovereignty. That relatively low tariff was to open the South-Netherland market for English and North-Netherland imports. It is true that the Conference soon felt obliged to levy extra duties over and above it, in order to obtain money for the war. The Dutch meanwhile with dogged persistence pursued their purpose of getting all these regulations confirmed in a barrier treaty.

The game was easily seen through by the Flemings and Brabanters. The particulars of the first barrier agreement between the States-General and England became common property when in February 1712 the Tory Government offered up the Townshend Treaty to the indignation of Parliament. But long before that the ambitions of the Republic had been sufficiently patent. That they aroused fierce animosity in Flanders and Brabant is a fact.

A good treaty for a barrier and for trade (*thus writes Goslinga when recording the year 1706*) would be hard to obtain. Both matters went against the grain with the ruler (*Charles III*) as well as with the population—which latter has always hated us on the grounds both of religious principle and of commercial jealousy.

And towards the end of the war, when efforts were being made to force the second agreement with England upon the Austrians, an English agent from Brussels wrote that 'the Dutch are considered the greatest enemies of this country'.

That Flemish intellectuals were capable of holding a different view even at that time is proved by a sonnet of De Swaen's:

Oh Holland, peace-loving country, where freedom lives—
In vain I looked for her among your neighbours:
The Frenchman and the Castilian disturb quiet and peace,
The citizens trembling before foreign masters.
Oh had I, beloved country, remained within your sphere,
How joyfully should my voice be urged to sing,
Be it on the river Rotte or on the river Maas.

The Dunkirker, whose town had been annexed to France from 1659, must have felt the lack of freedom particularly painfully. Moreover he had apparently got to know Holland on a personal visit. An utterance like his remains individual and unusual. Generally speaking it may be said that if any national feeling, any active public opinion, manifested itself in the Southern Netherlands during the later years of the War of the Spanish Succession, it was in aversion to and resistance against the domination exercised by the Naval Powers and especially by the Republic. But how weak were the reactions of the South-Netherland people, divided as it was and unschooled in any political action on its own account. Circumstances, indeed, were in every way unpropitious. The country's natural protector was Charles of Austria, but for him, both before and after his elevation to the Imperial dignity, other interests, Spanish or German, counted much more heavily than those of that distant possession, where he knew he would have to let the Republic have some control. And as a matter of fact, whenever it seemed the best way out, he did not scruple to sacrifice his Netherlands to the Naval Powers, who were actually more deeply interested in them than he was himself.

The opposition of the Flemings and Brabanters at first expressed itself mainly through the Council of State, which soon came to be on terms of tension with the Conference. In 1709 and again in 1711 clashes occurred, though it still proved possible to compose these after considerable discussion, exchange of notes, and deputations. If in 1711 Van den Bergh's desire that the Council should once and for all be forced to submit to its creators could not be fulfilled, it was only owing to the fact that these creators were now too much at loggerheads among themselves. As soon as unity had been restored by the yielding of the Republic, the latter could, with the co-operation of England, impose its will upon the recalcitrant Council.

That was by then urgently necessary, because the opposition was threatening to assume considerable dimensions. Towards the end of 1712, when it was becoming clear that peace was imminent, the States of Brabant approached those of Flanders and of Hainault in order to present at The Hague and at Utrecht to the assembled powers a request for the immediate transfer of their provinces to the rightful sovereign, the Emperor. Hainault joined in but waveringly, and in Flanders only Ghent was active. But what that deputation of abbots, barons, and counts (Ghent was represented by a marquess and two barons) discovered in the North was only that their fate was to be disposed of as the Powers thought fit. As regards its position in the Southern Netherlands, the Republic, however disappointed and humiliated, had its new treaty with England; the Austrians were powerless to interfere with that. When the South-Netherland gentlemen came to take leave of Heinsius (for they had at least been received by the most important statesmen), the Grand Pensionary told them:

Do not forget, sirs, that you have been conquered. (*A reminder of immense practical importance, for from this he deduced*) that the privileges, laws, constitutions and customs of these provinces were to him unknown.

With some truth the Louvain Burgomaster, Van de Ven (now a viscount), wrote from Utrecht:

The more I observe, the firmer becomes my opinion that we have been sold; handing us over is all that remains.

These reports caused such a stir in the South that Van den Bergh at Brussels urged more strongly than ever that measures be taken against the Council of State, whose 'dirty intrigues' he considered to be behind it all. He was convinced, however, that even though influence had been brought to bear upon the headmen of the Brussels 'Nations' (the guild groupings)—they had, for instance, 'been given their fill at the taverns'—

these attempts to make the people ripe for rebellion have been fruitless; and Your Honour (*the letter was directed to Fagel, the Greffier of the States-General*) may be assured that I need have no more fear of any molestation on the part of the citizenry here than I should have in any town of Holland.

Only if The Hague were to treat the matter 'with a continual yielding or with a sort of indifference'—so he went on to warn—the result might very well be 'an outburst into public commotion'. But on the contrary Van den Bergh was authorised to act as he desired. So in March 1713 the Council of State, which continued to appeal to the name of Charles VI and to the privileges of the land, was deposed and, under the chairmanship of one of the old members, the Count de Clairmont, who thus made a career for himself, a new Council was formed. And now it was seen that Van den Bergh had correctly estimated the weakness of the opposition. It is true that the States of Brabant bestirred themselves to support the unruly Councillors: in their minutes we read:

It is further resolved in the meanwhile not to recognise the newly appointed Council of State.

Brave words: but the States of Flanders again held aloof. Persons of standing accepted appointment to membership of the new Council, a Baron d'Hooghvorst, chairman of the Brabant Audit Department; the Vicar-general of Mechlin; a lord of Bouchoute, member of the Council of Flanders, who had already been proposed for that post by the States of the province in 1706. Vainly the discharged Councillors had climbed down somewhat, suggesting to the States-General and to the English and Austrian ambassadors in The Hague that it might be possible to arrange an amicable compromise. The Austrian ambassador replied evasively. The Conference asserted its authority, and from that moment the Council of State was its submissive servant. Whatever Königsegg (as we saw above) was to say about the mildness of its rule, it had in this instance performed an act of authority that Philip II might have been proud of, and it is a striking proof of the lack of cohesion among the provinces that they were not able to present a common front against its presumption.

The Anglo-Dutch Treaty of January 1713, for all that it did to strengthen the position of the States with respect to the Southern Netherlands, was far from leading to a rapid and definitive settlement with Charles VI (who could not in the meantime enter into possession). The Tory government in England gave very little support indeed to the States-General in their negotiations with Charles, carried on at Antwerp. The States were exultant when after the death of Anne in 1714 the Protestant Succession Act was carried into effect and the Elector of Hanover recognised as King, while their friends of some years ago, the Whigs, once more came to power. But the Whigs had only thought the Townshend Treaty inevitable in the circumstances of 1709; they did not dream of undoing the advantages which their opponents had gained for England by betraying the country's allies. Thus it was that the Dutch could not prevent, in the spring of 1715, a strong Austrian military force from entering and occupying the provinces; even the new

Consequences for the Republic

THE main political object of the Republic, then, had been attained, although the form in which it was achieved was far from propitious. The circumstances in which the settlement was reached, too, were profoundly humiliating. The diplomatic defeat the Republic had suffered at the hands of its ally, so suddenly grown imposingly powerful, could not have been more complete. Nor was loss of prestige all: for the first time the Republic lost, and tellingly, a round in its long economic struggle with England, who proved more dangerous as an ally than she had been formerly as an enemy. It was in order to protect its trade interests in the Spanish colonies against French penetration that the Republic had gone on with the heavy war, even after the danger of French absorption of the Southern Netherlands had been disposed of. Now it was faced with the result that instead of France England was ousting Dutch trade from Spanish America as well as from the Mediterranean. An advantageous trade treaty with France was obtained, just as at Rijswijk: England was not interested in French trade; but that was only a meagre compensation.

It will not do to ascribe the Republic's thus being outstripped by England solely to Bolingbroke's betrayal in 1711–12[1]: if England had not already surpassed the Republic in actual power he could not have risked treating the ally in that way. The successful manoeuvre brought to light a previously existing weakness. What was beginning to tell on the Republic was its neglect of overseas interests and opportunities, due to its omission to keep its naval forces up to standard. While it was engrossed entirely in the land war across its Southern frontier, England had been able to conduct a large-scale world policy, gaining supremacy in the Mediterranean and imposing its will on the King of Spain and of Spanish America, no matter whether he was called Charles III or Philip V. An unavoidable weakness and an unavoidable omission! That land war alone had already taxed the strength of the Republic too heavily. After all it was a small state with much slighter resources than England, which had only for a time been prevented by internal difficulties from vigorous development in the commercial and colonial sphere.

[1] See above, p. 320.

This had been one of the factors which made the tremendous prosperity of the Republic in the seventeenth century possible. During that same time other potential competitors had also been impeded by domestic confusion, disunity, and abuses, out of which they were now gradually emerging. What more particularly placed the Republic in a position of inferiority with respect to England—not for the first time, but it had never counted for so much as it did now—was that its situation kept it shackled to the continent, while England owed to its geographical position an enviable freedom of movement. It had been impossible for the States to withdraw from the war in the Southern Netherlands. And shackled to the continent the Republic remained. Because even though the long-standing menace from France had now been averted, the Republic had in the meantime become saddled with another troublesome neighbour in Prussia, which had laid hands on Upper Gelderland and was already reaching out for East Friesland; nor from that point of view was Austria a good exchange for Spain.

Utrecht closes the period of North-Netherland greatness. That so profound a decline should have followed, inexorably leading from one humiliation to the next and at last to the overthrow of the Republic, cannot directly be inferred from the events described here. It was due, also, to internal abuses, perhaps to a decline of the national spirit; it was a process which must form an important theme in any sequel of this story.

c. THE NORTH NETHERLANDERS
OUTSIDE EUROPE

1. THE EAST INDIA COMPANY

STARTING with *points d'appui* in the Moluccas, at Batavia, and along the coast of Coromandel, the Empire of the Dutch East India Company had, round about the middle of the seventeenth century, spread across the Malay Peninsula and Ceylon and still further along the coasts of Coromandel and of Malabar; moreover, by the settlement at the Cape access was assured. After

This assembly is of the greatest importance: it meant a big step forward in the process of the real subjection of Java.

It was darkened by a horrible incident. Among the rulers come to render homage to the Susuhunan there was also the Depati of Surabaya, who had been looked upon with suspicion by the Company ever since the campaign of 1706, and who was in any case considered to be more powerful than was compatible with the authority of the Susuhunan. The Depati was still maintaining himself as the overlord, under the Susuhunan, of a number of 'regents' in North-Eastern Java. Cnol had been left free by the government at Batavia to act with regard to him as he thought fit. According to his own report, he incited the Susuhunan 'to help' the redoubted vassal 'at last to get his long and well deserved reward', reminding him of the Depati's 'unruliness' and 'great exercise of authority'; and this to such effect that the Depati, coming to visit his overlord at the latter's invitation, was stabbed to death by the court attendants within the second gate of the palace;

without myself (*so Cnol concludes his report complacently*), or anybody on the part of the Company, meddling or being present or anywhere in the neighbourhood.

An affair which makes one feel how deeply the political morals of the Company's servants themselves could, in the conditions prevailing in that society, be corrupted. However that may be, the fall of the Depati had far-reaching effects; together with the humbling of Madura, it paved the way for a disintegration of all independent power under the Susuhunan's well-controlled sway. Three 'regencies', each wholly separate from the others, were now instituted and at the same time each of the 'regents' received instructions indicating which products, and in what quantity, he was to supply to the Company yearly.

Because that had now become the system. The Company through its coercive treaties no longer tried only to control the import and export trade of the various native territories, demanding that they buy from and sell to the Company; it prescribed what they were to produce. In the Batavian 'Ommelands', in Preanger and Cheribon, where it now directly instructed the 'regents', it had already been doing this for some time. Sugar was required of those districts, cotton, indigo, and coffee; the cultivation of the two last-named commodities having been introduced—sometimes in an improved fashion—from other regions with which the Company was entertaining relations, viz. Coromandel and Mocha. Bantam, which had always been a land for pepper, had to supply specified quantities of that spice. The beach 'regents' of Mataram already had to supply rice to Batavia, but at the assembly in question all the 'regents', at the command of the submissive Susuhunan, appeared before Cnol,

in order to specify which produce the lands under their authority are wont to supply every year, so that from their returns a project may be formed in writing of the merchandise taken or desired by the Noble Company.

This was a task to which the statesmanship of the Javanese 'regents' was not equal, but in a rough and ready manner an obligation was imposed on each of them and sealed with the Susuhunan's small seal. That measures like these must involve the Company very deeply in the affairs of the Javanese people, even though it left the execution to the native heads, goes without saying. The son of a Susuhunan banished to Ceylon, a Susuhunan created, the country's trade cut off from all contact with English, Portuguese, or Arabs, its production regulated, guided, promoted—the Company had indeed become a power on Java!

And now it was hoped, as the Governor-General and Council expressed it from the bottom of their hearts:

that the Company, Java's eastern shore having been reduced to peace, may at long last, in return for its heavy outlay, enjoy the benefit of the true riches of that island.

Financial worries; Monopoly, Supplies

THIS was all the more necessary because in the activities of the Company a serious decline was making itself felt on one point, namely in the inter-colonial trade. Already some years previously (in 1703 and 1705) the warnings addressed by the Supreme Government at Batavia to the Directors had sounded grave enough.

The profits have turned into losses, trade is declining, the competition of the English, French, Portuguese, Chinese, and Moors cannot along this extensive coast-line be checked, the spending capacity of the population is diminishing, the sale of cloths (*as the reader will remember,*[1] *this was what the profitable trade of Coromandel consisted in*) is not a fifth of what it used to be.

---

[1] See Part One, p. 188.

Thus, curiously enough, it came about that if one confines one's attention to the activities in the Indies—and in the Company's books these were kept separate from those in Europe—the most remunerative establishments were those where the Company had not assumed sovereign power, where it did not keep up any fortresses and garrisons, but traded in free competition: Japan, Surat, Persia, Bengal, Mocha; Coromandel also figured in that list, where it is true the Company had from the start maintained Fort Gelria, but where nevertheless it could not dream of excluding the English, French, or Portuguese. Siam and Tonkin, although free establishments, usually registered losses; for the rest, all the establishments figuring among the unprofitable category were such as claimed sovereign rights and aimed at monopolies: Palembang, Sumatra's west coast, Ceylon, Malabar, and then particularly Amboina, Banda, Ternate, Macassar, Bantam, Cheribon, Java's east coast, and the Cape. Well might the Governor-General and Council sigh out:

Time has shown clearly enough the poor effect for the Company's commerce yielded by these many imposed exclusive treaties and by our forcible interference with native navigation—apart from the hatred and other disadvantages which the Company suffers therefrom.

Bold words on the part of the Supreme Government, for in so speaking they touched the holy of holies. They more than hinted that to enforce the monopoly policy was a hopeless task, while it devoured vast sums of money.

Coen had advocated the admission of free citizens. What had become of their position appears from the case of Beeck and others. Jurriaan Beeck, a man of a good Dort family (he inherited the manor of Strevelshoek), had been born in Malaya, and had never set foot in Europe. He carried on trade at Batavia, no small-scale trade either: during sixteen years he had bought goods from the Company to an amount of 300,000 to 400,000 guilders annually. But in 1701 letters were intercepted and it came to light that with the help of bribed sailors, he had been trading direct with Europe, via England even, and the Supreme Government inexorably dispatched him to the 'fatherland' he had never seen. The same ship took along five other free citizens who had been caught out. But Beeck had, moreover, in one of his letters been guilty of 'serious slander and vilification of the authorities':

by impertinently abusing the High Government of these territories, calling their régime and the life led under its auspices one of slavish subjection imposed upon us, and more of suchlike expressions.

In Holland Beeck and his fellows sought redress, first from the Directors, and next from the States-General, persistently arguing that they had been unlawfully deprived of their livelihood. But the Directors were too well able to make their influence felt in the States-General for the High and Mighty assembly to treat the case otherwise than dilatorily. Practically it came to be established that free citizens might be removed from the Indies on account of private trading. Not that disapproving voices did not make themselves heard. In 1711, for instance, the retired ship's surgeon, Abraham Bogaert, a well-known man of letters, dealt with the matter from the point of view of the free citizens in his *Travels through Asia*. At Batavia, too, 'various arguments were to be heard', so he reports,

but, as the saying is, *under the rose*, since in the Netherlands Indies the least semblance of freedom can only wander surreptitiously.

Hardly an auspicious atmosphere for 'free citizens' to breathe in! But the Supreme Government was not thinking of the free citizens when it regretted the 'exclusive contracts and forcible interference with native navigation'. Both in its indifference to the former as well as in its disapproval of the latter it can be seen that Batavia had detached itself from Coen's tradition. Nobody had worked more zealously than Coen to destroy the old native trade—and now the consequences were making themselves felt. At a much earlier date, as a matter of fact, under Maetsuycker in 1675[1], the Supreme Government had suggested that the Company should keep its royal position intact by leaving trade to the natives and pluck the fruit of their 'prosperity' by means of taxation (a word of wide consequence was there pronounced).

At the turn of the century there was a whole group of high officials who wanted to move in that direction. With Camphuys and, after an interruption, again with Van Hoorn, men of this way of thinking even came to occupy the Governor-Generalship. In spite of this remarkably little was effected. Their ideas were expressed most strikingly by Cornelis Chastelein, a friend of the two 'Generals' mentioned, himself a member of

[1] See above, p. 184.

the Council of the Indies. An attractive feature of the mentality here becoming apparent is that these men seemed aware of other things than the vulgarly material side of the Company's trading activities. Camphuys, de St. Martin, and Chastelein went to a great deal of trouble to promote the publication of Rumphius' scientific works about Amboina.[1] Camphuys was personally a great collector. Chastelein bought land at some distance from Batavia, where 'in my quiet solitude', as he says himself, surrounded by his slaves, he led a patriarchal existence, experimenting with the cultivation of sugar and coffee. In those days there was a draughtsman and painter, Cornelis de Bruyn, of The Hague, who after travelling the length and breadth of Asia described his expeditions in some richly illustrated folio volumes, showing him to be interested in art and history as well as in nature and the customs of alien peoples. This man on one occasion also visited Chastelein's Seringsin—getting there on horse-back and partly by ox-cart—and in his book he depicts the Governor-General's 'house of pleasure' as well as the two Balinese slave women attending him. Both *Weltevreden* and *Buitenzorg*, the well-known resorts near Batavia of later days, took their origin from Chastelein's estate. Part of it, in his highly remarkable will, he bequeathed to his liberated Christian slaves and their progeny, who were still in possession when Dutch rule came to an end, some hundreds of them.

Now this man, too, who came to feel attached to the country as did few others, protested against 'the Noble Company's principles' which made it stake all on 'private trade of its own'. Chastelein's proposals at a first glance still remind one of Coen: he too recommends the settlement of Dutchmen as the best way of attaining so powerful a position that there would be no danger any longer of being 'kicked out' by other Europeans. He was apt also to indulge in animadversions against 'the lazy Javanese' and 'the insolent, self-assured Chinese'. Making the rulers tributable, and forcing the inhabitants to work—these were ideas much in his mind. And yet in his argument there is already a note of acquiescence in the fact that the chance had been lost; and what matters above all is that he considered the true wealth of the sovereign to lie in the agriculture and the other activities of the population—and if it must be, of the original population.

[1] See above, p. 183.

Thus he directed his energies not only to an improvement of agricultural methods, but to the creation of an orderly society. The safety of law and order, that primary requirement for prosperity, still left much to be desired in the territory under the sway of the Company, and Chastelein tried to draw the attention of the lords and masters at home to the reform of abuses precluding that safety, as also to the advantages that might result from a little more freedom for the inhabitants, freedom to plant pepper and weave their own cloths, instead of expecting everything from more stringent measures for maintaining a trade monopoly which had proved untenable in practice.

But the lords and masters at home remained deaf to the warnings of the officials on the spot. It was rather in *their* shortcomings that they looked for the cause of the decline. Van Rheede tot Drakestein's journey of inspection, as we know,[1] and the measures then attempted, had had no effect whatsoever. Private trade continued to flourish; everyone, from high to low, was bent on making his own fortune instead of thinking of the interests of the Noble Company. Punish the guilty among our own servants, do all that can be done to keep the foreign interlopers out: no other solution seemed acceptable to the Directors. The monopoly was not succeeding? Then have it carried out more strictly!

The conservatism of the direction of affairs at home is strikingly evident in the argument with which the powerful Company Solicitor, Pieter van Dam, in 1688, rejected proposals for improvement that had been suggested by a Committee of Investigation (for the situation was already then causing concern) and which Coenraad van Beuningen (a member of the Committee) was advocating with his customary impetuosity.

I am of opinion (*thus Van Dam*) that it would be a doubtful and even perilous proceeding to undertake anything that might in the slightest way weaken or subvert the foundations of the Company, foundations on which the edifice has rested for so many years to the great benefit of the State and of the shareholders. Experiments of that nature might yield quite different, even the opposite, results from what had been forecast or imagined in the council room.

Van Dam, who twenty-five years earlier, in the less responsible days of his youth, had ventured to criticise the monopoly

[1] See above, p. 184.

system, was a very different man now. The ideas of Van Beuningen which now roused his alarm were less thorough-going than had been his own. All Van Beuningen wanted was 'management'—retrenchment: how many useless officials were there not employed over yonder, how the money was poured out on 'donations' and 'fortifications'; compared with forty years ago expenses had multiplied, and nobody could find his way through the accounts drawn up in the Indies. Would it not clearly be in the interest of the Company if we at home (we Directors), instead of allowing ourselves to be led by the nose by the Company's servants over yonder, bound them to stricter regulations? All that was needed was that, 'after the style of a sensible merchant', we should for a change make careful calcu-lations ourselves. What might seem 'subversive' here was only the hint that to get the better of the abuses the independence of the Supreme Government at Batavia would have to be en-croached upon.

When the Directors could not even screw up courage for *that* policy—and it is a moot point whether it would have proved feasible—it could not but prove impossible to prevent the officials on the spot from taking their share of the profits. And what was more natural at a time when in the mother country itself those who took part in government were ever more and more openly intent on their own advantage, on 'jouissances' and 'douceurs'?

The community of officials in the East, infested as it was with shady characters, and lacking any principle capable of promoting self-renewal, could not live by any higher standards than those observed in the Netherlands itself. Even the clique spirit, which came to prevail in the regent society at home, was reflected in the Indies at the Castle of Batavia. The manner in which the Governor-General was elected conduced to this evil, because the new overlord was always recruited from the small circle of high officials; almost always was he appointed by the Council of the Indies itself. Since Speelman's unfortu-nate tenure of the office the Directors were repeatedly having trouble with the Supreme Government. Close family ties between the Governor-General and the Director-General, factions and feuds within the Council of the Indies—the in-corruptible Camphuys for instance met with a great deal of secret

z

and open opposition—such circumstances were not propitious for undertaking an all-embracing purification; and indeed officials were too badly paid to be able to live on their salaries.

Just as inevitably, the maintenance of the monopoly system kept on requiring new and unforeseen expenditure. Averse as the Directors still were to war, the one just ended could yet not remain the last. We shall see presently of how short duration 'the new period of quiet' was to be. It was not the monopoly system alone that was responsible for this, although it was more than anything else. The hatred, to which we heard the Supreme Government allude, sprang largely from those never-ending and yet never wholly efficacious attempts of the Dutch to cut off the peoples of the Moluccas, of Macassar, of Java, of Palembang, of Ceylon, and of Malabar from the free traffic they had been accustomed to, amongst themselves and with other European traders: attempts of which the sole aim was too obviously to force them to sell cheaply and to buy dearly.

(*The grandees of Bantam bitterly complained*) that the pepper was now to be sold exclusively to the Company, a state of affairs by which only the Sultan benefits; (*as regards the rest, so they say,*) whether of high state or of low, we are all equally poorly off.—(*And a few days before he was assassinated, the Depati of Surabaya expressed himself to the effect*) that the Company's commerce broke the backs of the poor Javanese inhabitants and that owing to the miserably low prices they could make for their products those poor people were being completely ruined.

We have here, no doubt, the explanation of the fact that the Company was no longer able to place the Coromandel cloths in the islands so profitably. In this way her own inter-colonial trade suffered under the paralysing effect of the monopoly. From early days on warnings had been sounded[1] that the monopoly policy was bound to come up against uncontrollable forces. The struggle was still going on, obstinately persisted in by the Directors, but ever more clearly the Company was becoming the losing party, at least if note is taken only of the business done in the Indies. For as a matter of fact the losses suffered there were for the time being amply counterbalanced by the unexampled prosperity enjoyed by the import trade in Europe. Asiatic products as a whole were fetching higher prices, but moreover, in addition to the spices, which had formerly yielded the highest profit, tea and coffee had now come into

[1] *The Netherlands in the Seventeenth Century*, Part One, p. 172.

vogue and were proving a mine of wealth for the Company. At the close of this period there opened a succession of years in which it regularly paid its shareholders a dividend of 40 per cent. No wonder that the Directors did not give up the old monopoly by which, after all, this too seemed to be guarded.

The voice of criticism, nevertheless, was again making itself heard in the mother country too. A pamphlet writer, examining the economic situation at the close of the war with considerable ability, argued that the charter of the Company laid unnecessary restrictions upon Dutch trade. Freedom for all to trade with the East was what he wanted: the English and the French did not let themselves be restrained by the Dutch charter anyhow, and was not Dutch private competition, 'owing to the industry and thrift of the Hollanders', the best means of ousting them? Moreover he recommended the founding of settlements (how often and each time how ineffectively do we see this idea keep cropping up!) in order to strengthen the position out there and to create markets for Dutch industry. The writer was thinking of the Cape—where it was said there were gold mines in the interior—of Ceylon, and of Java; and he did not omit to make an allusion to the Beeck case, saying that expulsion of free citizens on account of alleged trespassing in trade should never occur again.

It was without doubt a dangerous state of affairs that this enormous economic structure of Asiatic trade rested in Holland on a small privileged group, among whom a still smaller number of elect were entrusted with the actual direction.

It must be admitted that the system of obligatory supplies by which the monopoly policy was now rounded off had its promising traits for the Indian world. It stimulated the productive capacity of the Javanese population. It brought the Dutch into closer contact with them (as they were already with, for instance, the population of the subjected part of Ceylon), it roused their interest in the natives' welfare, and made them put their experience of other methods and of unfamiliar crops at the service of a conservative race resigned to its poverty. But that the possibilities one can here discern were also confined within too narrow bounds by the Company's appetite for monopoly was soon to become apparent.

The Cape under the Van der Stels: 1679–1707

THE number of citizens at the Cape had for a long time, since the days of Zacharias Wagenaer,[1] been growing very, very slowly. Soldiers or officials who requested citizenship after having completed their period of service came to grief almost regularly. There was no more than a thin trickle of fresh arrivals from Europe. The Directors asserted again and again that suitable emigrants were hard to get, even by promises of a free crossing and farms in full ownership, because craftsmen and farmers' sons too readily found employment at home. In 1672 there were, apart from some 300 officials and soldiers, no more than 64 citizens, 39 of whom were married, with 65 children; in 1687 the numbers had risen to 254, of whom 88 were married, with 231 children; the remainder was mostly but a floating and miscellaneous crowd.

But now a whole wave suddenly came in. The Directors found emigrants in the Huguenot refugees who were arriving in a more impecunious state after 1685 than before the repeal of the Edict of Nantes, which made it more difficult for them to convert into money their possessions in France. Not only were they promised a free crossing and a decent farm, but a minister was sent out with them so that the refugees, to whom their religion meant so much, would be able in that far-off country to commune in their own language. Some 160 French people came and settled at the Cape in 1688 and 1689, men, women, and children. Their case caused a stir and aroused sympathy: even in Batavia a not inconsiderable sum was collected to support the destitute among them in their difficult start. In the following years a few more arrived, but at the same time the stream of Dutch emigration flowed somewhat more fully; the prosperity of the colony became known and exercised an attraction.

In great part this was owing to Simon van der Stel, under whose Governorship fell the arrival of the French, but who promoted the settlement of Dutchmen with especial zeal. After a series of brief administrations Simon van der Stel started one in 1679 which was to last twenty years; and when he resigned he was succeeded by his son, Willem Adriaan. Simon van der

---

[1] See above, p. 66.

Stel had been born on Mauritius in 1639 as the son of a Company official (who soon after was murdered in Ceylon) and of 'a black, heathen woman slave' as his enemies put it. The Dort regent family from which the father sprang did not therefore fail to recognise the child; Simon even married into the Amsterdam Burgomasterly family of Six. In 1672 he commanded at Amsterdam a company of town militia; his son Willem Adriaan became alderman there in 1691. Simon at that time was in great favour with the Company: his title had been raised from Commander to that of Governor, and he had become an extraordinary member of the Council of the Indies. He had been sent out in 1679 from the office of the Amsterdam Chamber; the reader will remember that this had been the customary method with the West India Company, but the East India Company was luckier in its choice of Van der Stel than the other had been with Van Twiller or Kieft.[1] He was a man of unusual ability and enterprise. From the very first moment he looked upon South Africa as a country of great possibilities, which it would be his task to develop. That was the spirit in which, three weeks after he had stepped ashore, he undertook his first journey of inspection to 'Hottentot Holland', the region south-east of Fort Good Hope, where were to be found the only farmers outside the actual Cape peninsula. For that fertile land, shielded against the severe winds blowing at the Cape, he heartily wished to obtain more 'industrious farmers from home'. Still deeper was the impression made on him by

a certain region, situated 3 or 4 hours from there (*going north*), being a level valley containing several thousands of acres of fine meadowland, very suitable also for agriculture, provided with an excellent river for draining the water— a river decked out on both sides with fine, tall trees, fit for timber. We discovered an islet there, fresh water lapping both its sides, planted by nature with fine, tall trees, which his Honour the Commander took for a resting place that night, and, since no earlier Commander had ever set foot in that spot, it was named: *Stellen Bosch*.

The Commander immediately encouraged settlement in that delightful valley. Several citizens left their estates nearer Table Mountain, at Rondebosch and Wijnberg, in order to migrate further away, on the other side of the sandy and uninhabited Cape plain, to Stellenbosch. In 1683 some thirty landowners were to be found there, mostly with families, and a school was

[1] See *The Netherlands in the Seventeenth Century*, Part One, pp. 201, 203.

set up; the schoolmaster also acted as visitor of the sick and conducted a weekly church service. A few years later a church was built and a regular minister appointed. A local administration had already been set up, under the name, taken from the Holland countryside, of 'heemraad' (district council). At first it consisted of four citizens, who tried small offences, and also looked after the interests of the community; if in the mother country control of the water had claimed most attention, here it was measures against lions and other wild animals. At the Cape itself a Citizens' Council was established, and citizens sat also on the Council of Justice there. The supreme direction remained with a Political Council exclusively composed of officials, yet more room had been allowed to the citizen element than had been the case a generation before in New Netherland,[1] and the institution of 'heemraden' was as time went on to give a considerable amount of independence, with respect to Cape Town, to the outlying districts, of which Stellenbosch was only the first: this notwithstanding the fact that Van Rheede tot Drakenstein[2] when inspecting the Cape in 1685 had taken the precaution to appoint at the head of the heemraad at Stellenbosch a Bailiff to represent the Government. So relations between Simon van der Stel and the growing farming population were quite friendly. He felt especially well-disposed towards the settlement at Stellenbosch. He had an annual fair held there, to which the Cape farmers repaired in their wagons, and where the main attraction was shooting at the popinjay. Van der Stel used to celebrate his birthday at Stellenbosch, receiving the congratulations of the citizenry and the schoolchildren.

There had been a big change since Zacharias Wagenaar had complained about the citizens as 'lazy, sodden louts'. A real community was growing up now that there were Dutch wives and mothers in the colony: a community which kept up many of the best traditions of the homeland, with a sense of law and freedom, careful of school and church. Van der Stel saw to it that the immigration of orphan girls was promoted. The cares lavished on these both on the voyage and on their arrival gives anew the impression of a truly humane civilisation, and when one studies the regulations for the freeing of slaves, laid down by Van Rheede on his visit in 1683, one will notice once more

[1] See Part One, p. 205 ff.   [2] See above, p. 184.

that the immigrants were still in touch with the traditions of the mother country.

The vivacious and kind-hearted, hospitable Van der Stel fits very well into that picture. As the chief officials might otherwise have felt too keenly the lure of the (unlawful but certain) enrichment offered by the Indies and might therefore have sought a transfer, Van Rheede had allowed them to acquire land for private cultivation. The farmstead of the Governor, Constantia, became a famous spot; viticulture there yielded better results than elsewhere, the house had an air of distinction. Visitors to the Cape used to express the greatest admiration for the Company's garden in the Table Valley. It was no longer simply a vegetable garden for the provisioning of the fleets on their way home to Batavia, but under the personal supervision of Van der Stel it had been turned into one of the most beautiful ornamental parks, and at the same time experimental gardens, in the world.

The influx of the French element at first raised problems of its own. The new settlers were conscious of their cohesion as well as of their separateness. On their coming with a particular minister of their own, as arranged by the Directors, Van der Stel received them somewhat suspiciously. He wanted to scatter them among the Dutch colonists, and when they nevertheless settled, most of them, in a group at Drakenstein, beyond Stellenbosch, he gave them considerable offence by his demand that their congregation should be no more than a subdivision of the Stellenbosch church community. High words were uttered on both sides. In 1690 the Directors decided largely in favour of the Drakensteiners, but at the same time laid it down that the French schoolmaster should know Dutch and that the French children were to be taught that language, while in future the French colonists were to be endowed with land situated in between Dutch-occupied farms. Events occurring when Simon Van der Stel's son held the Governorship did presently more perhaps than these measures to promote feelings of solidarity among the citizens irrespective of their nationality, and to hasten the absorption of the French by the Dutch population (which was certainly six times their number).

As a matter of fact a situation developed in which the citizenry as a whole came to face the Governor and his officials in sharp antagonism, a situation in which it could not but feel its very existence threatened.

However considerably the colony had developed under Simon Van der Stel, the freedom of the citizen community, and especially its economic freedom, remained confined within very narrow limits. Such was the wish of the Lords and Masters at home. The Company kept all trade jealously in its own hands. It had the right of preemption with respect to whatever goods the farmers had to offer; not until the Company had been provided could they sell their cattle, their corn, their wines, to others, and even then only at fixed prices. In order to make life possible for the settlers, the Company had eased certain too rigid prohibitive regulations, but the situation still left them little breathing space. The fleets calling at the Cape were supplied with provisions, but there was no question of any export to Europe or Asia: the market consequently was sadly restricted. How greatly did the colonists feel injured therefore, when Willem Adriaan van der Stel, immediately after he had become Governor in 1699, started to farm on his own account on a much larger scale than his father had ever done at Constantia, and, inspired by avarice and unrestrained by any respect for law, abused his official power in the most shameless way. On his farm at Vergelegen the visitor might count 18,000 sheep, 1,000 cattle, 500,000 vines, and hundreds of servants; sixty lower-grade Company officials were employed there for his benefit, while the citizens were forced to supply wares and render services. The other higher officials acted likewise under his protection. By 1708 the eight of them already possessed as much land as did half of the free inhabitants together. They reviled the latter as the Company's bastards while in their arrogance they called themselves its lawful children. The 'second' (or 'second person') said triumphantly to the Governor:

in three or four years' time no citizens will be needed at the Cape any more; we (the officials) shall be in a position to provide the Company and the Cape with all that is required.

A free community of Dutch farmers; or four or five large estates worked with Hottentots, half-castes, and East-Indian slaves: it was a choice between this future or that. Small wonder that, apart from the officials, the Governor could only count on a small number of dependents. Between him and the whole of the citizenry, the farmers especially, a tension grew up that surpassed anything that had existed fifty years earlier in New Netherland. As had been the case there, the citizens at the Cape opposed to this official arbitrariness a strong consciousness of their unalienable rights as Dutchmen, and when at last they appealed to the Directors, they received a more favourable hearing. After all, Willem Adriaan was not oppressing the citizens in the interests of the Company, but had, for his own benefit, grossly harmed not only the citizens but the Company itself.

A number of the most important citizens, having consulted together in 1705, began by lodging a complaint with the Government at Batavia. A leading role had been played in this affair by a man who in fact kept carefully behind the scenes, Henning Huyser, an enterprising businessman, who, as such, felt the restrictions imposed by the new régime all the more painfully. He was not, indeed, a man of marked integrity, and, now that matters were being forced to an issue, various personal interests came into play on the part also of the citizens, and the means employed were not too fastidious. No answer was forthcoming from Batavia, and just when the plotters had drawn up a second, more detailed note for the Directors themselves, signed by sixty Burghers, French as well as Dutch, the Governor found out about this 'godless' plot of 'these sanctimonious scoundrels', these 'vile, ignorant farmers' and had the chief instigators arrested. The indictment against Van der Stel, Jr., was nevertheless smuggled to its destination by a surgeon, Abraham Bogaert, who happened to be in the harbour on a return-fleet, but while the citizens were waiting a whole year for the rulings of the Lords Seventeen, the Governor played the tyrant without let or hindrance.

From more than one point of view this is a most remarkable episode. We are well documented about it. The Bogaert in question was no other than the writer of *Reizen door Asia*, whose sympathy for the Batavian free burghers I touched upon above,[1] and soon he gave, as an appendix to his book, an indignant account of it all; the Governor subsequently defended himself before the home public in a contumelious *Deductie*, in answer to which there appeared a whole folio volume from the side of

[1] See p. 350.

the citizens, the *Contra-deductie;* and finally there was published in the thirties of this century the priceless diary of the man who had composed the indictment to the Directors—Adam Tas, a cousin of Henning Huyser's.

What strikes us most of all is the lawless high-handedness which the officials of the Company were able to indulge in on their outlying posts. W. A. van der Stel had been born in Amsterdam, he had been an alderman there; but he is typical of the later generation of Company officials, the sons and grandsons of officials, often half-castes, for these are now often to be found among the personnel. When the fortunes of the Company in Asia are considered, even worse examples of misconduct will obtrude themselves. But no less characteristic is the fierce resistance of the white population of settlers at the Cape holding fast to their Dutch principles. Adam Tas himself was almost thirty when he left Amsterdam. In the neighbourhood of Stellenbosch where he lived (at a distance even from Cape Town therefore) he kept up his intellectual contacts; he read the periodical *de Boekzaal*,[1] received new books about De Witt, about the course the war was taking in Europe, and so on. His diary presents us with a colourful picture of the sociable intercourse among the farmers, with their ever recurring feasts, 'nibblings' with 'a pipe of smoking weed' and 'glasses of wine' —indeed, there was a good deal of heavy drinking! He held himself as independent towards the minister of religion as towards 'the tyrant'. When the latter, before rightly knowing about the movement against him, is uttering threats, Tas notes down:

Children may be frightened, in our country, with a bogey-man, but men living honourably and virtuously should not have fear of anybody.

His arrest and the confiscation of his papers taught him differently.

This violence committed upon the person of a free citizen, a free farmer, an Amsterdammer (*so Bogaert writes*), made the signatories exclaim. They wanted to know what had become of the qualification 'free', what was left of the famed Holland freedom, and whether these great concepts were now nothing but vain sounds so that men did not even seem to have the privilege of complaining to their fathers, the Lords and Masters.

Several of the plotters allowed themselves to be intimidated, and retracted. Others, both French and Dutch, stood firm.

[1] In which foreign as well as Dutch literature was reviewed.

Jacobus van der Heiden, one of the prisoners, refused to answer the questions put to him by the official Council of Justice, whose competency he denied, since they were party to the affair and indeed had not even summoned him in the proper way. Twenty-seven days in a dark cellar with a negro slave who had been sentenced to death unnerved him, and at the same time made him so ill that the Governor had to release him for fear he might die on his hands. Tas remained in prison for over a year, when at last the decision of the Lords and Masters arrived by which the Governor and his chief henchmen were removed from office and recalled.

They were not punished, but the victory of the free Burghers was sufficiently complete. Willem Adriaan van der Stel and the other officials had to give up the estates by means of which they had competed so unfairly with the settlers. The aged Simon remained in possession of Constantia, but Vergelegen, which in many ways had been a model estate, was partitioned. The house Willem Adriaan had built there even had to be pulled down. The Directors agreed with the burghers in their dislike of a manor with outbuildings showing off in aristocratic grandeur compared with the simple level of the ordinary farmsteads. The decision meant that in the future development of the colony social equality was to prevail. It has been regretted that as a result conditions were inevitably marked by a certain pettiness and the country's culture by rusticity. But a victory for Van der Stel would have prevented the springing up of any Dutch settlement at all, because his system could only be based on negroes and Asiatics.

The citizens also, it must not be forgotten, worked with slaves. The difference was that they actually lived on, and managed, their 'places'.

The area now covered by the settlement was about equal to that of the provinces of Holland, Zealand, and Utrecht together: quite a big area for so small a number of colonists, but only a speck on the vast expanse of South Africa, which seemed to offer land to those who felt trek-minded both eastward and north-ward. During the whole of this first period and for a long time afterwards there were but few serious difficulties with the original inhabitants. The roaming, cattle-rearing Hottentots had too little grip on the soil not to make room fairly easily for the newcomers who attached themselves more closely to the land. Only, the latter were minded to move ever further inland, and also expeditions for the exchange of cattle sometimes led to blows. That was why the government was usually bent on keeping the Boers back from such adventures. It was not, however, until much later that the expansion was to come up against the more powerful Kaffir tribes, of whose movements in the interior the settlers had as yet only the vaguest knowledge.

2. THE WEST INDIA COMPANY

The West India Possessions during the War

THE West India Company had gone bankrupt in 1674. Starting on 1 January, the States-General had granted a charter to a new Company which took over 30 per cent of the debts of the old one together with all its possessions in the territory of the charter. Besides the stations on the West Coast of Africa (among which St. George d'Elmina ranked first) these embraced some islands in the Antilles (the group of St. Eustatius, and the group of Curaçao) and on the South American continent, on the Wild Coast as it used to be called, Essequibo and Berbice. In those two last-mentioned colonies the position of the Company was not so simple, however. Essequibo, which for a time had been administered by three Zealand towns,[1] had been transferred in 1669 by them to the States of Zealand, who in turn had handed them over the next year to the Zealand Chamber of the West India Company, with the stipulation that the colony was to be open for the ships and trading activities of all Zealand citizens on paying a recognition duty to the Company. Under the new charter the supreme authority of the Directors (they now numbered ten instead of the nineteen of former times) was recognised, but the day-to-day administration remained with the Zealand Chamber, whilst the inhabitants of Zealand were confirmed in their privilege of free trade. As regards Berbice, that region was under the patronage of the family of Van Pere,[2] with whose rights the new Company could not interfere. While the Commander of Essequibo, who with a few officials and a small garrison had his abode at Fort Kijkoveral, was appointed

[1] See Part One, p. 200.   [2] See above, p. 81.

by the Zealand Chamber, subject to the approval of the Council of the Ten, the Commander of the still very unimportant Berbice only had to do with the owner, Van Pere.

On those islands an end had by that time already been put to the patronages through the vicissitudes of the war, which in the long run were to make the position of the Van Peres in Berbice impossible too. In 1676 Tobago, which had belonged to the Zealand ship-owner Lampsins,[1] had been conquered for good by the French; in 1682 the heirs of Van Rhee and Van Pere sold St. Eustatius to the Company for 6,000 guilders: plundered in 1663, and again in 1665, it was once more occupied by the English in 1672, and although it had been promised back in 1674 it had actually only just been returned, thoroughly ruined. The Company was not able to protect it: as early as 1689 it was conquered by the French, and the new ally, England, who took it away from *them*, did not let it go again until the peace in 1697. The importance of the island did not lie in the plantations but in the slave trade, for which it provided a well-situated distribution centre; just as did Curaçao.

And then there was also Surinam, conquered by Crijnsen in 1667; Crijnsen's fleet had been equipped by the States of Zealand acting on their own, and as a result the colony had, after some wrangling with the States-General, virtually become the possession of that province. But it was a possession that was to cost a great deal of fresh capital and of patience. Almost immediately England had reconquered Surinam, but by then peace had already been concluded in Europe, so Zealand received it back again—as good as stripped bare: everything, particularly slaves, had been carried off, and most of the English planters had left. Discouraged by all this, Zealand sold the colony in 1682 to the new West India Company, and the latter presently got rid of a third of it to the town of Amsterdam, and a second third to Cornelis van Aerssen van Sommelsdijk: the three owners together (Amsterdam, Van Aerssen, Zealand) formed the Society of Surinam for the exploitation of their possession. Van Aerssen, disappointed in his ambitions at home, where he had courted the favour of De Witt too assiduously ever to be properly trusted by William III, had himself sent out as Governor.

[1] See above, p. 83.

He encouraged the immigration of French Huguenots; the name of his wife, of noble French stock, attracted a good many. Among the planters refugee Portuguese Jews from Brazil were already numerous. White society in the colony consequently displayed a strongly cosmopolitan aspect. But Van Aerssen at least created the order which is the indispensable condition for growth. He was 'more feared than loved' and a few years later lost his life in a small scale soldiers' revolt. The Council of officials and planters, now in charge according to the charter, managed to master the confused situation. Shortly afterwards, in 1689, the new Governor, Van Scharphuysen, manfully warded off an attack of French privateers. The French were more fortunate on the Pomeroon, where they utterly destroyed a new settlement, so that the Commandant had to flee back to Kijkoveral; and in Berbice, which they ravaged thoroughly, leaving with a bill on the patron, Van Pere, for no less than 20,000 guilders. Van Scharphuysen was able to get the claim diminished to 6,000 by means of the prisoners who had fallen into his hands.

Dreadful was the suffering inflicted upon the West Indian Colonies by the wars, as well with England as with France. It had been one of the factors contributing to the fall of the first Company, and it impeded development under the second. How different was the position from that in the East! There the East India Company, after having dismembered the Portuguese Empire by force of arms, stood as the naval power *par excellence*, capable of gloriously protecting its possessions and far-flung monopoly claims against the English and French. The West India Company, always in a languishing condition, never disposed of a considerable navy. The men-of-war of the State, which were never needed in the East, continually had to offer help in the West and repeatedly had to restore the declining state of affairs there. The result was that the West India Company, both before and after 1674, always had to heed the wishes of the States-General much more carefully than had its East Indian sister. As a matter of fact, however, the protection the State offered was by no means always sufficient. The West India colonies were situated in an area where the English and the French were present in at least equal strength, and towards which the attention of their governments was certainly directed more strongly. Particularly during the War of the Spanish Succession the enforced neglect of the navy—I already touched upon this in my account of the central course of events[1]—led to a whole series of calamities in the West Indies.

It was privateers, direct successors to the buccaneers who had at one time proved so dangerous to the Spaniards, who undertook all these raids; but they were now recognised by the French government, and enjoyed its support. In 1708 three French ships sailed up the river Essequibo. The planters fled from all sides to Fort Kijkoveral and furiously reproached the Commander, Van der Heyden, for allowing the enemy, unmolested, to play havoc with their plantations. But with his garrison of fifty men the Commander was powerless; he was obliged to conclude a capitulation which enabled the privateer chief to take his departure with a tribute of 50,000 guilders, one-third of it paid by the planters, and two-thirds by the Company, largely in slaves. A few months later other privateers visited the colony and destroyed and looted what was left. In that same year 1709 it was the turn of St. Eustatius. The Commander, Lamont, allowed himself to be surprised in his slippers and dressing-gown. A capitulation was not even possible. The French destroyed what they could not take with them, and then sailed to Martinique in vessels loaded to sinking-point with goods and slaves.

This humiliation of the Commander afforded his ill-wishers the opportunity of getting rid of him. The small community was torn by feuds. Lamont had come from the official ranks, but already possessed plantations on various islands; his ideal remained, one day 'to ride in his coach in Amsterdam'. At St. Eustatius the Council confronted him under the leadership of one of the inhabitants, Doncker by name; according to the latter Lamont was a dishonourable scoundrel, who used to try to persuade people over to his side by treating them to 'a dram of aniseed', cinnamon-water, or brandy and playing a game of cards with them; now he had to flee from the looted island in an English barque to seek refuge on his plantation at Curaçao; Doncker became Commander.

After a few quiet years the visitation was repeated and assumed worse form. In 1712 a formidable fleet of privateers

[1] See above, p. 39.

appeared in the West Indian seas, equipped by a few Marseilles merchants in partnership with the commander Cassard. His first exploit was directed against Surinam. In serried rows the sugar plantations there bordered the rivers which after merging flow out into the sea, the Surinam, the Commewijne, and the Cottica. Paramaribo, protected by Fort Zeelandia, where the Governor lived, had become a place of some hundreds of houses. Planters and town-dwellers were organised in citizens' companies; the Jews separately. In June Cassard's first assault was beaten off.

The inhabitants on that occasion had put up a brave fight under their civic captains, but they had seen more clearly than had the enemy how defenceless the colony must be against any determined attack. So they began urging the Governor and the Council of Police (that is to say the Political Council, mainly composed of elected planters) to take measures, offering to help at once to improve matters—the planters through the work of their slaves, the townsmen by means of money—but on the understanding that the Society would ultimately bear the expense. The Governor and Council had to consult the civic captains, authorised in writing by the colonists, about the construction of the defence works, but protests against taxes, which according to the citizens were contrary to the charter, were outside their competence. So it came about that the civic captains addressed the States-General directly with complaints about the Society for its neglect of the defence works and for unlawfully burdening the inhabitants.

That document had not long been sent off when Cassard appeared for the second time, with a stronger force, eight large ships and more than thirty small ones, and 3,000 soldiers. The small garrison and the armed planters and townsmen were located in Paramaribo and in Fort Zeelandia, while the French sailed up the river Surinam and had free play in the plantations. Women and children had been sent into the wooded interior with trusty slaves. Their most precious property, which would most readily serve the invader for booty, that is, the plantation slaves, many planters also tried to hide in the woods. From Paramaribo the citizens did make some sallies on Frenchmen who had taken up their stand in nearby plantations; but such skirmishings, in which the slaves, who were also used in the fighting, always soon ran away, took on the whole a discouraging course, so that a capitulation soon seemed the only solution.

Cassard consented to a truce so as to enable the Governor to consult the councillors who were in Fort Sommelsdijk, higher up on the Commewijne. After this had been done, all the citizens, as well as the captains and mates of the ships that happened to be in the road, were called together and the Governor, surrounded by his councillors, represented the hopeless situation to them. It was agreed upon to seek a capitulation. On the plantation Meerzorg, which belonged to one of the councillors and which Cassard had turned into his headquarters, negotiations were now held, and the councillors, who had been authorised to do so, finally signed an agreement for a tribute. A year's income had been taken as a basis, 15,000 hogsheads of sugar; together with some small additional costs the account came to 622,800 Dutch guilders. The sum was paid largely in merchandise, and for a considerable part also in slaves. According to the agreement:

The remainder will be made up through slaves, men and women, at 350 guilders (*Surinam guilders; worth about 300 Dutch*) a head.

From Surinam Cassard steered to Berbice, where he proved strong enough to encircle and bombard Fort Nassau. Very soon a capitulation followed, by which the colony, so much poorer than Surinam, promised to pay 300,000 guilders. The pirate admiral accepted well over three-fifths of that sum in the form of a bill on Messrs Van Pere, the patrons of Berbice. In spite of the unhappy fate awaiting the two hostages whom Cassard had carried off, the Van Peres refused to pay up; the whole colony was not worth such a sum, they asserted, and so Berbice fell to the holders of the bill. But those French merchants did not know what to do with it and sold their property for over 100,000 guilders to an Amsterdam combine, which after many years, in which the colony was left in a sad state of stagnation, set itself up as the Society of Berbice; not without difficulty the West India Company managed to get its overlordship recognised.

Cassard had meanwhile sailed on, and in January 1713, after a breathing space at Martinique, he appeared before St. Eustatius; resistance was not even thought of, but there was not yet much to be got after the raid of 1709: '34 slaves, 22 head of

cattle, 65 sheep, 23 turkeys, and 67 fowls. . . .' Now it was the
turn of Curaçao. That island was not only larger than St.
Eustatius, but much richer on account of the smuggling trade
with South America that went on under cover of the import of
slaves. The Director Van Collen attempted to organise a defence
with his handful of soldiers, strengthened with a band of sailors
of all nationalities got together from the ships that happened to
lie in the roadstead, and with the citizen guards. When the
French who had come ashore started to bombard Willemstad
such a panic arose that here too it soon ended in capitulation.
Cassard's first demand was for 400,000 pesos, about 1,200,000
guilders, almost double the sum Surinam had brought him!
After a great deal of haggling he contented himself with 115,000
pesos.

What a humiliating spectacle, the defencelessness of one
West Indian colony after another in the face of that enterprising
freebooter! A satirist who described the Curaçao adventure in
sarcastically high-flown language makes Van Collen snub the
citizens who still wanted to offer resistance in the following
lines:

> 'You impecunious louts have nothing to lose by the transaction.
> You possess nothing but debts and should be only too content
> To let the great ones suffer all the damage.
> But you will be out of your reckoning here and I shall, with the
>   other gentlemen,
> Presently sign the treaty even though all of you should be the worse
>   by it.'
> So spoke the Hero and with unshakable determination
> Concluded with his enemy an agreement
> To prevent any further calamities
> For just one hundred and another fifteen thousand pieces of eight.
> So an end was put to evil, hostility laid down,
> Through the Governor's wise conduct, for nothing but a handful
>   of money.
> What cannot the people hope from such a guide!

One would have expected that in the colonies the authority of
the Directors at home, whose Governors were already often
enough in difficulties with their Burgher councils, could hardly
survive all this. And indeed everywhere there were loud lamentations and protests, particularly in Surinam. There the griev-
ously afflicted inhabitants were bent on shifting their share in
the contribution on to the Society, the more so as they had not
by any means been able to recover all the slaves they had sent

into hiding in the woods. While the Governor and Council were proposing to levy an assessment of one-tenth from each citizen's property, the civic officers remonstrated more fiercely than ever with the States-General. They did not however get any comfort from the mother country. The States-General, who of course began by consulting the Directors—that is to say the Lords Ten of the West India Company, the powerful Burgomasters of Amsterdam, and the lord of Sommelsdijk—severely adjured the colonists to fulfil their obligations towards the Society and ordered the discontinuance of separate meetings: the inhabitants ought to be content with their representation on the Council of Policy. An agreement between the Directors and that Council about the apportionment of expenses for the fort, which had proved to be so badly needed at the point where the Surinam and the Commewijne divide, was also hanging fire; it was not until 1773 that a beginning was made with the execution of the plans for Fort New Amsterdam. In principle nothing had changed in the position of the colonies and their administration.

The above account will have made the reader feel what it must have meant to the West India Company that at Utrecht so lengthy a period of peace was inaugurated. However disappointing the whole peace settlement may have been, one important part of it, which in the ensuing period was going to give England an incomparable position in the South American trading area, and which had for that reason seemed more hateful than anything else to Amsterdam, brought an advantage to the Dutch plantation colonies: I mean the *asiento*.

The Guinea Coast and the Slave Trade

FOR the development of the plantation system an uninterrupted supply of negroes was indispensable. But to the West India Company, which notwithstanding all its vicissitudes had jealously reserved to itself the right to import slaves into all those colonies, however varying its position may have been in each, the Spanish colonies had in the seventeenth century, unfortunately for the planters, offered another, still more important, market. The Spanish government, it is true, also tried to preserve a monopoly in trade relations with its overseas territories, but the spirit of enterprise in the mother country was so inadequate that it could not be maintained effectively. Moreover Spain had no access to the African market in human beings and could not possibly therefore herself satisfy the need for slaves in her American colonies. The companies to which the Spanish government granted the right to import—by means of contracts which were called *asientos*—had after 1648 inevitably had to go to the Dutch supplier, that is to say that through their agents they bought at the depots to which the West India Company transported its cargoes of slaves straight from St. George d'Elmina on the African coast, mainly at Curaçao. To the great indignation and alarm of the clerical party at the Spanish Court the *asiento* itself was from 1685 to 1689 in the hands of a big Dutch *entrepreneur*, Balthasar Coymans of Amsterdam. But when this contract was annulled and the *asiento* granted to a group of Portuguese, the slave camp on Curaçao still remained one of the chief places to which the importer came to pick up his merchandise.

For the Dutch plantation colonies, and even for the plantation owners on Curaçao itself, this demand from Spanish America had the disadvantageous consequence that their own needs were badly served; and this in spite of the fact that in the various con-tracts or charters which regulated the complicated relationship of the Company with the mainland colonies, a sufficient number of slaves per annum was always stipulated. But complaints about pressing shortages were still regularly heard. Smuggling in slaves therefore remained a profitable activity. The governors of Spanish and of Dutch colonies alike were often unable to prevent their planters, hungry for slaves, from supplying themselves from some slaver trading on his own account—usually once more a Dutchman, often from Zealand.

In the War of the Spanish Succession, when the Spanish colonies recognised Philip V as their lord and the latter granted the *asiento* to Frenchmen, the Spanish American market became much less accessible to the Company. Nor did matters improve when at the peace England, as the price for her recognition of the Bourbon succession which she had at first wanted to combat so much more stubbornly than the Republic, obtained the *asiento* for her own subjects. From then onwards the Dutch slave trade, as well as the smuggling in goods that had gone along with it, lost its footing in Spanish America. The demand for slaves in the Dutch planters' colonies could now be satisfied much better, although the cry for more never ceased. At any rate, in the protracted period of peace that was now opening and in which a regular importation of labour could be ensured, the Dutch slave colonies, in Surinam, Essequibo, and Berbice, flourished. Here we shall look a little more closely only at the slave trade itself as carried on from the other side of the Atlantic, that slave trade which formed so important a source of income for the West India Company and on which the Guiana regions so largely depended.

Procuring slaves was not the only activity the Company practised on the Guinea coast on the opposite side of the Atlantic Ocean. On the contrary, its ten forts, spread over a stretch of nearly 300 miles and interspersed with English forts and some few Brandenburg or Danish ones, were all situated on the Gold Coast; and here gold was everybody's first concern. According to the calculations of Willem Bosman, who, after having served as head merchant in Guinea, published in the early years of the eighteenth century a lively and detailed account of the country and the people, the Dutch West India Company exported to the tune of 1,500 gold marks per year (3 marks = 1,000 florins) as against 1,200 exported by the English; while Brandenburgers, Danes, Portuguese, and French together accounted for another 1,800. The most serious competition, however, came from the smugglers: the Zealanders (one always comes across them in the history of the West India Company, either as partners or interlopers!) did quite as much business as the Company itself, the English interlopers until recently somewhat less, but now, Bosman believed, rather more.

When one compares the West India Company and the East India Company, it is the differences that strike one first. Here on the Gold Coast one may think at first sight that one is confronted with a position which in principle resembles that of the East Indies: no planters and citizens to form a Council by the side of the Governor, as was the case in the Antilles and Guiana, and such as the East India Company only had at the Cape, but a settlement consisting solely of officials trading for the Lords and Masters to the exclusion of everyone else. But how imperfectly was that exclusion enforced! The whole of that coast had to be shared with rival companies. That alone was enough to make it impossible to get so much authority over the natives as to be able to force them to let the intruding smugglers depart empty-handed. Between the companies of the different nations relations were strained. Each had its particular friends among the petty negro kings or negro republics in the neighbourhood, and if they did not openly fight each other, they were yet deeply involved in the feuds carried on by their black allies or protégés.

Bosman, in a tone of considerable irritation, relates the disputes occurring in his day with the tribes near to the chief posts of the two leading Companies, the Dutch St. George d'Elmina and the English Cabo Corso (Cape Coast Castle), and between these mutually. The English, who had the negro king murdered when the latter made overtures to the Dutch, had according to him stolen a march upon the Director-General of the Dutch Company. Our author retaliates by scornfully expatiating upon the 'evil way of living of the English'. The immoderate drinking of punch to which the leading men as well as the common soldiers were addicted caused an astonishing mortality in their castles, although it would be labour lost to try and make them understand that there was here a connection of cause and effect. . . . In fact the drinking habits and other excesses with which Bosman reproaches the English can only have been relatively bad. If the Guinea Coast had such a bad name in the Netherlands as well—a generation before this the comic poet, Van Focquenbroch, who later on met his death there, had already spoken of 'infernal Guinea'—then this was not only on account of the unhealthy vapours and the stench emanating from the negro villages, but also, according to Bosman himself, to 'the unmannerly toping' and 'the zealous offerings in the temple of Venus' which the officials could not forbear. It was not for lack of church-going:

We are on the contrary very pious and attend religious services regularly (*so scoffs Bosman*): we must go to church every day or pay half a dollar; except for Sundays and Thursdays when the fine amounts to a full dollar.

As a matter of fact the short spell of life meted out to the average official of the Company had its advantages for the survivors: they rose more quickly to the higher posts, without having occupied which it was unlikely one would come home from Guinea a wealthy man. And what other ambition could one cherish? There was little elevating in the trade carried on there, and to find satisfaction in it was the less easy as there were always the smugglers to get off with the best bargain. For these men could not only do business more cheaply because they did not have to bear the burden of forts and officials on the coast and of expensive Directors at home (as Bosman gives us to understand), but could take note of the taste of the fickle negroes much more quickly than could the Company's traders, whose suggestions were usually followed up too late by the cumbersome bureaucracy in the mother country. Nor was it possible to get much pleasure out of the primitive negro community. The servant of the West India Company was not called on to undertake any great task of constructive administration, or to build an Empire. Some sixty men was the sum total of the official personnel sprinkled over the forts on the Guinea coast; with here and there a small garrison of soldiers. The Director-General and his Council had their seat at St. George d'Elmina—not a council of more or less independent colonists, but a council of officials, a council of yes-men according to Bosman, who, it is true, in the second edition of his book prided himself on the fact that the Directors had taken his criticisms to heart and had somewhat curtailed the power of the Director.

All the Company's ships came to St. George d'Elmina—the finest castle of all on the coast—to unload their goods, which were distributed from there to the other trading stations. There also called the slaving ships before setting out upon their voyage to America. But the chief places for obtaining the slaves were situated further east, in Koto and Popo, and especially in Fida, in the present Dahomey, and then much more south, in Loango. From Fida and Loango the Company annually 'traded in' 3,000 negroes, according to a report dating from 1670. There the native populations and the kinglets made it their business to obtain, on the slave markets in the interior, and if necessary directly in wars or predatory raids against enemy tribes, the human merchandise which the whites of all nations came to seek so greedily.

Most of the slaves offered us (*so Bosman writes*) are men taken prisoner in war and sold by the victors as their booty. When these slaves arrive at Fida, they are all placed together in a shed or prison and when we are ready

to buy them, they are collected in a large square, where they are very carefully examined by our surgeons who are appointed for this task; they are
fingered over down to the smallest member of their bodies, men and women,
quite naked, without the least shame being shown. Those who are found
to be all right are ranged on one side, and the others in whom any defect is
detected are counted among the lame, or *macrons* as they are called here; that
is to say those who are over thirty-five years of age, or who are crippled in
arms, legs, hands or feet; also those who have lost a tooth, have grey hairs or
their eyes filmed over; all those who suffer from venereal disease or any other
illnesses. . . . After having sorted out these lame and crippled persons, the
rest are counted and their suppliers noted down. In the meantime a branding
iron is already in the fire, bearing the arms and name of the Society, in order
to brand on the breast all those who have been set apart as acceptable. This
is done so that we shall be able to distinguish them from the slaves of the
English, the French or any other owners, who are kept in the same prison-
house, for these have also branded theirs with their mark. This branding is
practised also in order that the blacks shall not exchange our good slaves for
bad ones (a trick they would otherwise play for sure).

You may think this way of treating them somewhat cruel and almost
barbaric, but since it is done under pressure of necessity it will have to be put
up with. In any case we see to it that they are not branded too severely,
especially the women, who are always a little softer.

The apologetic tone audible in the last sentence is rare enough
to be taken notice of. Yet how weak it remains! How quickly
does the momentarily disquieted writer comfort himself! But
truly there were worse terrors connected with this trade than the
branding. The crossing, with six or seven hundred mortally
alarmed people roughly torn out of their surroundings and
closely packed on top of each other, all secured in irons, groups
sometimes brought on deck for a breath of fresh air—the crossing was an abomination. Bosman was well satisfied with the
orderly way it was done on the Dutch slavers, 'clean and
spotless', whilst on the English, French, or Portuguese ones
'it is always dirty, foul, and smelly'. Nevertheless on board the
Dutch ships too mortality among the cargo that had with so
much medical care been pronounced healthy was as a rule high
enough, something like ten per cent at least. Some tribes stood
the uprooting better than others. Those who had been 'fetched'
out of the deep interior, sometimes, to Bosman's complacent
amusement, frightened themselves with awful imaginings that
their abductors had the intention of eating them. Suicides and
profound depression were of frequent occurrence.

And then in Surinam the selling, in groups or in couples,
families roughly parted, a second branding by the new owner,
and so under the whip-lash of the overseer to the plantation. Or

to Curaçao, to be bought up by the importers from Spanish America, or to St. Eustatius, where more particularly plantation owners from the other islands came to provide themselves. So long as the Company had the slaves under its control it prescribed 'good treatment'; on Curaçao there was a physician 'for the treatment of the negro slaves', there was for them a 'shack for small-pox' and one for fever patients—a choice of hospitals! The ministers of religion were even in their general instructions enjoined 'to teach the basic truths of the Christian religion' to the blacks as well as to the Indians, the Portuguese, and the Spaniards. That the blacks were human beings was not an unknown truth. Only, it was not acted upon in practice. The branding mark turned the slaves into cattle, as did the fixing of prices according to height and age, or a prescription like one from 1694 inculcating upon the Governor of Curaçao to promote 'breeding'.

The Dutch share the guilt of this inhumanity with all other European nations that sailed the seas. The buyers and the sellers, the skippers, the doctors and the overseers, are no guiltier than was the society that produced them and sent them out to do this work. The indifference of public opinion, of protestant ministers and of catholic priests, of the Directors from the regent class and of the diplomats negotiating about *asientos*, is astonishing. Let it not tempt us to condemn a culture which has other claims to our admiration; let it rather be a reminder to us of our own shortcomings. With how many crimes does not our day compromise! For that the slave trade was a crime, on account of the premium it put on kidnapping in the far interior of Africa, on account of the atrocities that accompanied it from one coast to another, and on account of the fate to which it condemned so many thousands from year to year for the rest of their lives and for their progeny, that is a fact which the general acceptance by contemporaries cannot obscure.

Sources of the Quotations

ABBREVIATIONS

W.H.G.U., B.M.H.G.U., K.H.G.U., B.H.G.U.: *Werken, Bijdragen en Mededelingen, Kroniek,* and *Berichten* van het Historisch Genootschap te Utrecht.

R.G.P., *Rijks Geschiedkundige Publicatiën.*

W.L.V., *Werken* van de Linschoten-Vereniging.

Knuttel: W.P.C. Knuttel, *Catalogus van de pamfletten-verzameling . . . in de Koninklijke Bibliotheek* (Den Haag).

Archives: Archives de la Maison d'Orange-Nassau, publ. par Groen van Prinsterer.

Aitzema: L. van Aitzema, *Saecken van staet en oorlogh;* quoted after the quarto-publication, 1650–71.

V.M.K.V.A.: *Verslagen en Mededelingen van de Koninklijke Vlaamse Academie.*

B.V.G.: *Bijdragen voor Vaderlandsche Geschiedenis.*

De Jonge: J. K. J. de Jonge, *De opkomst van het Nederlandsche gezag in Oost-Indië.*

PAGE

16. (*a*) Van der Capellen, *Gedenkschriften,* II, 308.
17. (*b*) *Openhertig discours tusschen een Hollander, een Zeeuw, een Vries, ende een Over-Ysselaer, rakende de subite dood S. H. Prins Wilhelm* (*onsterffel. mem.*); Rotterdam, 1651, *Knuttel,* 7040, 7.
17. (*a*) Cats, *Twee en tachtigjarig leven.*
18. (*b*) Memorie van Nanning-Keyser betreffende de gebeurtenissen van 1650, edited by G. W. Kernkamp, in B.M.H.G.U., XVIII, 1897; 356.
21. (*a*) *Aitzema,* VII, 127.
22. (*b*) *Op. cit.,* 211.
23. (*a*) *Op. cit.,* 442.
24. (*b*) *Op. cit.,* 223.
27. *Op. cit.,* 363.
31. (*a*) ('Frenzy') *Brieven aan De Witt,* W.H.G.U., I, 61.
31. (*b*) *Hollandsche Ruyker,* 1653; *Knuttel,* 7439.
32. (*a*) *Ernstig gesprek voorgevallen tusschen drie personen . . . gesteld door een recht liefhebber van den Hollandschen Leeu;* 1652, not in *Knuttel.*
32/33. (*b*) *Brieven van De Witt,* W.H.G.U., I, 95; 18 July 1653.
33. (*c*) Elias, *Schetsen uit de geschiedenis van ons zeewezen,* V, 149.
35. *Brieven van De Witt,* W.H.G.U., I, 161.
41. (*a*) *Op. cit.*
45. (*b*) L. Baeck to his cousin A. Hooft, 19 March 1655; *Brieven van Hooft,* IV, 239.
47. C. de Bie, *op. cit.*
50. *Dagverhaal van den oproer te Antwerpen in 1659,* edited by the *Maetschappij der Vlaemsche Bibliophilen,* I, 2.
50. *Op. cit.*
51. (*a*) *Op. cit.*
51. (*b*) *Aitzema,* IX, 323.

51/52. (c) *Dagverhaal* etc. (three notes).
54. (a) Geyl, *Oranje en Stuart* (paperback edition, 1963), 128.
55. (b) *Brieven van De Witt*, W.H.G.U., II, 279.
55. (c) *Brieven van De Witt*, 1725, V, 137.
57. (a) Downing to Nicholas, in Geyl, *Oranje en Stuart* (paperback edition, 1963), 151.
58. (b) 'Deductie van H. Gijsen', edited by Dr. S. van Brakel, in B.M.H.G.U., 1924, 58.
60. *Brieven van De Witt*, W.H.G.U., II, 583; April 1663.
62. Mignet, *Négociations relatives à la succession d'Espagne*, I, 266; in French translation.
65. (a) 1657; Godée Molsbergen, *De stichter van Hollands Zuid-Afrika*, 103.
66. (b) *Op. cit.*, 122.
67. (c) Quoted by Theal, *History of South Africa*, I, 164.
69. (a) Van Goens to the States-General of the Republic, 31 July 1656; in Aalbers, *Rijcklof van Goens*, 60.
69. (b) *Op. cit.*, 165.
71/72. *Daghregister gehouden op't Casteel van Batavia*, 1663, 127.
75. (a) *Documents relative* etc., I, 264.
76. (b) *Op. cit.*, 266.
77. (c) H. C. Murphy, *Jacob Steendam, a memoir of the first poet of New Netherland*, 1861.
78. (d) *Op. cit.*
85. (a) Quoted after Keith Feiling, *British Foreign Policy*, 119.
86. (b) *Scheepskroon der zeehelden van de vrije Nederlanden*, 1666, in Penon, IV, 283.
86. (c) *Brieven van De Witt*, W.H.G.U.
87. (d) *Aitzema*, XI, 1034.
87. H. T. Colenbrander, *Bescheiden uit vreemde archieven omtrent de zeeoorlogen, 1652–76*, R.G.P., I, 218. (French).
91. (a) The end of January 1666; B.M.H.G.U., XXVII, 559. (French).
91. (b) To Van Dorp, 4 September 1666; *Brieven van De Witt*, W.H.G.U., III.
91. (c) Quoted by Wicquefort, *Histoire des Pays-Bas*, ed. Chais van Buren, III, 262. (French).
92. (d) B.M.H.G.U., XXVII, 581. (French).
92. (e) 15 April; *Aitzema*, XII, 247.
94. (a) Quoted after Blok, *Michiel Adriaanszoon de Ruyter*, 275.
94. (b) *Brieven aan De Witt*, W.H.G.U., II, 336.
95. (c) Pepys, *Diary*, 29 July 1667.
100. (a) The medal in Van Loon, *Nederlandsche Historiepenningen*. (Latin).
101. (b) Temple to Bridgman, 27 January 1668; in Temple's *Works*.
104. (a) *Brieven aan De Witt*, W.H.G.U., II, 542.
104. (b) 10 December 1671; *Brieven van De Witt*, W.H.G.U., IV, 177.
105. (c) *Op. cit.*, 177.
107. (a) More detailed in Geyl, 'Opkomst en verval van het Noord Nederlandsch nationaliteitsbesef', in *Leiding*, July 1931, 10.
107. (b) Knuttel, *Acta der Zuid-Hollandsche Synode*, R.G.P., IV, 85.
107. (c) Knuttel, *Toestanden* etc. I, 276.
107. (d) Molhuysen, *Bronnen tot de geschiedenis der Leidsche Universiteit*, III, Appendix, 56.

PAGE

168. (*d*) Muller, *Wilhelm von Oranien und G. F. von Waldeck*, I, 272.
169. (*e*) Gebhardt, *Witsen*, II, 87.
173. *Op. cit.*, II, 170.
175. (*a*) P. van Dam, *Beschrijvinge van de Oost-Indische Compagnie;* ed. Stapel, R.G.P., second book, II, quoted foreword.
177. (*b*) Quoted by Stapel, *Bongaaisch Verdrag*, 226, 230.
181. (*a*) *Dictionary of Nat. Biography*, art. Josiah Child.
181. (*b*) N. de Graaff, *Oost-Indische Spieghel*, 1703, W.L.V.
181. (*c*) *Op. cit.*, 44.
182. (*d*) Theal, *op. cit.*
183. (*a*) P. van Dam, *Beschrijvinge*, R.G.P., second book, II, 315.
184. (*b*) De Graaff, *op. cit.*, 13.
185/186. (*a*) J. Nieuhof, *Gedenkwaerdige Zee- en Landreize door de voornaemste landschappen van Oost-en West-Indiën*, 1682, II, 208.
188. (*b*) Quoted by Knappert, *Bovenwindsche Eilanden in de 18e eeuw*, 102.
188. (*c*) C. Udemans, *Geestelijk roer*, quoted (modernised) by Dijkstra, *Het evangelie in onze Oost*, I, 155.
192. (*a*) *Interest van Holland ofte Gronden van Hollands-Welvaren, aangewezen door V.D.H.* (P. de la Court) 1662; 70.
193. (*b*) Jer. de Decker, *Rijmoefeningen* (edited 1726), I, 269 (1658).
194. (*a*) Temple, *Observations upon the United Provinces of the Netherlands;* 1673.
194/195. (*b*) Pallavicino, in B.M.H.G.U., 1911, 82. (Italian).
195. (*c*) A. P. Faugère, *Journal d'un voyage à Paris* . . . 1657–58.
200. (*a*) De Witte van Citters, *Contracten van correspondentie*, 45.
201. (*b*) *Briefwisseling tusschen de gebroeders Van der Goes*, W.H.G.U., II, 344; 11 February 1672.
201. (*c*) *Morgenwekker aan J. van den Vondel*, in Zoet, *Uitstekendste Digtkonstige Werken*, edited, 1714, II, 81.
201. (*d*) *Aitzema*, quoted by heart.
202. (*e*) *Aitzema*, VII, 279.
202. (*f*) *Ibid.*
204. Fruin, *Verspreide Geschriften*, IX, 194.
205. (*a*) De Witte van Citters, *op. cit.*, 9.
206. (*b*) *Stok in 't hondert op 't burgerlijck versoek*, in *Nederduitsche en Latijnsche Keurdigten, bijeenverzamelt door de Liefhebberen der Oude Hollandsche Vrijheit*, I, 1710; 400.
209. (*a*) *Mélanges Moeller* (1914), II. (French).
210/211. (*b*) The letter of the eight priests (originally in Latin), published in Dutch at Ghent, 1669.
214. (*a*) *Acta der Zuid-Hollandsche Synode*, VI, 169. (1691).
215. (*b*) *Op. cit.*, 207 (1692).
216. (*c*) Quoted from Knuttel, *Balthazar Bekker*, 323.
217. Ypey and Dermout, *Geschiedenis der Nederl. Hervormde Kerk*, III, 303.
220. (*a*) Zoet, *op. cit.*, 271.
220. (*b*) *Op. cit.*, 172.
220. (*c*) Quoted by Van Slee, *De Rijnsburger Collegianten*, 123.
220. (*d*) Quoted by Hylkema, *Reformateurs*, II, 327.
221. (*e*) *Uitroepinghe* (by Crisp?) I, 16; quoted by Hylkema, *op. cit.*, I, 168.
221. (*f*) Hylkema, *op. cit.*, I, 327.
222. (*g*) Meinsma, *Spinoza en zijn kring*, 278.
222. (*a*) Hylkema, *op. cit.*, II, 212.

223. (b) Knuttel, 'Ericus Walten en zijn proces', B.V.G., V, I, 432.
224. (c) Knuttel, Acta, V, 191.
228/229. (a) P. Harting, Christiaan Huygens, 55.
230. (b) A. J. J. van de Velde, Derde bijdrage tot de studie van de werken van de stichter der micrographie; V.M.K.V.A., 1922, 1040.
234. Steenhoff, Schilderkunst in het Rijksmuseum, III, 122.
236. (a) De Bie, Gulden Cabinet, 164.
236. (b) Had I been able to take note of vol. III of Vermeulen's Geschiedenis der Nederlandse Bouwkunst in good time, I should have shown earlier French influences on the architecture in the North, and have fixed more sharply the attitude of North and South against the Baroque.
238. (c) Quoted from Houbraken, Groote Schouwburg der Nederlandsche Konstschilders, 1718, III, 268.
239. (a) S. van Hoogstraten, Inleyding tot de Hoogeschool der Schilderkonst, 19.
239. (b) Op. cit., 287.
239. (c) Communicated by Voltaire; see Littré, Dictionnaire de la langue française, under 'magot'.
243. De Bie, Faem's Weergalm der Neder-duytsche Poësie, Aenleydinghe. The exact words are: 'naer den Hollantschen stijl en manier'.
245. (a) M. de Swaen, Werken, edited by Dr. Celen, II, 231.
246. (b) Edited by Sabbe, in V.M.K.V.A., 1934, 566.
246. (a) From the foreword of P. Dubbels' Hoogmoedige Prins of gelukkige staatzucht, 1665; quoted by Kronenberg, Nil Volentibus Arduum, 26.
247. (b) Quoted from Te Winkel, Ontwikkelingsgang der Nederlandsche letterkunde; Republiek, II, 256.
247. (c) Scheltema, Oud en Nieuw, II, 161.
249. (d) J. Oudaen, Lijk-gedachtenis van den groten Agrippijner, de Heer Joost van den Vondel.
249. (e) J. Vollenhove, Lijkzang over den groten poëet Joost van den Vondel.
252/253. J. Antonides van der Goes, Oorspronck van 's lands ongevallen; aen Joachim Oudaen.
256. (a) Correspondentie van Willem III en van H. W. Bentinck, edited by Japikse, R.G.P., little series, no. 23, 357 (1683).
257. (b) Journalen van C. Huygens den Zoon, I, 193. (W.H.G.U.).
258. (c) Gebhardt, Witsen, I, 249.
259. (a) Catalogus Atlas van Stolk, 249.
260. (b) Nederduitse en Latijnse Keurdigten, I, 229.
263/264. Sypesteyn, Geschiedkundige Bijdragen, III, 225.
264. (a) Wagenaar, Vaderlandsche Historie, XVI, 237.
266. (b) J. Z. Kannegieter, 'Amsterdam en de vrede van Rijswijk', B.M.H.G.U., 1927, 111.
267/268. (a) H. J. van der Heim, Het archief van den raadpensionaris A. Heinsius, III, 233.
269. (b) Quoted by H. C. Diferee, Geschiedenis van den Nederlandschen Handel, 337.
274. Archives, 3ᵉ série, III, 235.
275/276. (a) Ibid., 236; (b) ibid., 255; (c) ibid., 287.
278/279. (a) Ibid., 278; (b) ibid., 242.
279. (c) Wagenaar, Vaderlandsche Historie, XV, 207.
280. (d) Eenige politieke consideratiën rakende de Spaansche Nederlanden (1691), Knuttel 13588.

PAGE

281/283. For these pages are used the messages of the English resident Bulstrode (Public Record Office, London) which I read after the composition of my lecture, 'Een historische legende; het Zuid-Nederlandsch tarief van 21 December 1680', *Mededelingen der Kon. Nederl. Academie van Wetenschappen*, afd. Letterkunde, 1933. (reprinted in *Kernproblemen*, 1937). In fact, these messages confirm the opinion given in the lecture.

282/283. (a) Mertens and Torfs, *Geschiedenis van Antwerpen*, IV.

283. (b) L. Galesloot, *Mémoire secret d' A. Foppens* (1877), 28.

284. (a) J. Nève, *Gand sous l'occupation de Louis XIV*, (1931), 31.

285. (b) Brunot, *Histoire de la langue française*, V. 93.

291. (a) Prologue of 'De gedempte hoogmoed', in *Drie Brusselsche Kluchten uit de zeventiende eeuw*, 135.

291. (b) *Mémoires du Feldmaréchal comte Mérode-Westerloo*, publiés par son arrière petit-fils, (Bruxelles, 1840); I, 165.

298. Quoted by Gachard, *La Belgique au commencement du 18ᵉ siècle*, 33.

301. Du Parc de Bellegarde, *Vie de Van Espen* (1767), 25.

303. (a) Quoted by Van Vloten, in Arend's, *Algemene geschiedenis des Vaderlands*, IV, II, 846.

305. (b) *Keurdigten*, I, 266, presumable date, 1705.

305. (a) Quoted by Van Vloten, in the same work of Arend, 818.

305. (b) *Ibid.*, 821.

306. (c) Compare G. W. Kernkamp in *Verslag Algemene Vergadering*, Utrechts Provinciaal Genootschap, 1933, 98. (Latin).

321. (a) *Letters and Correspondence of Henry St. John, Viscount Bolingbroke*, (1798), I, 157. The letter is dated 20 April 1711 and addressed to the ambassador at The Hague, Lord Raby (the later Strafford)—Swift wrote in his pamphlet that appeared at the end of November: 'We have conquered a noble territory for the States, that will maintain sufficient troops to defend itself, feed many thousand inhabitants, where all encouragement will be given to introduce and improve manufactures, which was the only advantage they wanted; and which, added to their skill, industry and parcimony, will enable them to undersell us in every market of the world.'

321. (b) *Historical Manuscripts Commission, Portland Manuscripts*, IX (Harley Papers: letters from Strafford to Harley), 336 (9 August 1712).

322. (c) *Keurdigten*, continuation (1717), 40, 43.

322. *Op. cit.*, Fourth continuation, 45.

325. (a) Gachard, *Collection de documents inédits*, III, 459. (French).

326. (b) Request of the States of Flanders, in Van Houtte, an article on De Meulenmeester, in *Bulletin de la société d'histoire et d'archéologie de Gand*, 1928, 130. (French).

328. (a) *Verhael van den borgerlijken oproer binnen Gent*, (pamphlet from the Southern Netherlands).

330. (b) Gachard, *Collection de documents inédits*, III, 410.

331. (a) S. van Goslinga, *Mémoires*, 9. (French).

331. (b) Laws to Bromley, December 1713, quoted by Geikie-Montgomery, *The Dutch Barrier*, 319.

331. (c) The sonnet of De Swaen, in Yelen, *Fransch Vlaanderen*, 17.

333. (d) Gachard, *Histoire de la Belgique au commencement du* 18ᵉ *siècle*, 225, and Van Houtte, *Occupations etrangeres de la Belgique*, I, 340, note. (French).
Gachard gives the quotation in French.

That Heinsius in The Hague should have spoken French to the gentleman of Brabant, I consider to be improbable, likewise that an official letter to the States of Brabant should have been written in French (for Gachard drew from Régistre aux résolutions des Etats de Brabant: procès-verbal du 26 Janvier 1713). Belgian historians have often silently translated their quotations from documents in Dutch into French, similarly changing into French, Christian names, names of places, titles and so on. In that way the history of the Flemish provinces is covered with a deceitful French veneer, and the sharp difference between the 19th century situation and that of before the French Revolution gets obscured.

I took the trouble to write to the Record Office at Brussels to get the original text, but was told in reply that Gachard's note was not to be traced. Strangely enough the same happened with regard to the next quotation from a letter of Van Ven.

333. (a) Gachard, *op. cit.*, 225.
333. (b) Van Houtte, *Occupations étrangères*, II, 390.
334. (c) Gachard, *Histoire de la Belgique au commencement du* 18ᵉ *siècle*, 398.
336. (a) *Chronycke van Vlaenderen*, Brugge 1735.
336. (b) Quoted by Bussemaker, 'De Republiek der Verenigde Nederlanden en de Koning-Keurvorst George I', B.V.G., IV, 326. (Van der Dussen to Heinsius).
337. (c) Gachard, *op. cit.*, 469. (Dutch).
338. (a) Gachard, *op. cit.*, 460. (French).
339. (b) The text of the Barrier Treaty in Geikie-Montgomery, *The Dutch Barrier*, 398. (French).
339. (c) Edited by Sabbe, V.M.K.V.A., 1934, 25.
340. (d) *Ibid.*, 32.
344. *De Jonge*, VIII, 25.
347. (a) *De Jonge*, VIII, p. CXIII.
348. (b) Van Deventer, *De Nederlanders op Java*, II, 73, note.
348. (c) *De Jonge*, VIII, 150.
348. (d) *Op. cit.*, VIII, 116 ff.
349. (e) *Ibid.*, p. CXXI.
349. (a) Quoted by Mr. N. P. van den Berg in 'Een onderkruiper van 's Compagnies negotie', *Onze Eeuw*, 1903, 337.
350. (b) Bogaert, *Reisen door d' oostersche delen van Asia*.
350. (c) *Tijdschrift voor Indische Taal. Land-en Volkenkunde*, III, 1855, 104.
351. (d) Corn. de Bruin, *Reizen over Moscovien door Persien en Indien* (1714), 367.
352. (a) See Roldanus, *C. van Beuningen*, 115.
354. (b) *De Jonge*, VIII, p. CXXVI.
355. (c) *Korte schets van 's landswelvaren* . . . , 1714; *Knuttel* 16231, 37.
357. (a) Quoted by Godée Molsbergen, *Reizen in Zuid-Afrika in de Hollandsche tijd*, W.L.V., I, 139, note 3.
358. (b) *Op. cit.*, 140.
360. A. Bogaert, *Reisen door Asia*, 476.
362. (a) *Het dagboek van Adam Tas*, edited by L. Fouché, 1914, 66.

PAGE
362. (b) Bogaert, op. cit., 518.
366. Droste, Overblijfsels van Heuchenius.
367. Knappert, De Bovenwindsche Eilanden in de achttiende eeuw, 31, 33.
369. (a) Hartsinck, Beschrijving van Suriname, II, 715.
369/370. (b) Knappert, op. cit., 36.
370. (c) Nederduitse en Latijnse Keurdigten, continuation (1717), 12.
374. (a) Compare W. Bosman, Nauwkeurige beschrijving van de Guinese Goudkust, 104 ff.
375. (b) B.M.H.G.U., XXXV, 1914, 96.
375/376. (c) Bosman, op. cit., 149.
377. (d) Hamelberg, De Nederlanders op de West-Indische eilanden, 77, 100, 101.

Notes on Sources and Secondary Works

MUCH OF what was said in the *Notes on Sources and Secondary Works* on pp. 269–71 of Part One applies to the period dealt with in this volume. A few additional remarks is all that will be required here.

I remarked in Part One (p. 270) that for the period there dealt with there is a certain scarcity of intimate political correspondence. That cannot be said of the 'Stadholderless Period', for which De Witt's letters form a source of central importance: six quarto volumes containing his correspondence with envoys of the States abroad published between 1723 and 1725, and six more complementary volumes in the *Werken* of the Utrecht Historisch Genootschap, 1906–22, edited by G .W. Kernkamp and N. Japikse. Of great importance are also the memoirs of Hans Bontemantel, a member of the Amsterdam corporation, *De Regeeringe van Amsterdam*, two volumes, edited by Kernkamp for the same series 1897. For the ensuing period. Japikse's publication in the R(ijks) G(eschiedkundige) P(ublicatiën) of the correspondence of Portland (Bentinck) and of William III, five volumes, 1927–37, is an invaluable supplement of the material to be found in the *Archives de la Maison d'Orange-Nassau*. At a much earlier date, 1867–80, Van der Heim had already published three volumes based on the Heinsius archives, and containing among other correspondence numerous letters exchanged between that Grand Pensionary and William III; unfortunately the publication was not continued beyond August 1697. In 1951 van 't Hoff edited for the Historisch Genootschap, *The Correspondence of Marlborough and Heinsius*, 1701–11; Marlborough's letters preserved in the Heinsius archives (Algemeen Rijksarchief) had been presented in 1945 by Wilhelmina, Queen of the Netherlands, to Winston Churchill.

For the history of the Spanish Netherlands, especially of the central government, there is Lonchay, Cuvelier and Lefèvre, *Correspondance de la Cour d'Espagne sur les Affaires des Pays-Bas au XVIIᵉ siècle*, 6 vols., 1923–37.

Coming to historiography, I mention first the large *Algemeene Geschiedenis der Nederlanden*, completed with Vol. XII in 1958. (I ought to have mentioned it in Part One.) By *de Nederlanden* is here understood both the Northern and the Southern Netherlands, and among the numerous authors, as well as on the board of editors, Flemish historians are duly represented.

There is a number of monographs in English relating to this period of Netherlands history, but not all of them are satisfactory from the point of view of historical scholarship. Mary Trevelyan, *William III and the Defence of Holland, 1672–74*, 1930, is far too much under the influence of the Orangist legend and unfair to the regents' régime; much worse in this respect, and full of historical errors besides, is a more recent work, Nesca Robb, *William of Orange*, (1962). Of a much higher quality are Charles Wilson, *Profit and Power, a study of England and the Dutch Wars*, 1957; K. H. D. Haley, *William of Orange and the English Opposition*, 1953; Roderick Geikie and Isobel Montgomery, *The Dutch Barrier*, with a 'General Introduction' by myself, 1930; Herbert H. Rowen, *The Ambassador prepares for War*. (Pomponne in The Hague, 1669–71), 1957; and Douglas Coombs, *The Conduct of the Dutch, British Opinion and the Dutch Alliance during the War of the Spanish Succession*, 1958.

I pointed out years ago, in several articles in Dutch, the partiality with which English historians represented the treatment meted out by the Tory Government to the Dutch ally in 1711; a critical review from my hand of Wickham Legg's *British Diplomatic Instructions*, vol. II, appeared in *History*, 1926, and is reprinted, in English, together with the Dutch articles alluded to, in a volume of essays of mine, *Kernproblemen van onze geschiedenis*, 1937. G. M. Trevelyan refers to, and largely follows, these articles in his *England under Queen Anne*, vol. III, 1934.

Among special studies in Dutch there are several essays, especially on William III, by Robert Fruin, the leading nineteenth century Dutch historian. These used to set the tone, but it has lately been demonstrated, especially by J. W. Smit, *Fruin en de partijen in de Republiek* (1958) that Fruin's political philosophy, a liberalism conditioned by his period and the prevailing national circumstances, seriously detracts from his once famed impartiality; see also D. J. Roorda, *Partij en factie* (1961). Then there are Japikse's *Johan de Witt*, 1915, and *Prins Willem III*, two volumes, 1930 and 1933, books which remain indispensable even though in my own monograph, *Oranje en Stuart* (1939; paperback edition 1963), in which both De Witt and William III figure prominently, I stressed very different accents. On the history of the war of the Spanish Succession I mention two monographs, A. G. Veenendaal, *Het Engels-Nederlandse Condominium in de Zuidelijke Nederlanden, 1706–16* (1945) and Johanna Stork-Penning, *Het grote werk; vredesonderhandelingen gedurende de Spaanse Successie-oorlog, 1705–10* (1958), both doctoral theses produced under my auspices (as was J. W. Smit's work mentioned above).

Index

The dates given after the names of reigning sovereigns refer to the duration of their reign; other dates are those of birth and death.

PRINTED IN GREAT BRITAIN BY
J. AND J. GRAY, EDINBURGH